# FOUNDERS OF FAITH

**Michael Carrithers** is Lecturer in Anthropology at the University of Durham and author of *The Forest Monks of Sri Lanka* (also published by OUP).

**Raymond Dawson** is Lecturer in Chinese at the University of Oxford. His other books include *The Chinese Experience and Imperial China*, and he is the editor of *The Legacy of China* (also published by OUP).

Among **Humphrey Carpenter's** other books are biographies of Auden and Tolkien, and (with Mari Prichard) *The Oxford Companion to Children's Literature*.

**Michael Cook** is Professor of Near Eastern Studies at Princeton University. His other books include *Population Pressure In Rural Anatolia 1450–1600* (also published by OUP) and *Early Muslim Dogma: A Source-Critical Study*.

# Founders of Faith

*The Buddha*
Michael Carrithers

*Confucius*
Raymond Dawson

*Jesus*
Humphrey Carpenter

*Muhammad*
Michael Cook

Oxford   New York
OXFORD UNIVERSITY PRESS

Oxford University Press, Walton Street, Oxford OX2 6DP

Oxford New York Toronto
Delhi Bombay Calcutta Madras Karachi
Petaling Jaya Singapore Hong Kong Tokyo
Nairobi Dar es Salaam Cape Town
Melbourne Auckland

and associated companies in
Berlin Ibadan

Oxford is a trade mark of Oxford University Press

Each section was first published separately in the Past Masters series as an
Oxford University Press paperback and simultaneously in a hardback edition
This edition first published 1986
First issued as an Oxford University Press paperback 1989
Reprinted 1989

British Library Cataloguing in Publication Data
Founders of faith.
1. Religious biography
I. Carpenter, Humphrey. Jesus  II. Carrithers,
Michael. The Buddha  III. Cook, M. A. (Michael
Allan). Muhammad  IV. Dawson, Raymond. Confucius
291.6'092'  BL72
ISBN 0–19–283066–X

Library of Congress Cataloging in Publication Data
Main entry under title:
Founders of faith.
Bibliography: p.  Includes index.
Contents: Jesus / by Humphrey Carpenter—The
Buddha / by Michael Carrithers—Muhammad / by
Michael Cook—Confucius / by Raymond Dawson
1. Religions—Biography—Addresses, essays, lectures.  I. Carpenter, Humphrey.
BL72.F648 1986  291.6'3  85–15445
ISBN 0–19–283066–X

Printed in Great Britain by
The Guernsey Press Co. Ltd.
Guernsey, Channel Islands

# *Foreword*

This book comprises four self-contained studies of the founders of the world's greatest religious traditions: the Buddha, Confucius, Jesus, and Muhammad. They were originally written for the Past Masters series, which sets out to expound the ideas of notable thinkers of the past in a lucid, accessible, and authoritative manner. By reprinting them in one volume, Oxford University Press has provided a unique guide to what have proved to be some of the most influential ideas in human history. It is impossible to read these four accounts in succession without gaining a new awareness of the different ways in which men and women in different parts of the world have sought to make sense of some of the most intractable problems of human existence.

KEITH THOMAS
*General Editor*
*Past Masters*

# Contents

# THE BUDDHA

MICHAEL CARRITHERS

*To Elizabeth*

# *Preface*

Until the present century the Buddha was probably the most influential thinker in human history. His teaching prospered throughout the subcontinent of India for more than 1,500 years, and in that time it changed and diversified at least as much as Christianity did in its first 1,500 years in Europe. By the thirteenth century A.D., when the power of Buddhism was broken in its original home, it had long since spread to Tibet, Central Asia, China, Korea, Japan and Sri Lanka, and its was making its way into South-East Asia. Buddhism's history in those countries was as complicated as it had already been in India.

I have not attempted to explain such a vast matter in this short book. I have only recounted the life of the Buddha and described the genesis and significance of his teaching. I have tried, however, to phrase this account so the reader will be able to see why Buddhism moved so easily across continents and survived so well through the centuries.

# *Contents*

# Note on quotations

## Abbreviations

References to works in the Buddhist canon are to the Pali Text Society editions of the Theravāda canon. The letter refers to the appropriate *nikāya* (collection), the first number to the volume within the *nikāya*, and the second number to the page in the volume. Thus a reference to the *Majjhima Nikāya*, second volume, page 91 would be written M II 91. Where I have referred to a whole discourse I have given the number of the discourse, e.g. M I no. 15. The following abbreviations are used:

D   *Dīgha Nikāya*
M   *Majjhima Nikāya*
A   *Anguttara Nikāya*
S   *Saṃyutta Nikāya*

Other references are to the *Udāna* (U) and the *Paramatthajotikā* (P), also in Pali Text Society editions; and to the *Bṛhadāraṇyaka Upaniṣad* (B) and the *Chāndogya Upaniṣad* (C), which are cited giving book, chapter and section number so that any edition may be consulted.

## Translations and Terms

The translations are almost entirely my own. Anyone who wishes to trace citations to their context will find that the Pali Text Society's English translations are keyed so that one may light more or less on the appropriate passage, though one's aim is better if one can consult the Pali. A little experimentation will be necessary.

The technical terms are in Pali, except where I have noted that they are in Sanskrit.

## Pronunciation

To avoid really embarrassing mistakes in Pali pronunciation it need only be borne in mind that *c* is equivalent to English *ch*, so *cetanā* is pronounced very roughly chay-tuh-naa; and that *h* after a consonant means only an extra breathiness in pronunciation, as in the English pit*h*ead or dog*h*ouse. Those wishing to pronounce *Buddha* correctly will need to know that the doubled *d* is pronounced as such, rather as doubled consonants are pronounced in Italian. Thus it is roughly Bud-dhuh, *not* Booduh.

The special symbols that appear above or below certain letters in Pali and Sanskrit words transliterated in the text affect the pronunciation of those letters *roughly* as indicated in the following table of equivalence:

| | |
|---|---|
| ā | *ah* |
| ś | half-way between *s* and *sh* |
| ñ | *ny* as in ca*ny*on |
| ṭ ḷ ṇ | instead of the tongue touching the back of the teeth, as in English, it is taken further back towards the roof of the mouth. |
| ṣ | *sh* |
| ṃ | *ng* |

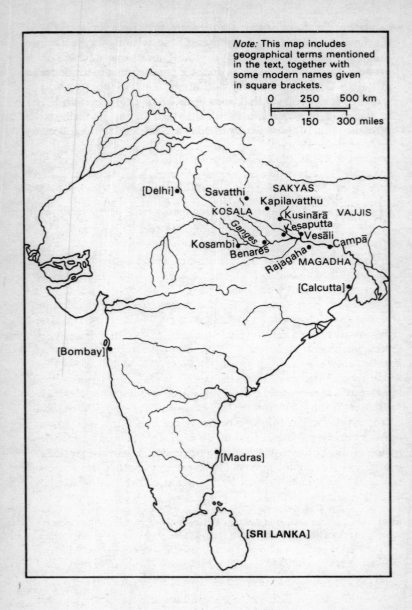

Note: This map includes geographical terms mentioned in the text, together with some modern names given in square brackets.

0     250     500 km
0   150   300 miles

[Delhi]

Savatthi

SAKYAS
Kapilavatthu

KOSALA

VAJJIS

Kusinārā
Kesaputta
Vesāli

Ganges

Kosambi

Benares

Campā

Rajagaha

MAGADHA

[Calcutta]

[Bombay]

[Madras]

[SRI LANKA]

# 1

## Introduction

Among the ruins of Anuradhapura, the ancient capital of Sri Lanka, there rests alone on a pedestal above the grass a seated image of the Buddha in stone, slightly larger than life. The statue is conventional, probably more than a thousand years old, of a type found throughout Buddhist Asia. The legs are folded in meditation, the hands laid one upon the other in the lap. Buddhists hold that it was in this posture, seated beneath a tree more than 2,500 years ago, that the Buddha was awakened, attaining decisive knowledge of the human condition and the unshakeable certainty that he was released from its suffering.

In its excellence, however, the Anuradhapura image is far from conventional. The back and head are disciplined and upright; but the arms are relaxed and the face reposes in tranquillity. The figure seems intelligent and serene, wed perfectly to the unmoving granite. Standing before it an elderly English socialist told me that in the whole mess of human history *this* at least — the statue and all its stands for — was something of which we could be proud. He said that he had no use for religion, but that he felt he had unknowingly been a follower of the Buddha all along.

An intensely private reflection, its disclosure prompted perhaps by the power of the figure: but what is remarkable is that it should be found in so many others. Here, for example, is the anthropologist Claude Lévi-Strauss, by no means a Buddhist, writing in a similar vein:

what have I learnt from the masters I have listened to, the philosophers I have read, the societies I have investigated, and that very science in which the West takes such pride? Simply a fragmentary lesson or two which, if laid end to end, would add up to the meditations of the Sage at the foot of his tree.

This testifies to the fascination the Buddha still holds for us. Is it justified? What does an Oriental seer, born in the middle of the first millennium before Christ among historical circumstances and a culture so different from our own, have to offer such very modern thinkers? This is the first question I have tried to answer.

And I have tried to answer it by writing a biography of the Buddha. That this is a reasonable strategy is by no means obvious, for history is full of figures whose significance lies very little in their personal lives and very much in their teachings alone. But the Buddha is peculiar in this regard, for his teaching and his life are intimately and inextricably mingled.

Let me illustrate this from traditional accounts of the Buddha's life, which have exerted tremendous influence over Buddhists and are now widely available in European languages. The Buddha was born the son of a king, and so grew up with wealth, pleasure and the prospect of power, all goods commonly desired by human beings. As he reached manhood, however, he was confronted with a sick man, an old man and a corpse. He had lived a sheltered life, and these affected him profoundly, for he realised that no wealth or power could prevent him too from experiencing illness, old age and death. He also saw a wandering ascetic, bent on escaping these sufferings. Reflecting on what he had seen, he reached the first great turning-point of his life: against the wishes of his family he renounced home, wife, child and position to become a homeless wanderer, seeking release from this apparently inevitable pain.

For some years he practised the trance-like meditation, and later the strenuous self-mortification, which were then current among such wanderers, but he found these ineffective. So he sat down to reflect quietly, with neither psychic nor physical rigours, on the common human plight. This led to the second great change in his life, for out of this reflection in tranquillity arose at last awakening and release. He had 'done what was to be done', he had solved the enigma of suffering. Deriving his philosophy from his experience he then taught for forty-five years, and his teaching touched most problems in the conduct of human life. He founded an order of monks who were to free themselves by following his example, and they spread his teaching abroad in the world. He eventually died of mortal causes, like others, but unlike others he was 'utterly extinguished' (*parinibbuto*), for he would never be reborn to suffer again.

There are good reasons to doubt even this very compressed

account, but at least the outline of the life must be true: birth, maturity, renunciation, search, awakening and liberation, teaching, death. This biography, with the two marked transformations, the renunciation and the awakening, gave the Buddha and his followers the dramatic plot with which to illustrate their belief and the psychological and philosophical model on which to found their thought. Dramatically the action centres on spiritual changes achieved by heroic personal application, while philosophically it centres on discoveries made within the Buddha's own mind and body.

Hence he said, 'it is within this fathom-long carcass, with its mind and its notions, that I declare there is the world, the origin of the world, the cessation of the world and the path leading to the cessation of the world' (S I 62). Within these bounds what he suffered was suffered in common with all mortal beings. For all mortals, in his words, 'birth is suffering, ageing is suffering, sickness is suffering.' In his view these inescapable and pressing facts were discoverable by anyone through introspection into their own experience. Similarly the means of release were available to everyone. The meditation methods which he developed, for example, are based on such simple and available phenomena as one's own breathing. The morality he espoused was founded in clear and practical principles derived from his own life. The Buddha's laboratory was himself, and he generalised his findings to cover all human beings.

So the second question is, how did the Buddha change and develop? For it is this development which is, in one way or another, the subject of his philosophy. It is a question which has been of central concern to Buddhists, and it is one which the Buddha himself frequently answered. Sometimes he answered it directly by recounting part of his life. Elsewhere he answered it indirectly by stating that if one did X, then the following deleterious consequences would ensue, but if one did Y, then the consequences would be wholesome and conducive to liberation. Behind this lay the assumption that the Buddha knew this because he had witnessed the alternatives. He required of himself, as of his monks, adherence to one rule of evidence: 'that which you affirm [must be] that which you have realised, seen, known for yourself' (M I 265).

It does not follow from the autobiographical nature of the

Buddha's philosophy, however, that an account of the Buddha alone would be adequate to explain it. For despite his taste for solitude he was part of his society and its history. He lived amid great and decisive social and intellectual changes, changes whose fruits he inherited and to whose further course he contributed substantially. His thought was revolutionary, but it was a revolution which had already been in the making for a long time. The image I have in mind is that of a wave of change which built up slowly, over centuries, touching every aspect of the lives of the ancient Indians. The Buddha was elevated to the crest of this wave, and he enjoyed a wide view across human affairs. The problem is to assess how much of his vision he owed to his elevation, to his position in history and to the work of his predecessors and contemporaries, and how much to the keenness of his own sight.

What evidence do we possess to recount the life and circumstances of a man who lived 2,500 years ago? For the life of the Buddha we rely almost entirely on the Buddhist scriptures, preserved in many oriental languages, which have at least the advantage of being very extensive. Those portions which are oldest and which most narrowly concern the Buddha, the *Basket of Discourses (Suttapiṭaka)* and the *Basket of the Disciplinary Code (Vinayapiṭaka)*, take up several library shelves in their various versions. Most of these, furthermore, are represented as being utterances of the Buddha, each spoken on a particular occasion in a particular place. The intention of the Buddha's followers was evidently to preserve the actual words of their teacher in their historical setting.

How well did they achieve this intention? Let us look first at the formation of the Buddhist canon. The canonical discourses take various forms: sometimes they are dialogues into which the Buddha entered with followers of other teachings; sometimes they are answers to specific questions brought to him by his own monks; sometimes they are lessons directed to his monks; and occasionally they are sermons addressed to the laymen who did not leave their homes but were content to support those who did.

The monks were chiefly responsible for preserving this teaching, since it was largely directed to them. The Buddha and his monks were peripatetic for much of the year, but gathered together in separate monasteries for the four months of the rainy season retreat, during the North Indian monsoon. While wandering, the

Buddha and his monks spread the message abroad, but while in retreat they discussed and rehearsed the teaching. Indeed, a few of the canonical discourses consist of discussions between monks. Throughout the canon are found slightly different versions of some doctrine or other, and this is no doubt partly attributable to elaborations at the hands of the monks, either during the Buddha's lifetime or after his death. But it also seems likely that the Buddha sometimes changed or improved his teachings, and that the dispersal of the monks allowed both earlier and later versions to be preserved among them, each in a different place.

It was after the Buddha's death that the real work of preservation began. The monks probably held a council shortly after that event, and almost certainly another was held a century later. At these councils they made an effort to establish or authenticate the then extant accounts of the life and teaching of the Buddha, and they were aware of systematic rules governing the acceptance or rejection of a discourse as authentic. Moreover the monks brought to the task of preservation a number of devices. They adopted from the culture around them or developed themselves methods of recitation and memorisation. They gave many of the discourses repetitious and formulaic shape, which facilitated such memorisation. They used poetry, which was probably sung — though the Buddha may have already done this as well. And, most important, they divided the discourses into distinct but largely overlapping bodies of material, each of which became the responsibilities of certain monks to memorise and pass on. The scriptures were not written down until three or four hundred years after the death of the Buddha, but these oral and social methods ensured that his words were probably kept better than our print-bound culture would recognise.

This is not to say that the canonical materials are wholly faithful. Some of the Buddha's words were lost, others misunderstood. Some became formulae which were repeated in inappropriate contexts. Moreover the monks added a good deal themselves, and in particular the figure of the Buddha tended to be magnified. Indeed none of the languages in which the canon now appears was the language of the Buddha himself, whatever it was, though one of them, Pali, is probably very close to it. From internal evidence it seems certain that these oldest texts had crystallised into roughly the shape in which we have them by the time of the second council or shortly thereafter. So at best we can hope to see the Buddha about as well as did his own disciples three generations after his death.

However, it took many Western scholars, working for more than a century, to conclude this much. For some time not too long after the second council the Buddhist order was riven by schisms, and as each group moved apart it preserved the old texts, but re-arranged them. And indeed the principle throughout Buddhist history was that, whatever rearrangements occurred, nothing was discarded. But to the old material different schools added new material, and the now expanded canons of each group represented different emphases, and new doctrines, in one or other of the related North Indian languages of Pali, Sanskrit or one of the Prakrits. These ancient developments took place within the Indian subcontinent, and of this period are preserved in an Indian language only the Pali canon in its entirety and some fragments in the other languages.

But much of the other material still exists in translation. For still later, slightly less than a thousand years after the death of the Buddha, Buddhism moved to China, and subsequently to Tibet, and a great deal of the material which has now been lost from Indian languages was translated into Chinese and Tibetan and thereby preserved. In these translated canons, however, the old teachings were now quite surrounded, and in effect obscured, by teachings different from those espoused by the Buddha. The Buddhist world, as Western scholarship found it in the nineteenth century, presented practices and opinions at least as varied among themselves as those among Christian churches.

It at first seemed easy to accept that the Pali canon, preserved by the Theravadins (School of the Elders) of Sri Lanka, Burma and Thailand, was the oldest and most genuine. This is what Theravadins themselves claimed. Since then, however, individual scholars have learned the Pali, Sanskrit, Tibetan and Chinese which are required to check such claims, and quite ancient texts have come to light from Central Asian hoards. It now appears that, though the Pali texts are still the single most useful source on the Buddha, in many respects they can be corrected and improved by readings from the Central Asian finds or from Tibetan and Chinese. Certainly the Tibetan and Chinese sources are indispensable for establishing what the oldest sources are. In this book the translations and terms are from the Pali sources, but I have used the conclusions of scholars working in other languages to supplement them.

These texts have many virtues, but they are peculiarly weak on one account, the facts that would make up the Buddha's *Who's Who* entry. Most troublesome is the Buddha's chronology. The scriptures give us license to accept that he lived to a ripe age, eighty years, and that he taught for forty-five years. But the actual dates are another matter. Sources preserved in Sri Lanka and corrected by Western scholars yield a date for the Buddha's death in 483 B.C. Sources preserved in Chinese suggest 368 B.C. The question is still being actively debated, and will probably go on being debated, for in either case the argument depends upon a long and tenuous chain of inference. The problem illustrates a trait characteristic of the ancient Indians altogether: that they were very little interested in chronology but much exercised over philosophy. Hence we are in the paradoxical situation of having a better idea of what the Buddha thought than of what century he lived in.

This is not to say, however, that the sources are weak on history. The Buddha was a practical man who often spoke through concrete examples from the life around him, and this reveals a great deal about his world. The monks' efforts to conserve the Buddha's words in a realistic setting have the same effect. We learn about what occupations people pursued, how people classified each other, what kind of political arrangements there were, and what religious institutions were current. It is possible to construct quite a rich and complex picture of the Buddha's India, a picture that can be corroborated from the scriptures of the Buddhists' rivals, the Jains. Indeed it may be said that with the Buddha India first enters history, for in any narrative account it is only at the Buddha's time that detail becomes clear enough to write with confidence of particular kings and states, particular economic arrangements, particular religious teachers and their doctrines.

This relatively static picture can moreover be set in motion by comparison with other sources. For the period preceding the Buddha we have the Sanskrit texts of the Brahmanical tradition (what was later to become Hinduism proper), the *Brahmanas* and *Upanishads*. These possess little of the revealing detail of the Buddhist scriptures, since they are the technical literature of a sacrificial, and later an esoteric, cult; nor do they refer to a single period, having been composed over many centuries. But they do testify that the earlier society was quite different in kind from that of the age of the Buddha. These differences are moreover confirmed by the archaeological record. A few centuries before the Buddha there were no cities proper and no states, only a series of small warrior principalities. At the time of the Buddha there were both cities and states, and a century or two after his death North India was to support the Mauryan empire, the greatest state in the subcontinent until the British Raj. The Buddha lived amidst the rise of Indian civilisation, just as Socrates lived amidst the rise of Western civilisation in ancient Greece.

There also developed in ancient India new and enduring habits of thought, which are in some respects so similiar to our own that we have difficulty recognising them at all. Here the comparison with ancient Greece is especially helpful, for only by looking back to that period of our own history do we find these habits actually being formed. We now take for granted a language and a way of thinking in which we can talk about human societies in general, or discuss what a universal morality might entail. We are acquainted with the notion that fundamental questions may be asked about ourselves, and that the answers might apply broadly to people in quite different situations. Moreover we easily suppose that such matters can be discussed according to impersonal criteria of truth available to anyone. In sum, we are familiar with thought which is general not particular; abstract not concrete; and argued rather than certified by supernatural sanction, illustrated by customary imagery or sanctioned by tradition.

But when we look to Socrates and his predecessors in Greece, and to the Buddha and his forebears in India, these habits seem fresh and newly acquired. This does not mean that the earlier Greeks or Indians were unable to consider their nature or their society. They certainly did so. But they did so in a way that constrained their reflections within the narrow viewpoint of their own group. They spoke best for themselves and to themselves, and only someone born within the society could fully participate in the fruits of their thought. For their thought was symbolic, in the specific sense that it evoked or expressed — rather than questioned or explained — the shared experience and values of a relatively small-scale community. So long as that experience was shared, and so long as that community did not embrace too many disparate elements, there was no reason, indeed no occasion, for questioning the values.

But with the rise of cities and the growth of a complex, cosmopolitan community, experience was no longer shared nor values unquestioned. The easy correspondence between traditional thought and life no longer held. There were substantial changes in the forms of common life, and with those changes arose the possibility that those forms could be reconsidered, discussed and reasoned over; people could now philosophise about them. This is the import of Cicero's dictum about Socrates, that he 'first called philosophy down from the skies, set it in the cities and even introduced it into homes, and compelled it to consider life and morals, good and evil'. Much the same could be said of the Buddha. Neither was much interested in God, gods or the supernatural, but both were passionately concerned with the ends and the conduct of human life.

# 2

## Early life and renunciation

Later traditions embroidered a great deal on the Buddha's early life
and appearance, but of this we can rely on little. The conventional
images of him are perhaps true to his characteristic posture in
meditation, but since such images were not made until centuries
after his death they cannot be portraits. There are some grounds for
believing that he was handsome according to the tastes of his time,
for a relatively early source, the *Aggañña Sutta*, praises his beauty
at the expense of the neighbouring king Pasenadi. As for his
character apart from his philosophy, little can be said, for in our
sources his character *is* his philosophy. We might justifiably
assume, however, that he was passionately intense and rebellious
in his youth, for no placid and obedient character could have set
out to do what he did, still less achieve it.

We are on firmer ground with two facts. First, the Buddha was
born among the Sakya people, probably at their capital,
Kapilavatthu, now the town of Lumbini in the lowland Terai
region of Nepal. Second, his family or clan name was Gotama
(Sanskrit *Gautama*; he was not called Buddha, 'awakened', until
after the awakening, but for convenience I will use the title
throughout). These facts reveal nothing about his childhood or
education, but they do place him in the wider Gangetic civilisation
of which he was a part, and they suggest something of the
circumstances which he inherited.

The Sakyas were one of a number of peoples spread along the
northern edge of the Ganges basin, at the periphery of the then
developing North Indian civilisation. When the Buddha was born
these peoples were still more or less independent and had roughly
similar systems of government. They were ruled by oligarchies or
councils of elders, or some mixture of the two, and might therefore
best be called tribal republics. Some of these might have elected a
leader for a fixed term, but they did not have kings in the strict

sense, and therefore the later tradition that the Buddha was a king's son must be dismissed. However the Sakyas considered themselves to have the effective rank of kings, nobles, and warriors in respect of the wider civilisation, and indeed they probably did not recognise, as others did, the ceremonial precedence of Brahmans, priests of high rank. They considered themselves an élite, and it is difficult to resist the impression that the Buddha had the confidence of high birth in his dealings with the wider world.

There is evidence that the Sakyans struggled to remain aloof from that world, but they were already deeply embroiled in it. The Buddha's clan name, Gotama, was itself used elsewhere, and probably originally, by Brahmans. Indeed the very scale against which the Sakyans claimed their high status really only made sense beyond their borders. Moreover they were already in effect tributaries to a king in the south, and were probably tied economically to southern commerce. The Sakyans, and the tribal republics as a whole, were more acted upon than acting. They were to contribute to Indian civilisation only their great kinsman, the Buddha, and certain of their values preserved in his teaching.

The centres of change, and of power, lay in the central Ganges basin. A collection of small heroic warrior societies had spread along the river centuries earlier, and these societies developed into centralised monarchical states. There was a traditional list of sixteen of these 'great countries', but already in the Buddha's youth some had swallowed others and were on the way to further conquests. One, Kosala, conquered the Sakyas in the Buddha's lifetime. Another, Magadha, already ruler of western Bengal and destined to be the nucleus of the Mauryan empire, was to engulf the Vajji confederacy of tribal republics after his death. The future lay with the kings, and not with the republics.

At the heart of these states appeared true urban centres where there had been none before. These swelling cities contained the kings' courts, and to the courts and cities were drawn the makings of an urban life: merchants and craftsmen with new skills, soldiers and labourers, conquered lords to render tribute, the displaced, the foreigners, the opportunists. There was a more complex division of labour and of status between people, and those of different languages and cultures were now thrown together to get along as best they could. The court and the city also drew the countryside into relation with this urban life, through force wielded by the king's soldiers and officials, through the subtler effect of long-distance commerce and through movements of population. The archaeological record shows no planning in these ancient Indian cities: they were chaotic, and that chaos perhaps best symbolises both the difficulties and the creative possibilities of these newly complex societies. Above all the question was, how were the Indians to understand themselves among these unprecedented forms of common life?

They began with one very old intellectual tool, a conception of the different estates in society. This was the property of the old heroic warrior societies, and is reminiscent of the medieval European division of society into those who pray, those who fight and those who labour: Church, nobility and peasants. In the Indian case there were four estates (Sanskrit *varṇa*). At the top were the Brahmans, priests of the sacrificial religion and intellectuals. Despite their rank, however, they did not wield power. That was left to the second estate, the Warriors (*khattiya*, Sanskrit *kṣatriya*), whose duty it was to fight, to rule and to pay for sacrifice. This is the rank claimed by the Sakyans, and into this category fell kings and nobility. The third estate were the commoners, the producers, Husbandmen (Sanskrit *vaiśya*). And the fourth estate were the Servants (Sanskrit *śudra*), those ineligible for the benefits of sacrificial religion and compelled to a life of servitude under the other three orders. This conception *prescribed* an orderly and hierarchical relationship between the estates, each having certain claims on the others and certain obligations towards them, and each owing respect to the ones above. It also more or less *described* society, for these were communities of rank in which a warrior élite, with their priests, ruled over commoners and the still lower populace of the conquered.

But, most important, this conception of estates was a deeply held and pervasive way of looking at the human world. It was not merely an ideology of different occupations or social ranks, for it also purported to describe the essential characteristics of the people in each estate. To call someone a Warrior, for example, was not just to designate him as a bearer of arms and a ruler, but also to say that he was rich, powerful, generous, heroic and of noble birth. A Brahman was not just a priest by function, but also inherently endowed with wisdom, virtue, learning, personal purity and purity of birth. And to call someone a Servant was not merely to refer to his job, but also to his poverty, weakness, vileness and low birth. Everything significant that was to be known about a person was known through his estate, whether for religious, psychological, political, economic or social purposes. A person's appearance, psychic and physical endowments, his very essence was determined by his estate. It was as if the estates were different species. In this conception there were no human beings, only Brahmans, Warriors, Husbandmen and Servants; rather as in the theory of apartheid there are only Blacks, Whites and Coloureds. In the texts of the older warrior societies, the *Brahmanas*, this order of estates is wholly taken for granted. It arose from the experience of the pre-urban Gangetic Indians and expressed the nature of their society. If it was unfair from our point of view, that unfairness was already built into their world in many ways.

However, the estates theory did not bear the same intimate and organic connection to the world centred upon the cities as it had to the earlier heroic world, and that for several reasons. First, it did not comprehend the new variety and complexity of occupation and position. In the older texts, for example, we read nothing of merchants; but in the Buddhist and Jain texts they are a very visible and active part of the scene. In the older texts there are only Warriors, but in the newer there are paid soldiers and salaried officials as well. These and other specialisations were dependent upon the new states and the use of money, which arrived in North India only with the cities. These new categories of persons presented the estates theory with formidable difficulties. The theory envisaged a simple agrarian and pastoral world inhabited by four kinds of people. Where did these new figures fit in? What sort of persons were they?

But that was by no means the most pressing challenge offered by the new circumstances, for there was another which struck at the very heart of the estates. This is adumbrated in a Buddhist discourse (M II no. 84) which makes two relevant points. First, it asserts that a criminal, whether Brahman or Servant, Warrior or Husbandman, would be sentenced by the king of a newly centralised state strictly according to the seriousness of his deed, not according to his estate. This was quite contrary to the old view, however, for there the punishment — envisaged as reparation or penance — was to be appropriate to the person, to the estate of the transgressor, not only to the crime. Were Brahmans and Warriors to be treated like common criminals? Were the estates not to be respected? And second, the discourse points out that, in the urbanising world of the Buddha, it was quite possible for someone born of high estate, a Brahman or a Warrior, to be employed as a servant by someone of low estate, a Servant or a Husbandman. Such an eventuality was wholly inconceivable under the old order: Servants could only serve, Brahmans and Warriors only command.

In the discourse these observations are meant to reveal the real state of the world, as opposed to the hollow pretensions of the Brahmans, the upholders of the estates theory. And it is plausible. If we compare the pre-Buddhist texts with another new literature which began to appear at about the Buddha's time, the *Dharmaśastra* (Science of Law; I refer to the earliest, the *Gautama Dharmaśastra*), we learn that kings were indeed taking new powers of judgment and punishment. In any case they could depose old élites, as in the tribal republics, and raise new ones. We also read in both Buddhist sources and the Law literature that new financial arrangements — credit and debt, interest, a market in land — had come into existence. This bore the possibility that a person of rank and wealth could lose everything through rapacious business practices, or that a person of low status could rise by the same means.

The difficulty for the estates theory was that it had described four ideal types of persons, and each type had been a harmonious blend of characteristics. A Warrior, for example, was a Warrior by birth, a Warrior by political power, and — since power was power over people and land, the only sources of wealth — a Warrior by wealth. But now this was too evidently contradicted by facts. There were Warriors by birth who had neither power nor wealth. There were wealthy men, merchants, who had neither birth nor power. And there were powerful men in the new states who were not Warriors by birth. A person in any of these positions could have found his actual plight at painful variance with the one attributed to him in the estates scheme. That old version of human nature and the human world simply did not express the new reality.

To this problem there were two responses. The first was that of the Brahmans, the theorists of the estates. In their Science of Law, a series of texts which appeared over many centuries after the Buddha, they gradually amended that theory. Their strategy, as in so much of Indian thought, was to keep the old but to build on new additions. They retained the hierarchical order of the estates simply by putting new occupations in old slots: merchants were placed with Husbandmen, while many craft specialities were put in the Servant estate. Regional groups or tribes were distributed among the lower three estates. They also devised a theory to explain the appearance of hereditary local or occupational groups — now called castes — as the result of intermarriage between different estates. In this enterprise they were, in the long run, so successful that Indians today still understand the complex order of castes according to the simple estates scheme.

But our interest lies with the other response. This was formed, quite in opposition to the Brahmans, by the ascetics and philosophical wanderers whose ranks the Buddha was to join. Their answer is found in both Buddhist and Jain sources, and it is so fundamental to the ascetics' point of view that it must have been already present, in rough form at least, when the Buddha arrived on the scene.

The Buddha expressed this common view in an especially clear form in dialogue with a Brahman (D I no. 4). In the dialogue he asks the Brahman the leading question, 'what makes a true Brahman?' This in effect amounts to asking, 'what makes the best, the supreme species of humankind?', for according to the estates scheme the Brahman is just that. In reply the Brahman claims that he and his fellows hold their elevated position by virtue of a number of qualities which they enjoy simultaneously. They are at once of highest birth, of greatest learning, the most beautiful, the wisest and the most virtuous.

This is perfectly orthodox: the Brahman believes himself to be an harmonious bundle of praiseworthy qualities. But then the Buddha dissects this claim by enquiring into its details. Could one fairly claim to be a Brahman without pure descent through seven generations on both sides? Well, apparently so. Could one claim to be a Brahman without mastery of Brahmanical learning? Yes. Could one claim to be a Brahman without physical beauty? Most assuredly. But could one claim Brahman status without wisdom and without virtue? No, replied the Brahman, for these were the very grounds on which Brahmans stood, the foundation of their claim to spiritual leadership and high rank.

Wisdom and virtue. One doubts that a Brahman could really have been forced to make these damning admissions, but the very fact that an argument of this form could be made points to a substantial change in intellectual climate. For now not only was the Brahmanical view challenged, but also those two qualities, wisdom and virtue, had become detached from traditional Brahmanical interpretations of them. Virtue: now there was some general view of what might constitute good behaviour quite apart from what might be appropriate to a particular estate. For the Buddha's point is that virtue is something anyone can have: it is not ascribed by birth, but achieved by application. And likewise wisdom is to be achieved and cannot just be ascribed. So the true Brahman is simply the person, born of whatever parentage, who has both wisdom and virtue.

The argument is directed against Brahman pretensions and favours the ascetics' claims to possess wisdom and virtue. But the implication is far greater, for it implies that there is some basic human nature, capable of wisdom and virtue, quite apart from one's estate or position. At a stroke the bewildering variety of different ranks and different fates was set in the background, while in the foreground was set one simple common endowment. In principle any human being can become wise and good. This assumption was made, in one way or another, by many of the Buddha's contemporaries. They spoke, not merely to this or that condition, to this or that estate, but to the human condition as such. It was a revolutionary step, for until it was taken the Indians had no way of speaking of human life beyond the narrow local conception of estates, bound to the older order of Indian society. They now had the opportunity to speak to a very much wider world, and it was an opportunity that the Buddha exploited more than any of his fellows.

★

This may seem momentous to us, but in fact it was but a small part of a much greater project which the Buddha inherited from the wanderers when he renounced the world. Their concern was not so much human society as its horizons: birth and death, and the vast spiritual cosmos which lay behind the fleeting appearances of this life. They looked upon the society of the Ganges basin as though from afar, and disdained it. They were indeed homeless wanderers (*paribbajakas*), spiritual strivers (*samaṇas*), renouncers of the world and all its fruits. But they were also perhaps India's only true cosmopolitans, citizens of the whole, not just of part.

Their cosmopolitanism is shown by the fact that the young Buddha-to-be knew enough of them in his provincial home to decide to join them. The earliest sources on his renunciation are bare and simple, but they attest well enough to the perspective of the renouncers. He was just 'a youth, with coal-black hair, in the early stages of life' (M I 163) when he left the world. This casts doubt on the existence of the wife and child later traditions awarded him, but it does illustrate that to leave the world was a whole life's vocation.

There was also a specific motive for renunciation: 'it occurred to me that life in the home is cramped and dirty, while the life gone forth into homelessness is wide open; it is difficult to live a spiritual life completely perfect and pure in all its parts while cabinned inside' (M I 241). From this we can infer some of the adventurous high-mindedness associated with the wanderer's life in the Buddha's time. They sought an ideal of perfection elevated beyond the squalid exigencies and mean quarrels of ordinary experience. They were bent not on their own pleasure, but on a lofty enterprise which sometimes brought them honour but also struggle and difficulty. To be a renouncer was a young man's, indeed a romantic's, aspiration, and from this point of view the Buddha was but one of many youths who left home, attracted by the challenge of the wandering life.

But the counterpart to this enthusiasm was a sombre and deeply serious view of such a life's task. First, the refined ideals of virtue and wisdom laid upon these wanderers a burden of perfection which perhaps few could achieve in detail. And second, they left ordinary life not just because of its irritations, but also because of its dangers. In the bare account of his reflections before renunciation the Buddha's first great change of heart is described thus:

Why, since I am myself subject to birth, ageing, disease, death, sorrow and defilement, do I seek after what is also subject to these things? Suppose, being myself subject to these things, seeing danger in them, I were to seek the unborn, unageing, undiseased, deathless, sorrowless, undefiled supreme surcease of bondage, the extinction of all these troubles?

This account is filtered through the Buddha's later thought, but what we can see through the filter is the starkness of the alternatives. The unexamined and uncontrolled life of the home leads only to sorrow and despair, endlessly repeated. Only the renouncer's life offers hope, the hope of looking down upon a morass of desire and suffering from an eminence of knowledge and dispassion. Western writers have often counted this view as unrelieved pessimism, but they have missed the optimism, the prospect of attaining 'the deathless'. The renouncers' attitude was compounded of dark bitterness and bright hope.

What rendered this attitude compelling was a larger theory which lay behind it, explaining and justifying the renouncers' rejection of the world. In this view the ordinary activity of the householder was contrasted with the extraordinary inactivity of the renouncer. For the householder must commit acts or deeds (Sanskrit *karman*) in pursuit of his worldly ends such as sexual pleasure, procreation, the acquisition of goods and power over others. Such deeds do not include inconsequential ones such as, say, brushing your teeth, but only those which are consequential or fruitful, which substantially affect your own or someone else's condition. Moreover these deeds have spiritual consequences beyond the purely visible ones, for they are charged with the power to create another body and life for the hapless householder, causing him to be reborn. (If this seems peculiar it should be remembered that it is no less rational than the belief that our deeds consign us to heaven or hell, or that they call down on us supernatural retribution.) And in being reborn he is condemned to suffer and desire in another life just as he does in this one. The suffering of one life, therefore, is but a sample of the endless suffering one will inevitably experience as one dies and is reborn again and again in the 'running on and on', *saṃsāra*, of life in the world, of desire and sorrow.

In contrast the renouncer lives in celibacy, poverty, harmlessness and desirelessness, which amount not so much to good activity as to inactivity, for he simply does not commit acts which are charged with the awful power to cause him to be reborn. Thereby the successful renouncer escapes the cycle of rebirth completely. True, the householder may achieve a better rebirth (in heaven or as a Brahman) by good deeds, or a worse one (in hell or as an animal) by bad deeds. The householder can control his fate to this extent. But this is as nothing beside the fact that, in whatever birth, even the most exalted, suffering, death and rebirth are inevitable. Only by renouncing the world entirely, by giving up all flawed activity, can one escape from this awesome mechanism into the 'unborn, unageing, undiseased, and deathless'.

This law of causation is impersonal, not administered by a god, and universal, for it applies to all sentient beings, animal, human or supernatural, who are reborn in accordance with their acts. Certainly it must have been the development of this view, and not just a criticism of the estate theory, which led the renouncers to discover human nature. For the Buddhist discourse which remarks that anyone can become a servant or that anyone is punished by a king according to his deeds, also appeals to this universal law of causation. Everyone, the discourse says, whether Brahman or Servant, must experience the consequences of his deeds in another life, but anyone, Brahman or Servant, may become a renouncer to escape rebirth entirely. These are the fundamental refutations of the estate theory: the social criticism was incidental. What the renouncers saw was the plight of all sentient beings, among whom the human condition was but a special case.

As a novice the Buddha must have found this clearer in outline than in its details. But in any case both the theory of moral causation and the project of escaping it were already established, though on the scale of centuries it was relatively new. In the older pre-Buddhist texts there are only a few hints of it. In later pre-Buddhist texts, the *Upanishads*, it had taken shape. And by the Buddha's time reincarnation was commonly accepted and the renouncers had become in effect a fifth estate, a notably important part of the life of society. There are many unanswered, and unanswerable, questions about how the renouncers and their world-view developed, but in any case their practices and their theory must have developed together. Only a body of men whose practices were moving away from ordinary life could have come to adopt such a distant and sombre view, and only such a grand, general, and all-embracing theory could have justified such a hard life or inspired people throughout the Ganges basin to respect and support the renouncers as mendicants.

The renouncers were made by their world, but they also made it, as teachers, preachers and exemplars. Their theory of reincarnation has frequently been treated as an irrational religious view, perhaps even a very old one which was already present when the warrior societies conquered North India. There may be some truth in this, but it ignores the power of the theory to explain a

complex world, as it ignores the theory's relative sophistication.
Whether one were favourably endowed by birth or not, whether
one were rising in the king's court or had lost one's ancestral lands,
whether one were successful in business or were defeated by the
king's armies, the theory could explain it. Success, beauty and
power in this world are the result of good acts in a previous life.
The humble goodness of the poor now will garner its just reward
in the next life, while prosperous wrongdoing will be punished.
Moreover, not only events within life, but its ultimate ends —
birth, old age and death — were set within a much larger scheme
within which they could be remedied. It is not at all surprising that
the theory was accepted so widely, in one form or another,
throughout Indian civilisation, and even by Brahmans. In its use
of abstract moral categories of good and evil to apply to all acts,
in its positing of a natural law of cause and effect, and in its
impersonality it was the product of generations or centuries of
intellectual effort. It would continue to be refined and developed by
the Buddha and his contemporaries.

★

In the earlier Brahmanical texts the discussion and debate which led
to these developments is relatively muted or even silent; but in the
Buddhist and Jain texts which reveal the Buddha's immediate
environment a multitude of contending voices speak, as though in
a tumultuous market-place of philosophical opinions and ascetic
practices. There were indeed public debating halls where ascetics of
all stamps gathered to dispute. The public lecture or sermon,
directed to disciples but also to potential lay supporters, was a
common institution. Certain practices were shared — begging,
wandering, celibacy, self-restraint — but upon this basic fabric
were embroidered a welter of different opinions and philosophies
and a fantastic variety of inventive self-torments.

There was an element of self-display in this. Some ate like dogs,
others adopted the posture of a chicken, many went naked. More
important, much of the self-display was intellectual: the Buddha
was later to inveigh against those who were 'clever, subtle, experienced in controversy, hairsplitters who writhe like worms in
argument'. But the very terms of abuse put in the mouths of such
'hairsplitters' demonstrate a heightened quality of debate and the

spread of those habits of mind which would allow people to decide between one argument and another: 'you conclude with your assumptions, you assume your conclusions'; 'work to clarify your views'; 'disentangle yourself if you can'. There were different schools of sceptics, philosophers doubtful of the possibility of effective knowledge in this or that matter, and their existence was perhaps the surest sign of the heat and sophistication of the intellectual climate. There were materialists who wholly denied the existence of that unseen spiritual cosmos of transmigration. There were predestinarians who believed in transmigration but who felt that every sentient being must pass through every possible fate before release was possible.

Most relevant to the Buddha, however, are three movements, the first of which can be traced through the Brahmanical texts. In the oldest sacrificial literature the sacrifice had been directed to the person of the sacrificer, in his bodily parts and faculties, in order to imbue him with magical power for the this-worldly ends of success, fertility and long life. This evolved towards a concern with the other world, life after death, and simultaneously towards a more inward conception of the sacrificer's person, now his Self. And in the *Upanishads*, composed perhaps not long before the time of the Buddha, it is the Self, the inner essence, which is the subject of transmigration, travelling from birth to birth.

The second movement was that of yoga, which in the relevant aspects was so similar to the Upanishadic movement that we may fairly speak of a spectrum of yogic/Upanishadic doctrines. Through the Buddhist scriptures which attack these yogic/ Upanishadic views we glimpse a wealth of speculation and many finely differentiated teachings proposing various views of the Self: some said that it was material, some that it was fine-material or made of mind only, while yet others held that each individual has several increasingly refined Selves. With each view went a slightly different construction of the spiritual cosmos and a panoply of meditation techniques aimed at attaining this Self so that one could sink into it, beyond the pain and confusion of the world and of transmigration.

The third movement is one which we associate today most closely with Jainism. The founder of Jainism was Mahāvīra, a contemporary of the Buddha; but there is ample evidence that his teaching was largely given in doctrines already in existence, and these doctrines enjoyed a wide influence. This school held a particularly strong version of the transmigration theory, to the effect that to hurt any living being, each of which has a soul, is to injure one's own soul by making defilement adhere to it, as dirt to a cloth. In order to cleanse oneself of defilement already acquired one was to undertake voluntary self-mortification such as fasting; and to avoid further defilement one was to avoid any injury to living beings, great or small: this is the doctrine of harmlessness or non-violence, *ahiṃ sa*. Jain self-mortification blended on one extreme with the self-restraint generally expected of all renouncers, and on the other with self-torments of a quite spectacular kind. And similarly harmlessness or non-violence was a common part of the renouncer's morality, practised perhaps most enthusiastically by Jains and proto-Jains but found among others as well.

The Buddha's relation to these movements was complex. In the first place he took some of their offerings and rejected others. He built upon the yogic/Upanishadic concern with introspection and he developed their meditative techniques, but he rejected the yogis' doctrines of the Self. He adapted the teaching of harmlessness to his own purposes, but he discarded self-mortification. However, it was never just a matter of borrowing what he found plausible or of being passively influenced by his predecessors and contemporaries, for what he did accept he transformed, and what he rejected he rejected for reasons which were original and creative. The Buddha found himself in a vigorous, competitive world which importuned him on all sides with predatory demands for total intellectual allegiance and total acceptance of one way of life or another. The relative simplicity and the cool, magisterial tone of the Buddha's teaching disguise the intensity of his struggle to find his own voice among so many others.

# 3

## To the awakening

When the Buddha left home he walked south towards the centres of population strung out along the central Ganges basin, and until his death he continued to wander throughout an area roughly 250 miles long and 150 miles wide, from Kosambi in the west to Campā in the east. There does exist a late and unreliable chronology of much of this period, but more to the point is the pattern of the Buddha's wandering life. He evidently spent time in the depths of the forest, and even sheltered in a cowshed. He had contact with both kings and prostitutes, merchants and Brahmans. His role as a peripatetic mendicant allowed him a freedom to see every way of life and every corner of his civilisation. He enjoyed a licence allowed to those, the religious beggars, who belonged to no particular part of society, free to move everywhere because in principle they threatened no one. Perhaps only a merchant or a pedlar — those other figures so characteristic of the Buddha's civilisation — would have seen so much of that world, would have had such a cosmopolitan experience.

But though the Buddha witnessed his world comprehensively, he was not of it. He was set apart by the high-minded personal morality of the renouncers: 'as a lotus flower is born in water, grows in water, and rises out of water to stand above it unsoiled, so I, born in the world, raised in the world, having overcome the world, live unsoiled by the world' (A II 38–9). He sometimes shared a roof with other wanderers, and stayed frequently for long periods of time in forested parks near the great cities — Rājagaha, Sāvatthi, Benares, Vesāli, Kosambi — which were reserved for wanderers or, later, for the growing Buddhist order.

What we know of this formative period of the Buddha's life, of his encounters with the other wanderers, is contained in a brief, bare account which, shorn of its repetitions and untrustworthy detail, would occupy but a page or two in translation: no very promising source for biography. However, this narrative is cast in terms which themselves can be glossed in considerable detail from other, doctrinal discourses of the Buddha, and once the narrative is unpacked in this way it becomes a more fruitful source than it first appears. To the keen sceptical scholarly eye there is no single detail of the narrative that could pass unquestioned; but the story as a whole is so well connected with the rest of the Buddha's teaching that it must bear a substantial burden of truth.

In that narrative (M I 163–6) the Buddha's first contacts among the renouncers are represented as having been with two teachers of yogic meditation, Āḷāra Kālāma and Uddaka Rāmaputta. The Buddha went first to Āḷāra Kālāma, and 'in no long time' mastered his teaching 'as far as lip reciting and repetition went'. Realising that this doctrine — itself significantly left undescribed in the narrative — was founded in the teacher's meditative experience, the Buddha asked him, 'To what extent do you declare you have attained this doctrine, witnessing it directly through meditative knowledge?' Āḷāra Kālāma replied that he had attained it as far as the Meditative Plane of nothingness. The Buddha then achieved this meditative state, and when he returned to describe his accomplishment to Āḷāra Kālāma, the latter was so pleased that he invited the Buddha to become his fellow teacher and leader. But the Buddha reflected that 'this teaching does not lead to dispassion, to the fading of desire, to cessation, to peace, to direct knowledge in meditation, to awakening, to release; it leads only to the Meditative Plane of nothingness'. He therefore left Āḷāra Kālāma and went to Uddaka Rāmaputta, where the same course of events took place, the only difference being that Uddaka Rāmaputta's teaching was found to lead, not to awakening, but only to the Meditative Plane of neither perception nor non-perception, so the Buddha left him as well.

This was in some ways the most important chapter of the Buddha's search, and clearly any understanding of its significance must turn on the Meditative Planes. What were they? And why did the Buddha reject them?

The fundamental practice used to attain such states is roughly similar in all Indian meditative systems, whether the Buddhist or the yogic/Upanishadic. One begins by sitting cross-legged with a straight back in some quiet place. The straightness of the back and the folded legs foster a degree of wakefulness which could not be obtained in a more comfortable position, such as lying down. One then concentrates on some object, in some versions at first a physical object but eventually in almost every case a mental image, a single sensation, or perhaps a silently repeated sound. In an Upanishadic version one might perhaps have concentrated on the Self dwelling in the heart, 'smaller than a mustard seed and golden' (C III 14). Or in a Buddhist version one might concentrate upon a colour such as blue; or in both a Buddhist and a yogic meditation on one's own breath. The counterpart to this concentration on one object is the strenuous exclusion from the attention of other sensations and indeed of merely adventitious thoughts. One is thereby absorbed in the object of meditation — and indeed some measure of this absorption is experienced by anyone who concentrates on some task.

But because the object is held unchanging before the mind's eye for long periods of time, quite extraordinary effects are achieved. Psychologists who have investigated such effects confirm not only that measurable physical changes accompany such meditation, but also that — quite apart from beliefs about what should happen — there are psychological changes such as a heightened awareness of the object of meditation, feelings of comfort and pleasure, and detachment from the surroundings and from one's own preoccupations. (These states are now much better known in the West than they were a generation ago.)

On the scale of meditative accomplishments these are relatively modest effects. There are others as well, such as the appearance of peculiar sensations or a light; and even entire complex visions may be witnessed. These further effects may, in some systems, become objects of meditation themselves and may represent the whole purpose of the discipline.

Since all meditative experiences are so radically subjective it seems difficult to find a language in which to couch an objective or value-free account of them. But there are nevertheless circumstantial accounts of a series of meditative states found in Buddhist texts, states which correspond roughly to those described in some yogic texts; and this Buddhist scheme has the advantage from our point of view of offering relatively unadorned descriptions of attitudes and experiences in meditation, descriptions which could as easily describe meditation in one system as in another. Indeed this Buddhist scheme is so untainted by dogma that it has been adopted by Western psychologists attempting to describe the phenomenon of meditation in general.

This scheme is that of the four Absorptions (*jhāna*), a graduated series of increasingly deep meditative states. In the first Absorption the meditator becomes oblivious to everything around him, though still capable of both casual and concerted thought, and his attention dwells unbrokenly on the object of meditation. In this state he enjoys both bodily comfort and the more refined mental pleasure attendant on such relaxed concentration. The meditator in this frame of mind is untroubled by unachieved desires, or by anger, or by torpor, or by doubt and restlessness.

In the second and third Absorptions the meditator gradually leaves off thinking entirely, becoming more and more absorbed in the object of meditation alone, and with this increased concentration and simplification he also transcends his feelings of comfort and intellectual pleasure. He is bent upon the object of meditation alone. And finally, in the fourth Absorption, the meditator is aware only of the object, and of an abiding sense of firm equanimity, beyond feelings of pain or pleasure. Indeed from his point of view he might be said to have increasingly *become* the object of meditation, in that he is aware of little else save the bare fact of his firm concentration or 'one-pointedness'. These four Absorptions were eventually to play a special part in the system of training elaborated by the Buddha, representing specific useful skills in the manipulation of one's own experience.

Beyond the Absorptions, however, there were further meditative accomplishments, the Meditative Planes (*āyatana*). These are described in the Buddhist literature in a relatively abstract and colourless way, but it is very likely that in the yogic systems where they originated they were actually held to be, in some sense, places or spheres, locations in the unseen spiritual cosmos. To reach them was perhaps even conceived as a sort of astral travel. There are hints of such regions in the spiritual cosmography of the *Upanishads* and yogic texts, and the Buddhist descriptions of other yogic systems suggest this as well. Indeed in later Buddhist cosmography these were spiritual planes inhabited by gods. Even the abstract early Buddhist account of them cannot disguise that they are not, like the Absorptions, a general description of meditation appropriate to any number of specific meditation theories, objectives and techniques. They are rather bound to some specific view of the topography of the unseen world. And this is not surprising, for once having resolutely set aside the world of everyday experience such a meditator was likely to supply himself with a map of the territory he had now entered.

In the Buddhist scheme of the Meditative Planes these states are achieved by leaving off 'perceptions of variety', a phrase which, though not entirely clear, seems to mean that the particular qualities perceived in the object of meditation are transcended, so that the meditator remains conscious though no longer with a detailed and defined object of consciousness. And we can see this in the first such state, the 'Meditative Plane of undelimited space'. Here the meditator is conscious of extension, though with no perception of a limitation or a quality in that extension. It is in effect infinite. In the second Meditative Plane, that of 'undelimited consciousness', the meditator is aware of consciousness alone, though with no awareness of a delimiting object of consciousness. In the third Meditative Plane the meditator is barely aware that 'there is nothing' — an awareness, according to more detailed later Buddhist texts, rather like that of coming into a room and finding no one there: it is not an awareness of *who* is not there, but just an awareness of absence. This is the Meditative Plane of nothingness. It can only be transcended in the Meditative Plane of neither perception nor non-perception, in which consciousness is so refined, or suppressed, that the meditator can only just retrieve from such a state an awareness of its existence.

I suspect that such deep trances may account for some of the more spectacular feats of yogic athleticism attested in India today. Breathing is almost wholly suppressed, the heart rate markedly slowed, and other physiological signs yet further altered. Of course this modern Western physiological description was not how the yogis viewed the matter, nor can they have seen it with quite the colourless abstraction of the Buddhist description. In their eyes such experience, being after all the consummation of their efforts, was located in some more highly coloured spiritual landscape. It may have been something like that found in the *Upanishads*, where there is considerable concern with the Self as found in deep sleep, which might have been thought to be equivalent to such profound meditation. Or it may have been like the 'meditation without qualities' found in some early yogic texts of the Indian epic, the *Mahābhārata*. But in any case the achievement of such states must be regarded as a testimony to human self-discipline and self-transcendence.

Yet the Buddha rejected such states; or, to be more accurate, he rejected the yogic teachers' assertions that they represented the culmination of the spiritual life. Why? A first approximation to an answer can be found in the *Sallekha Sutta* (M I 40–6), the Discourse on Complete Expunging. There the Buddha outlines the meditative states, both the Absorptions and the Meditative Planes, and he refers to all these as 'tranquil abidings' and as 'comfortable abidings in the here and now'. But these are distinguished from 'complete expunging', i.e. total release from the sufferings of birth and death, which is achieved by following the elaborated path that the Buddha promulgated after his awakening. From this point of view the meditative states are finally inadequate for two reasons. First, they are *merely* temporary states, *only* abidings in the here and now. This criticism is echoed more clearly elsewhere (M III 243–5), where the Buddha notes that, though the skilled meditator can remain for a very long period of time in a meditative state, that state is nevertheless impermanent, liable eventually to dissolve. And again (M III 236–7), a meditator who believes himself to have achieved final and decisive relief through such states is in fact doing something quite different: he is in fact scurrying back and forth pointlessly between 'distress' (ordinary consciousness) and 'the physical comfort of solitude', or at best between 'the fleshless pleasure [of meditation]' and 'the [mere] feeling of neither pleasure nor pain'. So in other words, though these meditative accomplishments offer temporary, even quite long-standing, release, they do not offer a decisive and permanent end to suffering. One must finally emerge only to find that one is still unchanged.

Second, as is implicit in the Discourse on Complete Expunging, such meditative skills are, when compared to the rounded fullness of the Buddha's post-awakening system of training, one-dimensional and narrow, leaving untouched both intellectual and moral development. We can see how this might be so from an analogy with mountain climbing: though the abilities and mental traits developed in such an enterprise might be conducive to some wider development of character in the climber, they do not necessarily do so. Courage and endurance can be used to quite immoral and destructive ends. So though the Buddha had mastered the meditative skills, they did not in themselves release him from ordinary waking life.

It is important, however, to gain a balanced view of what the Buddha was rejecting. On the one hand, he rejected the yogic teachers' claims that their particular accomplishments led to final release. But on the other hand, he implicitly accepted that meditation is, in some ways, the spiritual tool *par excellence*. The Absorptions in particular appear throughout his discourses as accomplishments of great usefulness. A meditator thus skilled would have great powers of concentration; for him there would 'remain an equanimity, cleansed and purified, soft, malleable, and resplendent' (M III 243), like the gold melted and purified by a goldsmith before it is fashioned into an ornament. This concentrated equanimity — of course by no means the sole property of Buddhist meditators — could then be used to attain the final goal of specifically Buddhist awakening and release.

His final view of the Meditative Planes is more difficult to pin down. On the one hand they are sometimes mentioned, in passages sprinkled through the canon, as achievements very near to final release. One could indeed take them a step further to 'complete cessation of what is perceived or felt' by a little more of the same kind of effort. But broadly speaking the canon makes it clear that this 'complete cessation' is not yet final liberation, for beyond that is still required an intellectual and emotional change, the acquisition of a Buddhist wisdom. The Buddha was evidently willing to accept many paths to release, even ones very near those of his yogic teachers; but the final goal still had to be achieved by a quite different step, a change in quality of thought and feeling, not in quantity of meditative effort.

★

The usefulness of the narrative of the Buddha's encounter with the yogis does not end there, however, for it also points to the positive and creative direction the Buddha was to take. This is implicit in the terms in which the yogis are criticised: for it is not their theories which the Buddha here finds wanting — though theories such as they must have held are attacked in many places in his discourses — but their practice. They fall short because, whatever view of the spiritual cosmos clothed their meditative techniques, it was the techniques themselves which were inadequate. On the one hand this signals that the Buddha was to move towards creating his own special forms of meditation, forms beside which methods such as the Absorptions were to take a subsidiary place. On the other hand it betokens the formation of an abiding attitude which must have marked the man as it deeply marked his teaching, an attitude which might be called a stubbornly disciplined pragmatism. Whatever teachings or practices the well-stocked market-place of ancient Indian thought offered him, they had to be shown to be useful in his own experience for him to accept them.

We can understand the significance of this attitude by looking at the Buddha's milieu. Centuries later, India recognised certain authorities or criteria of valid knowledge, by which spiritual truth could be tested, and these criteria were already implicitly present at the Buddha's time. One such criterion was simply whether a teaching appeared in the Brahmanical scriptures, including the *Upanishads*; and we can see that the Buddha was not inclined to accept this, in his view, pretentious and foreign tradition. A second authority the Buddha showed no sign of accepting was the testimony of august inspired teachers of the past on the basis of their supernormal experience. For the Buddha was self-confident, even rebellious, sure that if the problem of suffering were to be solved it had to be of such a nature that he could solve it; and in any case these teachers were not separated from him by centuries in which their knowledge could have gained an unassailable super-human authority, but were present to him in the flesh and insistent that he could himself experience their knowledge and the liberating fruit of that knowledge. A third authority, that of sheer reasoning or inference, was hardly amenable to him, perhaps because of his already formed commitment to meditation. So he depended wholly upon a fourth criterion, that of direct personal knowledge, direct personal experience, 'direct witnessing in the here and now'. As the Buddha expresses it this criterion seems such ordinary common sense that we can hardly say he invented it, but he was unique and original in insisting on its rigorous and exclusive application.

The consequences of this attitude appear throughout the Buddha's mature teaching. 'Know not by hearsay, nor by tradition . . . nor by indulgence in speculation . . . nor because you honour [the word of] an ascetic; but know for yourselves' (A I 189). The Buddha's monks were not to speculate about the future or the past, or about such recondite questions as the beginning or end of the world. They were to limit their concern and efforts to one thing, the arising and cessation of suffering within 'this fathom-long carcass'. There are many possible kinds of knowledge, asserted the Buddha, but only those touching this immediate experience were of relevance to his disciples in their search for liberation.

In the Buddha's own search this attitude of circumscribed pragmatism was however not merely a matter of clinging blindly to meditative practices alone. It also led him to reject outright the sort of theories which must have accompanied his yogic teachers' practices. This is not surprising, for, after all, meditative practices must be carried out in the light of some theory of their purpose, of the human constitution and its spiritual environment, and if the techniques fail then doubt must be cast on the theories themselves. We do not of course know just what his teachers' theories were, but we may be fairly certain that they fell within the range of yogic/Upanishadic thought. Moreover, it is clear from those discourses in which the Buddha assails such theories that they shared, from his point of view, certain common characteristics. They were all theories of the Self (Sanskrit *ātman*), though the term used for that indwelling personal principle might have differed from system to system.

At issue was the peculiarly yogic conception of knowledge. For the knowledge of the Self promulgated in such systems was radically different from other sorts of knowledge. From the yogic point of view the knower (the Self) is identical with the known (the Self), and these in turn are identical with the knower's frame of mind.

To get the measure of this let us begin with a contrasting example of ordinary knowledge, that of a skilled goldsmith. (Such examples were frequently used by the Buddha himself, since they already have stamped on them his peculiarly pragmatic turn of mind.) In this case there can be no doubt that the knower, the goldsmith, is inherently different from what he knows. As a craftsman and as a knowing subject he is clearly to be distinguished from his knowledge of the gold, of its properties and uses, and of the skills by which gold may be manipulated. Though we might admit that he would not be much of a goldsmith without the knowledge, we would never in the ordinary course of things be tempted to say that he was identical with his knowledge. The man is one thing, the knowledge another.

Nor would we be tempted to say that a goldsmith's frame of mind was identical with the goldsmith himself. A goldsmith might be angry and upset, or tranquil and alert, and he would still be a goldsmith. Nor, again, would we confuse his frame of mind with his knowledge. Whether angry or tranquil he would still have the knowledge of goldsmithing. In the case of the goldsmith the knower, the known and the frame of mind are clearly separate things even if associated in one goldsmith.

But the introspective yogic knowledge of the Self is quite another matter. For, in the first place, in this yogic knowledge the knower is the same as the known: the Self with a capital 'S', that which is to be known, is the same as the knowing self with a small 's': indeed the Upanishadic texts which proclaim this do not differentiate between the two senses of 'self'. To 'know' oneself in this yogic sense is also to 'attain' or 'become' one's Self. The power of the Upanishadic vision lies precisely here, in that the witness, the subject of knowledge, reaches a condition in which it witnesses only itself. It is a vision of radical simplification, of the perfect self-identity of the Self. 'There is in it [the Self] no diversity' (B IV 4 19). To realise this Self the yogi has only to turn inward upon himself.

This radical simplification has other consequences as well. Since there is no duality of perceived and perceiver, there are also no perceivable or analysable qualities in the Self (B IV 4 13). If, for example, what is to be realised in meditation is the Self as (meditative) Bliss — one Upanishadic formulation — then the Self is, from the point of view of the meditator, identical with Bliss. The Bliss cannot be separated out, distinguished, from the Self. Or again, if the Self to be realised is the 'Self without qualities' (perhaps in what Buddhists would call a Meditative Plane), then there is no frame of mind 'without qualities' separate from the Self; for in the Self there is 'no diversity'. One can see the plausibility of this from the yogi's point of view, for in accomplished states of meditation he may feel precisely this sense of *becoming* an object of meditation, of total simplification of his experience.

Moreover, such an experience of radical simplification also implies the immutability of the Self: for, since the Self is so perfectly unified, it cannot be thought of as changing, as losing old qualities and taking on new ones. Indeed the 'Self without qualities' could never, by its very definition, be shown to change. And to say immutable is to say eternal. The Buddha's answer to this was that, precisely because such meditative states stop sometimes, they cannot be eternal: but for a meditator bolstered by the conviction that what he sought was eternal, the very experience of stability and simplification in meditation would confirm the conviction of eternity. It would confirm as well the conviction that this eternal, immutable, radically simple Self was beyond the world of cause and effect, uncreated, 'unborn' (B IV 4 20). It could not be analysed, broken down into constituent parts (B IV 4 13). It would for him be the all-embracing and undifferentiated 'ground of the universe' (*Brahman*).

The Self, in short, is an eternal, seamless whole, self-identical, beyond phenomenal appearances and unanalysable, yet to be achieved and known through yogic meditation. This yogic vision was a powerful and persuasive one, perhaps precisely because it cut through all the diversity and potential confusion of ordinary experience and offered at a stroke a decisively simple view of the ultimate reality. Any one feature of the vision — the experience of deep meditation, the question of what lies beyond the painful world of appearances, or the nature of Self-knowledge — leads inexorably towards each of its other features. It is no wonder that, despite the Buddha's best efforts, its career continued and expanded in Hindu India.

But, on the other hand, once one bit of it begins to unravel, the rest follows swiftly. We can reconstruct how the Buddha's pragmatic reasoning about meditation led him to reject the Self theories through a discourse in which the Buddha replies to the questions of ascetic Poṭṭhapāda (D I 185 ff.). If — to pick up the thread at the experience of deep meditation — the meditator is able to witness the Self directly and thereby attain knowledge of it, it could be asked, and was asked by Poṭṭhapāda, whether the frame of mind of deep meditation arises first, and only afterwards the knowledge of the Self appropriate to that frame of mind, or whether the knowledge of the Self comes first, and then the frame of mind, or whether they are simultaneous. That is, could Poṭṭhapāda expect to reach some meditative state and then cast about for the Self, or would the attainment of the state automatically entail the attainment of the Self?

To this the Buddha quite plausibly answered that a particular consciousness or frame of mind arises first, and then the knowledge which accompanies that consciousness. This is the Buddha's meditative pragmatism speaking. For the skilled meditator, having trained to achieve that consciousness, 'knows that it is from such and such conditions that such a consciousness has arisen in me'. The meditator's practical skill is in manipulating the causes and conditions in himself which give rise to progressively more refined states of consciousness. It is upon that achievement, and upon the practical knowledge of introspective psychology that goes with it, that his eventual knowledge of the Self rests.

One can see how even the yogic teachers might have given away this much, for after all there is a good deal of training and skill, and of practical advice to go with it, in any meditative system. But once this is admitted the whole yogic system begins to crumble. For from this radically practical point of view the meditative state, caused and conditioned by the yogi's training, cannot be equivalent to an uncaused, unborn, unanalysable Self: the state itself is quite analysable and clearly caused by something.

In the discouse the Buddha continues to spin out the implications of this pragmatism. Potthapāda asks another question: 'is the consciousness or frame of mind the same as the Self, or are the Self and the consciousness different?' To this the Buddha posed the counter-question, 'but what is the Self you profess to believe in?' The sense of this question lies in the fact that, though the basic form of Self-theories were the same from the Buddha's point of view, there were evidently many variants in the theory. Different theories might place their version of the Self in rather different spiritual landscapes, or one theory might contain a teaching of several increasingly refined Selves leading up to the ultimate one. So Potthapāda first offered this: 'I profess a material Self, having a specific form, made of the four elements and nourished by solid food.' The Buddha then replied that 'if there were such a material Self, then the frame of mind and the Self would be different; . . . for even granting such a Self, still some frames of mind would come into being, and others would pass away'. When Potthapāda then changed tack, and proposed first a Self made not of material, but of mind-stuff, and then one of consciousness alone, the Buddha reiterated his argument; the Self so constituted must be one thing, the frame of mind or state of consciousness quite another. And the reason for this is quite clear: by a yogic definition the Self, whether it is material, immaterial or made of consciousness, must be eternal, unchanging and independent of the causes and conditions of this world. But it is a fact of meditative experience that states of consciousness come and go, for reasons that the meditator himself can understand and, to some limited extent, control. So whatever might be eternal, it is not the states of consciousness, and they must therefore be different from the eternal Self.

The Buddha was aided in this judgment by the use of a word which he took into his vocabulary and made his own. The root meaning of the word (*saṃkhata*) is something like 'prepared' or 'composed'. It covers a rather wider field than 'prepared', however, and in fact it has two meanings which are relevant here: it means 'willed' or 'intended' and it also means 'caused' or 'conditioned'. Meditative states are *saṃkhata*. They are attained by the will or intention of the meditator, and this also means that they are caused and conditioned. They are attributable to certain preceding causes and dependent on certain contemporaneous conditions being fulfilled. As such they are not at all 'unborn', nor are they independent of circumstances.

One might speculate that this is as far as he took his investigation of meditation and the Self at the time of his encounter with the yoga teachers, but in his mature teaching the Buddha unravels their theory of the Self a great deal further; so far, in fact, that he was to reject it entirely and propose in its place the characteristic Buddhist doctrine of non-self, *anatta*, the absence of an eternal, independent Self, whether in ordinary consciousness, in meditative states or anywhere else. This teaching was well integrated with his other thought on both ethics and psychology. In his mature view this eternal Self could not be witnessed at all, and those who believe in it are likened to a man who says that he is in love with the most beautiful woman in the land, but is unable to specify her name, her family or her appearance (D I 193).

This eternal Self is, in other words, a product of speculation, of falsely understood meditative experience, or of hearsay. The Buddha was willing to admit the existence of a self — and here the lower-case 's' is very appropriate — but that self was merely 'an agreed term, a common form of words, a worldly usage, a practical designation' (D I 202). One could reasonably say 'discipline yourself' or 'know yourself', but in so saying one would not be assuming the existence of an eternal entity. The Buddha drew an analogy with milk. Milk can become curds, then butter, and then ghee, but there would be no point in speaking of an abiding entity (milkness?) which would persist through these changes: milk is just milk, butter just butter. The British scholar T. W. Rhys Davids put it in these terms:

when the change (in the composition of the personality) has reached a certain point, it is convenient to change the designation, the name, by which the personality is known — just as in the products of the cow. But the abstract term is only a convenient *form of expression*. There never was any personality, *as a separate entity*, all the time.

So when we say, 'I feel as if I am a different person today', we are in fact alluding to an important truth about human nature.

This is a difficult doctrine, and a courageous one, in that it led into waters uncharted by the meditators of the Buddha's time. One difficulty is that of purely intellectual understanding. When the Buddha went on to develop a new method of meditation it was aimed at analysing in detail the self (small 's') of the meditator. By this method one could see how this self was in fact 'composed', made up from previous causes and subsisting on contemporaneous conditions. The doctrine in detail is one of formidable complexity, but its basic principle is simple. Just as milk progressively changes, so the self which we experience changes continually for specifiable reasons.

The real difficulty is not, however, one of intellectual understanding, but of emotional plausibility. Anyone might ask with alarm: how can I, with my well-developed sense of myself, be expected to accept that I have no self? The intellectual answer is that one has a self, but no eternal Self. But it is the emotional answer which is important. Since anyone attempting to attain or witness an eternal unchanging Self was, in the Buddha's view, bound to failure, the doctrine of the Self was an invitation to further suffering: 'such [a doctrine of the eternal Self] is merely a sensation, a writhing in discomfort, of those venerable ascetics and Brahmans who neither know nor see, and who have fallen victim to desire [for such a Self]' (D I 40–1). So to give up such a doctrine was to give up a potent source of frustration. The emotional tone of the teaching of non-self was that of a calm and relieved detachment. It was a liberation which transcended the frustrated strivings of those who revolve around a Self 'like a dog tied to a post' (M II 232–3).

★

But let us return for the moment to that point at which the Buddha realised that these yogic systems of meditation in their very nature led to mutable states of consciousness quite different from their avowed object, the eternal Self. From such a conclusion two further consequences might follow. One is that there is indeed no eternal Self, and that is the path the Buddha eventually took. The other is that the Self exists, but is not to be obtained by yogic methods. Another discipline, however, might lead to its achievement, and there was such a discipline at hand: the method of self-mortification and extreme asceticism which we know best through Jainism. On such a view the eternal principle in the individual, called the *jīva*, the 'life' or 'soul', is held in the world of suffering by the effects of transgressions committed in earlier lives, and these effects adhere to the soul like dirt. By avoiding further transgressions one obviates further bondage in the world of suffering, and by self-mortification and voluntary penances one burns away the effects of former transgressions from the soul, so that it rises to bliss and eternal freedom from pain. Here there is no necessity for meditation, nor for the application of introspective knowledge, though the theory probably did hold, as Jainism does, that knowledge, indeed omniscience, would miraculously result from the successful prosecution of such asceticism.

So after leaving Uddaka Rāmaputta, the yogic teacher, the Buddha turned to self-mortification, and the canonical discourses leave no doubt about the sincerity of his efforts in this direction. He stopped breathing completely, so that 'violent winds racked my head . . . and violent winds carved up my belly, as a skilled butcher . . . carves up an ox's belly with a sharp knife' (M I 244). Passing deities thought he was dead. Then he gave up eating more than a handful of food daily, so that 'my spine stood out like a corded rope, my ribs projected like the jutting rafters of an old roofless cowshed, and the light of my eyes sunk down in their sockets looked like the gleam of water sunk in a deep well' (M I 245). Passersby thought him a black man, so much had his austerities affected his clear complexion. By the extremity of these exertions the Buddha came to the conclusion that 'in the past, present, or future, whatever ascetic or Brahman might experience such painful, racking, and piercing feelings, he will not exceed this' (M I 246).

But he also came to the conclusion that 'by these gruelling exertions I have by no means gone beyond the common human condition to an eminence of knowledge and vision appropriate to those who are truly (spiritually) noble'. Or, in other words, all he had to show for it was a prominent rib cage. 'There must be another path to wisdom.'

★

In the traditional narrative this conclusion brought the Buddha to the threshold of awakening. But it also brings us to substantial difficulties in the interpretation of the sources. For, on the one hand, the Buddha is represented in the narrative as having reached, in a relatively short time, the saving knowledge, the certainty that 'birth is exhausted, the ascetic's life has been consummated, what was to be done has been done' (M I 249). Indeed the awakening is meant to have taken place within one night. However, it is already clear that the Buddha's progress towards awakening was long and complex, a process in which he gradually transformed himself by various disciplines and worked out an acceptable view of himself and the world. This was recognised in later discourses: 'just as the ocean slopes gradually, falls away gradually, shelves gradually, with no sudden drop, so in this teaching the training, the practice, the path are gradual, with no sudden penetration of knowledge' (A IV 200–1).

How are we to resolve this contradiction? In the first place, we must accept that the purely biographical narratives are compressed accounts: they are stories, and they are stories which march at a smart pace. Their material was meant not only to be historical, but to be an inspiration to later disciples, so they were fitted into a relatively manageable span. They had dramatic tension. Hence, even if we accept that the awakening, as a moment of certainty in the Buddha's mind that he was indeed on the right path, did take place on a single night, that certainty was long in the making and longer in the elaboration of its implications.

In the traditional account the Buddha, realising the pointlessness of extreme asceticism, accepted a reasonable meal and sat down to find that other path. In effect, that is, he accepted a still relatively disciplined asceticism, but one which avoided extremes of sensual indulgence or of self-mortification. He was soon to designate this more measured asceticism as the 'Middle Path'.

He also recollected a time when, as a child, he had sat under a rose-apple tree while his father had worked in the fields. He had on that occasion entered the first Absorption, 'accompanied with casual and applied thought, and with bodily happiness and the mental pleasure born of seclusion'. And he recognised that 'this might well be the way to awakening' (M I 246).

This account alludes only indirectly to the Buddha's original meditative accomplishments before the awakening. These accomplishments were composed, on the one hand, of his already established habit of meditative pragmatism, of his concentration upon what he could witness by, and within, himself; and on the other, of his now hardened inclination to analysis and criticism. For despite his rejection of the yogis' doctrine, he continued to cultivate the awareness of mental and physical states, an awareness which had arisen out of the yogis' psychic technology. If it was impossible to find an enduring entity, a Self with a capital 'S', through and behind these mutable experiences, it was possible at least to have an insight into the nature of these evanescent psychophysical processes themselves. Here were matters which could be directly witnessed and directly understood, and it was upon these processes that the Buddha turned the full weight of his concentration and driving curiosity. For if he could not find a Self, he could at least find release.

What these efforts gave rise to was a distinguishable meditative skill, quite different from that practised by other yogis. For this concern with immediate experience required not only a power of concentration, but also a kind of mindfulness and self-possession through which the Buddha could in fact see what was going on in his mind and body. Indeed it was just these qualities, mindfulness and self-possession (*satisampajañña*), which were to be taught throughout the Buddha's mature discourses. They demanded the ability to witness here and now with full lucidity the inner and outer states of oneself (and, by extension, the analogous experiences of others). The single most important text for the training of his own disciples was to be the Great Discourse on the Foundations of Mindfulness (D II 290 ff.), and these foundations are the dispassionate, immediate and clear perceptions of the meditator's own body, feelings, state of mind and mental contents. Such alert perceptions presupposed to an extent the one-pointedness and equanimity of the Absorptions, but they required at the same time a bright awareness of the smallest perception. This emphasis on, and elaboration of, wakeful and energetic introspection constituted the Buddha's unique contribution to meditative technology. From the conclusions based on this introspection the awakening was to flow.

How can one treat objectively, and analyse, one's own immediate feelings and attitudes? Would not the effort to perceive passions dispassionately, for example, destroy the object of study itself? The answer to these questions lies in the course of training to which the Buddha had already subjected himself, albeit unsystematically, in his search. In the pursuit of both meditative accomplishments and asceticism the Buddha had repeatedly disciplined himself to ignore those sensations and impulses which ordinarily issue in action or reaction, and which would thereby have deflected him from his purpose. He had ignored the calls of hunger and thirst which accompanied his fast, as he ignored those pains of the body and distractions of the mind which accompany long and arduous meditation. The effect of such long discipline — as meditators today attest — is not only to achieve a reproduceable tranquillity, but also to break long-standing, automatic and unconscious habits. One would ordinarily break a fast to eat, but the ascetic does not. One would ordinarily shift from a physical position which grows increasingly uncomfortable, but the meditator does not. To get the measure of this meditation, try this experiment: sit in the most comfortable possible position in a comfortable chair, and try to hold that position without moving for an hour. The Buddhist prediction is that within minutes you will wish to scratch the nose, twitch the finger, shift the leg. What if one could watch these urges arise and pass away with no movement at all?

But this is not to say that impulses to respond to such calls disappear, for they do not, or at least not permanently. In the meditator such impulses simply do not issue in a reaction. He is tranquil, his mind is malleable (*kammañña*). He can temporarily ignore such impulses completely if he chooses, as in an Absorption, but his long-term relationship to such impulses is also changed, for he can now respond to such impulses in a reasoned rather than an automatic way.

Moreover, just because such sensations and impulses do not disappear, he can choose to exercise mindfulness, securely founded in his now habitual equanimity, to observe and analyse them. Whereas the ordinary unskilled person can with clarity contemplate painful or pleasurable sensations, and the accompanying impulses and emotions, only in the tranquillity of memory, safely removed from their effects by time, the meditator learns to do so immediately, as they actually occur. It must be the case that, because of his long training, the meditating ascetic perceives his pains, pleasures and urges as being less poignant and pressing, but this does not change their fundamental nature. And in any case the meditator may still use memory, and the observation of other people, to confirm that what he observes of his relatively controlled emotions must also be true of less controlled emotions.

This new form of meditation was to be called insight (*vip assanā*) meditation. It was the Buddha's experimental method, his way of gathering information, and upon this information about his presently occurring states of body and mind his analysis of the human condition was to be erected.

# 4

# *The awakening*

In Buddhist countries the awakening is thought to have occurred on a single night of the full moon of the lunar month Vesakha, April–May, as the Buddha sat beneath a huge Bodhi tree (*ficus religiosus*). With the awakening (*sambodhi*) the Buddha attained, first, a knowledge of the nature of the human condition that would lead to salvation and, second, the certainty that he himself had attained liberation from the sorrows of that condition. The early scriptures attribute many doctrines, and certainly the most important ones, to the night of the awakening itself, so that the awakening is made to bear the weight of the whole of the Buddha's mature teaching. Even if this is not literally true, the knowledge and certainty of that night must lie at the base of the mature teaching.

The awakening grew out of a creative tension between two governing convictions. One was that the answer was to be sought in painstaking attention to the minutiae of experience as witnessed in insight meditation (though the articulated method of that meditation may not yet have been fully formed). But if this consideration alone had informed the Buddha, he might have become only a minor contributor to yogic thought. The other conviction, however, was that of the truth of transmigration, and the Buddha's conception of this gave his teaching a scope and a purchasing power in human life which transcended the narrow yogic concerns. The Buddha's originality stemmed from his close analysis of individual experience, but his importance stemmed from his acceptance of this common Indian belief in rebirth.

In the Buddha's case this belief came down to a deep moral seriousness. In other teachings the doctrine of transmigration went with an elaborate view of the spiritual cosmos within which transmigration occurs. One moves up and down, becoming now an animal, now a god, now the denizen of some hell, and again a

Warrior or Brahman, a slave or a king (Buddhism itself was later to be prolific in the production of such views). But for the Buddha the specific details of transmigration were never so important as the principle underlying it: human action has moral consequences, consequences which are inescapable, returning upon one whether in this life or another. There *is* a fundamental moral order. One cannot steal, lie, commit adultery or 'go along the banks of the Ganges striking, slaying, mutilating and commanding others to mutilate, oppressing and commanding others to oppress' (D I 52), without reaping the consequences. There *is* an impersonal moral causation to which all are subjected. Misdeeds lead to misery in this life or in later lives. The Buddha's teaching was devoted to the apparently selfish purpose of self-liberation, being directed to sentient beings in so far as they are capable of misery and final liberation from misery. But the teaching also touched sentient beings as moral agents, as agents capable of affecting the welfare not only of themselves but of others as well. Some of his teachings seem to treat only personal liberation, others morality, but for the Buddha the two matters were always intimately and necessarily connected.

The teaching most closely connected with the awakening chiefly concerns personal misery and personal liberation. This is the doctrine of the Four Noble Truths (*cattāri ariyasaccāni*), which cover under their spacious umbrella the central tenets of Buddhism. These are phrased after the pattern of a medical diagnosis: this is the disease, these are the causes of the disease, this is the judgment of whether it is curable, this is the method of treatment. The disease is 'suffering' (*dukkha*) — a condition which covers all that is meant in English by 'suffering' but more as well, and this wider sphere of meaning must be borne in mind. The first Noble Truth is that there does indeed exist the disease, suffering, and this is the Truth of Suffering. The second Noble Truth is that there are discernible causes of suffering: this is the Noble Truth of the Arising of Suffering, which contains an account of those causes. The third Noble Truth is that there is in fact a cure for suffering, and this is the Truth of the Cessation of Suffering. The fourth Noble Truth is that of the cure for suffering, the Truth of the Path Leading to the Cessation of Suffering.

Let us take the first Truth, that of the existence of suffering, in a form in which the Buddha is traditionally thought to have explained it shortly after the awakening. That description begins thus: 'What is the Noble Truth of Suffering? Birth is suffering, ageing is suffering, sorrow and lamentation, pain, grief, and despair are suffering' (S V 421). Here there is no problem in translating *dukkha* as 'suffering'. This is suffering viewed as we might commonly view it, on a large time-scale, a concomitant of any human life as a whole: in so far as we are born, we are bound to suffer in being born, in sickness, in growing old, in the loss of loved ones and in death. This long-term view considers that the continuous process of birth and death could not be anything but a magnification in one life after another of the sorrow which falls to any one human life. All our experience, even that of common happiness, is bracketed by pain and sorrow. Since in the long run we are all dead, the problem of suffering is a pressing one, demanding a solution.

At this level the Truth of Suffering resembles other views, common among renouncers, that worldly life is a morass of pain. But what saves it from conventional pessimism is its connection with a more carefully worked-out view of human fate. This view is progressively revealed as the description of the Truth of Suffering continues: 'association with what is disliked is suffering, dissociation from what is desired is suffering, not to get what one wants is suffering'. This is suffering on a more intimate time-scale, as it might appear within a year, a day or even an hour, and is closer to the Buddha's characteristic concern with what is immediately observable. It is also a more general description of suffering, not only as it accompanies the crises of life, but as it appears in everyday situations, situations which might not occasion lamentation but rather an acute consciousness of failure, or of frustration, or of unfulfilled yearning: the missed opportunity, the baffled effort, the irksome routine, the petty irritation of life with others. Here *dukkha* might be translated not as 'suffering', but as something less grand but more pervasive: discomfort, dissatisfaction or discontent. This is illustrated in the canon by tales of, for example, the insecurity of office-seekers, the anxieties of husbandmen, the irritations and frustrations of household life. This teaching brings suffering within the ambit of daily experience, for it points to the inescapably changing nature of life, which engulfs all the things we believe to be secure and stable.

But such a viewpoint was also shared with others at the Buddha's time, so for a doctrine which is quite uniquely Buddhist, we shall have to turn to the end of this description of the first Truth: 'in sum, all the aspects of experience in the mind and body . . . are suffering'. This is the definition of suffering which leads to the heart of what is original in the Buddha's teaching, and to that part of his view of suffering which is thoroughly argued in the canonical sources as a dispassionate description of the human plight. Here suffering is seen as being woven most finely into the texture of human experience; here experience is considered on the smallest time-scale, from second to second, under a microscope, under the clinical eye of the introspecting meditator. Under this microscope *dukkha* falls within another range of meanings, such as imperfection, impermanence, evanescence, inadequacy, insubstantiality, incompleteness, uncontrollability. The great crises which occasion lamentation, and the small desperations which occasion discontent, are but especially visible examples of the fundamental imperfection-cum-impermanence — suffering — which is inherent in all experience. In so far as it is dynamic, changing, uncontrollable and not finally satisfactory, experience is itself precisely suffering.

To see how this works let us take the case of feeling (*vedanā*) as a paradigm. Feeling is one of the objects of immediate introspection recommended in insight meditation, and it is also one of the 'aspects of experience in the mind and body'. Feeling may be physical or mental, and it may be adjudged pleasant, unpleasant or neither pleasant nor unpleasant, i.e. neutral. So, as he contemplates his presently occurring experience, the insight meditator is to discern, as each actually arises, that this feeling is pleasant, or that feeling unpleasant, or another feeling quite neutral. For example, the pains in one's knees as one tries to sit cross-legged in meditation are unpleasant; the exhilaration of actually managing to sit for a long period and gain some concentration is pleasant; and many feelings in between, such as that of the process of calm breathing, are neutral. Or again, the blowing of a car horn just outside the room in which one is meditating might occasion unpleasant feelings, the song of a nightingale might occasion pleasant ones, or the sound of rain might occasion neither. Though some of the feelings which thus arise and clamour for attention may last for a while — such as the pains in the knees — or may come back again and again, it does not require deep meditative insight to see why

the Buddha came to regard feelings as impermanent. They are soon
chased away by other feelings, and even in the great meditative
attainments cannot be made to abide. The question which underlay
the Buddha's quest was, 'in what may I place lasting reliance?' On
this diagnosis, certainly not in feeling, for even pleasant feelings are
'suffering by virtue of change'; that is, though pleasant at the
moment, they bear within them the seed of insecurity, of their own
imminent destruction. The introspectively discovered Truth of
Suffering is one of ceaseless movement, of a dynamic process which
is suffering by virtue of being uncontrollable, ever-changing, and
therefore inadequate and unsatisfying.

Furthermore this inadequacy rules throughout the experience of
both the mind and body of the individual. The Buddha proposed
several different analytic descriptions of the mind and body, each
fitted to a different context; but generally these descriptions are of
a process, not a stable entity. The individual is seen by the Buddha
more as, say, a burning fire or a swiftly moving stream than as a
solid vessel for holding experience or an unmoving slate upon
which perceptions are written. Our own language tends to obscure
this, for we tend to think of a relatively stable body and mind
which receive a dynamic and changing experience, and we therefore tend to think that mind and body can be described apart from
experience. But the Buddha's language was one in which both
experience and the mind-body complex were described together, as
part of a single process. Here, for example, is such a description:

In dependence upon the eye and upon visible objects visual
consciousness arises. The union of these three [i.e. the eye, objects, and
visual consciousness] constitutes contact. Dependent upon this contact
feeling is constituted. One perceives what is thus felt; what one perceives
one considers; and what one considers one develops all sorts of notions
about. (M I 111–12)

In this view, objects of experience, the organs of experience such
as the eye, and the consequent consciousness of experience, 'the
mind', are indissolubly linked. None of the three is conceivable
without the other: they lean upon each other as one sheaf of reeds
leans upon another, to use a canonical simile.

Furthermore, those features of experience which might be said
to lie within the 'mind' itself, such as perception, feeling and
consciousness, are themselves 'conjoined, not disjoined, and it is

impossible to separate them in order to specify their individual characteristics' (M I 293). So right from the objects of perception, through the physical organs of perception, to feeling, consciousness, thought and volition, there is one dynamic, interdependent, ever-changing complex, which might be called an 'individual' or a 'self', but which has nothing lasting in it.

Indeed the very term which I have translated as 'all aspects of experience in the mind and body' is one of the analytic descriptions of this process, a description in which the impersonal, dynamic and interdependent nature of the process is already implicit. This term is the 'five aggregates' (*pañcakkhanda*). The first 'aggregate' is materiality, which includes physical objects, the body, and sense organs. The other four 'aggregates' are feeling, perceptions, impulses and consciousness. Within these 'aggregates', this process, are included all that pertains to an individual and his experience. Feeling is but one face of this process, a face available to insight meditation. The mutability and inadequacy of feeling are characteristic of the whole process: 'all aspects of experience in the mind and body are suffering'. Or, as the Buddha said elsewhere, 'as the aggregates arise, decay, and die, O monk, so from moment to moment you are born, decay, and die' (P I 78).

This seems a gloomy doctrine, and a common instinct is to question it. Surely there must be some happiness in the world? However, the Buddha's teaching does not deny that there are satisfactions in experience: the exercise of insight assumes that the meditator sees such happiness clearly. Pain is to be seen as pain, pleasure as pleasure. What is denied is that such happiness will be secure and lasting.

But this does not fully answer the doubt, for the real grounds of it lie elsewhere, in a radical difference between the experience of the questioner and that of the Buddha. The doctrine of suffering presupposes a vulnerability to disease, death, natural calamity and human oppression that characterised the Buddha's world, as it does much of the world today. It is in these terms that the doctrine is illustrated in the canon. But for many in the societies of the West this vulnerability is suppressed or rendered inconspicuous — by prosperity, by medical advances and by those peculiar institutions surrounding death which render it invisible. Without that sense of vulnerability there might be little reason to connect suffering as unsatisfactoriness on the small scale, with death, disease and

lasting failure on the grand scale: one could just put up with the
discomforts (as indeed Buddhist monks learn to do). However, for
those whose experience includes vulnerability — a vulnerability
that might be psychological or social as well as material — the
connection can have a compelling cogency.

★

Though the announcement of the Four Noble Truths is in fact brief
and bare, there is a good deal of dramatic tension in it. For if
suffering is such a pervasive and unending process, what could be
its cause? How could one break into the cycle to see what makes
it revolve? And from this point of view the discovery of the second
Noble Truth (that there are discernible causes of suffering), the
Truth of the Arising of Suffering, is the centre-piece of the awakening. Some Buddhists celebrate this as a dramatic moment in which
the Buddha saw the 'house-builder', the cause of this flawed and
unsatisfactory existence. He is said on that occasion to have uttered
this verse:

> Seeking but not finding the house-builder
> I travelled through life after life.
> How painful is repeated birth!
> House-builder, you have now been seen.
> You will not build the house again.
>
> (*Dhammapada* 153–4)

We can already see the directions in which the Buddha would
look for this cause. One direction is given by the Buddha's
pragmatic turn of mind. He tended to think of causes not in a
purely abstract way, but rather by using analogies from practical
activity. The meditator, for example, is likened to a goldsmith, or
to a fletcher straightening the mind like an arrow. In one passage
(M I 240–3), concerning the Buddha's search before the awakening,
he speaks of his efforts on the analogy of a man trying to start a
fire: just as a man could not start a fire by rubbing a dry stick upon
a wet one lying in water, or by rubbing it upon a wet stick lying
on dry land, but only by rubbing a dry stick on another dry stick
on dry land, so a meditator must be *bodily* withdrawn from sensual
pleasures (a stick out of water), and also *mentally* withdrawn from
such pleasures (a *dry* stick out of water). This way of thinking has
a good deal of subtlety in it, for it recognises that there are
subsidiary, enabling causes and conditions, such as the dryness of

the stick and so forth. But it places the chief cause with the agent, the meditator, the man making the fire. The chief cause is conceived as being *agent-like*, like a person bringing about a result. This is certainly the sense of describing the cause of suffering metaphorically as the 'house-builder'. The pieces of that 'house' had to be lying to hand, but there also had to be a 'builder', a *purposive* and *active* principle. Hence, in seeking the cause of suffering, the Buddha was seeking something active and purposive, which was to that extent like an agent, a person.

Moreover, this principle had to be agent-like in other ways as well. First, just as the meditator can, to an extent, control himself in order to perfect his meditative skill, so this principle had to respond to corrective action. Like a person or agent, it had to be corrigible: it had to be possible to deal with the 'house-builder' as one deals with oneself, for otherwise there would be no possibility of liberation. Second, just because the activities of this principle had moral consequences, upon others and upon oneself in the process of rebirth, it had to be like a *moral agent*, a person whose acts are good or evil. These considerations may seem so abstract as to be inconsistent with the Buddha's pragmatism, but they point to the practical obstacle he had to overcome. The simplest explanation of all this might be just that the purposive, active principle is an agent, a Self or 'person' or soul. But the Buddha had good reason for rejecting this idea. Indeed in his insight meditation he had found only an *impersonal* process, that of suffering. He had to break through to find a principle which was in many ways like an agent or person, but which was finally impersonal, not an agent or person at all.

This is what he discovered:

And this, O monks, is the Truth of the Arising of Suffering. It is just thirst or craving [*taṇhā*] which gives rise to repeated existence, which is bound up with impassioned appetite, and which seeks fresh pleasure now here and now there, namely, thirst for sensual pleasures, thirst for existence, thirst for non-existence. (S V 421)

So thirst or craving is that which drives the whole mass of suffering experience forward. The word *taṇhā* bears the literal sense of 'thirst', and it is this meaning that lends the term its vividness. Its technical sense, however, is 'craving' or 'desire'. In this sense it is insatiable craving, 'which seeks fresh pleasure now here and now there', not only in this life but in the lives beyond, and because of this it 'gives rise to repeated existence'. Moreover, in so far as craving is 'bound up with impassioned appetite', the metaphor of fire was never far from the Buddha's mind, and indeed in a discourse traditionally placed very early in his career, the Fire Sermon (S IV 19), each facet of experience is described as 'aflame with desire'.

This way of thinking is in many ways poetical rather than soberly technical, and a good deal of the Buddha's effort around and after the awakening must have been devoted to drawing out the implications of this pregnant idea. Certainly craving could be shown to be purposive: to crave is to crave something, to be thirsty is to be thirsty *for* something. 'Where does this craving come into being and settle itself? Wherever there is what seems lovable and gratifying, there it comes into being and settles' (D II 308). In most descriptions of craving there is a tendency to emphasise this positive desire, 'desire for sensual pleasure'.

This was the puritanism of the renouncers speaking. Indeed, the idea of desire was common among the renouncers: it was the great obstacle to achieving the Self or purifying the soul. But in elevating it to an autonomous principle the Buddha expanded its definition. For him craving also included aversion, and that is probably the sense of 'thirst for non-existence'. One craves not only what is attractive but also relief or escape from what is unpleasant or undesirable. And we crave a great deal. We crave all sensual pleasures — sexual, gustatory, olfactory, tactile or whatever. We yearn keenly to escape pain. We crave wealth, power, position. We even lust sensually after our own bodies, or in rebirth a new body. There is even a 'thirst for views', the urge to be right, to be in the know, to have an answer for every question.

Craving may be spoken of comprehensively as 'thirst for existence'. This is, to be sure, the 'thirst which gives rise to repeated existence', but perhaps a better way to think of it is as *the desire for becoming other than what present experience gives*. Under many guises it is a ceaseless striving for some new state, some new being, some new experience, at the same time as being a striving for satiety and permanence, and it is a striving always frustrated. 'The world [in the sense of all common individuals in the world], whose nature is to become other, is committed to becoming, has exposed itself to becoming; it relishes only becoming, yet what it relishes brings fear, and what it fears is pain' (U III 10, Ñāṇamoli's reading). Rebirth may be rebirth from moment to moment of experience, or it may be rebirth in another life, but in either case it is the consequence of this lust *to be something else*.

This is the purposive activity of craving on a large scale, as it embraces all sentient life. But this grand vision is to be justified, as ever in the Buddha's teaching, by reference to the fine grain of experience. In this perspective craving was in fact already written into the five 'aggregates', that comprehensive description of mental and physical experience, as impulses (*saṃkhāra*). Let us return to the example of the pains in the knees one feels when trying to sit for long periods in insight meditation. Just because one feels these as unpleasant, one also feels an urge to change position, an impulse to seek comfort and relief by moving. This impulse is, in effect, just the active, purposive aspect of the unpleasant feeling: it arises with the unpleasant feeling, is indeed inseparable from it. In ordinary circumstances one would simply shift position automatically, without reflecting or perhaps even without being conscious of it. The same might be said for pleasant feelings: while meditating one might feel sleepy and dreamy, and one is moved automatically to follow and indulge such feelings. Or one feels hungry and thinks of having a little snack before continuing. Without the attempt at meditation many such impulses would hardly be noticed, so instantly do they follow one another. In this microscopic view, experience is revealed as having a foundation of ceaseless activity, of short-lived purposive impulses. The Buddha indeed thought of this activity as *making* experience. 'What is called "mentality" and "mind" and "consciousness" arises and ceases, in one way and another, through day and night; just as a monkey ranging through a forest seizes a branch and, letting go, seizes another' (S II 95).

This perception through insight meditation of an animating principle of existence ruled the Buddha's thought. It was the evidence which guided his understanding of the human condition. Because impulse is habitual and automatic, fundamentally unreflective and not a function of decision, there was no reason to think of it as the work of some person or Self, as other renouncers thought. It was just a propensity, an active disposition at the base of life which had the special and disastrous ability to reproduce itself endlessly. As a propensity he called it 'clinging' (*upādāna*). This propensity was in fact already written into the Noble Truth of Suffering, for the full form of that reads: 'all aspects of experience in the mind and body, *in which clinging inheres*, are suffering' (S V 421). The different terms — clinging, craving, impulse, thirst — each shed a different light on the activity behind and within sentient life. They all point to one thing, the impersonal active principle, the discovery of which answered the Buddha's question, 'how did I come to be in this sorry plight?'

The Buddha did not consider, however, that craving acts alone — his idea of causes by no means required a single or a simple solution to the problem. While craving might be the chief motive cause in the painful process of rebirth, there was room for subsidiary, enabling causes, conditions without which it could not take hold. And among these there was one which had an especially important place: ignorance or delusion. The idea was current among the wanderers and yogis: they enjoyed a special knowledge of which others were ignorant. In the Buddha's usage, however, his knowledge was not so much an esoteric truth like the knowledge of the Self, but rather a penetrating understanding of *things as they are*. By comparison people are ordinarily not so much uninformed — as one might be uninformed of tax laws or of the Self — but positively deluded. They hold that the world contains lasting and secure satisfactions, whereas in fact it is riddled with suffering. They are mistaken, so craving has its way with them. The relationship between craving, ignorance and suffering is rather like the relationship between heat, oxygen and fire. Heat is the motive force, but without oxygen fire could not arise. 'Thirst for existence, O monks, has a specific condition; it is nourished by something, it does not go without support. And what is that nourishment? It is ignorance' (A V 116).

★

So far these teachings are amoral. They are the utterances of a detached specialist, a renouncer, addressing himself to others with the same concern for personal salvation. But the Buddha was also convinced that sentient beings are subjected to a law of moral causation, and he was deeply concerned with the evaluation of behaviour and its effects on others. So these amoral teachings are indissolubly linked in his thought with others that point to a radically moral significance in the human condition.

Let us begin with impulses. As I have so far described them

impulses hardly have a moral significance, but they may be regarded from another point of view. They may be considered as intentions of choices, both of which are included in the key term *cetanā*. Sometimes 'choice' is the best translation, in so far as it is a mental movement which precedes action or speech. But intentions are also included, for the Buddha thought that unexpressed intentions could themselves have an effect, if not outwardly then inwardly in the mind. The Buddha held that in human affairs it is the mental choice or intention which is of ultimate significance: 'the world is led by mind' (S I 39). Hence, for example, in the legal system developed for the Buddhist order, only intentional actions are regarded as transgressions, and unintentional acts — such as those committed while asleep, or mad, or under duress — are not culpable.

This has great implications. It means that intentions are not negligible, that they have consequences. They do work, are in themselves actions. This is the sense of the term 'karma', whose primary meaning is just 'work' or 'deed', but in this Buddhist sense 'mental action'. (Karma does not refer to the *results* of action, as we now assume in ordinary usage in the West.) 'It is choice or intention that I call karma — mental work —, for having chosen a man acts by body, speech and mind' (A III 415). Intentions make one's world; it is they that do the work whose consequences we must reap in suffering. They form the subsequent history of our psychic life as surely as wars or treaties, plagues or prosperity form the subsequent history of a nation.

To speak of impulses and urges is not necessarily to speak in moral terms, but choices and actions are the very stuff of moral discourse. One may make good or bad choices, one's actions may be good or evil. And in fact from the Buddha's point of view *unconscious* impulses are really to be equated with *conscious* choices, the only difference being that impulses occur in ignorance of their nature as choices: they are choices made under the delusion that there is no better choice, no better way of acting. In this light the relatively neutral term thirst (craving) may itself be considered as greed, something morally reprehensible, and frequently the Buddha spoke in just this way. Greed may be supported by sheer delusion about the nature of the world, but it is also immoral, a propensity to be condemned and, in oneself, to be improved upon. Moreover greed is always coupled in the discourses with hatred or aversion. Hence from a radically moral standpoint it is by choosing badly, by being greedy and hateful, that we bring upon ourselves the suffering we meet in birth after birth. The ill that we cause ourselves and the ill that we cause others are of a piece, stemming from the same roots. The Noble Truth of the Arising of Suffering could be rephrased thus: 'inflamed by greed, incensed by hate, confused by delusion, overcome by them, obsessed in mind, a man chooses for his own affliction, for others' affliction, for the affliction of both, and experiences pain and grief' (A III 55).

Or in other words the propensities of greed, hatred and delusion which cause us to injure others through evil deeds are exactly the same propensities which cause us to suffer ourselves by being reborn in life after life. The moral cause in transmigration is equivalent to the cause of suffering. But this raises a fundamental question: how exactly does this cause work? For a doctrine of a Self or soul it is easy enough. The Self acts, causes consequences to itself, and is reborn again according to its deserts. The basic structure is in its own terms plausible, so the details are not so important. But what if there is no Self?

The answer (as it appears at D II no. 15) works backwards from the appearance of a new body and mind, a new psychophysical entity. How did this appear? It appeared through the descent of consciousness into a mother's womb. On the face of it this is primitive, going back to earlier Indian ideas of an homunculus descending into the womb; and it is speculative, going beyond the Buddha's brief of attending only to what he could witness himself. But later Buddhist commentators are clear that this descent is metaphorical, as we might say 'darkness descended on him' if someone fell unconscious. Moreover this enlivening consciousness is not an independent entity, a disguised Self, but is composed of causes and conditions.

So what in turn were these preceding conditions? One was the act of physical generation, but more important was a previous impulse. Here impulse is to be understood as intention or mental action, bearing a moral quality and informing by that quality the nature of the new psychophysical entity. If the impulse was good the new body and mind will be well endowed and fortunately placed, if not it will be poorly endowed and unfortunate.

And now comes the key question: what is this mysterious impulse? It is in fact nothing other than the final impulse, the dying thought, of the previous mind and body. It is nothing like a Self, but is merely a last energy which leaps the gap from life to life rather like — as a later Buddhist source puts it — a flame leaping from one candle wick to another. Nor is it free of preceding conditions, for it is the product of the dispositions formed by habitual mental actions conducted under the veil of ignorance and desire within the previous life. And thus one can trace the process back — to beginningless time, in fact.

In this account there is no underlying entity, but there is a stream of events which has its own history. This history is borne forward, not by a Self or soul, but by the complex interaction of the causes, conditions and effects summarised under craving and suffering. To understand this interaction is to understand the nature and origins of the human condition. Many canonical accounts treat this as the substance of the awakening itself: the Buddha called it dependent co-origination (*paṭicca samuppāda*). It was dependent in that the causes and conditions necessarily interact with each other, as do fuel, heat, oxygen and so forth in the production of fire. No one of them is finally independent, as a Self or soul might be. So dependent co-origination served two functions: it refuted the idea of an independent permanent soul, and it described the origin of suffering. The doctrine attached to dependent co-origination includes everything I have discussed under the first two Noble Truths, though it is phrased somewhat differently. It usually (but not always) comprises twelve factors. These range from those describing the psychophysical entity, such as sense organs and feeling, to the descriptions of the sources of suffering, namely ignorance, craving, clinging and impulses. And of course it includes suffering as well. Though we might speculate that, as a doctrine, dependent co-origination appeared after the Four Noble Truths, it was in fact already inherent in them, in the Buddha's understanding of craving and suffering, and of the interactions through which craving causes suffering.

★

The third Noble Truth, the Truth of the Cessation of Suffering, certifies that the disease of suffering is actually curable. Though there is no permanent moral person, the impersonal process is corrigible. One can achieve liberation. Within the Four Noble Truths this is a relatively colourless doctrine, fulfilling the form of the medical diagnosis. But it did speak to an important body of opinion held at the Buddha's time. This was represented especially by the Ājīvikas, who held that the process of rebirth is an automatic, mechanical one: every being must, whatever he does, be reborn in every possible condition, and every being is destined ultimately to attain salvation, so special effort is pointless. An Ājīvika might well have asked the Buddha whether his own doctrine of dependent co-origination did not in effect lead to just such a conclusion. Do not these causes and conditions, however complex, lead in the end to a mechanically predestined result, rather like an intricate clockwork wound up and set ticking? To this the Buddha's answer was that, though one's endowments and capacities are formed by circumstances in previous lives, one still has the ability, within the confines of this present life, to alter voluntarily one's behaviour. One can dispel ignorance by seeing the world as it is, as it is described in the Four Noble Truths. And one can control craving by the measured renouncer's discipline promulgated by the Buddha.

The fourth Noble Truth is the Truth of the Path Leading to the Cessation of Suffering. This contains the prescription, the medicine. This is usually given as the Noble Eightfold Path, but already in canonical sources this list is conveniently broken down into three constituents: moral self-discipline or morality, meditation, and wisdom (*sīla, samādhi, paññā*). Morality consists of a pacific, truthful, upright and thoroughly disciplined way of life, reasoned to cause harm neither to oneself nor to others. For the Buddha's monks this meant a life of mendicancy, or poverty but not of self-mortification, of celibacy and of gentle honesty. Though the Buddha and his renunciant disciples elaborated a monastic disciplinary code consistent with Buddhist principles, this was probably in essence not far different from the code with which the Buddha began, a code inspired by the moral ideals then current among the wanderers and renouncers.

The second part of the path is meditation. Part of meditation is allied with morality: the attempt to restrain one's senses from what is immoral and to create good, wholesome and skilful frames of mind within which to work. The counterpart to this is the avoidance not only of bad actions but of bad frames of mind, which lead not to clarity but to delusion. Against this background the basic skill is concentration, coupled with equanimity, and this meditative control is then the basis of insight meditation. Insight meditation, however, is not practised only by sitting in quiet solitude. For it demands a general attitude of self-recollection, of clear consciousness, of awareness of one's surroundings, one's experiences, and one's actions and their consequences moment by moment, day by day. As it was taught to his pupils this meditative discipline is relatively systematised, but the Buddha fulfilled it unsystematically in the course of his search. These first two parts of the path could be thought of as a battery of skills rather like those a painter: draftsmanship, the use of colour, the depiction of perspective and so forth. As these skills blend into a greater skill, that of painting itself, so all the individual exercises of morality and meditation blend into a single alert and calm way of life.

But the abilities of the painter must be wedded to a sensibility, a way of seeing the world. And analogously the third part of the path — wisdom — demands a radically new way of perceiving experience. One facet of this new perception is, quite simply, seeing the world as it is, and for the Buddha this meant seeing by means of the Four Noble Truths and dependent co-origination: in such-and-such a way is experience evanescent, devoid of abiding self and painfully flawed. In such-and-such a way does craving reproduce this suffering again and again.

The other facet is a new attitude, a new habit of mind, which grows out of the equanimity of meditation. One can now stand aloof from experience. One can see the dangers in it and turn away. One can observe, yet not pursue, even fleeting pleasures and aspirations as they flicker before the mind's eye. Perhaps the most compact statement of this sensibility is found in the stock prescription that the monk should 'not cling to the here and now, not grasp after situations, relinquish easily'. Or again:

[the monk] neither constructs in his mind, nor wills in order to produce, any state of mind or body, or the destruction of any such state. By not so willing anything in the world, he grasps after nothing; by not grasping, he is not anxious; he is therefore fully calmed within.          (M III 244)

One should neither look forward to coming experiences, nor clutch at present ones, but let them all slip easily through one's fingers.

The Buddha took this to great lengths. In the Simile of the Raft (M I no. 22) he instances the case of a man who, faced by a flood, builds a raft from wood lying about and floats safely to the other side. The Buddha asks whether it would be rational for the man, having reached the other side, to put the raft on his head and carry it with him. The answer is that it would assuredly not be rational. Just so, concludes the Buddha, it is irrational to cling even to the profitable states of mind created by morality and meditation, still less to unprofitable states of mind. (This presupposes, of course, that through habituation and training the profitable practices are now second nature to the monk.) The same applies to ideas: to indulge in speculations and theories about the past or future, eternity, the fate of the world and so forth, is to lose oneself in 'a tangle of views, a thicket of views'. Instead one is to view the world simply, directly, with the perception achieved in insight meditation. This perception, like the artist's way of seeing, is highly cultivated, but it is nevertheless immediate and uncomplicated by reflection. One is to hover in a sensibility of liberation, where the flood refers to the painful stream of birth and death: 'if I stood still, I sank; if I struggled, I was carried away. Thus by neither standing still nor struggling, I crossed the flood' (S I 1).

This is Nirvana, the 'blowing out' of the passions and frustrations of existence. The Buddha asserted that to speculate about the frame of mind of one thus awakened and liberated is to invite confusion and madness. But despite this useful advice, such speculation played a great part in subsequent Buddhist history, as it must in our assessment of the claims of Buddhism to our assent. The accounts of awakening in the canon foster the impression that one is either awakened or not, liberated or not, and that the switch from one to the other is practically instantaneous and irreversible. However, one of the issues in the first great schism in Buddhism, a few generations after the Buddha's death, was whether a liberated person can, even temporarily, backslide from awakening. And by the same token later schools conducted debates over whether awakening was instantaneous or gradual.

What these difficulties point to is a problem inherent in the language used in the canon to describe such impalpable matters: for the purposes of a narrative, the story of the Buddha's *awakening*, a sudden, dramatic and decisive transformation is required. And this is plausible to the extent that the awakening was a matter of certainty, of the knowledge that 'what was to be done has been done'. The Buddha realised that he had fulfilled all the requirements for liberation and no longer had to struggle arduously forward. But the *liberation* is a different matter, for here we are speaking of a wholesale transformation in the human constitution. It seems implausible that this transformation, as it is described in the canonical sources, could be other than gradual, a slow mastering of the whole field of one's behaviour and thought. In this respect the awakening had to be further certified and shown to be practically effective in the course of subsequent experience. We may accept that the Buddha was awakened one moon-lit night, but the liberation was an extended, indeed a life-long affair.

The question of whether the Buddha's notion of liberation is a believable or a practicable one must I think be answered in the affirmative. True, we cannot say anything useful about the claim that liberation puts an end to the rigours of death and rebirth. That is beyond our ability to argue cogently and bring evidence. But this claim is — as is so characteristic of the Buddha's style — linked to another more concrete claim, that liberation may be achieved in this life, and on this the Buddhist texts offer some grounds for discussion. It is not claimed that liberation puts an end to physical pain this side of the grave, for painfulness is admitted to be the nature of the body. (Someone accomplished in the Absorptions or Meditative Planes, however, might be able temporarily to anaesthetise himself by such meditation.) It is rather mental suffering, the extra and unnecessary anguish of existence, that is progressively dispelled by the Buddhist training. Moreover, the sources give us a relatively clear view of the effect of the training: the Buddha's monks 'do not repent the past nor brood over the future. They live in the present. Hence they are radiant' (S I 5).

The principle underlying the elaborate training is one directed precisely to this end of living radiantly in the present. The Buddha called the principle 'thorough reflection' (*yoniso manasikāra*), a considered and meticulous pragmatism about the consequences of each practice in the Middle Path. 'For him who reflects thoroughly, cares and troubles which have not yet arisen do not arise, and those already arisen disappear' (M I 7). What this means in effect is that any practice must be seen to conduce to present welfare *as well as* to long-term transformation. There is no doubt a tension here. On the one hand, the monk's life is strenuous, and he must undertake practices which are at first quite uncomfortable. But on the other hand, since the practices are not designed as self-mortification, their fruits are not deferred indefinitely, but are witnessed and

adjudged useful within a manageable period. What was difficult
becomes second nature, an occasion not for anguish but for cool,
indeed intellectually pleasurable, reflection on the nature and
demands of experience in the mind and body. Furthermore, the
monk is bolstered in this by the evaluation, repeatedly stressed in
the texts, that such a life is not merely escape, but a noble and
heroic vocation; and this evaluation is in turn certified by his fellow
monks and by the surrounding society which prizes such fortitude.

Moreover, the present mastery of one field of the training not
only produces benefits in itself, but also is seen as leading forward
naturally to further mastery. Thus, for example, the monk's
mastery of moral discipline produces a lack of remorse, a freedom
from regret and anxiety. Because one commits no injury to oneself
or others, one's conscience is clear, and this leads of itself to a
serenity upon which meditative accomplishments may then be
founded. This progressive mastery is considered to lead to the very
summit, an aloofness from all the accidents of experience.

From our point of view what is important about this process is
its naturalness. One of the most intractable problems of a project
such as the Buddha's is that desire is an enemy, but the final goal
of liberation is one that the monk desires, wills. How is it possible
to give up that impassioned will towards liberation itself? On the
Buddha's account one wills the present object of training — e.g. to
attain moral discipline — and the consequences fall into place. Thus,
for example, 'there is no need for one well disciplined, endowed
with moral discipline, to will with the intention "let me do away
with remorse". For this is the way of things, O monks, that moral
discipline does away with remorse' (A V 2). As one wills, and then
relaxes into, each stage of practice the next stage is prepared. The
final stage is attained not by strenuous willing at all, but by the
now habitual relaxation.

The Buddha held the human constitution to be such that it could
be laid bare to fruitful investigation through insight meditation and
decisively transformed through the Buddhist training. The internal
coherence of this view is difficult to fault, but our ultimate assent
must be founded in experience, in empirical evidence. I can offer
only my experience from fieldwork with meditating forest monks
in contemporary Sri Lanka. Many monks were evidently healthy
and content, 'radiant' and 'without remorse', and this in itself
impressed me. Yet to be fair this may have been only the fruit of

a quiet life, since I simply was not with any of the monks for the long years necessary to have witnessed and understood some slow metamorphosis of character through the Buddhist discipline.

There were, however, three traits of the monks which did seem directly pursuant upon the Buddhist training. The first was an interested, indeed fascinated, absorption in what they called their 'work', which referred to the hour-by-hour, minute-by-minute prosecution of the daily round — study, careful eating, hygiene, meditation, exercise — which makes up the monk's life. In the reflective execution of these ordinary tasks they clearly found tremendous satisfaction. But, second, some did nevertheless also pour tremendous energy and years of their lives into long-term projects, such as the founding of forest hermitages. Yet they still remained without anxiety and relatively indifferent to the results of their efforts. They were both remarkably successful and remarkably uninterested in success. These deep-seated attitudes were far enough from ordinary life and close enough to the Buddhist ideal of living in the present that I had no difficulty in attributing them to the monastic discipline.

It was the third trait, however, which most persuaded me of the discipline's effectiveness, and that was the monks' courage in the face of wild forest animals. On two occasions while on foot in the jungle there stood between me and a surprised and threatening animal — once a wild boar and once an elephant — only the slight body and unmoving equanimity of a monk. On both occasions the monk took a firm but unaggressive stance and spoke calmly to the animal, which crashed off into the underbrush. No behaviour could be further from ordinary expectations, and it attested vividly to the depth of transformation achievable through the Buddhist training. None of this, of course, proves the truth of the Buddha's teaching, but it does invite us to consider his philosophy seriously as one which has something to tell us about the nature and capacities of the human constitution.

# 5

## *The mission and the death*

In the very long run Buddhism was strikingly successful: it became a world religion which until recently reigned over the Far East and mainland South-East Asia, the most populous areas of the globe, and now it is making its way in the West. However, we need only look a little closer to see that this is not to be explained simply as the triumphant progress of the truth. In the Buddha's time and for many centuries afterwards in India his teaching competed with others on a more or less equal footing. It was not until the middle of the first millennium after Christ, ten to fifteen centuries after the Buddha, that its hegemony was firmly established in the rest of Asia, and shortly thereafter it was on its way to extinction in India itself. Buddhism's history is one of many different episodes, and in each episode different social, economic and political factors — factors often quite extraneous to Buddhism — have played a part. So even if we agree that the Buddha's teaching was insightful and practicable, these virtues alone can hardly in themselves be regarded as the motive force in Buddhism's successes.

Nevertheless, Buddhism did have properties which, if they did not actively motivate Buddhism's expansion, did at least make that expansion possible. The evidence of these is found in Buddhism's relatively easy adaptation to other, native religious traditions in the area it colonised. Buddhism coexisted with archaic Hinduism in India and Sri Lanka, Taoism and Confucianism in China, the Bon religion in Tibet and Shinto in Japan. Indeed Buddhism is presently adapting to Marxism in the East and to liberal humanism and liberal Christianity in the West. In all these circumstances it has been possible for Buddhists to cleave to indigenous beliefs for certain worldly, religious or civil purposes, while simultaneously holding Buddhist views about their own psychological nature and the ultimate ends of human action. Buddhism, in other words, has had little of the imperiousness which has characterised missionary religions such as Christianity and Islam. It is quintessentially tolerant, cosmopolitan and portable, and hence it has been able to respond to opportunities created by circumstances quite beyond its control.

The foundations of this portability lie in three interconnected features of the Buddha's own teaching. First, it was explicitly directed to human beings by virtue of characteristics they held in common: the capacity for pleasure and suffering, the ability to affect their own and others' welfare. One could, of course, object that other Indian religions, and indeed other world religions, embodied similar attempts to speak to all humanity. But, second, in the Buddha's case this universalistic project was relatively good at actually being universalistic because it was abstract. We have seen this abstraction at work, for example, in the Buddha's description of the Absorptions, a description which is consistent with many systems of meditation and with different purposes in meditation. And in the same spirit the Buddha's conception of wisdom and virtue neither opposed nor condoned India's nascent caste system, but rather spoke of human action in abstract terms which were indifferent to the presence or absence of caste: it could exist within or without caste society. Third, this abstraction was always linked in the Buddha's teaching with a deliberately limited concern to apply it to the structure of individual human experience alone. There was a great deal about the world upon which he simply refused to pronounce. Hence, on the one hand, it has always been possible for people to agree in Buddhism while living in quite different cultures and holding quite different views about the world. And on the other hand it has been possible for Buddhists themselves in the course of history to add to the Buddha's own teaching the most varied doctrines — doctrines which fitted in with local traditions and circumstances.

However, this leaves unanswered one fundamental and troublesome question. As I have so far described the Buddha's teaching it is really directed only to that handful who are willing and able to pursue the life of a monk with total devotion. Yet the acceptance of Buddhism by whole peoples meant that it was embraced by a laity who did not 'go forth from home into homelessness'. How did Buddhism develop from a teaching for the few into a teaching for the many? What did this élitist message have to offer people in the world? These questions were answered in the course of the Buddha's career after the awakening.

The most plausible accounts of the Buddha's life before and

during the awakening are found in bare and simple narratives in
which the Buddha seems to speak of his own experience. It is easy
to accept that these have an ancestry, however distant, in edifying
discourses the Buddha actually imparted to his monks. In contrast,
the oldest legends of the Buddha's life after the awakening (I speak
here and hereafter of the beginning of *Mahāvagga*) are in the third
person, evidently took form some generations after the Buddha's
death, and are full of mythical detail. They are therefore far from
trustworthy. They do, however, convey at least some sense of how
the Buddha's personal liberation was metamorphosed into a
mission to the world at large.

The seed of the Buddha's mission is wrapped in an especially
mythic guise in the legend. While the Buddha was still mulling over
in solitude the consequences of his discoveries, he decided that it
would be pointless and tiresome to announce them to a world sunk
in ignorance. But a god intervened: as is characteristic in Buddhist
legend, the god is merely a walk-on character who supports the
central plot of human self-transformation. He pleaded to the
Buddha on behalf of all those creatures who had 'only a little dust
in their eyes', who would respond well and gratefully to the
Buddha's message. To this plea the Buddha responded generously,
undertaking to spread abroad his remedy for suffering, 'out of
compassion for creatures'. And thus was born that resolve which
Buddhists regard as bringing light to the world's darkness.

The truth of the matter is impossible to discern, but this
legendary vignette is nevertheless revealing. In the first place, it
points to a fundamental feature of the Buddha's mature teaching,
that it embodied not only the governing value of liberation, but
also the second governing value of compassion: concern for others.
And indeed something like compassion was inherent in the
Buddha's moral seriousness and in his propensity for describing the
mind in moral terms, in terms of the effects of mental actions on
others. Compassion for the Buddha was intimately intertwined
with liberation as a human purpose and guiding sentiment.
However, in the legend compassion has a significance narrower
than it and its corollaries were to have in the elaborated teaching.
Here compassion is a personal attribute of the Buddha and the
sufficient motive for his decision to teach. Moreover it is a
compassion directed to a specific end, the imparting of the
Buddha's version of the renunciant life.

A good deal of this section of the legendary biography is concerned with the consequences of this compassion, the formation of an order of monks following the Buddha. The Buddha arose from solitude and wandered by stages to the city of Benares, where he stayed in the Deer Park at Isipatana. There he met five ascetics who had been with him before the awakening, but who had left in disgust when he gave up self-mortification. To them he addressed his first sermon, the Setting in Motion of the Wheel of the Teaching, which enunciated the Middle Path and the Four Noble Truths. This they accepted, they became his disciples, and from that time on many of his converts were drawn from the body of wanderers and ascetics. This is historically plausible to the extent that many of the Buddha's discourses were addressed to such wanderers, who were at the time a fluid group, moving easily from one teacher to another. But what was now at stake was the foundation of a new and enduring institution, the Order (*sangha*) of monks following the Buddha, and indeed one senses that the general fluidity was now crystallising everywhere into separate religious corporations with their own constitutions.

However, the Buddha was addressing an audience broader than just the religious virtuosi. The next convert was Yasa, a rich young layman, who awoke one morning suddenly filled with disgust at the sight of the courtesans with whom he had taken his pleasure, now lying about him in drunken slumber. He wandered disconsolately to the Deer Park, and there he met the Buddha, who announced to him the Four Noble Truths. So Yasa left the world to join the Buddha and his small band. Yasa was a merchant's son, and according to the legend four of Yasa's friends 'from the leading merchant families of Benares' then became disciples, and then a further fifty 'youths from the countryside'. These were the kernel of the new Order, and indeed it was they who spread the teaching abroad: for in the legend the Buddha now adjured them to 'go out and wander for the well-being and happiness of the many, out of compassion for the world. . . ' But they were no Protestant evangelists creating a church of laymen, for they were to 'propound the absolutely perfect and wholly pure life of celibate mendicancy'.

Certain elements of this ring true. There was an elective affinity between Buddhism and city merchants, who were among the founding members of the complex urbane society which the

Buddha's teaching addressed. But his was also a universal message, and many besides merchants — perhaps the youths 'of the country-side' — must also have joined the Order. The emphasis on the celibate life seems especially plausible, for it expressed the *esprit de corps* of the Order, and it is consistent with the message of many of the discourses, that the only truly rational course is to renounce the world. However, even if this uncompromising purpose was the original brief of the Order, the missionary activity held within it the possibility of a profound involvement with the laity: for it was after all the laymen's food which sustained, and their cloth which protected the mendicant missionaries as they spread along the trade routes through India and later throughout Asia.

So laymen do appear in the legendary biography. Immediately after Yasa joined the Order, Yasa's father came looking for him and met the Buddha, who preached to him. The father was converted, 'he gained confidence' in the Buddha's teaching, and he thereupon 'went for refuge to the Buddha as long as breath lasts'. This 'going for refuge' today marks formally a layman's commitment to the Buddha, his Order and his teaching, and it seems likely that it had a similar significance at the time of the compilation of the legend and earlier. Yasa's father then invited the Buddha for a meal, and while at the father's home the Buddha converted Yasa's former wife and his mother as well, who also 'went for refuge' to the Buddha. These events at Yasa's father's home convey the substance of the relationship between Buddhist monks and laymen. The laymen offer food and physical support to the monks, while the monks offer the laymen wisdom and other spiritual goods. Anthropologists are fond of discovering institutions based on long-term gift exchange, in which two parties establish a relationship by giving gifts to each other and continue the relationship by the continued exchange of gifts, and this is such a case. On the laymen's part liberality, and especially generosity towards monks, is enjoined, whereas on the monk's side 'the gift of the Buddha's teaching is the best gift', as the canon repeatedly asserts. The gifts are different in kind, but they are given freely, and through them lasting ties are created. Upon this mutual exchange there was thus formed the Buddhist community as a whole, the 'fourfold assembly', which included monks, nuns (whom the Buddha later sanctioned), laymen and laywomen. It was this community as a whole that achieved Buddhism's lasting success.

So what the Buddha's teaching had to offer the laity was certain spiritual goods. Some of these goods were not offered by Buddhism alone, however. One was merit, an immaterial reward garnered by a layman simply by feeding a monk and listening to his sermon. Merit could be laid up to secure a better rebirth: the more merit in the spiritual account, so to speak, the better the rebirth. Hence, as there was a high spiritual purpose appropriate to the monk, namely liberation, so there was a lower one appropriate to the layman, better rebirth (and the hope that one would eventually be reborn in circumstances allowing one to become a monk and achieve liberation). This was a good reason for patronising the Buddhist Order; but in fact it was also a reason for patronising others such as the Jain order as well, for they too held a similar conception of merit.

Another spiritual good offered to the laity was a high moral teaching, composed of injunctions against such acts as lying, killing and stealing; against gaining one's livelihood in harmful ways; and against destructive attitudes of greed, hatred and folly. The monk, with his strenuous discipline of self-control, represented the perfection of human virtue, but the basic principles of that perfection were adaptable to a lower level, to a morality fitting the compromised circumstances of a laity who had to make their living and bear their children in the world. The Buddha, however, held no monopoly of such teachings, whose novelty and popularity were linked with the relative newness and wide distribution of the now developing urbanised forms of social life. Now there were merchants who, through command of the impersonal instruments of money and trade, could wreak a new damage on others; now there were states and armies with new capabilities of harm; now there were offices to seek at others' expense. Moreover, life in the new cities required that groups who had no natural mutual interest or mutually inherited moral code had to devise ways of living together with at least a bare minimum of trust. Much of the adaptation to new forms of life must have occurred quite apart from the renouncers, but the renouncers gave form and voice to the change. They embodied the virtues of harmlessness and poverty (the Buddha's monks were not even to touch gold or silver). They sought no offices. And in their preaching they advocated virtues whose practice — whatever theory went with them — could render the new social world habitable.

The teachings of merit and lay morality explain the renouncers', and not merely the Buddha's, success. Indeed in ancient India Buddhism would probably seldom have seemed markedly more successful than other movements, and taken singly many of the Buddha's teachings to the laity could be found in other doctrines. However, the Buddha achieved a synthesis of the various elements which made the whole more than the sum of the parts. This synthesis is formed upon the Buddha's tendency to think in practical terms, on the analogy of craftsmanship, and also upon his concern with psychological explanations.

The key to this way of thinking is embodied in a term found frequently in his discourses. This term is *kusala*, whose primary meaning is 'skilful', as a goldsmith may be skilful at making gold ornaments. It is a term which the Buddha made his own, and he used it in the first place to refer to skill in meditation. But he also used it widely to apply to skill in moral discipline and in the acquisition of merit. In this application 'skilful' also means morally good, as we might say 'he is a good man' or 'that was a good act'. Indeed in many contexts 'skilful' is the opposite of evil, and refers to the same kind of sharp distinction that is made in Christianity between good and evil. But for the Buddha 'skilful/good' always had a practical, not a metaphysical or absolute flavour to it. The dead centre of the term is best conveyed by a sense lost to us (but still alive among the ancient Greeks), that just as one could be skilful or *good at* a craft, so one could be *good at* being a sentient being, and hence one could be *good*.

This term was animated by 'thorough reflection' upon the consequences of deeds and in particular of the attitudes, the mental actions, behind deeds. For the Buddha skilfulness cut two ways: its consequences were good for oneself, but good for others as well. For example, the act of giving food to a monk gained one merit, and indeed with the characteristic Buddhist emphasis upon the mental side of things this merit was conceived as being also a psychological good, a wholesome frame of mind pursuant upon liberality. But giving is also good for the monk, at the very least because the monk thereby assuages his hunger. By the same token, to cultivate moral discipline is simultaneously to avoid harm to others and to create good/skilful frames of mind in oneself. We tend to think of doing good as involving the sacrifice of one's own interests for someone else's, but for the Buddha to do good was

precisely to act in both one's own *and* in someone else's interest.
For the monk the stress was on one's own interest, liberation, while
the means — exemplary moral discipline — incidentally achieved
others' interests. But this way of thought was easily turned around
to apply to laymen, who by being good to others achieved the end
of being good to themselves. This reasoning was further bolstered
by the teaching that to be kind, gentle, honest and harmless to
others was in fact to invite them to behave in the same manner to
oneself: do good to others that they may do good to you. By wise
reflection and moral action Buddhists, whether monks or laymen,
could achieve the fruit of their skilfulness 'both here and in the next
world'.

The Buddha's doctrine for laymen, therefore, was intimately and
organically connected to his thought on his monks' training. But
this connection was not limited to the level of morality alone. For
the monk the moral discipline underpins cultivation of the mind in
meditation; but for both monks and laymen the cultivation of
certain mental skills and attitudes could in turn underpin morality.
It is here that compassion, concern for others, enters the picture
again, now as an attitude to be cultivated meditatively and as a
value directed to others' welfare in general. One can transform
oneself not only for liberation, but also for love. In the Buddhist
texts compassion is analysed into three: first, compassion proper,
defined as sympathy with others' suffering; second, sympathetic
joy, the enjoyment of others' good fortune; and third, loving-
kindness, the Buddhist sentiment *par excellence*. The attitude
cultivated by monks and laymen in loving-kindness is expressed in
this famous passage of very early Buddhist poetry:

Whatever beings may exist — weak or strong, tall, broad, medium or
short, fine-material or gross, seen or unseen, those born and those pressing
to be born — may they all without exception be happy in heart!

Let no one deceive anyone else, nor despise anyone anywhere! May no
one wish harm to another in anger or ill-will!

Let one's thoughts of boundless loving-kindness pervade the whole
world, above, below, across, without obstruction, without hatred, without
enmity! (S 146–8, 150)

This passage compresses the attitudes underlying the morality
taught by the Buddha into a single sentiment, capturing the positive
spirit that is to accompany the negative injunctions. Indeed loving-
kindness is absolutely necessary both in the monk's training and in

the lay morality, since for Buddhists it is the mental action, the intention or attitude, which counts and not the deed itself. The sentiment of loving-kindness is certainly impersonal, and in this the Olympian detachment of the renouncer shows through. One must treat all equally, regardless of position or relationship. Indeed in this universal sentiment the Buddha's moral reasoning has a place, for in prescriptions for loving-kindness the meditator is to 'identify oneself with all' (A II 129). That is, just as I am subject to pain and pleasure, so are others, and just as I wish myself well, so I should wish well to others. Throughout the Buddhist world loving-kindness, supplemented by compassion for suffering, was to become the model for social sentiments beyond the family and a value in its own right. In later Buddhist folklore and thought these sentiments grew so prominent as to overshadow even the premier value of liberation.

★

The assembled structure of the Buddha's teaching to laymen is revealed in the Discourse to the Kālāmans (A I 188–93), a people on the northern fringe of the Gangetic civilisation. In that discourse the Buddha is represented as touring with a body of monks through the area. A group of Kālāmans learn of his presence and go to him in the village of Kesaputta with a problem: various wandering ascetics and Brahmans have travelled through expounding and recommending their own views to the Kālāmans, while attacking and rebutting the views of others. The Kālāmans are confused, and seek advice from the Buddha. Whom should they believe? To this confusion the Buddha replies with a teaching which has frequently been quoted to demonstrate the Buddha's lack of dogmatism and advocacy of individual judgment. He asserts that the Kālāmans should not rely on 'hearsay, on tradition, on legends, on learning, nor on mere inference or extrapolation or cogitation, nor on consideration and approval of some theory or other, nor because it seems fitting, nor out of respect for some ascetic'.

This is not recommendation for capricious individual fancy, however, for what the Buddha recommends is his own moral reasoning from wise reflection and skilfulness, and he is confident that if the Kālāmans so reason they will each one arrive at the Buddha's moral teaching:

when you know for yourselves that this is unskilful and that skilful, this

blameworthy and that blameless, this deprecated by the wise because it
conduces to suffering and ill, and that praised because it conduces to well-
being and happiness. . . when you know this for yourselves, Kālāmans,
you will reject the one and make a practice of the other.

The moral teaching at which they will arrive is a straightforward
one. The Kālāmans will not kill, they will not take what is not
given, they will not take another's wife, they will not incite others
to their own harm. These injunctions will arise naturally out of the
Kālāmans' experience and their reflection upon skilfulness.

In the first place it is possible to infer a certain topicality in the
discourse. There is reason to believe that the Kālāmans, like their
neighbours the Sakyans, the Buddha's people, had had an
independent oligarchic republican government and had been, in the
remembered past, a relatively autonomous people. But now they
were subjected to the power of the Kosalan king, as the Sakyans
were soon to be, and in their economic life they must have felt the
magnetic pull of the distant Kosalan capital. These political and
economic forces were drawing the Kālāmans out of a relatively
simple and closed tribal society into the complex world of Gangetic
civilisation, and these dislocations were compounded by new
cultural forms, embodied in the conflicting advice of those
messengers of the Gangetic civilisation, the wandering ascetics.

It is impossible to believe that the injunctions against killing,
lying, stealing and so forth were wholly new to the Kālāmans: their
own ancestral culture must have offered analogous injunctions. It
is difficult to conceive the survival of a society which did not hold
these values in some form, at least as touches the members of the
society itself. However, it is characteristic of societies like the older
Kālāman one that such values are not reasoned, but are rather held
by virtue of tradition and custom, and dramatised in legend and
ritual. Under the new conditions these inherited moral traditions
had lost their unquestioned hegemony, though, and hence there
was occasion for the Buddha to offer a new form of moral
reasoning which grew out of the most basic conditions of human
life. The proposed morality was not a specifically Kālāman thing,
but grew out of the sheer fact of being in society at all, of having
a common life, of being able to reason for one's own and others'
ends, whoever was involved. This morality was meant to hold for
all conditions.

But the Buddha envisaged more than just a new foundation for

Kālāman morality. For the injunctions are meant to apply not only within Kālāman society, but to all individuals, Kālāman or not, with whom a Kālāman might deal: and the Kālāmans were already implicated with many other peoples. It is typical of small-scale societies, and of small groups within a larger society, that their members alone are treated as full constituents of the moral community. But now the Kālāmans were invited into a larger world to embrace within their moral community all living beings, and certainly all the people of the Gangetic plain. The Buddha promulgated a universal morality to fit the Kālāmans' enforcedly more cosmopolitan life.

To this extent the Buddha's teaching to laymen was founded on his moral reasoning, but in the discourse this moral reasoning is in turn founded more deeply in his teaching and experience, in his analysis of the human constitution and his project for self-transformation. When he taught the monks the Buddha emphasised that the sources of suffering — greed, hatred, delusion — lead to one's own harm. But in this teaching to laymen he stressed that they are generally harmful, not only harmful to oneself.

When greed rises within a man does it not conduce to harm? Or when hatred and delusion arise within a man? Is it not when his mind is overcome with greed, hatred, and delusion that a man murders, steals, lies, and so forth? And is it not by having a mind unconquered by these things that he is able to avoid all these acts?

In this passage 'harm' refers to harm caused both to oneself and to others: just as to be skilful is to serve both one's own ends and others' ends, so to be harmful is to harm both oneself and others. The point is worth emphasising, because not only Westerners but also later schools of Buddhism have wished to reject or improve on the Buddha's teaching on the grounds that it is oblivious to others' welfare or to the existence of society. Although on balance the Buddha was more concerned with the anatomy of individual experience than with the anatomy of society, his teaching always recognised that to be human is to be a social being.

Moreover the Buddha's view of how a layman is to mend himself so that his mind is 'unconquered' relies on more than just wise reflection. On the one hand, the Buddha presupposes in laymen a rational faculty which, if rightly directed, will produce skilful solutions to moral problems. Laymen can calculate what to do. But on the other hand this view of laymen as having a capacity for rationality is only part of the story, for the Buddha also felt that laymen could — to an extent appropriate to their station — transform themselves. Hence in the Discourse to the Kālāmans the Buddha recommends the meditation on the social sentiments, especially loving-kindness. Laymen are to practise by directing loving-kindness to all quarters and all beings, 'identifying oneself with all . . . having a heart free of anger and hatred'. The effect of this mental exercise is to establish loving-kindness sooner or later as a lasting habit and motivation in action.

This has two important implications. First, it means that the Buddha recommended not only *why* one should act skilfully, but also *how* the sometimes intractable human constitution can be made to do so. The Buddha was an optimist in that he thought humans capable of skilful rationality, but a realist in that he knew this rationality to require an emotional transformation as well. One may calculate an act to be good and skilful, and yet be unable to carry it out, and this common weakness was taken fully into account. Second, this practice of self-transformation is portable, in the sense that in principle it may be practised effectively by anyone. This is important because much of human experience, and especially that beyond the bounds of an enclosed group such as the Buddhist Order, cannot be manipulated to one's own ends. The Kālāmans were subject to natural changes but also, and increasingly, to social changes which were beyond anyone's power to control or even to understand fully. But here at least was a matter which one could effectively handle: one's own habits and motivations. If one cannot change the world, one can at least change oneself. True, a practice for laymen such as the meditation on loving-kindness must be partly dependent for its effectiveness on one's being part of a Buddhist community which cleaves to such values; but the final effort is one's own and the focus of effort is oneself. A Kālāman travelling to the Kosalan capital or a Kālāman working his ancestral fields could both equally well practise loving-kindness and compassion.

The Discourse to the Kālāmans is perhaps quite topical, but as the Buddha phrased it the discourse, like many of his other teachings to laymen, is applicable to anyone in a similar plight. In this the Buddha is strikingly modern, for today it is difficult to find a people which has not been drawn into a wider, more complex, more confusing social world, as the Kālāmans were drawn into

Gangetic civilisation. The Buddha addressed himself by the very generality of his discourse to the wide variety of possible fates in the experience of a complex society, and that experience of complexity is ours at least as much as it was the ancient Indians'. On the surface people now, as then, obey the dictates of a bewildering variety of different necessities and values, but there are some traits which they all share: the capacity for misery or happiness, the capacity to harm or benefit others.

Indeed this modernity corresponds to certain hard-won views of our own. The Buddha was original in his consciousness of the varieties of culture in his milieu, and he was capable of recommending in the canon, for example, that different groups adhere each to its own ancestral morality and religion. The Buddha recognised, that is, that peoples' values are relative to their own history and culture. We too have come to recognise this irreducible difference of values: we call it cultural relativism, and we take this to mean that other societies are not to be judged by our own. But just as cultural relativism cannot realistically be thought to mean that people can live according to just any values or with no values, so the Buddha advocated that people adhere to ancestral standards *only in so far as* those standards are consistent with moral skilfulness. Similarly the Buddha taught that human individuals are not to be seen as isolated from each other, but as conjoined to each other in a weighty and consequential relationship. This is consistent with another modern view, a growing awareness that individuals are not to be understood in isolation, but as being inextricably involved in a social context.

There is another kind of modernity, however, which the Buddha did not have, and that is an overriding preoccupation with the political dimension of human affairs. For the most part the Buddha's discourses define three areas of concern which, between them, make up the human world as it is seen by the Buddha: an individual's concern with the events of his own mind and body, his concern with his face-to-face personal relations with others, and his concern with the welfare of all sentient beings. For these three areas, the psychic, the socially very small-scale, and the universal collectivity of all beings, he was willing to lay down both the way things are and the way they should be. But these descriptions and prescriptions say little about how men do and should behave as members of political collectivities, and how political collectivities should be organised. Certainly this relative indifference to the specifics of political affairs must have contributed to the ease with which the Buddha's teaching has been found relevant in very different political climates.

But this is not to say that the Buddha's teaching is devoid of political interest or political implications. In so far as we can infer the Buddha's own preferences, they were for the sort of oligarchic egalitarian or republican political organisation that seems to have held among his own people. And we know this because his prescriptions for the organisation of the Buddhist Order, which appear in a long biographical text on his last days, are set beside very similar prescriptions for another such people. The Order (or the people) are to conduct their business in concord, their decisions are to be unanimous, they are to respect and defer to elders, but where elders' views conflict with the teaching and disciplinary code (or the tradition of the group), one is to follow the teaching. Had such oligarchies prospered and expanded, we might have had ancient Indian theories of democracy and citizenship such as ancient Greece gave us. But oligarchies had probably never been the principal form of government in India: they were very much on their way out when the Buddha lived, and very soon they were gone forever. Most of the Buddha's experience was with kingdoms, and no kings wishes to hear radical political thought.

So the Buddha was left to talk about kings if he was to talk about politics at all. There are left to us a number of fascinating discourses which must have taken their complex literary form after the Buddha's death but some of which quite possibly represent the Buddha's views, and in these he expounds on kingship. The chief message is that kings, no less than anyone else, are subject to the moral order, to considerations of what is morally and socially skilful. When there came to be Buddhist kings these discourses where taken at face value to construct a specifically Buddhist theory of ethical kingship. Other messages include what seems to be a recommendation for state capitalism, to the effect that the king should finance enterprises in order to bring prosperity to the people; and a contract theory of the monarchy, to the effect that the king is elected because he is the handsomest and best and able to keep people in line. But these messages are set in highly ironical and even humorous frames, in which the Buddha tells a fanciful story to an imaginary figure (e.g. Sharptooth the Brahman), and the consequence is that the Buddha is distanced very far from the messages he seems to convey. Part of this distancing is that of a world renouncer looking down from the perspective of liberation upon the folly and pettiness of even grand state affairs. But there is a keen edge to this commentary which implies that the Buddha must have been a very perspicacious observer of the political scene.

In the light of our deeply disillusioning experience of the teachings of the past as they have been applied in the world, we might very well doubt that any past master still bears cogency and relevance. And one might further object in the case of the Buddha that his mastery is not *world-wide*, but is grounded upon views of the cosmos, such as transmigration, which can never be accepted by the West. But I have tried to show that the philosophy of the Buddha was concerned with matters that do make his mastery available to everyone, that do bring him within Western history, though the West must — quite appropriately — expand its view of its own history beyond parochial preoccupations to embrace him. The Buddha was concerned with the physical and psychological bases upon which human self-transformation is possible: such a mastery could not be lost to us. His teaching was suited to a world of different political philosophies and different religions, but a world in which certain basic values must guide personal relations if we are to live together at all, and it is difficult to see how that mastery could be irrelevant to us.

The story of the Buddha's death is recounted in a long text (D II no. 16) which, shorn of its mythical elements, portrays the last journey of an old man. Accompanied by his now continual companion, the loving but, as the text portrays him, rather bumbling Ānanda, the Buddha made his way northward over hundreds of miles, plagued by illness. Finally the Buddha was struck down by food poisoning and came to rest in the obscure village of Kusinārā.

When Ānanda realised that the Buddha was about to die, 'he went into a house and leaned against the doorframe weeping'. The Buddha called Ānanda to himself and told him,

do not mourn, do not weep. Haven't I told you that we are separated, parted, cut off from everything dear and beloved? . . . You have served me long with love, helpfully, gladly, sincerely and without reserve, in body, word, and thought. You have done well by yourself, Ānanda. Keep trying and you will soon be liberated.

# Further reading

A great deal has been published in English about Buddhism, some of it very technical, some of it misleading and some of it very good indeed. These are suggestions which will lead to a more comprehensive understanding of the Buddha, of his teaching, and of the history of Buddhism.

Quite a different approach to the Buddha's biography was taken by Bhikkhu Ñāṇamoḷi in *The Life of the Buddha* (Buddhist Publication Society, Kandy, 1972), which is available from the Society in Kandy, Sri Lanka. He tells the story of the Buddha entirely through accurate translations from the Pali texts themselves. This book is perhaps the best introduction to the Pali texts, with their peculiarly meticulous and laconic style. Yet another approach was taken by Michael Pye in *The Buddha* (Duckworth, 1979). He conveys a vivid sense of the Buddha's life as well as of the stories and myths through which the early Buddhist community came to see the Buddha. Both of these would very usefully supplement the picture I have given.

For the Buddha's teaching there is nothing better than Walpola Rahula's *What the Buddha Taught* (Gordon Fraser, 1967). This combines lucidity with a warm advocacy of Buddhism from the point of view of a practising monk. Nyanaponika Thera has written a similarly lucid book on insight meditation, *The Heart of Buddhist Meditation* (Rider, 1969). These are both based on the Theravāda tradition.

For a broader introduction to the breadth of Buddhist philosophy and history Richard Robinson and Willard L. Johnson's book, *The Buddhist Religion* (Dickenson, 1982), is especially good. This may then be followed by Heinz Bechert and Richard Gombrich (eds.), *The World of Buddhism* (Thames and Hudson, 1984), which is composed of articles on Buddhism and the Buddhist order in each of the Buddhist countries. Though written for a general readership each article represents the latest scholarship on each area.

It would be well to supplement such reading with an acquaintance with the Buddhist texts themselves, which can be consulted in Henry C. Warren's *Buddhism in Translations* (Atheneum, 1963) or in Stephen Beyer's more recent *Buddhist Experience: Sources and Interpretations* (Dickenson, 1974).

Many of these books have useful bibliographies which will then lead the reader further into the subject he or she wishes to study. My own interest has been in the actual practice of Buddhism in Buddhist lands today. On this Holmes Welch's *The Practice of Chinese Buddhism, 1900–1950* (Harvard University Press, 1967) is particularly thorough. My own understanding of Buddhism is based on field work in Sri Lanka, and I have written of that in *The Forest Monks of Sri Lanka* (Oxford University Press, 1983). This picture of strict meditative practitioners is complemented by Richard Gombrich's *Precept and Practice* (Oxford University Press, 1971), which concerns the beliefs and practices of popular Buddhism in Sri Lanka.

# CONFUCIUS

RAYMOND DAWSON

# *Preface* and *Historical introduction*

There are remarkably few books on Confucius in Western languages and fewer still which combine a high standard of scholarship with general readability. Indeed Arthur Waley's *The Analects of Confucius*, published in the thirties, is still essential reading. This little work is very different from anything else that has appeared. To the Western reader who knows nothing of Chinese civilisation the sayings of the Master may seem obscure or banal, so that the only way to appreciate them is to understand their formative influence on Chinese civilisation. In this book I am therefore as much concerned with the impact of the message as with the man himself. Since this involves some excursions into later Chinese history, I append a list of the major dynasties to help the reader to get his bearings. The names of some unfamiliar historical personages need to be mentioned, and these are dated and described in the index.

A preliminary sketch of China in Confucius's time is also necessary. It is impossible to bring his period into sharp focus since we have much less detailed information about life in fifth-century-B.C. China than is available concerning fifth-century-B.C. Athens. That city comes to life in the masterpieces of Euripides and Aristophanes, but there are no surviving works of literature to bear contemporary witness to life in Confucius's state of Lu. The age had no Herodotus or Thucydides to provide vivid accounts of the drama of war and politics.

The China of Confucius's lifetime was still nominally under the Chou Dynasty. The founders of that dynasty, Confucius's hero King Wen (the Cultured King), who paved the way, and his son King Wu (the Martial King), who made the actual conquest, had originally been satellites of the previous dynasty, the Shang. They came from the valley of the Wei, a tributary of the Yellow River, in the vicinity of present-day Sian. The Chou people cherished the tradition that they had conquered the Shang because that dynasty's last ruler had forfeited the Mandate of Heaven by his tyrannical and licentious behaviour.

At first the Chou sovereigns headed a confederation of city-states linked by kinship ties, which gradually increased their control over the countryside in the Yellow River valley and the North China Plain. Some of these city-states gradually developed into large virtually independent countries, which by the eighth century were giving only nominal allegiance to a much weakened Chou, while *de facto* hegemony was wielded by the most powerful among them. These were times of constant warfare, on three different fronts: first, the alliance of these northern Chinese states had to contend with the large expansionist state of Ch'u in the Yangtze valley, which had its own distinct culture and was not merged with North China until the end of the Chou Dynasty in the third century B.C.; secondly, these states were subject to harassment by the nomadic peoples living not only beyond the frontiers of Chinese settlement but also within the more mountainous and inaccessible regions of their own territories (just as aboriginal non-Chinese people have continued to occupy areas of China right up to the present day); and thirdly, these states were engaged in internecine conflict in which the smaller were absorbed by the larger until the unification of China by the state of Ch'in in 221 B.C. and the dawn of the imperial age.

These political changes were closely linked with great social and economic transformations, from hereditary aristocratic rule towards meritocracy, from serfdom towards a free peasantry, from a barter economy towards a widespread use of currency, from aristocratic chariot-warfare towards conflict between huge armies of peasants. But it was not until after Confucius's time that the pace of these changes accelerated so that they sparked off an era of wide-ranging speculation without parallel in Chinese history, as the so-called Hundred Schools sought solutions to the problems of man in society. This was the age of Confucius's great successors, Mencius (c. 371–289 B.C.) and Hsün Tzu (c. 298–238 B.C.); but Confucius himself had lived at a time when it was still possible to look back to a Golden Age rather than forward to a Utopia.

## Major Chinese dynasties

Chou ?1027–256 B.C.

Ch'in 221–206 B.C.   Ch'in Shih Huang Ti unifies China and builds the Great Wall to defend it from the northern nomads. The Confucian books and much other ancient literature are destroyed in the 'Burning of the Books' in 213 B.C., part of Ch'in Shih Huang Ti's totalitarian attempt to wipe out opposition.

Former Han 206 B.C.–A.D. 9 This is the first great imperial dynasty. Much of the old literature is recovered and restored, and Confucianism becomes the dominant philosophy and heart of the educational system.

Later Han 25–220 Buddhism, the chief foreign rival of Confucianism, is introduced to China.

Sui 581–618 China is reunified after nearly four centuries of division, for most of which time North China has been split between various non-Chinese states.

T'ang 618–907 Buddhism is at the height of its influence but Confucian influence is restored as the revived civil service examination system grows in importance.

Sung 960–1279 This is the heyday of Neo-Confucian philosophy, and a period of great technological and industrial progress.

Yüan 1279–1368 China is ruled by Mongols, and Confucianism suffers a setback with the suspension of the examinations for several decades.

Ming 1368–1644 Following Mongol rule, this is a conservative and autocratic regime.

Ch'ing 1644–1912 China is governed by Manchus, whose rulers adopt Confucian culture to show themselves worthy of the Mandate of Heaven. Examinations dominated by Confucian Classics are abolished in 1905.

## Note on romanisation

I have retained the more familiar Wade-Giles system, which has been used for most English-language books on China, in preference to the new *pinyin* system introduced by the Chinese, which gives even less idea how the words are actually pronounced.

## Note on references

References to the *Analects* are given by book and chapter as numbered in Waley's translation; to *Mencius* by the standard enumeration of book and chapter; to Hsün Tzu by the page number in B. Watson's *Hsün Tzu: Basic Writings*; and to the *Record of Rites* by volume and page number of James Legge's translation, which is to be found in volumes 27 and 28 of *Sacred Books of the East*, ed. Max Müller. The references are preceded by the letters A, M, H, and L respectively.

## Acknowledgements

I should like to express my gratitude for the helpful suggestions I have received from my wife, from Keith Thomas, the general editor of the series, and from Henry Hardy and Robert Knowles of Oxford University Press.

# Contents

# 1

## *Confucius and K'ung Fu-tzu*

K'ung Fu-tzu lived 2,500 years ago, but he was not born for the Western world until the late sixteenth century, when his name was Latinised into Confucius, and the message of the ancient Chinese sage was first brought, in somewhat European guise, to the European consciousness. Marco Polo and other medieval European visitors to China had marvelled at the great cities, the teeming market-places, and the huge quantity of shipping which thronged the waterways; but they had been conscious only of the outer manifestations of this rich civilisation, and no Europeans had sampled the wealth of its literature and philosophy before the arrival of the Jesuits.

The Jesuit missionaries reached China in 1583 and established themselves at Peking under the leadership of Matteo Ricci at the beginning of the seventeenth century. It was the general policy of Jesuit missions to try to secure the conversion of a country by first winning the sympathy of its ruler, and Matteo Ricci and his colleagues soon became aware that, to gain the respect of the emperor, they had to make themselves congenial to the scholar-bureaucrats by whom he was surrounded. To achieve this they needed to become Chinese scholars themselves. So, while steeping themselves in the classical literature, they became strongly influenced by the attitudes of the Chinese literati, who thought of China as a country governed by philosophers, whose wisdom and virtue derived from the study of the ancient Confucian literature which they had had to master for the purpose of passing the civil service examinations.

The Jesuit version of Confucian doctrine and of the benevolent despotism which, in their view, administered the country in conformity with Confucian doctrine so aroused the admiration of contemporary European thinkers that Confucius himself has been described as 'the patron saint of the Enlightenment'. On the other hand the Protestant missionaries, who came to China in the

nineteenth century, could see little to praise in Confucius since he
lacked the light of God. Even James Legge, whose monumental
work entitled *The Chinese Classics* was so authoritative as to have
been reprinted on its hundredth birthday in the middle of the
twentieth century, concluded that Confucius 'threw no new light
on any of the questions that have a world-wide interest. He gave
no impulse to religion. He had no sympathy with progress. His
influence has been wonderful, but it will henceforth wane.' So we
in the Western world are heirs to two conflicting attitudes to the
Chinese sage.

The first work of translation from the Confucian literature
was a book entitled *Confucius Sinarum Philosophus, sive Scientia
Sinensis*, which was published in Paris by four Jesuit missionaries
in the year 1687. It contained a version of the *Analects* of
Confucius and of two short works known as the *Great Learning*
and the *Mean*, which were extracted from an ancient collection of
materials on ritual entitled the *Record of Rites*. Special attention
was paid to these texts, together with the book named after
Mencius, Confucius's most distinguished successor, since these four
books were required reading for the civil service examinations
throughout the last six centuries of imperial Chinese history. They
had to be studied with the commentary of Chu Hsi, the twelfth-
century Neo-Confucian philosopher, rather than with those written
nearer Confucius's own time, so European versions too were much
influenced by the interpretation of the Neo-Confucian master.

It was not until 1905, in the dying years of the imperial regime,
that the old-fashioned civil service examinations were abolished,
and the Four Books and other canonical writings yielded to the
advance of modern Western knowledge. Even in the late nineteenth
century reformers had had to defend their proposals for change by
enlisting the support of Confucius. With the advent of the Republic
the former veneration of the classical texts was replaced by a new
mood of extreme scepticism about knowledge of antiquity. Later
still the predominant mood shifted back towards defence of
Chinese culture against the inroads of the West, especially after the
First World War had exposed the darker side of European culture.
This made the Chinese mindful again of the values of their
Confucian heritage, and they were glad to throw its ethical
superiority into the scales against the material superiority of the
West. In Europe too, although nineteenth-century arrogance

towards the 'heathen Chinese' had reduced Confucius to a figure of fun in the eyes of the man in the street, he was taken more seriously in the old universities. When they at last began to pay serious attention to Chinese studies, it was the Confucian literature, rather than contemporary affairs, which became the cornerstone of their interests.

The Four Books formed part of a much larger collection of ancient literature called the Thirteen Classics. This corpus, which includes works of poetry, philosophy, and history, as well as ritual texts and a book of divination, was traditionally treated by the Chinese as an entirely separate category of literature, hallowed above the rest as the repository of truth. In antiquity only five of these works had had canonical status: they were the *Book of Changes*, the *Book of History*, the *Book of Songs*, the *Ritual* (which included the *Record of Rites*), and the *Spring and Autumn*. One reason for Confucius's pre-eminence is that he was thought to have had a hand in all of these five works, either as compiler, commentator, or editor.

However, this group of Classics should not be thought of as the special province of a Confucian school. In European writings Confucianism is often referred to as one of the 'three religions' of China, the other two being Taoism and Buddhism; but this gives a very misleading impression of the nature of Chinese religion. 'Three teachings' or 'three doctrines' would be more appropriate translations of the term. A Chinese did not normally adhere to just one of these doctrines. For the vast majority religion consisted of a motley collection of beliefs and practices to which these three schools of thought each made their contributions. The use of the term Confucianism is also misleading, since the Chinese equivalent, *ju chiao*, means 'the doctrine of the literati', so that the name of Confucius does not in fact occur in the title of this school of thought. Far from being the concern of one school, this canonical literature was a curriculum for all: it originated as a collection of material intended to provide an education suitable for the bureaucrats needed to govern the rapidly expanding Chinese empire during the Former Han Dynasty in the second and first centuries B.C. The Classics are at the forefront of the literary heritage of the Chinese people as a whole.

Confronted with these ancient classical texts, how are we to isolate and discuss the authentic teachings of Confucius? There are enormous difficulties. Confucius flourished about 500 B.C., three centuries before texts can be reliably dated. Long after his time the conception of individual authorship was still not firmly established, so that the names under which ancient philosophical writings are known are generally those of the thinkers to whom the teachings are attributed. These works consequently include not only genuine material assembled by disciples, but also extraneous matter interpolated by those who wished to give their views respectability by foisting them onto a venerable figure from the past. In the book named after Mencius, the great philosopher who was born a century after Confucius's death and who established him as founder of the tradition which was to dominate Chinese thought, Confucius is already venerated as the greatest of the sages in the words 'Ever since man came into this world there has never been anyone greater than Confucius' (M 2a.2). In such circumstances it is not surprising that his name is used prominently in ancient literature as an advertisement for doctrines not necessarily his own. In the *Record of Rites* he is naturally depicted as a great expert on correct ritual, and in the *Book of Filial Piety* he praises filial piety as the chief virtue. In the great Taoist classic *Chuang Tzu*, on the other hand, Confucius is depicted either as a student of Taoism sitting at Lao Tzu's feet, or as an expert on Taoism himself, or alternatively as a trickster and charlatan who curries favour with rulers by means of his nonsensical talk about moral duty and ritual observance. The earliest biography of Confucius was composed by the great historian Ssu-ma Ch'ien, but since he was writing in about 100 B.C., almost four centuries after Confucius's death, it is not surprising that his account is a hotchpotch of material of varying degrees of credibility.

If we want to get as near as possible to the real Confucius, the best thing we can do is look at the *Analects*. This is a collection of sayings and brief anecdotes, which at least has the advantage of treating Confucius as an ordinary human being and shows little trace of the adoration later lavished upon him. Even the *Analects* does not take us very close to the sage, since it is clear from internal evidence that the work was compiled long after his death, apparently by the disciples of disciples, and presumably at a time when a written record was felt necessary to replace fading memories. Surprisingly little familiarity with the book is shown in literature dating from before the Han Dynasty, which began in

206 B.C. Mencius clearly had available to him a quite different compilation of sayings: some of the material corresponds closely with passages from the *Analects*, but many more of his references to Confucius are not traceable in the *Analects* at all. Other pre-Han texts also share sayings with the *Analects*, but only once is the *Analects* acknowledged as the source.

The archaic nature of the language and the very rudimentary arrangement of material give an air of authenticity to the work and suggest that the composition is early enough to preserve some of the spirit of Confucius. To the modern reader it appears to be slapdash. Some pieces are duplicated. Some sayings are set in brief anecdotes, but others are so terse and devoid of context that their meaning is very elusive. Some of the sayings are attributed to Confucius's disciples rather than to the Master himself, and it is clear also that much material from alien sources has infiltrated the work. The tenth book, for example, seems to have been extracted from a work on ritual, the conduct advocated in it being attributed to Confucius rather than commended to the attention of the reader, so that the Master is here represented as a stickler for the finicky detail of ceremonious behaviour. Some passages seem to be late and alien to the work since the style in which they are written is uncharacteristically elaborate and sophisticated. It looks as if Books 3–9 (out of a total of twenty books) may form the oldest stratum, but even they may contain later insertions; and although they have a clearer ring of authenticity, it is impossible to vouch for the genuineness of any of the sayings included in them. Nevertheless, in spite of the disparate nature of the material, even some recently published books persist in treating it all as of equal value and trying to extract every ounce of information they can to produce a coherent picture of Confucius and his philosophy.

Caution is necessary, too, in evaluating the biographical material which appears in various sources. Confucius is said to have lived from 551 to 479, but the fact that firm dates are given is cause for suspicion since he lived in an era when the dates of private individuals were not preserved. For example, the dates of Mencius, who lived in the fourth century B.C., can only be worked out approximately from evidence drawn from the book named after him. As for Confucius, his death date derives from a legendary account of the capture of a unicorn in 481 B.C., which was thought to herald the death of the sage. His birth date was probably worked out from that, since the *Analects* refers to him at the age of seventy and there was a tradition that he actually lived until his seventy-third year. The great French sinologist Henri Maspero felt that he could have lived a quarter of a century later than the traditional dates, but on the other hand he would need to have been born earlier than 551 B.C.to fit in with some of the references to him in the *Tso Tradition*, which is the only detailed historical account of the period dating from pre-Han times.

Confucius's ancestors are said to have claimed descent from the royal family of the state of Sung, where a member of the royal house of the recently defeated Shang Dynasty had been set up by the Chou conquerors in the eleventh century B.C. to continue the Shang sacrifices; but this may be just an example of a lofty pedigree being invented to match up to his later eminence. His father died when he was very young and he was brought up in poverty by his mother. As a young man he held office as keeper of granaries and director of public pastures, but is extremely unlikely to have attained to the posts of Minister of Works and Minister of Crime with which the later tradition of his school invested him. He was ambitious to serve in high office in the hope that he could restore to public life the old morality of the founders of the Chou Dynasty; but making no progress in his own state of Lu, which at the time was controlled by usurpers, he travelled from state to state accompanied by some of his disciples, trying to find a more congenial home for his teachings. It became a common practice for philosophers and political advisers to peddle their wares from court to court in this way during the Warring States period, the two centuries of strife which preceded the unification of China by the state of Ch'in in 221 B.C., when its ruler inaugurated the first of the great imperial dynasties to govern much of China as we know it today. Failing to make progress in the political arena, Confucius spent the last period of his life as a private teacher, giving instruction to the humbly born as well as to young men of rank, hoping that those who obtained careers in government would be more successful than himself in putting his ideas into effect. He had a son, who predeceased him, and a daughter; otherwise few details of his private life are mentioned in the *Analects*. But despite the fact that the evidence about his life is difficult to evaluate, the *Analects* does give us a glimpse of a credible personality, a man who was brought up in humble circumstances and was prepared to accept

poverty rather than compromise his beliefs, a man who never tired
of learning and who stuck doggedly to his task ('He's the one who
knows it's no good but goes on trying', A 14.41), a man with a
strong sense that he had a divinely appointed mission to restore the
Way of the revered founders of the Chou Dynasty.

We can never hope to find out what Confucius was really like
and precisely what his teachings consisted of. Even the obituaries
in this morning's paper do not tell the whole truth about men
known to thousands still living. The task of trying to separate the
man from the myth is doomed to failure. But the fact that the real
Confucius is irretrievable should not be counted a disaster since it
was the myth rather than the reality which was important. The
story of his life and work provided a model and inspiration for
future generations of scholars and teachers. For greater philosophical interest one has to look at his two famous successors,
Mencius and Hsün Tzu. The appeal of the *Analects* is that it gives
us a hazy glimpse of the disciples' memory of one whose example
was to be set before the intellectuals of the most populous nation
on earth. The sayings attributed to him have served as texts to
which much of Chinese life and thought have been appended as
commentary, and the *Analects* is the oldest record of one who set
the pattern for the Confucian society which China has been for
much of the time since he lived.

The sayings attributed to Confucius can be manipulated into
some sort of coherent philosophy, but the best way to understand
the importance of the Master is to ignore the inevitable inconsistencies in the statements attributed to him and to forget about
problems of authenticity. Throughout Chinese history before the
present century few have questioned the authenticity of even the
most hagiographical references to him. The best way of dealing
with Confucius is therefore to take some of the most famous and
influential sayings, and to try to show both what they meant in the
context of late Chou Dynasty China and how the ideas they
contain became characteristic features of Chinese thought and
culture. Although the reader who has little knowledge of Chinese
civilisation may sometimes find these sayings trivial and inconsequential, this method should give him an impression of their
formative influence on Chinese civilisation, and hence a heightened
understanding of the nature of that civilisation. The method will
have the further advantage of affinity with the long Chinese

tradition of commentary on classical texts, in which brief passages of the original work alternate with lengthy explanations. This too is how the sayings appeared to many generations of scholars in the examination halls — as isolated quotations set for commentary. Thus we shall be looking at the *Analects* in a more characteristically Chinese way than we would if we attempted a very abstract distillation of Confucius's thought. And since Confucius saw himself primarily as scholar and teacher, it will be appropriate to start with a chapter based on his sayings about education.

# 2

## Learning and teaching

### The Master's love of learning

'I silently accumulate knowledge; I study and do not get bored; I teach others and do not grow weary — for these things come naturally to me.' (A 7.2)

'In a hamlet of ten houses there will certainly be someone as loyal and true to his word as I am, but not someone so fond of learning.' (A 5.27)

'At fifteen I set my heart on learning.' (A 2.4)

In spite of all the difficulties inherent in trying to assess the authenticity of the *Analects* and of other material about Confucius, it is impossible to deny that — although there is no telling whether we have a fairly accurate portrait of the Master or one made much glossier by the memory of his disciples — a recognisable personality does shine through the haze. One of the most important ingredients in his make-up was his love of learning. As an old man in his seventies he gave a terse description of the six stages of his life, which will be easier to understand when we meet it later in this book rather than here at the beginning. But at least the first stage is clear enough: at the age of fifteen he devoted his life to learning. This formed the basis of his whole life's work, for when he made no progress in public affairs or in gaining public recognition for his doctrines, he devoted himself solely to the role of private teacher, in order to distribute the fruits of his learning to others who might prove more successful in giving effect to it.

Thus he served as a model and inspiration for countless scholars of the imperial age, who often had to undertake half a lifetime of study before they at last succeeded in passing the civil service examinations — their only hope of playing a part in affairs. If they were unsuccessful in these ambitions, for them too teaching was the only obvious alternative outlet for their talents. The great significance of Confucius in Chinese history is that in many different ways he served as an example for his fellow-countrymen to follow; and the thought of the Master, patiently devoted to learning and not disheartened by his lack of worldly success, must have been an inspiration to many a frustrated scholar in later times.

Even those who were successful in the examinations had to continue with their studies in order to keep fresh the qualities of character which the Classics had instilled into them; and emperors, who had undergone a rigorous Confucian training before ascending the throne, continued to keep scholars at court to expound the Classics to them. If self-sacrifice, following Christ's example, is the key to the Christian message, then learning, after the fashion of the Master, is the vital ingredient of the Confucian message. But, in the case of China, the message did really get across. As Hsün Tzu put it, 'Learning continues until death and only then does it cease' (H 19). Learning was the occupation of a lifetime, and high office could be its reward. More than any other society China has given status to learning.

## Learning does not imply bookishness

'A gentleman who, when he eats, avoids seeking to satisfy his appetite to the full and, when he is at home, avoids seeking comfort, who is diligent in deed and cautious in word, and who associates with those who possess the Way and is rectified by them, may be said to be fond of learning.' (A 1.14)

For Confucius, and for the Chinese tradition in general, learning did not usually mean the accumulation of facts for their own sake. It meant the gathering of knowledge for the sake of guiding one's conduct. Therefore a person who had shown himself to have learnt certain moral lessons could be described as 'fond of learning', even if he were not at all bookish. The word *hsüeh*, which is normally translated as 'learning' or 'to study', often means the study and imitation of moral exemplars. Confucius himself was later seen as the kind of moral exemplar who was an appropriate object of *hsüeh* ('study and imitation'). For instance, Mencius is reported to have said: 'As to what I should like, it is to follow the example of [*hsüeh*, study and imitate] Confucius' (M 2a.2). So the main object of learning was the imitation of models, and an important part of a teacher's role was to act as a model himself and to provide an example of what the morally conscious human being should be like. The importance of following good examples is illustrated in the quotation above when it refers to the gentleman 'who associates with those who possess the Way and is rectified by them'.

It is a commonplace of ancient Chinese literature to equate education with moral training. In the *Book of History* and also in the *Mencius* it is reported that the legendary sage-emperor Shun appointed a Minister of Education to give instruction to the people because they were not observing the five relationships (i.e. the duties involved in the relationships between father and son, ruler and subject, husband and wife, elder brother and younger brother, and friend and friend). And in the nineteenth century it was still widely believed that such moral training was the cure for the ills which had beset the country, so it was urged that colleges should be established in troubled provinces to educate the people in Confucian principles.

The stereotype of the gentleman provided in this quotation also gives prominence to the virtue of frugality which was much admired by Confucius. This virtue was exemplified by his favourite disciple Yen Hui, who remained cheerful although he lived in squalid surroundings and only had a little rice and water to sustain him (A 6.9). Later it was a necessary part of the equipment of that virtuous figure, the poor scholar who strove for examination success despite his humble origins. Confucian frugality stood in stark contrast with the luxury and extravagance of imperial courts.

## The Master's love of antiquity

'I transmit but do not create. I have been faithful to and loved antiquity. In this I venture to compare myself to our old P'eng.' (A 7.1)

'If by keeping the old warm one can provide understanding of the new, one is fit to be a teacher.' (A 2.11)

In the opinion of Confucius models which were supremely worth imitating had to be sought in antiquity. The Master himself lived at a time of social and political instability consequent on the disintegration of the feudal type of society which characterised the early Chou period. Although the Chinese world was still nominally under the leadership of the Chou king, it had long since broken up into independent states. By the time of Confucius's successor Mencius, the age when inter-state tensions were building up to the climax of the unification of China by the state of Ch'in in 221 B.C., the obvious response to the prevailing instability was the reunification of China under any one of the independent states; and

Mencius himself argued that any ruler who put his teachings into practice would easily win over 'all under Heaven'. But, living almost two centuries earlier, Confucius had thought that the solution to China's social and political problems still lay in a revival of early Chou values. The commonly held doctrine of the Mandate of Heaven meant that the Chou founders had won the approval of Heaven by their virtue and had therefore been granted the right to replace the preceding Shang Dynasty, whose last ruler had forfeited the Mandate because of his evil and tyrannical behaviour. So the obvious reaction, in the view of Confucius, was a general return to those virtues which had secured the Mandate in the first place.

Since China was isolated from other major civilisations and unaware of any great cultural tradition apart from its own, it could not seek a solution to its difficulties by borrowing ideas from another society. It did not have experience of alternative systems of government, such as democracy or oligarchy, so that the only obvious means of salvation was a ruler who would govern virtuously in the manner of the Chou founders and restore unity to 'all under Heaven'. Therefore what was of supreme importance in Confucius's eyes was the investigation and transmission of the correct traditions concerning the Golden Age of antiquity. If there was an ideal Way to be rediscovered, transmission of that ideal was what was needed and creativity was unnecessary — and indeed both arrogant and harmful. As a lover of antiquity and transmitter of its message Confucius compared himself to P'eng, an obscure figure from ancient times whose name was proverbial for lon-gevity, a Chinese equivalent of Methuselah. Men of great age, whose memory reaches far back into the past, are obviously the best equipped to hand down traditions.

However, despite his reverence for the past, Confucius did not believe in a blind and unthinking traditionalism, and this may be clearly seen in the second saying at the beginning of this section. By keeping the old warm one can provide understanding of the new. Although he disclaimed creativity, there is a sort of creativity in using the past to serve the present. This theme echoes down the ages, for later periods of decline were blamed on failure to transmit the truth about the Golden Age of the Chou Dynasty, so that salvation was to be sought by looking again at the ancient texts and trying to discover a more accurate interpretation of them. Thus, for example, the Neo-Confucian movement arose in the late T'ang Dynasty in response to the country's decline after the tragedy of the An Lu-shan Rebellion; and in the late nineteenth century opposing interpretations of Confucius were still used in support of policies to meet the new challenge of the West.

So again we find that Confucius occupied his usual role of exemplar: he was the supreme example of that love of antiquity and eagerness to go on investigating it which was characteristic of the later Chinese intellectual tradition. Throughout imperial Chinese history men looked back on the feudal period of the Chou Dynasty as a Golden Age, and at the forefront of scholarship there stood a tradition of scholarly commentaries on the ancient texts, interpreting their message for contemporary readers. At the same time the Master's words 'I transmit, but do not create' could serve as a motto for traditional Chinese historiography, which always placed great stress on the transmission of documents. The written word was sacred, and the facts would speak for themselves if only they were handed down. But it was equally true that history's purpose was to serve as a moral guide to present conduct; for in the common Chinese metaphor history was a mirror in which men could see their own actions, understand their own motives, and judge their own behaviour. So Chinese history-writing had twin ideals: the past should be thoroughly transmitted, and the past should be used to understand the present. The seeds of both of these ideals could be found in these two sayings attributed to Confucius.

## The Master's association with early Chou culture

When the Master was intimidated at K'uang, he said: 'When King Wen [the Cultured King] died, did culture cease to exist? If Heaven had intended to put an end to such culture, a later mortal like myself would not have succeeded in associating himself with it. If Heaven does not yet put an end to this culture, what can the people of K'uang do to me?' (A 9.5)

Confucius was said to have found himself in difficulties in K'uang because he was mistaken for an adventurer called Yang Huo who had previously created a disturbance in that small frontier town. This is one of four occasions during his travels when his life was said to have been endangered, providing appropriate opportunities for sage-like behaviour and utterances. In this passage Confucius is represented as believing that no harm can befall him since he has

a Heaven-sent destiny to preserve the cultural values of the Chou
founders.

The antiquity which Confucius particularly loved and wished to
transmit to his own generation was the period of the founding of
the Chou Dynasty about five hundred years before his birth. This
was the period of moral excellence which the Master would have
liked to see imitated in order to secure a return to a sound political
order in China. King Wen was not the actual founder of the Chou
Dynasty, but the one who paved the way for its establishment. His
name means 'the Cultured King' and it was probably given to him
posthumously because of his style of leadership. He is mentioned
only twice in the *Analects*, but it is clear that before Confucius's
time he was already thought of as an ideal ruler who laid the
foundations for the conquest of the preceding Shang Dynasty by
his civilisatory achievements. Mencius was a great admirer of King
Wen and in the *Mencius* book he is portrayed as a leader whose
kindness to the people gained him such widespread support that,
although he initially ruled over only a tiny domain, he was able
to prepare the ground for the successful conquest of the Shang
Dynasty by his son and successor King Wu, 'the Martial King'.

As a result of these early Confucian writings the belief that every
successful armed conquest needed to be preceded by a period of
cultural preparation became an important feature of Chinese
political thought. The idea was that, through their skill in civil
administration and the arts of peace, the conquerors built up a
store of moral power which helped them to attract and win over
the neighbouring peoples, who then welcomed them with open
arms. The conception of the ideal ruler as a successful
administrator, skilful in the arts of peace, and attractive to the
outside world because of the cultural achievements of his regime,
a conception already in existence before Confucius's time and
adopted by him, has been profoundly influential throughout the
course of Chinese history. The civilian ideal continued to prevail,
and military virtues were given a very low place in the scale of
values. Ideally the enemy should be won over by a display of
China's cultural superiority rather than, or prior to, being
conquered militarily. Interesting examples of cultural preparation
for military conquest can be seen in the course of Chinese history,
and indeed the idea was borrowed by the Manchus who, by
immersing themselves in the Confucian literature and traditions,

were able to commend themselves to the Chinese as a suitable replacement for the decadent Ming Dynasty.

The word *wen*, here translated 'culture', originally meant 'striped', and consequently 'patterned', 'decorated', or 'adorned'. It therefore came to be applied to things which were not mere necessities of existence, but which gave beauty and variety to civilised life and distinguished it from barbarism. It was the attraction of this decorative element in life — the appeal of fine *objets d'art*, or of grand ritual celebrations and musical performances, together of course with the Chinese script (itself a work of art) and the literature written in it — which was thought to dazzle the untutored barbarian and win him over to the Chinese side. So, as far as the Chinese were concerned, the difference between civilisation and barbarism was neither a matter of social or political organisation, nor a question of race or religion. It was entirely a matter of cultural attainment.

Apart from King Wen, Confucius was thought to have had a special regard for the Duke of Chou, the brother of King Wu who acted as regent during the minority of the latter's son and successor King Ch'eng. It was natural that he should have been venerated in the state of Lu, where Confucius lived, since he was traditionally regarded as the founder and first ruler of that state. Accounts of Confucius's own veneration for the Duke of Chou rest on only two passages in the *Analects*, including the lament 'Alas, extreme is my decline; it is long since I dreamt I saw the Duke of Chou!' (A 7.5). There are in fact very few references to him in early texts; and it is not till the *Mencius* that he is treated as such a sage that, like Confucius, it is necessary to explain why he never ruled over 'all under Heaven'. Here in this passage it is King Wen who is shown to be the inspiration of Confucius and the model which a latter-day ruler should aspire to emulate.

## The materials for study are within everyone

Kung-sun Ch'ao of Wei asked Tzu-kung: 'From whom did Confucius derive his learning?' Tsu-kung said: 'The Way of Kings Wen and Wu has not yet collapsed to the ground. It is here present among us, and men of wisdom and talent remember the more important principles of the Way, and men who lack wisdom and talent remember its less important principles. So everyone has the Way of Wen and Wu within himself. From whom then does the Master not learn, and yet what regular teacher does he have?' (A 19.22)

'When I walk with two others, I always receive instruction from them. I select their good qualities and follow them, and avoid their bad qualities.' (A 7.21)

'In the presence of a worthy man, think of equalling him. In the presence of a worthless man, turn your gaze within.' (A 4.17)

In the only other reference to King Wen which occurs in the *Analects* a disciple of Confucius called Tzu-kung expresses the conviction that the Way of Wen and Wu has not entirely faded; but the burden of all of these three passages is that, since the object of learning is to learn how to behave, the materials for study are all around us all the time. The constant learning to which Confucius was devoted was aimed at self-improvement as the prerequisite to achieving improvement in others. Since the principal object of education was the moral training of the young, which is obviously also part of the normal parental role, education was naturally regarded not as something novel but as something which had been in existence since the beginning of time. Learning is as much part of our lives as breathing. Indeed learning can occur unconsciously through the unthinking imitation of our neighbours. So it is extremely important to live in the right district. As Confucius put it, 'It is humaneness which is the attraction of a neighbourhood. If from choice a man does not dwell in the midst of humaneness, how can he attain to wisdom?' (A 4.1). Mencius's mother had a legendary reputation for wisdom in choosing the right environment in which to bring up her son. She moved from the vicinity of a market, where Mencius had played all day at being a hawker, to the neighbourhood of a school, under the influence of which the boy abandoned his former pastimes and played at ritual instead (as Confucius was said to have done as a child). But although the moral lessons one learns from parents and from observing neighbours were thought extremely valuable, there are casual references to schools in the *Mencius* and other early sources, and it was taken for granted in antiquity that formal education had existed for as long as society had existed. Mencius himself quotes the *Book of History* saying: 'Heaven sent down the people who are on earth below, provided rulers for them, and provided teachers for them' (M Ib.3).

## Education should be available to all

'From the bringer of a bundle of dried meat upwards, I have never refused instruction to anyone.' (A 7.7)

When the Master went to Wei, Jan Yu drove his carriage. 'How dense is the population!' exclaimed the Master. 'When the people have multiplied, what more should be done for them?' asked Jan Yu. 'Enrich them', he replied. 'And when they have been enriched?' 'Educate them', replied the Master. (A 13.9)

'If there is education there are no class-distinctions.' (A 15.38)

A bundle of dried meat was an extremely humble offering, but Confucius, who endured poverty in his own youth, was prepared to teach anyone who showed a genuine willingness and capacity to learn. The principle that education should be readily available to all who seek it follows naturally from the idea that all men are born equal in the sense that every man has the innate capacity to develop into a sage. This belief was expressly held by Mencius, who declared that 'Everyone may become a Yao or Shun' (M 6b.2). Although Confucius did not express himself so clearly on the subject, there are indications that he inclined in this direction and believed that men were naturally close to each other and were set far apart from each other by their different experiences of life (see quotation on p. 135). So environmental factors like a person's economic situation and education are extremely important; and in equity all should receive both an adequate livelihood so that, freed from want, they can cultivate the virtues, and an equal opportunity of education so that they can fully develop their potential. Mencius was also a powerful advocate of these policies, but they could be traced back to Confucius, as can be seen in his replies to Jan Yu.

Confucius is credited with being the earliest man in China to have accepted these principles. He was more interested in the pupils' eagerness to learn than in their class status, and the majority of the disciples referred to in the *Analects* seem to have come from relatively humble backgrounds. As a consequence of this example set by Confucius the ideal of a nation-wide educational system was set before the Chinese long before other peoples had such a conception. In pre-modern conditions this could never lead to a serious attempt at the introduction of universal education, but it gave a stimulus to the widespread establishment of schools in response to imperial exhortations. As a result of their studies with

Confucius his pupils, however humble, were equipped to hold important official appointments. Similarly in late imperial China, when the civil service examination system was well established, the humble could obtain advancement in the government, since entry to the civil service through competitive examination was open to all males, with the exception of members of certain disadvantaged professions, which included actors and policemen.

The third quotation, consisting of a mere four characters in the original, is so condensed that its meaning is not entirely clear. The word *lei*, translated as 'class-distinctions', has a wider sense and means simply 'categories' or 'classification'. Indeed one commentator thought that it meant that there should be no distinction of race, so that it could be taken as an injunction to propagate Confucianism among the barbarians. But the saying has generally been adopted as a slogan for classless education, and as such it used to be displayed on school buildings in China.

The extent to which the humble could achieve greatness through study was always of course limited by economic factors, but there were cases of men from very humble backgrounds rising to the very top of the civil service, and there are many edifying accounts of ambitious scholars studying at night while supporting their widowed mothers by day. Many talented but poor young men received an education through the charity of wealthy relatives or in village schools financed by the more prosperous local farmers. Many combined a life of scholarship with agricultural labour, or 'ploughed with the writing-brush', as it was sometimes called. And as inspiration for all this the Chinese would look back to the one who thought there should be no class-distinction in education and was prepared to teach anyone, however poor, who would respond to his message.

## Subjects taught by the Master

The Master took four subjects for his teaching: culture, conduct, loyalty, and good faith. (A 7.24)

'Young men should be filial when at home and respectful to elders when away from home. They should be earnest and keep their promises. They should extend their love to all, but be intimate only with the humane. If they have any energy to spare after the performance of these duties, they should use it to study 'culture'. (A 1.6)

There are, in the *Analects*, various references to the topics included in Confucius's teaching, all of which he saw as contributing to the moral training of the individual. The standard content of education in antiquity was known as the six arts. These were rites, music, archery, charioteering, writing and mathematics, a collection of subjects of largely practical value essential to the upbringing of the young aristocrat. It was not at all a literary type of education, and only under the heading of 'rites' would there be any place for the kind of moral training in which Confucius specialised. For Confucius, too, literature was of no importance except in so far as it served the purpose of moral training. It was as a consequence of the teachings of Hsün Tzu that the Confucian approach to education developed the bookishness which was characteristic of the imperial age: he wrote that 'education begins with the recitation of the Classics and ends with the reading of ritual texts' (H 19), and it was he who recommended a list of Classics which were to become the nucleus of the curriculum for budding bureaucrats under the Former Han Dynasty, thus establishing the pattern for an educational system which would always set great store by the canonical writings.

Of the subjects listed, loyalty and good faith will have to be considered later in connection with the other Confucian virtues. The importance of culture for Confucius's teaching has already been noted. It was the culture of the Chou founders, the hallmark of civilisation which distinguished the Chinese from the untutored barbarians by whom they were surrounded, that Confucius was anxious to preserve and restore. Although this is an essential component of Confucius's message, he sometimes seemed to subordinate it to a man's duty to fulfil his social obligations. The study of culture was only to be pursued if there was energy to spare from such more serious occupations, as the second quotation indicates. But although Confucius seemed to make a distinction between moral self-cultivation and the pursuit of the polite arts and put the latter in a secondary position, it is clear from other passages that culture was a very important element of the moral training necessary for the production of ideal gentlemen to administer a harmonious society (A 6.25). Yen Hui, the favourite disciple, also claimed that the Master had broadened him with culture (A 9.10).

## The Master's use of the Songs

'One is roused by the *Songs*, established by ritual, and perfected by music.' (A 8.8)

'My young friends, why do none of you study the *Songs*? The *Songs* may be used to stimulate emotions, to observe people and share their company, and to express grievances. At home they enable one to serve one's father, and abroad to serve one's ruler.' (A 17.9)

'A man may know by heart the three hundred *Songs*, but if he is given a post in government and cannot successfully carry out his duties, and if he is sent to far places and cannot report in detail on his mission, then even if he has learnt many of them, of what use is this to him?' (A 13.5)

Other important materials for study are the *Songs*, ritual and music. The *Book of Songs* is a collection of poems which had already become part of the common literary heritage before Confucius's time. The traditional account of its completion is that Confucius selected 305 out of 3,000 poems which had been assembled by a music master of the state of Lu, but it is extremely unlikely that he had anything to do with the selection or editing of the pieces. The work was advocated by Hsün Tzu in his educational programme and in the Former Han Dynasty it was given the status of a Classic; and the alleged link with Confucius obviously derives from the fact that, once he began to be revered as a sage, his role in the establishment of the classical tradition was bound to be greatly exaggerated.

The *Book of Songs* consists partly of folk songs and partly of formal odes used for ceremonial occasions. It has considerable literary appeal, in this respect surpassing everything else which has come down to us from the Chou Dynasty, but it is not this aspect of the *Songs* which interested Confucius. Indeed the Master showed no interest in literature as such or any awareness that writing could be appreciated for its aesthetic appeal. All study, even of literature, is undertaken for a purely practical purpose. My translation of the difficult second sentence of the second quotation in the above group is somewhat tentative, but the whole passage certainly shows that the *Songs* were considered by Confucius to heighten a man's sensibilities and enable him the better to perform the social duties which were his primary responsibility. Also, in dealing with the *Songs*, Confucius did not forget that the ultimate aim of education was to obtain a post in government. As the final quotation insists, it is no use being able to recite the three hundred *Songs* unless this fits one for the task of administration and diplomacy.

The specific reason why a knowledge of the *Songs* was helpful to statesmanship is that quotations were used to oil the wheels of diplomatic exchanges. It was conventionally accepted that the words could be taken out of context and made to bear any meaning required by the speaker. Some idea of the technique can be gained by seeing how Confucius used the book for educational purposes. For example, there is a passage in the *Songs* which runs: 'As cut, as filed, as chiselled, as polished'. It is a simile referring to the jade-like elegance of a princely young lover, but for educational purposes it must be given a more high-minded interpretation, so when it is quoted in the *Analects* the simile is used to refer to the polishing and refinement of a man's character (A 1.15). As a result of this use of the expression in the *Analects*, it became a stock reference in Chinese literature for moral refinement rather than the physical elegance intended in the original poem. The disciple Tzu-kung received the Master's congratulations on this reinterpretation of the passage, which amounts to a deliberate misconstruction of the lines for the purpose of using them as a moral tag. The use of this kind of device enabled courtiers and diplomats to refer guardedly and obliquely to delicate and dangerous topics and so feel their way towards solutions which blunt and straightforward language might have rendered impossible.

In such exchanges the meanings of words could, if necessary, be completely altered. For example, the Master said: 'If out of the three hundred *Songs* I took one phrase to cover their meaning, it would be "Let there be no depravity in your thoughts" ' (A 2.2). But in fact this comes from a description of horses and the words taken here to mean 'no depravity' meant 'without swerving' in the original context, while the word rendered as 'thoughts' does not carry that sense in the passage in the *Songs*, but is merely used as an exclamation. This particular example of Confucius's technique is interesting not only because he uses this device of misinterpretation, but also because the end product, 'Let there be no depravity in your thoughts', firmly indicates that Confucius thought of the *Songs* as a sourcebook for moral training. Many of the *Songs* are simple love poems, but these had to be given a more solemn interpretation befitting the dignity of their inclusion in the canon of Five Classics during the Former Han period, especially as Confucius was thought responsible for selecting them from a much larger corpus of poems. The Master himself had provided a technique of reinterpretation, so such poems were generally misconstrued as allusions to the loyalty inherent in the ruler-minister relationship which was at the heart of Confucian ethics, rather than as descriptions of the dalliance of lovers.

Another classic which has been especially closely associated with Confucius is the *Spring and Autumn* annals, which, like the *Book of Songs*, was incorporated in the canon in the Former Han Dynasty. There is no reference to the work in the *Analects* itself, but in the *Mencius* Confucius is reported to have made the prophetic statement 'It is the *Spring and Autumn* which will make men understand me; it is the *Spring and Autumn* which will make men condemn me.' Later Mencius went on to say: 'When Confucius completed the *Spring and Autumn*, rebellious ministers and unruly sons were struck with terror.' The *Spring and Autumn* is a sparse, annalistic account of the state of Lu, which Confucius was traditionally believed to have compiled, indicating by subtle variations in the use of language his praise or blame for the participants in the historical events described. In fact no such theory about the composition of the *Spring and Autumn*, or at any rate of the work which at present goes under that name will survive careful scrutiny; so it is probable that the Master merely used the book as a source from which to illustrate his message and demonstrate the decadence of the age.

Later, as I have already mentioned, it became one of the principal aims of traditional Chinese historians to hold up a mirror to mankind, so that the acts of famous and notorious historical characters might provide examples for later men either to follow or to avoid. This tradition mainly derived from the conventional interpretation of the *Spring and Autumn*, and was especially evident in biographical writing. The standard dynastic histories each have biographical sections, which give accounts of the public careers of the prominent men of the age; and the value of these accounts is not so much that they portray the truth about the individuals concerned, but that they give examples of what their successors in public life should imitate or avoid. Since learning primarily consisted of the accumulation of knowledge for the purpose of guiding one's conduct, the reading of history shared this aim; and the classical example of this attitude to history, which had a powerful influence on later historical writing, was the *Spring and Autumn*, which was traditionally attributed to Confucius. So in connection with both the *Spring and Autumn* and the *Songs*

Confucius served as the earliest exemplar of the use of literature for moral purposes.

It is clear from his references to the *Book of Songs* that Confucius had no conception of literature as a subject of independent enquiry and interest. The *Songs* were merely a tool of diplomacy and a guide to morality and social conduct. It would have been surprising if it had been otherwise, for after the *Book of Songs* there was an extraordinary lack of poetry and of other writing for purely literary purposes right through until the end of the Chou Dynasty. Throughout imperial Chinese history literature's *raison d'être* was generally conceived as the teaching of truth and virtue, so Confucian bureaucrats tried to restrict the influence of popular plays and novels which disregarded the orthodox morality. Such attitudes lingered on, and it was still as true under the regime of Chairman Mao as it had been in ancient China that politics was in command and that literature was its servant.

# 3

# Ritual and music

## The importance of ritual in government

'If one can govern a country by ritual and deference, there is no more to be said; but if one cannot govern a country by ritual and deference, then what has one to do with ritual?' (A 4.13)

In the previous chapter there is a quotation from the *Analects* in which Confucius is reported to have said that one is 'aroused by the *Songs*, established by ritual, and perfected by music'; and it is now time to consider the part played by ritual in Confucius's teaching, and its impact on later Chinese thought. The individual was 'established by ritual' and so it was an important tool in the process of self-cultivation; but ultimately, like a knowledge of the *Book of Songs*, it was only valuable in so far as it assisted in the government of the country.

The word *li*, translated here as 'ritual', originally meant 'to sacrifice', and so its first extension of usage was restricted to ritual in the context of religion. Later, however, the meaning spread to include ceremonious behaviour in secular contexts, initially at those important occasions which were imbued with quasi-religious solemnity, such as court audiences, the reception of envoys from other states, challenges to battle, archery contests, and the like. At such events a ritualised protocol and code of behaviour had to be observed; and from use on such ceremonial occasions *li* became further diffused so that it coloured all social occasions and all human relationships, in such everyday contexts meaning 'propriety', 'politeness', or 'good form'. The virtue of deference or yielding (*jang*), which is associated with ritual in this passage, could also be used in ordinary social intercourse, to mean 'yielding precedence'; but its main significance in Confucian ethics is that it is the characteristic quality of the ruler who cedes his throne to a successor chosen for his virtue, for which the model was the legendary sage-emperor Yao's abdication in favour of Shun. It is the opposite of self-assertiveness and so a virtue which is valuable in government and diplomacy as well as in social relations.

The importance of ritual in Chinese society may partly be due to the fact that the Chinese did not share our concept of a divine lawgiver, so that human conduct had to depend much more on codes of behaviour based on precedent (as well as on the imitation of models, the importance of which has already been stressed in connection with education). At the same time the early Chou sovereigns had been overlords of a vast area of present-day north China at a time of primitive communications, so the political system of this period depended very heavily on the family ties which linked the rulers of the various states which recognised their suzerainty; and this cohesiveness could be more securely preserved if the family links and social hierarchies involved were solemnised and reinforced by a code of conduct which was heavily imbued with ritual. So ritual, which had originally been entirely devoted to the service of the spirits, became a means of controlling social behaviour and preserving political hierarchies.

This preoccupation with ritual is not solely a Chinese concern. We are familiar with a similar concept in our own society, a ceremoniousness ranging from the pomp displayed on grand royal occasions or important military parades to the ordinary courtesies of the informal handshake or the polite gesture of deference; but with us ritual is not carried to such extremes of detail, nor is it codified and treated as an all-embracing system, as it has been by the Chinese. There are other important differences. For example, *li* 'ritual' has something in common with mores, but the word 'mores' is used to mean the customary norms of a particular society, whereas the Chinese, being unfamiliar with other advanced societies, considered *li* to be universally valid. Another way in which ritual was more pervasive in the Chinese system than in ours was that it was not sufficient just to repeat the appropriate words and perform the appropriate actions. There was an added dimension to the performance of *li*: each rite had to be accompanied by the appropriate attitude, and there evolved a rich vocabulary describing the various ritual postures and expressions. These words were sometimes used to describe people's appearance, not only when performing ceremonies, but also when engaged in the ordinary business of life. An example from Book 10 of the *Analects*, the section which seems to have been extracted from a work on ritual, will give an impression of how *li* pervades the most trivial activities:

> In bed he does not lie in the posture of a corpse. When at home he does not use ritual attitudes. When he sees anyone in mourning, even if he knows him well, he must change countenance; and when he sees anyone in sacrificial garb, or a blind man, even if he is in informal dress, he must be sure to adopt the appropriate attitude. On meeting anyone in deep mourning he must bow across the bar of his carriage; he also bows in the same way to people carrying official tablets. When he is given a dish of delicacies, he must change countenance and rise to his feet. At a sudden clap of thunder or a violent gust of wind he must change countenance. (A 10.16)

In the ancient Chinese world Confucius must have been seen by the many who could not appreciate his moral and political teachings as primarily a specialist on ritual. In the *Tso Tradition*, the main historical source for the period, he is referred to as a teacher of ritual; and on one occasion, when a ruler consulted him about the advisability of attacking another state, the Master is reported to have said that he had learnt about sacrificial vessels and not about warfare, and then to have left the state in a huff, declaring: 'The bird chooses its tree; the tree does not choose the bird' (Duke Ai, year II; see also A 15.1 for a briefer version). It became a cliché of biographical writing that a great man's career was foreshadowed by his youthful activities; and, sure enough, Ssu-ma Ch'ien's biography shows the boy Confucius playing at arranging sacrificial vessels and performing ceremonies. In the *Record of Rites* the Master naturally appears as an expert on ritual, and in the *Analects* there is much evidence of his concern with this subject, although apparently not enough to please some of his followers, who seem to have inserted the material in Book 10 to provide more detail on the Master's ritual postures and attitudes.

The correct performance of ritual by the ruler was held to be essential to the welfare of the state. The ancient belief in the interaction between heaven and earth meant that, not only in the Chou period but also throughout the imperial age, it was thought that the correct performance of the appropriate rituals by the Son of Heaven was necessary to secure the harmonious operation of the cosmos. Ritually incorrect actions by the Son of Heaven were bound to be followed by natural disasters. Confucius saw the regretted decline from the standards of early Chou culture partly in terms of departure from appropriate rituals. During his time the powers of the Duke of Lu, his own state, had largely been taken over by three families; and the head of one of these families was described by Confucius as intolerable for usurping the ruler's prerogative of having eight teams of dancers performing at a ceremony (A 3.1). But although he did show his deep concern that such matters of detail should be correct, he was much more involved with the fundamental principles and meaning of *li* than with the outward forms. He stressed the ethical significance of ritual and saw it as a means of bringing order into the life of the individual and into his relations with the family and his dealings with society as a whole, so that one is 'established by ritual'. If the emotions and attitudes of mind associated with religious ceremonies could be carried over into the secular world, this would strengthen and beautify human relationships.

The words 'employ the people as though you were officiating at a great sacrifice' (A 12.2, see also p. 133) encapsulate the important Confucian view that the sacred is not something set apart from ordinary life, but something which one should be conscious of in all life's activities. Confucius appreciated that ritual was a powerful device for securing the harmonious human order which he craved; so he constantly stressed the important role of ritual in government, suggesting, as in the opening quotation, that ritual was useless unless it was employed in governing the country, for that was the supreme task for which it was most vitally needed. So he maintained that 'if the ruler loves ritual, then the people will be easy to employ' (A 14.44), an idea which is spelt out more fully in the *Mean*, where the Master says: 'If a ruler understands the rites at the altars of Heaven and Earth and comprehends the meaning of the ancestral sacrifices, then ruling his kingdom will be as easy as pointing to the palm of his hand' (Ch. 19).

## The relationship between ritual and humaneness

'If a man is not humane, what has he to do with ritual? If a man is not humane, what has he to do with music?' (A 3.3)

Yen Hui asked about humaneness. The Master said: 'To subdue oneself and return to ritual is humane. If for one day a ruler could subdue himself and return to ritual, then all under Heaven would respond to the humaneness in him. For does humaneness proceed from the man himself, or does it proceed from others?' Yen Hui said: 'I beg to ask for the details of this.' The Master said: 'Do not look at what is contrary to ritual, do not listen to what is contrary to ritual, do not speak what is contrary to ritual, and make no movement which is contrary to ritual.' (A 12.1)

The omnipresence of ritual in all kinds of social situations raises the question of its relationship to the social virtues. Here are two passages in which ritual is related to humaneness, the chief of the Confucian virtues, which will be discussed in more detail in the following chapter. From the first of these quotations it is clear that Confucius gives priority to humaneness. Humaneness is the essential virtue, and ritual (which could, after all, be conducted with regard for form rather than meaning) is, as stated elsewhere in the *Analects*, 'secondary' (A 3.8). The social virtues are thus the foundation on which ritual must be built. On the other hand in conversation with Yen Hui the Master says that 'to subdue oneself and return to ritual is humane', so that in this passage ritual is being given primacy and humaneness is being defined in terms of adherence to it. This conflict illustrates the difficulty of interpreting Confucius's thought on the basis of the *Analects*. One could argue that the two passages are not in serious conflict with each other but merely illustrate the close links which are bound to exist between the supreme virtue of humaneness and the Confucian conception of ritual, with its important role in social relationships. On the other hand it is equally true that the second passage comes from Book 12, and so may be a later interpolation emanating from a source which, like Hsün Tzu, elevates ritual to a supreme position. Certainly this passage's insistence that one should heed the dictates of ritual in every word and deed could be taken as a source of inspiration by extreme ritualists and could help to give Confucius the reputation of being an unsophisticated stickler for the empty forms of ritual.

The sterile pursuit of ritual expertise for its own sake was an inevitable consequence of the inability of lesser minds to comprehend the true virtues of Confucius's conception of ritual. When so much of human behaviour was subject to the demands of ritual, it tended to become mere habit; and the empty show of ritual, especially if accompanied by extravagance, was an easy target for criticism, so that in hostile writings Confucius was tarred with the same brush as the less perceptive of his followers.

On the other hand the discussion of the relationship between *li* and the social virtues was carried further by Mencius, who concerned himself with the nature of the human personality which was reflected by these social virtues. He regarded *li* (together with humaneness, dutifulness and wisdom) as one of the four basic virtues which derive from the cultivation of four so-called 'shoots' or 'sprouts' — as essential a part of the human personality as the four limbs are an essential part of the human body. Hsün Tzu had an even grander conception of *li*. Confucius had claimed for *li* a vital role in social relationships and in government as well as in religion, and *li*, unlike mores, was thought to have universal validity, so Hsün Tzu took the matter a stage further and elevated *li* to the status of a cosmic principle. 'Heaven and Earth gave birth to the *li*', he declared, and it was his view that the social distinctions and the rules of conduct whereby men observed them were as natural as the four seasons. 'Through rites', he declared, 'Heaven and Earth join in harmony, the sun and moon shine, the four seasons proceed in order, the stars and constellations march, the rivers flow and all things flourish, men's likes and dislikes are regulated and their joys and hates made appropriate' (H 94).

A statement on the supreme importance of *li* is attributed to Confucius in the *Record of Rites*: 'Of all things to which the people owe their lives the rites are the most important. If it were not for the rites, they would have no means of regulating the services paid to the spirits of Heaven and Earth; if it were not for the rites, they would have no means of distinguishing the positions of ruler and subject, high and low, old and young; if it were not for the rites, they would have no means of differentiating the relationships between male and female, between father and son, and between elder and younger brother, and of linking far and near by the ceremony of marriage' (L 2.261). By the incorporation of this work into the classical canon in the Former Han Dynasty the place of ritual was firmly established in the educational and governmental tradition of imperial China. Just as in antiquity Confucius and others of his kind (rather than priests) were the experts on ritual, both in its religious and in its secular manifestations, so the literati, educated in the Confucian Classics (which included the ritual texts), were the experts on ritual throughout imperial Chinese history. As such they, rather than any priesthood, played their part in the religious ritual authorised by the state. Among the common people in late imperial China the concept of *li* was propagated by the widespread dissemination of such works as Chu Hsi's *Family Rituals*, which were often commended in the rules published by clans for the edification of their members. And in the apparatus of bureaucracy the Board of Rites took its place alongside the Boards of Civil Office, Revenue, Punishments, War, and Works as one of the six government departments which remained a constant feature of the imperial administrative system.

Ceremoniousness and excessive politeness were features of Chinese civilisation which became a familiar part of the European image of China, and the language — with its many honorific and humilific expressions — was exploited for its quaintness by European writers. But beneath these superficialities there lies something deeply important, a philosophy which embraced within the one concept of *li* all rituals and ceremonies, whether religious or secular, as well as all common acts of politeness. At its finest this concept could give added dignity and meaning to ordinary human relationships. In this sphere too Confucius has been regarded as the chief inspiration. Not only because of the many references to *li* in the *Analects*, but also because the *Record of Rites* and other ancient sources treat him as an expert on *li*, Confucius has been regarded as the chief mentor of the Chinese people in matters of ritual.

## Mourning rites and music

Lin Fang asked about the main principles to be observed in connection with ritual. The Master said: 'An important question indeed! In ritual it is better to be frugal than lavish. In mourning rites it is better to be sorrowful than fearful.' (A 3.4)

Tsai Yü asked about the three years' mourning, and said that one year was already long enough. 'If gentlemen do not practise the rites for three years,' he said, 'the rites will certainly decay. If for three years they do not make music, music will certainly die. In a year the old crops have gone and the new crops have come up, so after a completed year the mourning should stop'. The Master said: 'If you were then to eat good rice and wear embroidered clothes, would you feel at ease?' 'Yes', he replied. 'If you would be at ease, then do so', said the Master. 'But when a gentleman is in mourning, if he eats dainties he does not relish them, and if he hears music he does not enjoy it, and if he sits in his usual place he is not at ease. That is why he abstains from these things. But if you feel at ease, then do them!' When Tsai Yü had left, the Master said: 'How inhumane Yü is! It is not until a child is three years old that it leaves its parents' arms. The three years' mourning is the mourning universally adopted by all under Heaven. Surely Yü had those three years of parental love?' (A 17.21)

Before we leave this important topic of ritual here are two more examples of its treatment in the *Analects*. The response to the disciple Lin Fang shows that Confucius believed that rites should be informed with genuine emotion and should not be conducted with extravagant display. Frugality became a strong Confucian tradition, and Mencius was constantly critical of rulers for taking people away from productive labours on the land to provide them with luxuries. But the tradition of frugality has run counter not only to the luxuriousness of imperial courts, but also to the desire of ordinary individuals in Chinese society to impress the neighbours at times of importance in family history such as weddings and funerals.

The conversation with Tsai Yü, a disciple in whom Confucius was much disappointed, is in a style which seems to indicate that it is a late addition to the text. The passage claims Confucius's support for the three years' mourning, a practice which was probably not very ancient and was by no means universal, as Confucius is reported to have stated. The justification attributed to the Master is absurd, as also is Tsai Yü's attack on the practice; but it appears not only in the *Analects* but also in the section of the *Record of Rites* dealing with the three years' mourning (Book 35). Consequently the Master's support for the three years' mourning became enshrined in the Confucian tradition; and this was sufficient to ensure that the practice became mandatory, so that even men in high office had to resign and return home to mourn for their parents. Although the practice is known as the three years' mourning, according to the *Record of Rites* it should only last for twenty-seven months, so a more accurate translation would be 'mourning unto the third year'.

Music is, as often, mentioned in parallel with ritual in the conversation with Tsai Yü. There is a further reference to music in the same conversation: the Master says that, when in mourning, the gentleman does not enjoy music. Confucius himself is said to have been fond of music. He played the zithern and sang (A 7.31 and 17.20). The words for 'enjoy' and 'music' are written with the same character, so that 'enjoy music' and 'enjoy enjoyments' or 'enjoy entertainments' are written identically in ancient Chinese. There is a passage in *Mencius* which puns on the two meanings. A king expresses his anxiety about his love of music, because he feels embarrassed that he can only appreciate the popular music of the day and not the music of antiquity. Mencius's response is typical: it does not matter what kind of music the king enjoys as long as he shares his music/enjoyments with the people (M 1b.1).

The ancient Chinese were indeed fully conscious of the sheer joy obtained from listening to music and the powerful effect it had on the emotions. But there was something far more valuable in music than the mere provision of pleasure. It is often closely associated with ritual, as in Tsai Yü's opening remarks, for ritual ceremony did often include dance, mime and music. Hence it was thought that just as the ancient kings established ritual practices which assisted in the maintenance of cosmic harmony, they also sponsored the composition of music which had a similarly beneficial effect. It was taken for granted that sound could have magical influences. There was a story current in antiquity which illustrated the dramatic effect that music could have. A certain ruler wished to listen to a piece of music which his music master said he was not worthy to hear since he was deficient in virtue. When he insisted in spite of his music master's warning, black clouds came up in the west, and a fierce wind was followed by violent rain that tore the curtains and hangings, overturned the cups and bowls, and shook tiles down from the roof. Afterwards his country suffered a great drought for three years, and sores broke out all over the ruler's body. Some music was also considered wild and licentious, so that it could have devastating effects not only on human personality but also on cosmic order. It was therefore a vital necessity of statecraft to institute the playing of music which fostered the harmony of the cosmos.

The influence of ritual music was especially great at the time of important cosmic events like the solstices. The *History of the Former Han Dynasty* has a description of the playing of cosmic music at the time of the winter solstice. This music was intended to facilitate the passage from *yin* to *yang* which took place at that particular season. There is a parallel here between music and architecture. The ancient ritual texts indicated how the capital city should be laid out to conform with the cardinal directions, so that the heart of the political system was patterned on the cosmic order. Music did for time what architecture did for space; for appropriate music and ritual were performed to accompany the cosmic events which marked the passage of the seasons. Music therefore had the most profound significance. When he heard the Shao music, Confucius is said not to have 'known the taste of meat' for three months, and to have exclaimed that he did not picture that music-making could have attained to such a level (A 7.13). This extraordinary impact on the Master did not mean that he was bowled over by aesthetic pleasure. Obviously the music referred to must have been of great ritual importance. According to later tradition it was the music that accompanied the dance miming the peaceful accession of the legendary sage-emperor Shun, which was an event of great cosmic importance: his matchless qualifications for ruling over all under Heaven would ensure harmony not merely on earth, but in Heaven as well.

Because of the close integration between the human and the cosmic order music was naturally also important in the lives of individual human beings. By ensuring that his people listened to the right kind of music a ruler could cultivate harmony and virtue among them. So rites and music stand side by side as the means whereby the ruler could transform and complete the nature of his people. That is why, in the quotation on p. 115, Confucius says: 'One is roused by the *Songs*, established by ritual, and perfected by music.' Music has a detached, magical, cosmic quality, which completes the task of bringing human beings in tune with the cosmic harmonies.

# 4

# Humaneness and other virtues

## The nature of humaneness

Fan Ch'ih asked about humaneness. The master said: 'It is to love others.' (A 12.22)

Tzu-chang asked Confucius about humaneness. Confucius said: 'He who could put five things into practice everywhere under Heaven would be humane.' Tzu-chang begged to ask what they were and he replied: 'Courtesy, generosity, good faith, diligence and kindness. If you behave with courtesy, then you will not be insulted; if you are generous, then you will win the multitude; if you are of good faith, then other men will put their trust in you; if you are diligent, then you will have success; and if you are kind, then you will be able to command others.' (A 17.6)

The chapters on education and ritual have included several references to virtues, including humaneness. Indeed the quotations which introduce the topic of ritual revealed a close link between it and humaneness, for the Master said: 'To subdue oneself and return to ritual is humane,' and again 'If a man is not humane, what has he to do with ritual?' The link with education is also close. Since according to the Confucian tradition education was primarily concerned with learning how to behave, it was natural that Confucius and his followers should have developed an interest in man's moral capacities and evolved theories about the general characteristics of human nature. This has in fact been one of the fundamental concerns of Confucian philosophy, and much later discussion is focused on *jen* (humaneness), which first appeared as a term of philosophical importance and interest in the pages of the *Analects*.

The problem of translating Chinese ethical terms is very great. Whatever English words are used are bound to have their own special associations which are alien to Chinese attitudes. For *jen* nobody has found an entirely satisfactory solution. Benevolence, love, altruism, kindness, charity, compassion, magnanimity, perfect virtue, goodness, human-heartedness, humaneness, humanity, and man-to-manness have all been used. One scholar even coined the word 'hominity', which certainly has the merit of avoiding irrelevant associations, but outlandish neologisms can never provide an answer to problems of translation, which are at their most insoluble in an area like moral philosophy, where a deep knowledge of the culture is necessary before one can understand all the implications of the terms used. Waley's version of *jen* is 'Goodness' and Legge translates it as 'perfect virtue'. Both versions do justice to the fact that *jen* is the supreme virtue in the *Analects*, but they sacrifice the etymological connection with *jen* meaning 'man'. So although 'goodness' (and 'benevolence' for *jen* in *Mencius*) often provides a close and smooth translation, for the purpose of more serious study it is preferable to use the words 'humane' and 'humaneness' and try to clear one's mind of the inappropriate associations which cling to them and think only of the essential meaning of the words. Basically *jen* means the manifestation of ideal human nature; and since Confucian ethics is concerned not so much with qualities of mind and heart as with activities and not so much with man in isolation as with man relating to his fellow human beings, so that man's virtues are social virtues manifested in the conduct of human relationships, then *jen* may be defined as dealing with other human beings as a man ideally should. Although Confucius was concerned that a man should achieve individual perfection, the achievement of that perfection was impossible in isolation from society. It needed to be manifested in dealing with others. This is even demonstrated in the construction of the character for *jen*, which is written with two elements, man + two, thus constituting a kind of shorthand for human relationships, which the translation 'man-to-manness' tries to render literally.

Humaneness is obviously closely related to other social virtues like filial piety. Indeed filial piety and brotherly respect are specifically described in the *Analects* as the roots of *jen* (A 1.2), but the words are attributed not to Confucius but to his disciple Yu Tzu, and they appear in the first book, which gives a disproportionate amount of attention to filial piety and probably belongs to a later stratum of the book compiled when that virtue was in the ascendant. The simplest description of *jen* in the *Analects* is that given in the reply to the disciple Fan Ch'ih, 'to love others'; but, as the supreme virtue and sum of human moral achievements, it may be analysed into various components, as in the reply to the disciple Tzu-chang. From this description it is clear that 'altruism' is not a satisfactory translation. Humaneness is not entirely selfless. The social virtues have their give and take. Just as filial piety is rewarded with parental care, so humane rule is rewarded by the allegiance of the people.

An important part of learning was, as we have seen, the imitation of exemplars, so an important part of moral education would be the discussion of what contemporary or historical paragons could be described as showing exemplary adherence to humaneness or one of the other virtues. The word *jen* — used here as an adjective (humane) rather than as a noun (humaneness) — would be an appropriate label to attach to someone proverbially responsible for supremely virtuous behaviour, someone who has dealt with other human beings as a man ideally should. It was not the kind of virtue which, like filial piety, could be unpacked into a list of specific duties. It was the supreme accolade for moral behaviour. So for Confucius's disciples a stock question was whether so-and-so could be described as *jen* (humane).

Unfortunately, however, they seem to have found difficulty in getting a consistent answer. References to *jen* in the *Analects* are somewhat paradoxical. Confucius is depicted as extremely reluctant to ascribe this quality to any given individual. Indeed he expresses doubt that anyone is capable of concentrating his whole effort on humaneness for a single day (A 4.6). This reluctance to admit that anyone attains to *jen* is due to the fact that it is the quality of ideal human nature. On the other hand, since *jen* is an essential ingredient of the human being, not something which depends on anything outside himself, it should in theory be easily attainable, if men were true to their natures. 'Is humaneness really so far away?', he asks. 'If we really wished for it, it would come' (A 7.29). In fact the passage expressing doubt whether anyone was capable of concentrating on humaneness for a single day is directly contradicted by another passage claiming that the Master's favourite disciple Yen Hui was capable of having nothing contrary to humaneness on his mind for three months at a stretch (A 6.5). Although these discrepancies may be due to the composite nature of the work, it is consistent with Confucius's apparent attitudes to suppose that in the case of *jen* there was a difference in the Master's mind between the ideal manifestation of the virtue as attained only in the Golden Age of antiquity and the striving towards it which could be attributed to some of his contemporaries even in the decadent times in which he lived.

## Reverence and sensibility as signs of humaneness

Jan Yung asked about humaneness. The Master said: 'When you are away from home, behave as if receiving an important guest. Employ the people as if you were officiating at a great sacrifice. Do not do to others what you would not like yourself. Then there will be no resentment against you, either in the family or in the state.' (A 12.2)

Tzu-kung said: 'Suppose there were a ruler who benefitted the people far and wide and was capable of bringing salvation to the multitude, what would you think of him? Might he be called humane?' The Master said: 'Why only humane? He would undoubtedly be a sage. Even Yao and Shun would have had to strive to achieve this. Now the humane man, wishing himself to be established, sees that others are established, and wishing himself to be successful, sees that others are successful. To be able to take one's own feelings as a guide may be called the art of humaneness.' (A 6.28)

Despite Confucius's reluctance to apply the label of *jen* to any given individual, these two quotations again show the worldliness and sense of mutual benefit which are at the heart of 'humaneness'. The reply to the disciple Jan Yung (already referred to on p. 123) starts by emphasising the close relationship between *jen* and *li* (ritual). The first ingredient of humaneness is to have an attitude of reverence in human relationships, as if one were taking part in a religious ceremony, or at least to behave with the ceremoniousness and sense of propriety required when receiving an honoured guest. The second ingredient is to show consideration for the feelings of others by not doing to them what you would not like them to do to you, a sentiment which has been compared unfavourably with the golden rule of the Gospels: 'Do ye unto others as ye would that others should do unto you.' The *Analects* has a special term for this ingredient of *jen*, namely *shu*, which is sometimes translated as 'reciprocity'. The passage reveals the same basic element of self-interest in *jen*, which appeared in the reply to Tzu-chang above: if one does not treat others inhumanely, they will not treat one inhumanely in return. In the reply to the disciple Tzu-kung, Confucius again gives a more positive version of the virtue. Both of these sayings maintain that one should take one's own feelings and ambitions as a guide to the desires and needs of others, so that one can treat them with humaneness. The supreme virtue advocated by Confucius is deeply concerned with mutual benefit.

## Humane government

'If there existed a true king, after a generation humaneness would certainly prevail.' (A 13.12)

Both of the quotations on p. 133 refer to humaneness as exhibited by a ruler. Obviously humaneness will be more effective and all-embracing when displayed by an ideal sovereign, whose *jen* is such that he is able to protect all the people under his care. *Jen* does not occur very commonly in pre-Confucian texts, but when it does it usually refers to a ruler's kindness towards his subjects. Mencius also, coming after Confucius, was much concerned that rulers should bestow humane government upon their people; and it was the great hope of both thinkers that a true king might arise, a man who had both political power and the necessary kingly qualities, so that through his humaneness he would succeed in converting the whole country to virtuous behaviour. This would be achieved partly by force of example, reinforced with the people's acceptance of the principle that enlightened self-interest leads to the treatment of others as one would like to be treated. But apart from the force of example on human beings, the ruler's act also had cosmic importance. By the performance of the appropriate rituals he could help to secure universal harmony, so that his moral and ritual behaviour had a certain magical quality which could ensure the moral transformation of the people. *Jen* in the ideal sense can only occur as the result of such a complete transformation brought about by the perfect ruler.

The highest political ideal of the Chinese throughout the imperial period was that of an empire presided over by a Son of Heaven who, having received the Mandate of Heaven, ruled as a true king. The ideal is more fully expounded in the teachings of Mencius, but the above quotation, from one of the later chapters and so possibly from a later stratum of the book, does give Confucian authority for the important doctrine of the transforming power of the virtuous ruler. This doctrine had an influence not only in China but also in Europe, where the high ideal of the benevolent despot (rather than the less impressive reality of imperial rule in China) was what greatly impressed Europeans when they first heard of it from the Jesuit missionaries.

## All men have equal potentiality for moral growth

'By nature near together; by practice far apart.' (A 17.2)

In considering man's ethical nature the Confucian tradition came up against the question whether human beings were born with equal potentiality for moral growth. Mencius emphatically believed that this was so. He expressed his belief in uncompromising terms: 'Everyone may become a Yao or Shun' (M 6b.2). Coming from a predominantly agricultural society, he conceived of human moral development on the analogy of plant growth. He believed that man's moral personality had four shoots or growth-points, the cultivation of which produced the four basic virtues of humaneness, ritual observance, dutifulness and wisdom. If these young shoots were not properly tended they would wither, but all men were born with an equal capacity for moral development.

It is not easy to say precisely why such an egalitarian philosophy developed in ancient China. Some hold that the belief in natural equality springs from that growth of opposition to hereditary privilege which was characteristic of the late Chou period, but it is hard to see any necessary connection between the two or any evidence from the history of other societies to substantiate this theory. On the other hand a belief in the equality and indeed in the innate goodness of man (a belief which Mencius placed in the forefront of the Confucian tradition) seems a natural corollary of the deeply held Chinese conviction that the universe is a harmony and that mankind is an integral part of that harmony. For Europeans the idea of natural equality is very difficult to accept because they judge in terms of intellectual rather than moral capacity. 'Everyone may become an Einstein' is sheer nonsense, but 'Everyone may become a Yao or Shun' is a hopeful slogan which is not belied by experience.

Although the classical Confucian theory of the equality and goodness of human nature must be attributed to Mencius, the germ of these ideas may be found in the *Analects* by those who really want to find it there. The quotation at the head of this section comes from a book which clearly contains much late material, and it is also very brief and consequently its meaning is uncertain. But in spite of the fact that elsewhere Confucius is reported to have said that men are born with different capacities, distinguishing those who are born with knowledge from those who are not (A 16.9), this passage has been taken to lend Confucian authority to the sentiment that man's differences are due to disparities in education rather than in their nature. This sentiment is then used to support a plea for equal opportunity. The influence of this saying was very powerful because of its prominence as the second couplet in the elementary textbook known as the *Three-Character Classic*, which was committed to memory by many generations of schoolboys. And indeed this simple observation of Confucius was still effective in the mid-twentieth century, when it was accepted as the essential truth with regard to human nature and racial differences by a group of international experts in the UNESCO 'Statement on Race' which was published in July 1950.

## The Master's attitude towards ghosts and spirits

Tzu-lu asked about serving ghosts and spirits. The Master said: 'If one is not capable of serving men, how can one serve ghosts?' He ventured to ask about the dead, and the Master said: 'If one does not understand life, how can one understand death?' (A 11.11)

Fan Ch'ih asked about wisdom. The Master said: 'To devote oneself earnestly to securing what is right for the people, and to show reverence for ghosts and spirits so as to keep them at a distance may be called wisdom.' (A 6.20)

The central concern of Confucius was the moral guidance of mankind, and the chief virtue for Confucius was humaneness. Such humanism seems bound to leave less room for concern with ghosts and spirits. If his purpose was to restore a paradise on this earth, there was little room for religion. The reply to Tzu-lu is the *locus classicus* in the *Analects* for the agnosticism and this-worldliness attributed to the Master. It is the main text quoted in support of the argument that Confucianism in general is an agnostic creed, so that the Chinese people have not been burdened with the kind of religious heritage which has sometimes tormented Europe. The most uncompromising critic of religious devotion was in fact Hsün Tzu, who said: 'You pray for rain and it rains. Why? For no particular reason, I say. It is just as though you had not prayed for rain and it rained anyway' (H 85). He thought that sacrifice was totally ineffectual, but merely had social and psychological value. His doctrine that prayer and divination were only taken seriously by the common people, but were viewed by the ruling class as mere manifestations of culture (*wen*), has had a strong influence within the Confucian tradition, and in modern times has particularly appealed to those who have sought to claim superiority for Chinese agnosticism over the turbulent religious tradition of Christianity. But in reality it is plain that Confucius himself did not detach himself from the religious tradition of his people. He shared the common belief in an impersonal Heaven or Providence, which dealt out life and death, wealth and rank (cf. the first quotation on p. 158). He was also regarded as an expert on ritual and sacrifice. 'Sacrifice to the spirits as if the spirits were in one's presence' (A 3.12) was the main theme of his advice. Just as with all ritual, sacrifice must be meaningful and must not lapse into empty ceremony. It must be fresh and sincere, as if the spirits were actually there. The same note is struck in the *Record of Rites*, which says: 'At all sacrifices the bearing and appearance of the worshippers were as if they saw those to whom they were sacrificing' (L 2.26).

The reply to Fan Ch'ih, however, shows the other side of the Chinese reaction to spirits. There has always been an ambivalence, which appears most striking in attitudes towards ancestor-worship. On the one hand there is deep respect for the venerable departed, but on the other hand there is a dark fear of the spirit world, which must be appeased by sacrifice so that it will not harm the living, for hungry ghosts will not let people dwell in peace. Accordingly Confucius talks of the wisdom of keeping the ghosts and spirits at a distance by showing them proper respect.

So although the reply to Tzu-lu does show Confucius giving a remarkably rational priority to this world, this does not mean that the demands of ghosts and spirits could be totally ignored. Although the humanism of Confucius and his followers set its stamp on later Chinese society, China, like all other societies, has been riddled with belief in supernatural intervention in human affairs. This has affected the intellectuals as well as the common people. The great pressure to succeed meant that the civil service examinations were a hotbed of superstitious ideas about success or failure being decided by the intervention of spirits. Scholars' literary functions were often held at the local temple of the God of Literature, and if they succeeded in obtaining a post as district magistrate their official duties included the responsibility of dealing with the city god and other local deities. Among all classes the ancestral spirits and household gods demanded constant attention. Nevertheless the humanism and agnosticism at the core of Confucian belief was reflected in a society in which no church, not even Buddhism at its heyday in the T'ang Dynasty, ever succeeded in consolidating a powerful and independent position *vis à vis* the state; so that education, for example, always remained a purely secular activity aimed at this-worldly ends.

The late Chou period in general showed much less interest in the world of the spirits than the men of the early Chou period had done. There was much more concern with the problems of men in society. The belief that priority should be given to these problems rather than to the other world, which we can know nothing about, receives its classic formulation in the simple question 'If one does not understand life, how can one understand death?' — yet another of those texts to which the unfolding of Chinese civilisation provides an eloquent sermon.

## Filial piety to be shown towards the living and the dead

The master (on being asked about filial piety) said: 'When they are alive serve them in accordance with ritual; and when they are dead, bury them in accordance with ritual and sacrifice to them in accordance with ritual.' (A 2.5)

'When the father is alive, you only see the son's intentions. It is when he is dead that you see the son's actions. If for three years he makes no change from the ways of his father, he may be called filial.' (A 1.11)

After humaneness, the supreme virtue, it is necessary to consider filial piety, which has already been referred to (together with the twin virtue of brotherly respect) as the root of humaneness. Filial piety consisted of duties towards both the living and the dead. The former aspect included not only obedience to parents but also the responsibility for caring for them and providing food for them in their old age. The latter comprised furnishing a worthy funeral for the dead and offering the proper sacrifices thereafter. These dual responsibilities, and the importance of concern for ritual in carrying them out, are succinctly described in the first quotation. The second quotation epitomises the power of paternal influence over a son's thoughts and actions, which is again typical of Chinese society.

Filial piety, however, is rarely mentioned in the *Analects*, except in the first two books, which may not be part of the oldest stratum of the work. It was certainly the special emphasis laid on family ties by the early Confucians that stimulated Mo Tzu, who was born at about the time of Confucius's death, to become a strong advocate of universal love as opposed to the graded affection he attributed to his antagonists; but in the surviving literature it is the *Book of Filial Piety* — composed probably in the third century B.C. — that first gives the virtue a pre-eminent position. In that book filial piety is described as the 'root of virtue and the source of all teaching' (Ch. 1). It is again to Confucius that this doctrine is attributed. This first chapter puts into the Master's mouth a description of filial piety which neatly summarises much of what the virtue has stood for in the context of Chinese civilisation. It states that the beginning of filial piety is that one should not dare to harm the physical body which one receives from one's parents, and that the end of filial piety is that one should establish one's character and practise the Way so as to make one's reputation known to later generations and thus bring glory upon one's parents.

So in this work Confucius is represented as the great advocate of a virtue which is of relatively minor interest in the *Analects*, and his opening description of it echoes down the centuries. The *Book of Filial Piety* is presented as a dialogue between the Master and his disciple Tseng Tzu, who was especially famous as a practitioner of this virtue: on his death bed he is said to have ordered that he be stripped naked so that those present could see that he had preserved the perfect body which his parents had given him at birth. He was thus one who observed what the opening chapter of the Classic described as the beginning of filial piety. The 'end of filial piety', the injunction to virtuous conduct in order that the reputation gained thereby might bring glory to the ancestors, had a powerful impact on many generations of Confucian scholars. It stimulated their ambition to study hard to pass the examinations and enter a bureaucratic career, so that their fame might be known to later generations and reflect glory on their parents.

The concept of filial piety was subsequently recognised as an excellent preserver of social stability, for it cemented the family and clan system on which the state depended for order and cohesion. The tensions inherent in the large family which was the Chinese ideal were undoubtedly eased by the need to observe the duties of filial piety and the sense of hierarchy which this virtue produced. Clans had their own published rules of conduct, which stressed

filial piety, often quoting the *Analects* or *Book of Filial Piety* in
support of their arguments. The legal system, too, was
progressively Confucianised during the course of imperial Chinese
history, so that it took special account of the duties of filial piety
and the rights of a father over his son. Penalties were made more
severe if the crime were committed by a son against his father, and
conversely the father could deal harshly with his son with
impunity. In the late empire the Six Edicts of the Shun-chih
emperor (who reigned from 1644 to 1661) and the Sacred Edict of
the K'ang-hsi emperor (1661–1722) were collections of
commandments which both listed filial piety as the first duty. In
order to instil morality into the populace fortnightly lectures were
supposed to be delivered by district magistrates, taking these
commandments as their texts.

The virtue also had an important influence at the highest level,
since it made for extreme conservatism in politics. Respect for the
imperial ancestors demanded that emperors retain the institutions
handed down to them, and especially those initiated by the
dynastic founder, the manifest recipient of the Mandate of Heaven.
Filial duty towards the emperor's mother could also have disastrous
and far-reaching effects. In the Former Han Dynasty, when the
word Filial precedes the title of all the emperors — so that the one
known as the Emperor Wu is really the Filial Emperor Wu — these
monarchs demonstrated their filial piety by piling high honours
onto their mothers' male relatives; and it was through this practice
that the dynasty toppled, being superseded by Wang Mang, who
owed his power to such a relationship.

Not only filial piety but also the rites of ancestor worship were
seen as a means of cultivating moral values among the people. As
the disciple Tseng Tzu said, 'Show solicitude for parents at their
end and continue this with sacrifices when they are far away, and
the people's virtue will be abundantly restored' (A 1.9). The
sceptical Hsün Tzu also took the view that ancestor worship was
only taken at its face value by the lower orders: 'Among gentlemen
it is regarded as a part of the human Way; among the common
people it is considered to be the serving of ghosts and spirits' (H
110). The same attitude could be found in the *Record of Rites*,
whose authority in these matters was supreme. Sacrifice was
'simply the expression of human feelings'. Its value lay in securing
the moral welfare and social harmony of the people.

Among children the doctrine of filial piety was propagated by means of the famous twenty-four examples of that virtue. In keeping with the traditional Chinese idea that education depends on the imitation of models as well as the adoption of rules, children learned the stories of paragons like Wu Meng, who let himself be eaten by mosquitoes in order to divert them from his parents, and Lao Lai-tzu, who in adult life still dressed as a child and played with his toys to make his parents happy. However, the ultimate source of inspiration for filial piety could again be found in words attributed to Confucius, especially in the *Book of Filial Piety* but also in the *Analects*.

## Loyalty, *and other virtues mentioned in the* Analects

Duke Ting asked about a ruler's employment of his ministers, and ministers' service to rulers. Confucius replied: 'A ruler in employing his ministers accords with ritual, and a minister in serving his ruler accords with loyalty.' (A 3.19)

'If one loves people, can one not exact effort from them? If one is loyal to a person, can one not instruct him?' (A 14.8)

Filial piety was the key virtue within the family, but for the Confucian gentleman there was another field of operations, the state. Family and state were often contrasted as 'inside' and 'outside', and it was natural that there should be a virtue which corresponded exactly with filial piety, but was relevant to this wider field of political activity. That virtue was loyalty (*chung*), the duty owed by a minister to his lord and by the people to their ruler. Loyalty is often mentioned in association with good faith (*hsin*), another essential virtue of the political arena, but one which obtains between friends and equals as well as between inferiors and superiors. These virtues were part of everyday social intercourse and were well understood, so Confucius did not need to describe them so much as to advocate them; but in his reply to Duke Ting the Master did make the point that the loyalty of the minister corresponded with the treatment according to ritual which he was supposed to receive from the ruler.

In imperial China the virtue of loyalty was naturally exploited by the autocratic regime. A spurious composition known as the *Book of Loyalty*, a forgery of the late T'ang or early Sung, was widely accepted as a genuine work of antiquity in the Sung and later periods. It was somewhat similar in format to the *Book of Filial*

*Piety* and it taught blind and undeviating loyalty to the ruler. In the later empire, as the state became increasingly despotic, the concept of loyalty became transformed into that of unquestioning subservience, and the support of Confucius himself was claimed for the view that ministers owed absolute loyalty to ruler and dynasty. An ancient hero called Kuan Yü was deified and worshipped as the symbol of loyalty. In the Ch'ing Dynasty he was worshipped in thousands of temples throughout the country, and during the crisis of the middle of the nineteenth century, when the Taiping Rebellion cost millions of lives and almost toppled the dynasty, he was even decreed to be the equal of Confucius. But earlier in the imperial age there had been much more conflict in the minds of scholar-bureaucrats about the nature of loyalty. In antiquity Mencius had set his authority against the unquestioning loyalty of ministers and had strongly proclaimed the duty of ministers to remonstrate with their sovereigns in the interest of wise government; as a consequence remonstrance became not only the right but also the duty of all officials in the Confucian state. Although the reply to Duke Ting might have been used as ammunition by the advocates of blind loyalty, the following quotation attributes the responsibility for admonishing or instructing the object of one's loyalty to Confucius himself. In the *Analects*, *chung* certainly meant 'doing one's best for' rather than blind obedience to the dictates of one's superior.

A short list of the main virtues mentioned in the *Analects* would include humaneness, filial piety, loyalty, good faith, and behaviour in accordance with ritual. Other virtues are mentioned rarely, but have considerable importance in the ethics of Confucianism. There is *shu* (reciprocity — the virtue of not doing to others that which we would not like done to ourselves), and *jang* (deference — the virtue of, for example, the sage monarch who abdicates in favour of another sage). But no complete list of virtues is set out and there is nothing like the four basic virtues of Mencius (humaneness, dutifulness, observance of ritual, and wisdom). The so-called five Confucian virtues (which are these four with the addition of good faith) do not appear as a set in the *Analects* at all, but are a much later categorisation invented by a numerological school of thought which needed to find five virtues to correlate with the five elements and other sets of five.

What all these virtues have in common is that they belong to relationships between human beings, and are all essentially actions rather than states. For us it is possible to conceive of man being virtuous in isolation, to attribute virtue to qualities like calmness and patience which do not necessarily involve positive behaviour towards others. But in the Confucian tradition virtues were not attributes of the recluse. They were to be seen in everyday actions which could be assessed and evaluated. For example, they were used as criteria for evaluating the performance of officials in the civil service. The Confucian virtues still survived in the language of the nineteenth century, when the foreign barbarians were condemned, as ancient rulers had been condemned, because they talked only of profit and had nothing to say about humaneness or filial piety.

There is one virtue of some importance which we have not yet met in the *Analects* and that is *i* (dutifulness), one of the four Mencian virtues, sometimes also translated as righteousness, rightness, or justice. Its original sense seems to have been natural justice, what seemed just to the natural man before concepts like law and ritual were evolved. In the *Analects* there are only a handful of references to this virtue in the oldest stratum, and it is not specifically mentioned as a topic of Confucius's teaching; but it is clearly regarded as the ultimate yardstick against which matters of law and ritual must be judged. Two things about the use of *i* in the *Analects* stand out: it is treated as the opposite of profit (as in the quotation at the beginning of p. 146), and it is regarded as the especial concern of the gentleman, who is the main topic of the chapter which now follows.

# 5

## Gentlemen and knights

### The nature of the gentleman

Tzu-lu asked about the gentleman. The Master said: 'He cultivates himself in order to show reverence.' 'Is that all?' asked Tzu-lu. The Master said: 'He cultivates himself so as to bring tranquillity to others.' 'Is that all?', Tzu-lu again asked. The Master said: 'He cultivates himself so as to bring tranquillity to all the people. Even Yao and Shun would have found this a difficult task.' (A 14.45)

Confucius and his followers used various words to describe men of virtue, and the most important of these was *chün-tzu* (gentleman). This passage sets out for posterity the essence of the gentleman's role. The reference to reverence (*ching*) — a word used elsewhere specifically to describe the demeanour which should accompany the performance of ritual (A 3.26) — can be understood by recalling Confucius's insistence that rulers should behave in accordance with ritual when dealing with their ministers (cf. the first quotation on p. 141). But the main message lies in what follows. The gentleman practises self-cultivation, or cultivates his moral personality, in order to bring tranquillity to all men. This puts in a nutshell the Confucian ideal of government: that it is an agency for ensuring that the influence and example of men of superior moral qualities is brought to bear on the population. For the *Analects*, and especially the *Great Learning*, self-cultivation and the ordering of family and society were different aspects of the gentleman's indivisible task; but unfortunately, as Confucius himself discovered, reality did not always permit the deployment of the true gentleman's talents in the political arena. His great tragedy was that he could not find the opportunity in government to match his superior attainments in self-cultivation. He had to content himself with continuing the process of self-cultivation while proclaiming his message about the kind of society in which his ideal of the gentleman, practising self-cultivation and at the same time bringing tranquillity to the people, would be realised. So for Confucian literati down the ages the Master's reply to Tzu-lu provided a description of the ideal role of the gentleman, while his own life served as an inspiration for those who had to adapt the ideal to reality when the times were unfavourable.

The word *chün-tzu*, which is here translated as 'gentleman' and is often rendered as 'superior man', really means 'son of a ruler'; but the meaning extended to include descendants of rulers and then members of the upper class in general. The *chün-tzu* was a gentleman primarily in the class sense, although at the same time he would naturally be expected to follow a code of behaviour appropriate to his rank. Before Confucius the term had always been used to mean gentleman in this primarily social sense, but the Master introduced the idea that social status was irrelevant. A man could be a gentleman without benefit of high birth. So in the *Analects*, as in our own use of 'gentleman', *chün-tzu* implied either superior social status or superior moral accomplishments or both. Since the important task of government was to transform the people through education, and since this involved the study and imitation of models, it followed that Confucius thought of the person in political power, not primarily as a man who could cope skilfully with administrative problems, but as one who would act as an example to the people because of his moral qualities. The gentleman, in Confucius's view, should be one who combined the possession of office with cultivation of his moral personality; and he hoped that men who lacked the advantage of high birth but possessed the moral qualities required of a gentleman could thereby achieve status and play their part in government. Confucius taught a philosophy of government by men serving as moral exemplars rather than government by laws and institutions framed and administered by men.

## Further qualities of the gentleman

'If the gentleman is not grave, then he will not inspire awe in others. If he is not learned, then he will not be on firm ground. He should take loyalty and good faith as his first principles, and have no friends who are not up to his own standard. If he commits a fault, he should not shrink from mending his ways.' (A 1.8)

'The gentleman, with his studies broadened by culture and yet restrained by the requirements of ritual, surely cannot overstep the mark.' (A 6.25)

'The gentleman is concerned with what is right, just as the small man is concerned with profit.' (A 4.16)

Some of the qualities which the gentleman must possess are set out in these three quotations. The first begins with a reference to gravity of demeanour, just as the reply to Tzu-lu at the beginning of the chapter commenced with a reference to reverence. This reminds us that behaviour in accordance with ritual is an important responsibility of rulers, and that the appropriate attitude and demeanour are an important aspect of ritual behaviour. The quotation goes on to stress the importance of learning, meaning primarily the moral training necessary for the production of a gentleman, and loyalty and good faith, which are essential components of an aristocratic code of honour. Finally Confucius insists on a willingness to correct faults, which was later also stressed by Mencius, who believed that gentlemen of his day contrasted unfavourably with gentlemen of antiquity, because they did not correct their faults, but instead persisted in them (M 2b.9).

The next quotation makes a contrast between the broadening effect of culture and the restraining influence of ritual, a schematic comparison between these two important components of education which became a commonplace in ancient Chinese literature. Ritual involves a disciplined adherence to rules of conduct, but culture releases man from a life concerned with the mere necessities of existence and exerts a broadening and civilising influence upon him; so the contrast made in this saying is clear enough. The reference to 'studies broadened by culture' gave much food for thought to readers of the *Analects* in late imperial China who fretted against the narrow and sterile intellectual life involved in preparation for the civil service examinations. The saying gave good canonical authority for their disenchantment.

The third of these quotations epitomises the difference between the gentleman and his opposite, the *hsiao jen*, which literally means 'the small man', but is often translated as 'the inferior man' in contrast with 'the superior man', which is sometimes used to translate *chün-tzu*. The gentleman is concerned with what is right or just (*i*), while the small man is concerned only with profit. Lacking moral training, he can only be concerned with his material welfare. Mencius followed Confucius in being very hostile to the profit motive. If a ruler wanted to profit his state, all his subjects would follow his example and strive with each other for profit (M

1a.1). The social class which characteristically pursued profit, that of the merchants and traders, was relegated to the lowest position among the four traditional classes in Chinese society (scholars, farmers, artisans, merchants), so this saying of Confucius not only encapsulates a class distinction based on concern for moral values, but at the same time provides a slogan for that constant subordination of mercantile interests, which has been a distinctive feature of Chinese society.

## The rectification of names

'If a gentleman abandons humaneness, how can he fulfil the name?' (A 4.5)

The gentleman, as the supremely moral man, must set his sights on the supreme virtue of humaneness. The saying indicates that this is implicit in the meaning of the word 'gentleman'. The concept of 'fulfilling the name', i.e. acting completely in accordance with the label one bears, is familiar in ancient Chinese philosophy from the doctrine of the rectification of names (*cheng ming*). This expression only occurs once in the *Analects* (13.13), where Confucius is reported to have told the disciple Tzu-lu, much to his astonishment, that the rectification of names was the first priority in government. The style of this passage suggests that it is an interpolation dating from the last century of the Chou Dynasty, when the doctrine of the rectification of names was widely current. Nevertheless the sentiment is certainly present in the *Analects*, even if not formulated as a theory. Confucius was obsessed with the decline from the ancient mores of the early Chou period, with the usurpation of titles and ceremonies, and with the fact that the gentleman (in the class sense) could no longer be trusted to behave as a gentleman (in the moral sense). This is what is implied in the advice the Master gave to Duke Ching of Ch'i when he asked about government: 'Let the prince be a prince, the minister a minister, the father a father, and the son a son' (A 12.11). This was a most appropriate recommendation, since the security of the duke's dynasty was menaced by ministers who were not content to be ministers, and the succession was being squabbled over by sons who were not content to accept their father's authority.

'Rectification of names' is not a very satisfactory term, for it is actualities rather than names which have to be rectified. The doctrine simply means that names originally had firm meanings and that actualities must correspond with them. It is merely another way of referring to the need to return to the Golden Age of the early Chou period, when the implications of the word 'prince' were clearly understood to include duties and responsibilities as well as power, so that princes always acted as princes, which they no longer did in the decadent age in which Confucius lived. If the name 'prince' were rectified, then the prince would always act in a princely fashion, and nobody else would try to usurp his position. As Hsün Tzu explained it, 'When the kings created names, the names were fixed and actualities distinguished from each other. When this principle was carried out so that their intentions were understood, then they were able to guide the people with care and give them unity' (H 140). Hsün Tzu believed that no new words should have been created since they confused the clearcut correspondence between name and thing laid down in the beginning. Those who were guilty of this crime should be punished in the same way as those who tampered with weights and measures. The Legalists, whose ideology toughened the sinews of the all-conquering Ch'in state in the late Chou period, also made use of this theory. They thought that, if names could be made to correspond exactly with the responsibilities they implied, this would be an aid towards the impersonal system of administration they wished to introduce. This depended on the automatic implementation of laws and regulations without any discretion being left to human judgement — the exact opposite of Confucian reliance on government by morally qualified human beings.

The idea that in the beginning there was a planned correspondence between things and the names given to them is obviously more credible to people who write with a script which was pictographic in origin. But the doctrine as universalised by Hsün Tzu and the Legalists seems naïve and bizarre. For Confucius the rectification of names was not meant to apply to all names. He merely wanted princes and ministers and others with moral responsibilities to live up to the full meaning of those terms, as had happened at the beginning of the Chou Dynasty, and in this sense the Master's alleged claim that the rectification of names is the first priority in government, although occurring in what is apparently a late interpolation in the text, is not in conflict with the rest of his philosophy as we understand it from the *Analects*.

## The gentleman is not a specialist, but a leader

'A gentleman is not an implement.' (A 2.12)

This saying sums up the idea that the gentleman's training should not be confined to particular skills so that he may become the tool or implement of others. It must instead develop his moral qualities and powers of leadership. In a passage in the *Analects* Confucius himself is accused of having many special skills, but he exculpates himself on the grounds that youthful poverty made it necessary for him to earn his living (A 9.6). Confucius also continued to be treated as a specialist on ritual, but this was tolerable since it was not a mere matter of technical knowledge. It was one of the six arts of the traditional education and was closely associated with morality. Of course the conventional education of the well-born young man included not only ritual but such practical accomplishments as archery and charioteering, but the Confucian literature in general regards those who have special skills as inferior to those who have the moral qualities appropriate to the leadership and organisation of these lesser talents. Hsün Tzu put the case for the generalist against the specialist very clearly:

The farmer is skilled in agriculture, but he cannot do the job of a supervisor of agriculture. The merchant is skilled in marketing, but he cannot do the job of a supervisor of markets. The artisan is skilled in craftsmanship, but he cannot do the job of a supervisor of crafts. But there are men who, although they are incapable of these three skills, may be employed to fill these three supervisory posts. This is because they are skilled in the Way. (H 130)

This philosophy obviously suited a class which could depend on the labour of others, and it became crystallised in the imperial civil service examination system, which was designed to recruit for the service of the state people who had had the training for moral and political leadership which was thought to derive from an intensive study of the Classics. The result was that many generations of bureaucrats in China received an education which, although it sometimes included more practical elements like law, was dominated by classical literature. In more modern times the efficacy of an education in self-cultivation and the niceties of ritual may have been called in question because of its inappropriateness for dealing with the specialised problems of a society more complicated than that of ancient China. It could nevertheless be argued that the kind of problems with which bureaucrats had to deal required a basic understanding of human nature and of the ethical relationships between human beings, and demanded the application to concrete situations of general principles derived from the country's cultural heritage, rather than the kind of specialist knowledge which could, when needed, be supplied by underlings. Certainly the idea that gentlemen should be generalists who do not get their hands dirty is very deep-rooted in China and has proved very durable even in the face of persistent Communist attempts to break down class barriers. The saying 'The gentleman is not an implement' is the classic Confucian expression of this ideal.

## Gentlemen do not form parties

'Gentlemen are proud but not quarrelsome. They are sociable, but do not form parties.' (A 15.21)

In *chün-tzu pu tang*, 'Gentlemen are not partisan, do not form parties', *tang* is the word which is used in modern times for political parties, as in Kuomintang. The meaning of the original is not clear, since in the *Analects* and the *Mencius tang* normally means a village. However, it does mean 'partisan' or 'party' in other ancient texts as well as in modern usage; and so, interpreted in this sense, this is another of the slogans taken from the *Analects* which must have had a powerful effect on bureaucratic attitudes. The role of ministers in ancient China was conditioned by the model of the individual wise man giving advice to the ruler, who listened and then decided the issue on the basis of that advice; indeed the word *t'ing*, meaning 'to listen', was often used in the sense of 'to govern'. The forming of parties or factions was likely to be interpreted as a means of pushing the interests of an individual, of espousing the cause of a younger son against the claim of an heir apparent, or even of attempting to overthrow the regime. Similarly in imperial China officials had the right and indeed the duty to remonstrate as individuals, and criticism of the regime was also channelled through the institution of the Censorate; which enabled the Censors, again as individuals, to remonstrate with the ruler. In the bureaucracy at large the formation of factions was suspect because it conflicted with the holistic conception of political organisation. Ties of kinship and of friendship between former fellow-students provided forms of association more congenial to Confucian ideology, and these had some influence in the political arena, though for the

purpose of securing personal advancement rather than the achievement of purely political ends. Any such establishment of parties for
political purposes was generally thought of as a disruptive element
in political life. Factionalism was a dirty word, and not a proper
occupation for gentlemen, as Confucius himself had indicated.

## The qualities of the knight

'A knight whose heart is set on the Way, but who is ashamed of bad clothes
and bad food, is not fit to be consulted.' (A 4.9)

Tzu-kung asked: 'What must a man be like to be called a knight?' The
Master said: 'One who in conducting himself maintains a sense of honour,
and who when sent to the four quarters of the world does not disgrace his
prince's commission, may be called a knight.' (A 13.20)

'The determined knight and the humane man never seek life at the expense
of injuring humaneness. They will even sacrifice their lives in order to
achieve humaneness.' (A 15.8)

Between the gentleman (*chün-tzu*) and the common people there
was another class known as the *shih*, which Arthur Waley
translated as 'knight'. This class consisted of the younger sons of
aristocrats, who had no opportunities of holding hereditary office,
together with the descendants of ruling families who were
dispossessed when their states were wiped out during this period of
history, in which the large states continued to eliminate their
smaller neighbours. They served as officers in time of war and held
administrative positions in time of peace. They were schooled in
the six arts of the traditional education; and therefore, in addition
to military skills, they had the literacy and numeracy and
knowledge of ritual which made them a reservoir of talent available
at a time when promotion increasingly went to the meritorious.
The society of the late Chou period was not only more egalitarian,
but also increasingly complex and therefore in greater need of the
specialist skills which the *shih* class had to offer. Their talent and
ambition continued to stimulate the process of change from
hereditary rule to meritocracy.

Confucius himself was a member of this class, and he provided
the training necessary for other members of it as well as people of
humbler birth to fit themselves for work in government; but in
conformity with the rest of his philosophy he insisted on the moral
implications of knighthood, so the simple code of loyalty and good

faith which the *shih* observed in pre-Confucian times was broadened and given new moral content by the Master and his disciples. A careful study of the *Analects* lends support to the view that this development did not reach its climax until after Confucius's time, for in that book the word *shih* occurs surprisingly rarely, and there is only one instance in the supposedly earliest stratum of the book in which the word is put into the mouth of the Master himself — the first of the quotations given above.

Here in these few references we see some of the essential qualities of the knight. He is oblivious to comfort, as Confucius himself was. Mencius also emphasised this characteristic by saying that it was only the knight who was capable of maintaining a constant heart without having a constant livelihood (M 1a.7). Secondly, in employment in the affairs of state he must be the true counterpart of the morally excellent gentleman who employs him. And, thirdly, he must also be a defender of the supreme virtue of humaneness even at the cost of his life. This call to martyrdom was taken seriously by many generations of Confucian scholar-bureaucrats. Some gave their lives for daring to criticise their rulers. A famous case of a man who courted martyrdom was Han Yü, the literary giant of the T'ang Dynasty, who bitterly attacked the emperor's veneration of a Buddhist relic. Fortunately he was saved from paying the ultimate penalty by the intervention of powerful friends. He was banished to a remote and unhealthy part of the country, where he could bear his exile with fortitude in the knowledge that he had kept faith with the Confucian Way.

In the long run the word *shih*, which had orginally implied military status rather than civil accomplishment, came to be used as the name for one of the four classes in Chinese society in addition to farmers, artisans and merchants. In this sense it meant the scholar-bureaucrat ruling class. So the Confucian writings, in establishing a code of conduct for the new administrative middle class known as *shih*, at the same time provided a code for the ruling scholar-bureaucrat class in imperial China, because they were also known as *shih*. Because of its later usage the word *shih* in ancient texts has frequently been mistranslated as 'scholar', for example in James Legge's version of the *Analects*. But the *shih* of the *Analects* is still very much the man of action, the knight whose heart is set on the Way and who is willing to sacrifice his life for humaneness.

# 6

# Government and people

## Governments must have the confidence of the people

Tzu-kung asked about government. The Master said: 'Enough food, enough weapons, and the confidence of the people.' Tzu-kung said: 'Suppose you definitely had no alternative but to give up one of these three, which would you relinquish first?' The Master said: 'Weapons.' Tzu-kung said: 'Suppose you definitely had no alternative but to give up one of the remaining two, which would you relinquish first?' The Master said: 'Food. From of old death has come to all men, but a people without confidence in its rulers will not stand.' (A 12.7)

The response to moral and humane government by gentlemen (*chün-tzu*) and knights (*shih*) will be the respect, loyalty, and confidence of the people. The supreme importance of winning the confidence of the people is expressed in this striking reply to the disciple Tzu-kung. The political importance of the people was not a new idea. In the *Book of History* we read: 'Heaven sees and hears as the people see and hear'; and the doctrine of the Mandate of Heaven justified rebellion to get rid of a tyrannical ruler. Confucius himself had nothing to say about the confidence of the people being won by actually consulting them and taking their opinion into account, but Mencius went so far as to say that the views of the people should be canvassed concerning cases of promotion, dismissal, or crimes meriting the death penalty (M 1b.7). So government for the people and in consultation with the people was a basic Confucian ideal, but the further step of government by the people was never an issue in traditional China.

The original strength of this doctrine clearly derived from the political situation in late Chou China, when the contending states needed to attract larger populations to help build up their military power. Unlike their contemporaries in Greece, who went off to find new territories overseas and colonise them, the Chinese states of the time had plenty of undeveloped land for their peasants to exploit; so, in the opinion of Mencius, the way to attract a sufficient population was to win the confidence of the people by a humane government which saw to it that their interests were consulted. This theme remained a powerful one in Chinese history, not only in the hearts of political idealists, but also in the more pragmatic calculations of governments, which constantly tried to maintain the confidence of the people by demonstrating that the regime had supernatural help and therefore obviously retained the Mandate of Heaven. At the local level, too, the task of maintaining peace by suppressing bandits was thought to depend much on considering the people's welfare so that they would extend their loyalty to the officials rather than collaborate with the anti-government forces. In the twentieth century the Communist victory could be seen as a triumph for the belief that a small and isolated force suffering from a serious shortage of both food and weapons, could eventually triumph through winning the minds of the people, a striking confirmation of the fact that Confucius had got his priorities right. The idea that the state was a co-operative enterprise, not a business run for the benefit of the rulers, was deeply rooted in the Confucian tradition.

## The people must be properly instructed

'The people may be made to follow it, but may not be made to understand it.' (A 8.9)

Chi K'ang-tzu asked Confucius about government, saying: 'Suppose I were to kill those who lack the Way in order to advance those who have the Way, would that be all right?' Confucius replied: 'You are running the government, so what is the point of killing? If you desire good, the people will be good. The nature of the gentleman is like the wind, and the nature of the small people is like the grass. When the wind blows over the grass it always bends.' (A 12.19)

'Only when good men have instructed the people for seven years, may they take up arms. . . To lead an uninstructed people into battle may be described as throwing them away.' (A 13.29 and 30)

In Mencius's view consultation with the people was possible, and indeed necessary for the sake of political harmony; but the further step of government by the people is incompatible with the Confucian idea that men have distinct roles which they must perform for the sake of the orderly arrangement of society ('Let the prince be a prince, the minister a minister, the father a father, and the son a son'). It is in direct conflict with the idea that the prerequisite for the restoration of the Golden Age is the rectification of names so that all these roles are properly performed. In the Confucian philosophy government has to be the function of a specialist ruling group.

As compared with Mencius who, reflecting the social turmoil of a later era, envisaged a more active role for the people, Confucius still looked upon them as a largely passive force. Although the winning of their confidence was essential to government, they were to be moulded and influenced rather than consulted. This is the idea behind the first saying above, which has caused some anxiety among defenders of Confucius, since it apparently takes too dismissive an attitude towards the people, who in theory are generally capable of moral understanding if presented with virtuous models to follow. But obviously the gentleman, who has the advantage of a thorough education, will have a level of moral understanding which is denied to the ordinary people, who cannot be expected to have the requisite vision and must take things on trust.

The reply to Chi K'ang-tzu, the usurper who was acting as dictator of Lu, contains the famous simile of the wind and the grass, which was also used by Mencius and became a cliché in later literature. Taken out of context it might be thought to mean that the people always gave way to the gentleman or were beaten down by him; but, as the context makes clear, it illustrates the familiar theme of the powerful moral influence which the gentleman exerts on the people.

The morale of the people and their confidence in their rulers were regarded as the most vital factor in warfare, as we have already seen. Therefore the people must not be used in battle unless they have been subjected to the kind of training in moral values which will prepare them for the fray. This is not just philosophical fantasy. In the historical writings also there are references to the people being trained in the virtues of good faith, dutifulness, and behaviour in accordance with ritual before they are thought fit to go into action. The fact that government was thought of as a matter of instruction and example is clearly demonstrated in the above three quotations.

## Government is a matter of setting a moral example

Chi K'ang-tzu asked about inducing the people to be respectful and loyal so that they might be encouraged to support him. The Master said: 'If you approach them with dignity, they will respect you. If you are dutiful towards your parents and kind to your children, then they will be loyal. If you promote the good and instruct the incompetent, then they will be encouraged.' (A 2.20)

Someone said to Confucius: 'Why do you not take part in government?' The Master said: 'What does the *Book of History* say about filial piety? "Only be dutiful towards your parents and friendly towards your brothers, and you will be contributing to government." These virtues also constitute taking part in government.' (A 2.21)

Chi K'ang-tzu asked Confucius about government. Confucius replied saying: 'To govern means to rectify. If you were to lead the people by means of rectification, who would dare not to be rectified?' (A 12.17)

The first of these three quotations shows how the moral example of the ruler is expected to be reciprocated by the people. Government was largely a matter of operating in the wider context of the state with virtues which were really more appropriate within the narrower context of the family. The ruler must practise filial piety and then his subjects will practise the parallel virtue of loyalty towards him. He must instruct and encourage his subjects as a father instructs and encourages his children. The saying also mentions promotion on merit, a common theme in the late Chou period when there was general hostility towards the old system of hereditary office.

The second quotation gives consolation to those who have no political power by saying that the practice of social virtues within the family must itself make a real contribution to government, since it is contributing to the social harmony which is the purpose of government. So this is the Confucian version of the people's participation in government: they respond to examples sent down from above and contribute to the order of the state by securing harmony within the family, one of the microcosmic units of which the macrocosm of the state is composed. As we saw earlier, this Confucian message was used by imperial governments for the purpose of political control. If clans had their own moral codes and were largely capable of policing themselves, the task of the government in trying to secure civil order was made much easier. From the state's point of view it was convenient if the people contributed to stability and harmony by contentedly practising the constant norms of human behaviour within their families. The precepts of Confucius about government often seem appropriate only to a small and cosy community, and it is remarkable that they should have provided the ideology of an enormous bureaucratic state. This could only happen because of the age-old dogma that the state was the family writ large, and the belief that the family virtues were a structural part of the cosmic order.

Finally, the reply to Chi K'ang-tzu depends on the fact that the words for 'to govern' and 'to rectify' were etymologically related to each other. The task of government was to rectify society and so restore it to ancient virtues. The same word is used in the expression *cheng ming*, 'the rectification of names'. This emphasis on rectification remained a keynote of Chinese political thought, so that political reform has generally been seen as rectification rather than innovation. It has generally been regarded as an attempt to get back to ancient wisdoms and ancient ways, and to understand the teaching of the ancients more clearly and restore society to the norms that they laid down.

## Miscellaneous advice on government

'To lead a country of a thousand chariots, the ruler must attend reverentially to business and be of good faith. He must practise economy in expenditure and love all men, and employ the people in accordance with the seasons.' (A 1.5)

Much other miscellaneous advice on government is given in the *Analects*, and this passage is included here as a good example of the difficulty of evaluating the book, for it is an amalgam of ideas more readily associated with other texts. 'Economy in expenditure' is the name of a section of the *Mo Tzu*, in which that philosopher takes a most utilitarian view of production, and will not allow anything decorative in the manufacture of clothing, houses, weapons, boats, or vehicles, an argument which is out of sympathy with Confucian support of culture (*wen*). The love of all men equally was also advocated by Mo Tzu in opposition to the graded love, giving preference to the claims of kinship, which he regarded as characteristic of Confucianism. Finally the employment of the people in accordance with the seasons was a favourite theme of Mencius, who criticised rulers for switching the peasants from their agricultural labours to the provision of luxuries for their palaces.

On the other hand, the Mohist school soon faded into oblivion, and the two Mohist principles included in this saying are not in the long run inimical to Confucianism. The frugality suggested by the words 'economy in expenditure', the pursuit of ideals despite a life of hardship, was regarded as a virtue by Confucius. And, despite Mo Tzu's criticism of the graded love associated with Confucianism, the love of all men is inherent in the Confucian notion of humaneness, which, if displayed by a ruler, is capable of protecting all within the Four Seas.

## All men are brothers: even barbarians can learn from example

'Other men all have brothers,' said Ssu-ma Niu in his distress, 'but I alone have none.' Tzu-hsia said: 'I have heard that death and life are predestined, and riches and honours depend on Heaven. If a gentleman is reverent and avoids error, if he is courteous with others and observes the obligations of ritual, then all within the Four Seas are his brothers. Why should a gentleman be distressed at having no brothers?' (A 12.5)

The Master wished to dwell among the nine wild tribes of the East. Someone said: 'They are uncivilised, so what will you do about that?' The Master said: 'If a gentleman dwelt among them, what lack of civility would they show?' (A 9.13)

Ssu-ma Niu's anxiety is said to have stemmed from the fact that his brother could no longer be regarded as a brother because he had attempted to kill Confucius. The reply is put into the mouth of the disciple Tzu-hsia, but the commentators claim without any evidence at all that it was from Confucius that he had heard the saying. Consequently the famous tag 'All within the Four Seas are brothers' is taken out of context and attributed to Confucius. The ancient Chinese believed that the inhabited world was surrounded on all four sides by oceans, which encompassed not only the Chinese people themselves but also those whom they recognised as culturally distinct. The idea that all within the Four Seas are brothers states dramatically what is implicit in Confucius's concept of the virtue of humaneness. The further implication is that in the long run the whole of the inhabited world is ideally and potentially subject to the one political regime administered by the moral and ritual-conscious Confucian gentleman. This then is the high-minded theory behind Confucian attitudes to barbarians. It is just a question of time before all are absorbed into the Chinese world as a result of the transforming power of Confucian virtue.

The passage referring to Confucius's desire to live among the eastern barbarians puts plainly this idea that a Confucian gentleman only has to go and dwell among foreigners for them to be affected by the transforming power of his virtue. As explained before, the difference between the Chinese and barbarians was seen as cultural rather than racial. Among the peoples which inhabited this part of the world there were no striking racial distinctions in physical appearance, so it was those people who had not absorbed Chinese culture who were thought of as alien. After the upsurge of Confucianism during the reign of Emperor Wu of the Former Han Dynasty, who was on the throne from 140 to 87 B.C., local officials were trained in Confucian studies. As the empire extended to embrace barbarian areas in the South, these officials, inspired with the aim of transforming the people in accordance with Confucian ideals, not only introduced improved agricultural technology to enable them to provide themselves with an adequate livelihood (without which, according to Mencius, they could not be expected to lead virtuous lives), but also gave the ignorant natives the blessing of instruction in filial piety itself, introducing the concept of marriage to people who were unfamiliar with the whole idea, so that for the first time men began to know who their fathers were.

The inspiration for all these arduous activities among remote peoples living in appalling climates lay in the words of Confucius and Mencius. The latter, as often, pushed the argument a stage further than Confucius, for he spoke of barbarians positively clamouring for their domains to be conquered by the exemplary King T'ang, founder of the Shang Dynasty (M 1b.11). Mencius's attitude suggests that the Confucian's duty was a crusade to liberate the barbarian peoples from their oppressive rulers. But the ultimate model was the quieter example of Confucius, who was supremely confident that, by living according to the prescriptions of ritual and ethics, one gentleman would be able by his mere presence to convert the barbarians from their coarse, untutored ways.

## The Master's antipathy to litigation

'At hearing legal proceedings I am just like anybody else, but what is necessary is to bring it about that there is no litigation.' (A 12.13)

A further indicator of the importance attached by the Confucians to government by virtuous example is their very negative attitude to litigation. They felt that, if everyone observed the moral code, there would be no need to invoke the processes of law. Confucian belief in the emulation of virtuous models came into direct conflict with the Legalists, who believed that it was necessary to control people through fear of punishments. The Confucian attitude is seen not only in the philosophical writings but also in the *Tso Tradition*, the main historical source for the period, where it is reported that in 513 B.C., when the state of Cheng cast bronze vessels on which were inscribed a code of penal laws, Confucius was critical. He argued that 'the people will study the vessels and not care to honour their men of rank. But when there is no distinction of noble and mean, how can a state continue to exist?' This is a classic statement of the Confucian belief that a hierarchical society is essential to the achievement of political order. It sounds like the sort of thing that Hsün Tzu might have said, put into the mouth of Confucius to give it greater weight.

The most important argument against controlling the people by penal law was as set out in this saying attributed to Confucius: universally applied laws would militate against the natural distinction in society between noble and base. The second argument was that, since laws cannot take all possible circumstances into account, it is better to leave matters to the judgement of morally qualified persons rather than to the mechanical application of a legal code. The third argument was that law merely controls through fear of punishment and does not play any part in the moulding of character. It does not educate, or rectify, or make any contribution towards the Confucian aim of transforming the people, as does the emulation of virtuous models. In Europe law has had a fairly good name, but in China, where it had no divine sanction and was thought of as man-made, arbitrary, and inferior to the requirements of ritual, it had a bad name, which became worse when the hated Legalists — literally the 'School of Law' — provided the inspiration for the ruthless Ch'in Dynasty, which caused much suffering to the people in its attempt at rapidly consolidating the unification of China in the late third century B.C.

Quite apart from ideological considerations, the Confucians, who were the experts on ritual, had a vested interest in ensuring that its role in providing rules for society was not entirely taken away by law. Inevitably, however, the need for law increased, since a great empire cannot be administered without a complex and pervasive legal system. It may seem therefore that this was one battle that the Confucians lost to the Legalists, but in fact in imperial China the law took on a distinctly Confucian complexion. Not only did it fix a scale of penalties which varied according to the relationship between the perpetrator and the victim of the crime; it was also much influenced by the principle set out in the *Record of Rites* to the effect that the code of ritual was appropriate for the gentleman and law should apply only to the common people (L 1.90). Throughout imperial Chinese history officials, whether active or retired, enjoyed a very privileged position in matters of law, a distinction ultimately deriving from the idea that the educated man's sense of honour should be sufficient to ensure that he conforms with the demands of *li* and does not need to be controlled by fear of punishment.

The ancient debate between the opposing ideals of the rule of law and rule by good men continued right through to the nineteenth century. The hostility to litigation which Confucius had expressed continued to be a characteristic of Chinese society. It was often featured in clan rules, perhaps less out of good Confucian principle than because of a vivid awareness that the harshness of the state's legal processes was exacerbated by the extortionate behaviour of the police and other underlings, so that it was much better to settle matters without recourse to the law.

## The people should be led by virtue rather than by fear

'If you lead the people by means of regulations and keep order among them by means of punishments, they will be without conscience in trying to avoid them. If you lead them by virtue and keep order among them by ritual, they will have a conscience and will reform themselves.' (A 2.3)

'He who rules by means of virtue may be compared to the pole-star, which keeps its place while all the other stars pay homage to it.' (A 2.1)

The first of these two quotations again contrasts ritual with law, and argues that punishments inflicted in accordance with the law do not have the capacity to give people the conscience and sense of morality which will make them obedient to the ruler's wishes. It also contrasts 'regulations' with the word *te*, which I have translated as 'virtue'. This is an extremely important concept in ancient Chinese thought. It is the word that occurs in the title of the Taoist classic *Tao Te Ching*, which Arthur Waley translated as *The Way and its Power*. 'Moral power' or 'moral influence' may often be a more appropriate translation, but the advantage of the word 'virtue' is that, like *te*, it does denote inherent nature or quality as well as moral excellence. *Te*, like virtue, can be used in contexts in which it has nothing to do with morality, as for example in the second quotation on page 154, where it is used to mean 'nature' in 'the nature of the gentleman is like the wind'. The difficulty of retaining it as the translation of this word in all circumstances is that it can be misleading since *te* does not mean virtue as contrasted with vice, for this polarity was alien to the thought-patterns of the ancient Chinese, who conceived of the universe as a kind of harmonious structure. This structure could break down, but there was no room in the concept for vice as a positive element.

The word *te* has played a very important part in Confucian political theory. At the beginning of its reign a dynasty was thought to have an abundant store of virtue or moral influence as a corollary of the fact that it had been entrusted with the Mandate of Heaven. Referring to the days of King Wen, Confucius said that the *te* of Chou could be described as perfect (A 8.20). This stock of *te* would decline as the dynasty deteriorated from its early excellence and lost the moral qualities which had won it the Mandate. In the first quotation *te* is used in contrast with regulations, but often it is used in opposition to *li*, meaning 'force' (a different character from *li* 'ritual'). In Mencius's schematic philosophy the men who ruled by force were the *pa* or paramount princes who became the *de facto* leaders of the Chinese world. Mencius abhorred them because they wielded authority which properly belonged to the Chou rulers, who were now too weak to exert more than a purely symbolical leadership. He contrasted the *pa* with the *wang* or true king, who did not rule by force but by his virtue or moral power (*te*). Rule by *te* rather than by force was traditionally thought to be the means to secure the allegiance of the barbarian peoples on China's frontiers, so later on in Chinese history it was very difficult to explain why the highly civilised Sung were conquered by the barbarous Mongols. The quotation also shows the close relationship between *te* and *li* (ritual): the inherent virtue of the ruler would be manifested in the appropriate ritual behaviour.

The second quotation seems to suggest that Confucius himself believed that the virtuous ruler had a kind of cosmic role. This idea is not fully set out in the *Analects*, but later theory held that the ruler, governing by means of virtue, secured harmony not only in the human world, but also in the cosmos. Throughout imperial Chinese history it was the belief that the virtuous conduct of the emperor at the apex of human society was necessary in order to ensure the smooth operation of nature. If he contravened the dictates of ritual and neglected the requirements of virtuous government, natural calamities were bound to ensue. The comparison with the pole-star also contains a flavour of the idea of rule by inactivity, the belief that, if a ruler's *te* or moral power were sufficiently great, government would run so smoothly that he would not need to take any action. But this is a fundamentally Taoist notion, which occurs in more blatant form in A 15.4, where the legendary sage-emperor Shun is said to have ruled by the Taoist principle of non-action, merely placing himself reverently with his face to the south and doing nothing. Such a concept is alien to the philosophy of the *Analects* and of Confucianism in general and should therefore be discounted in evaluations of Confucius's thought. According to the Confucian teachings, activity meant to benefit others is an essential part of virtue.

## Men's lives should conform with the Way

'Be of unwavering good faith and love learning. Be steadfast unto death in pursuit of the good Way. Do not enter a state which is in peril, nor reside in one in which the people have rebelled. When the Way prevails in the world, then show yourself. When it does not, then hide. When the Way prevails in your own state, to be poor and obscure is a disgrace; but when the Way does not prevail in your own state, to be rich and honoured is a disgrace.' (A 8.13)

'Riches and honours are what men desire, but if this cannot be achieved in accordance with the Way, I do not cling to them. Poverty and obscurity are what men hate, but if this cannot be achieved in accordance with the Way, I do not avoid them.' (A 4.5)

'What I call a great minister serves his ruler in accordance with the Way, and when it is impossible to do so he resigns.' (A 11.23)

'In the morning, hear the Way; in the evening die content!' (A 4.8)

An ideal ethico-political system such as Confucius believed to have existed in the early part of the Chou Dynasty is known as the Way (*Tao*). *Tao* is a very important word in ancient Chinese literature. It is the key concept in the philosophy of Taoism, but in that context it is the Way of Nature, a much broader and more metaphysical notion than the this-worldly Way of Confucius, the Way of running a state so that good order and harmony can prevail among men. *Tao* literally means a path or road, and this literal sense is still present in the words attributed to Tseng Tzu: 'The knight must be broad-shouldered and stout of heart. His burden is heavy and his *way* is long. For humaneness is the burden he has taken upon himself; is it not true that it is a heavy one to bear? Only with death does his journey end; is it not true that he has far to go?' (A 8.7). In the metaphorical and philosophical sense of Way there are really two distinct usages. Sometimes it seems to be regarded as something which existed in remote antiquity and is now almost unattainable, but other passages accept the possibility of the Way existing in the present decadent age. The final brief quotation is an example of the former usage: it suggests that to comprehend the Way is such a sublime experience that it would be worth having even if death immediately followed. On the other hand the first two quotations suggest that some kind of harmonious political order is sometimes achieved, and so in a sense the Way does sometimes prevail even in this imperfect world.

These two senses of Way reflect a conflict at the heart of Confucianism, between the belief that true fulfilment for the gentleman lay in political activity, and the frequent experience that the world was not a fit place for him to deploy his talents in. However deplorable the political situation in the state of Lu and however dark the prospect of improvement, Confucius was training his disciples to hold office. Several of them did achieve positions in government, and he would have been glad to obtain employment himself so that he could try to get his ideals accepted. Sometimes he is depicted as showing great distress at not finding scope for his talents. 'Am I a bitter gourd,' he cried, 'fit to hang up but not to eat?' (A 17.7). Talent he regarded as a precious object, which should not be kept hidden away; and when the disciple Tzu-kung asked: 'Suppose one has a beautiful jade, should one wrap it up, put it in a box, and keep it, or try to get a good price and sell it?', the Master said: 'Sell it indeed! Sell it! I too am one who is waiting for an offer' (A 9.12). One should be involved in the political world, and one should indeed even be prepared to die for the good Way, as the first of the above quotations says, just as one should be prepared to die for humaneness (cf. the last quotation on p. 151). And if the Way does prevail, it is quite acceptable to be rich and honoured. Indeed it is a positive disgrace to be obscure in such circumstances.

The dilemma for good Confucians would always be that one must take office to help realise the Way, but one must not, by staying in office, compromise one's commitment to the Way. The duty of resignation if the Way does not prevail is equally compelling, and the third quotation is an uncompromising message to countless generations of Confucians wondering whether they could reconcile service with their Confucian consciences. Renunciation of office and of political ambition was no easy step since participation in government was the goal of all educated men. Indeed renunciation of official life was regarded by the Chinese as a form of eccentricity comparable with being a hermit in other cultures. But, if divorced from political life, a man could still pursue his commitment to the Way by practising self-cultivation and finding scope for the exercise of his virtues within the family and the local community, reflecting that the frustration of not being employed in affairs of state had once been endured by the Master himself.

The alternative to the Way is disorder. The attainment of the Way is essentially the attainment of harmony. Therefore states which enjoyed a period of relative tranquillity might be described as having the *Tao*, even if it were not the *Tao* of the ancients. *Tao* resembles *jen* (humaneness) in that, despite its being — in its perfect form — something which belonged only to the Golden Age of antiquity and was therefore almost beyond hope of attainment, it was — in the sense of being the natural state of humanity — easily attainable or at any rate the most obvious goal. Just as Confucius said: 'Is humaneness really so far away? If we really wished for it, it would come' (A 7.29), so in the case of *Tao* he said: 'Who can go out without using the door? So why does nobody follow the Way?' (A 6.15). Confucius believed that the universe was characterised by order, and that it was possible for human beings to understand that order.

Confucius does not ever define what he means by *Tao*. It is not anything which can be defined. It is a model of political order which can be best understood by studying the Way of the ancients, a model to be studied and followed just as moral training consisted of the study and imitation of model individuals. It meant a society in which all the highest moral and political ideas were followed. To devote oneself to the study of the Way and to attempt to bring it into being for one's own generation was the highest calling of the gentleman.

# 7

# A Confucian China

Throughout this book I have, as a matter of convenience, frequently referred to the sayings or doctrines of Confucius when it would have been more accurate, although more clumsy, to have written of the sayings and doctrines 'attributed to Confucius in the *Analects*'. In the introductory chapter I maintained that it was difficult to write a book about the Master because of the lack of reliable knowledge about the man and his teachings. It was impossible to be sure that Confucius actually made any of the remarks attributed to him. The men who wrote about him either idolised him or tried to claim his support for doctrines which did not belong to him. Even the *Analects* showed much evidence of later additions; and, even in the apparently more authentic parts, the material was extremely sketchy, consisting largely of brief pronouncements rather than reasoned argument in support of a philosophical system.

My method of dealing with this unpromising situation was to point out that the importance of Confucius for China consists precisely in the transmission of these brief tags, since they have served as slogans for the guidance of Chinese social and political life throughout the ages. In these circumstances what the Western reader with no great knowledge of Chinese civilisation needed to be shown was, not simply what these often mysterious sayings had meant in the context of the China of the later Chou Dynasty, but also how they provided inspiration for Chinese institutions and attitudes right through until the present century. Just as in the Maoist era the sayings of the Chairman were reference points for policy decisions, so in imperial China the sayings of Confucius were often the ultimate authority in all spheres of social and political life.

Nevertheless, after treating the subject as concretely as possible by focusing attention on the significance of individual sayings, it is possible and desirable to summarise the message of the book by means of a general survey of the influence of Confucius (or rather of the sayings and writings associated with his name) on Chinese civilisation.

This influence may be observed firstly in the field of education. His name was closely linked with all the works in the canon of Five Classics set at the forefront of the educational system in the Former Han Dynasty. This was the culmination of a sequence of events which now needs to be described. After the Master's death a Confucian school gradually grew in strength as the disciples preserved and transmitted his teachings and other major figures like Mencius and Hsün Tzu added their contributions to the tradition; but Confucianism was only one of the so-called Hundred Schools which flourished during an age when it became fashionable for rulers to patronise well-known men of learning and gather them together to discuss matters of morals and politics at their courts. All this freedom of thought was swept away when the state of Ch'in triumphed and unified China. In 213 B.C. the new dynasty staged the execrated 'burning of the books', which was intended to remove from circulation the writings of the philosophical schools antagonistic to the state-sponsored Legalism, and indeed all literature apart from the historical records of Ch'in and books on certain practical subjects. Although copies of the banned works were preserved in the palace library for the benefit of the regime's own scholars, these also perished in the great conflagration which accompanied the downfall of the dynasty.

Eventually much of the older literature was recovered and restored, but only Confucianism and Taoism had the resilience to survive and go on to be joined by Buddhism in the trinity of 'teachings' which dominated Chinese thought during the imperial age. An education based on the Classics linked with the name of Confucius had been advocated by Hsün Tzu; so, as the prestige of the resurgent Confucian school grew, these books were well placed to be chosen as the curriculum for the growing bureaucracy. Hereafter a new brand of Confucianism, which had absorbed some Legalist and Taoist elements, became the official philosophy of the state. Its future dominance was assured when the centuries of division following the downfall of the Later Han Dynasty early in the third century A.D. coincided with a period when Buddhism had much political influence; for when unity was restored to China in the late sixth century A.D. it was to Confucianism (the creed of the great Han empire and the only available model of a successful ideology of imperial government) that the Sui rulers and eventually their T'ang successors naturally turned for an educational programme and a political philosophy.

The system of open examinations based on the study of ancient texts which would give students the general moral training needed by a ruling élite owed much to Confucius's own ideals and practices, such as his belief that there should be no class-distinctions in education, his use of the *Songs* in teaching, and his concept of the gentleman as a generalist and not one whose special skills might make him the implement of others. For the intellectuals of imperial China he also provided a personal example of conduct to which both student and teacher should aspire, with his lifelong commitment to learning despite poverty and discouragement, which was echoed in the life-style of his favourite disciple Yen Hui. For Confucius the purpose of learning was to fit oneself for official employment or, failing that, to teach others with the same aim in view; and this very same task was set before the scholars of imperial China. The content of learning was not the nuts and bolts of administrative practice, but the moral training aimed at producing officials whose conduct would be a model for the people to imitate and reciprocate; so self-cultivation or the cultivation of the moral personality was the heart of the matter. This concentration on self-cultivation was always to be an important feature of the ethos of the scholar-bureaucrat. It deeply affected his attitudes to cultural activities such as painting and writing poetry, which often seemed to be viewed primarily as exercises in self-cultivation.

In considering the subject-matter of education we became aware of the supreme importance attached to the handing on of tradition. Confucius himself claimed to be a transmitter and not a creator, entrusted with the task of handing down traditions about the Golden Age of the early Chou Dynasty. His essential message was that harmony could be restored by imitating the Way of an ideal past. The books in which the deeds of the ancients were recorded were consequently destined to be at the forefront of education and culture, and Chinese society became imbued with a powerful traditionalism in which the primary concern of scholarship was the preservation and interpretation of the ancient literature. This traditionalism inevitably resulted in a high degree of cultural unity. Despite the great regional diversity of China and the numerous distinct local cultures, the intellectuals were dominated by a 'great tradition' based on this single orthodoxy. At the same time it was culture which distinguished the Chinese from barbarians, and it was a cultural rather than a racial unity which had its embodiment in the Chinese state. Everyone could and would become Chinese. The Classics associated with Confucius were not the property of a single sect. The Confucian literature was the heritage of the whole people. The language in which this literature was written was kept artificially alive as the appropriate medium for all serious writing, a further powerful promoter of cultural unity and traditionalism. The script also played its part: like numerals, which are universally intelligible to the eye although pronounced differently in different languages, Chinese characters provided a common means of communication which united people even if they spoke mutually unintelligible dialects. But the inspiration for cultural unity and traditionalism may be clearly seen in words attributed to Confucius.

An important feature of the cultural unity inspired by the Confucian writings was the role of *li* (ritual), the rules of which, as we have seen, were thought of, not as the mores of a particular society, but as a universally valid system. Similarly the filial piety associated with the name of Confucius was universalised in the *Book of Filial Piety* and regarded as a cosmic principle. The ancient Confucian literature regarded the family as the microcosm of the state, so that the essence of government was to provide an example of adherence to family virtues for the people to follow and reciprocate in the form of loyalty. This image was preserved in imperial China and utilised by governments which saw the family and clan as convenient implements of political control. If the clans stressed the family virtues and thus secured order among their own members, they were doing the government's job for it. In a society in which order was ideally preserved by the constraints of ritual and the family virtues, the use of law was, as Confucius had suggested, a confession of failure; but in the real world there had to be a legal system. However, such was the domination of the Confucian ethos that not only were penalties graded in accordance with the pattern of family obligations, but also the law reflected the class distinction between the gentleman, for whom the obligations of ritual made it strictly speaking unnecessary, and the small man, who needed to be controlled by fear of punishments. Confucius's contrast between the gentleman motivated by justice and the small man motivated by profit was also reflected in the class system in imperial China, which placed the scholars on top and the merchants at the bottom. The ruling élite, as Confucius would have wished, was increasingly recruited on the basis of intellectual and ethical qualifications rather than birth. The imperial role was also in theory based on the ancient ideal of the benevolent ruler entrusted with the Mandate of Heaven, whose manifestation of exemplary virtue brings tranquillity to his own people and wins over the barbarians.

We have seen that the sayings attributed to Confucius have had a profound influence on educational, social, and political ideals and practices in China. If we turn now to literature and art, we shall see that the Confucian influence also permeates these areas of the Chinese experience. We have already noticed the pre-eminent position among the categories of literature which had been assigned to the Classics ever since Hsün Tzu stressed their educational value. We have seen that historical writing is imbued with such Confucian ideals as the provision of model characters for emulation or avoidance, as well as the belief that the recording of virtuous deeds brings lasting glory to one's ancestors. We have noticed that Confucius's use of the *Songs* sets the pattern for the utilisation of literature for the purpose of moral training; while novels and short stories have been disesteemed for not being vehicles for the dissemination of the orthodox Confucian morality.

Art is generally considered an area in which Taoism and Buddhism have more to say than Confucianism, but Confucian scholar-officials were the main arbiters of taste and the largest body of art patrons the world has ever known. The work of the scholar-painters, who were at the forefront of the Chinese artistic tradition, was naturally imbued with Confucian ideals. The business of painting, like the writing of poetry, was conceived as part of the regime of self-cultivation; and the resultant works always conformed with the Confucian sense of propriety and harmony. The demands of *li* were imperative in art as in social life. Chinese paintings did not show scenes of horror or violence. Art had educational value since it reflected the self-cultivation of the Confucian gentleman. The contemplation of portraits of exemplary figures from the past was as morally inspiring as reading their biographies in the dynastic histories; and another edifying *genre* was the illustration of morally enlightening episodes from life or literature. Landscape paintings too were full of a Confucian tranquillity and decorum, merging with the Taoist concept of man's communion with that nature of which he was himself a part.

Because of the agnostic sayings attributed to him Confucius is sometimes thought not to have had much influence on the religious lives of the Chinese people, especially in view of the powerful influence of Buddhism and other creeds. But the *Record of Rites*, which features Confucius as an expert on ritual, did provide detailed instructions for marriages, funerals, ancestor-worship, and for the celebration of other important religious occasions; and in imperial China scholars played important parts in religious ceremonies because of their command of this literature. It should also be remembered that Confucius himself was worshipped as a god. He had rejected the lesser honour of sagehood and would have been horrified at this development; but he was so venerated in the Later Han Dynasty that regular worship of him was conducted in government schools, and in the T'ang Dynasty temples to the Master were erected throughout the empire. In these temples the chief disciples and distinguished Confucians of later ages were also honoured. Above the altar were the words 'The teacher of ten thousand generations', and only scholars could take part in the sacrifices. As the patron deity of scholars and officials Confucius became an important figure in the state pantheon. In this capacity his role was somewhat comparable with that of the patron deities of the various crafts, which were communally worshipped by practitioners of those crafts at their guild meetings. But the supreme craft was scholarship. Confucius owes his supremacy in Chinese eyes to the fact that this deeply education-conscious people regarded him as the patron and model for the whole scholar-bureaucrat class.

So much for Confucius's influence on traditional China. How has his reputation fared in the modern world? His image was bound to crumble as the atmosphere became polluted by foreign ideas. A doctrine which embraced all under Heaven could not survive China's acknowledgement of the existence of a world split into separate nation states. In the early twentieth century attempts were made to use the Master's teachings to develop a home-grown ethical system for the new China; but in the country's reduced circumstances this could not really work. Moreover, in the eyes of the revolutionary spirits who wanted to switch off the past and turn on the future it was 'Confucius and Co.' who were responsible for the humiliations of the Chinese present. It was Confucius who was to blame for the rigid and hierarchical society of the past: when the young wanted to assert themselves, they pointed the finger of scorn at the Confucian subordination of children to their parents; when women's rights were at issue, reformers could blame Confucian literature for the fact that the traditional female role was first and foremost to bear children for the perpetuation of the family line so as to ensure the continuity of ancestor-worship, which many now regarded with increasing scepticism. Those who marvelled at the wonders of Western science and technology and saw that China was helpless against the military strength of Western nations could blame Confucius's opposition to specialisation and deplore past concentration on the Confucian Classics to the detriment of study of the external world. They could, for example, observe how the development of surgery had been hindered by the doctrine of filial piety, which refused to allow the body to be tampered with since it was a precious gift received from one's parents. The ancient criticisms of Confucius as a pedlar of ritual and a trickster who duped rulers with his moralistic nonsense resurfaced in the work of leading twentieth-century writers.

On the other hand there have also been those who have regarded Confucius as a progressive figure in his own age, believing that his emphasis on the importance of the people and his willingness to train prospective officials from whatever social background did much to undermine the old aristocratic predominance. This attitude to Confucius's historical role was still alive in the early years of the People's Republic. But eventually impatience at the difficulty of rooting out the deeply implanted conservatism of Chinese society led to Confucius being pilloried again during the Great Proletarian Cultural Revolution. After the downfall of the Gang of Four, figurines of the Master went on sale again in China, but in the world of the late twentieth century one has to look for evidence of the influence of Confucian thought in a diffused form rather than as an established and formally recognised doctrine.

Among the overseas Chinese the legacy of Confucianism may be observed most clearly in a strong sense of family unity. On mainland China, too, many echoes of Confucianism have continued to reverberate during the past three decades. Early communist writers consciously assimilated their ideas to familiar philosophical themes from the native tradition, just as many centuries earlier the foreign religion of Buddhism had been assimilated to native Chinese doctrines. The communist idea of remoulding the personality to acquire the correct proletarian class attitudes is far from alien to a people used to the Confucian emphasis on self-cultivation and moulding of the personality as the basis for moral and political life. A strict orthodoxy based on the Confucian Classics has its modern counterpart in the adoption of the sayings and writings of Chairman Mao as the repository of truth. Very traditional, too, is the use of exemplars in political education; for model workers, model communes and model industrial enterprises remind us that traditional Chinese education laid great stress on the imitation of models. Traditional and modern China have also shared a preference for political correctness to the detriment of technical expertise. Just as Confucius disparaged specialisation and the imperial civil service consequently favoured generalists schooled in the ethico-political orthodoxy, so until recently the party line has generally held that it is more important to be 'red' than 'expert', since nothing worthwhile can be achieved except on the basis of right thinking.

So the Confucian tradition is still far from dead. What I have written about him has much to do with the impact of the myth rather than the man, but despite the caution and scepticism it is necessary to bring to such an investigation, in reading the *Analects* we seem to be in touch with a real personality, not just an anthology of sayings. We seem to get glimpses of what Confucius was really like. His own distillation of a lifetime's experience is a highly personal account of his moral development: 'At fifteen I set my heart on learning, at thirty I was established, at forty I had no perplexities, at fifty I understood the decrees of Heaven, at sixty my ear obeyed them, and at seventy I could follow what my heart desired without transgressing what was right' (A 2.4). This account of self-cultivation and of the internalisation of moral imperatives seems remarkably consistent with the message of his teaching. Many of his qualities have an endearing familiarity: on his death bed he showed a typical hostility to sham; for, when his disciples dressed up as official retainers to enhance the dignity of his passing, he reproved them, saying that he would rather die in the arms of disciples than underlings (A 9.11). Indeed it is his relationships with his disciples, his different reactions to the studious Yen Hui and the extrovert Tzu-lu and others, which have the clearest ring of truth and seem to argue for the genuineness of the portrait which can be derived from a judicious selection of the material. The glimpses of personal life, the frugality and devotion to learning and sense of mission, accord so well with the teachings attributed to the man that one is left with a sense of unity of man and message which suggests that there might be more of the original Confucius surviving to us than cautious scholarship would permit us to believe.

I have presented the story of how his image inspired an alien society, but that is not to say that his message is entirely without universal appeal. Some of the sayings could profitably be adopted by anyone as mottoes, such as 'I am not worried about not being appointed; I am concerned about how I may fit myself for appointment. I am not worried that nobody knows me; I seek to become fit to be known' (A 4.14). His major concern, too, was a universal one — that political power should be wielded by men of wisdom and virtue. This was also Plato's ideal, and it remains the greatest anxiety of our world today. And his message to the individual also transcends cultural and racial differences: it is that one should strive for humaneness, seeking to cultivate the moral qualities within one so that one fully realises one's humanity.

Perhaps the most remarkable feature of the Confucian moulding of Chinese civilisation was that the sage and his disciples did not achieve this by introducing sophisticated new concepts such as justice, liberty, or democracy, which have elsewhere been valued as the hallmarks of civilised society. On the contrary they may be seen as bringing to completion the process whereby basic animal instincts developed into the guidelines of a great civilisation. Their concept of education developed out of the basic instinct of the young to imitate their elders. The family virtues derived from the basic instinct of family collaboration for survival. *Jen* (humaneness) was a sublimation of the fundamental need of human beings to collaborate for the sake of their own self-interest. And *li* (ritual) was founded on the desire of primitive man to try to gain control over his environment by means of magic. Confucianism shows how basic animal instincts can be transformed into the stuff of high civilisation by means of self-cultivation within society.

At the heart of Confucianism there was a rare humanism and a cry for mankind to be guided by moral considerations, which could not long survive in its purest form in this imperfect world. The Confucian message was adapted by politicians to suit the needs of an autocratic state, although the Master's original vision was preserved in the hearts of many individuals. Despite the distortions that his doctrine suffered during the imperial age, no human being has ever shaped his country's civilisation more thoroughly than Confucius. No human being has been set up as an example to more of his fellow human beings than Confucius. The stature which he already enjoyed more than two thousand years ago is summed up in Ssu-ma Ch'ien's biography. Since the main purpose of this book has been to explain Confucius's impact on his own people, the final assessment of him by his country's greatest historian may provide a fitting conclusion:

The world has seen many men, from kings down to ordinary men of talent and virtue, who have found glory during their lives which has come to an end with their deaths. But Confucius, although he wore the cotton gown of a commoner, has maintained his reputation for more than ten generations, and men of learning exalt him. From the Son of Heaven and the princes and nobles downwards, all those in the Middle Kingdom who speak of the six arts are guided and corrected by the Master, and this may be regarded as perfect sagehood.

# Sources and further reading

While writing this book I have been very conscious that I have had space
to mention only a relatively small proportion of the sayings of Confucius.
The translations of the *Analects* most commonly referred to are J. Legge,
*The Chinese Classics*, vol. 1 (reprinted by Hong Kong University Press,
1961) and A. Waley, *The Analects of Confucius* (Allen and Unwin,
London, 1938). Although heavily Victorian in tone, the former is still a
useful reference, with text, translation, and comment; and Waley's stylish
translation has a useful introduction which has stood the test of time quite
well. Waley's work stratifies the *Analects*, but the very recently published
version by D. C. Lau (Penguin Books, Harmondsworth, 1979) treats the
text as a unity. It has an introduction which contains a valuable exposition
of Confucius's moral philosophy. A large number of chapters are also
translated, with introductory material, in E. R. Hughes, *Chinese Philosophy in Classical Times* (Dent, London, 1942), W. T. Chan, *A Source
Book in Chinese Philosophy* (Princeton University Press, 1963) and W. T.
de Bary, ed., *Sources of Chinese Tradition* (Columbia University Press,
New York, 1960).

These three volumes also include material on other works of the ancient
Confucian school, notably *Mencius*, the best translation of which is D. C.
Lau's *Mencius* (Penguin Books, Harmondsworth, 1970), and *Hsün Tzu*, on
whom see B. Watson, *Hsün Tzu: Basic Writings* (Columbia University
Press, New York, 1963). Another translation of early Confucian material
is E. R. Hughes, *The Great Learning and the Mean in Action* (Dent,
London, 1942), and the *Record of Rites* is translated by J. Legge in books
27–8 of M. Müller, ed., *Sacred Books of the East* (Clarendon Press,
Oxford, 1879–1910). Ssu-ma Ch'ien's biography of Confucius is translated
by Lin Yutang in *The Wisdom of Confucius* (Modern Library, New York,
1938). Other books on ancient Chinese philosophy which contain valuable
material on Confucianism are D. Munro, *The Concept of Man in Early
China* (Stanford University Press, 1969) and K. C. Hsiao, *A History of
Chinese Political Thought*, vol. 1 (Princeton University Press, 1979). H. G.
Creel's *Confucius, the Man and the Myth* (John Day, New York, 1949)
is an imaginative but occasionally over-popularised account by a
distinguished scholar. D. H. Smith's *Confucius* (Temple Smith, London,
1973) is by a former missionary. Both these books devote much space
to the history of Confucianism after the Master's death. J. Ching,
*Confucianism and Christianity* (Kodansha International, Tokyo, 1977) is

a recent comparative study. On Confucius as a god the standard work is J. K. Shryock, *The Origin and Development of the State Cult of Confucianism* (Century, New York, 1932); and C. K. Yang's *Religion in Chinese Society* (University of California Press, Berkeley and Los Angeles, 1961) contains some excellent material on the religious aspects of Confucianism. Other general works about later Confucianism which can be consulted with much profit are D. S. Nivison and A. F. Wright, eds., *Confucianism in Action* (Stanford University Press, 1959) and A. F. Wright, ed., *The Confucian Persuasion* (Stanford University Press, 1960).

# References to the Analects

# JESUS

HUMPHREY CARPENTER

# *Preface*

This is one of a series of short books on leading intellectual figures of the past, written to give an account of the nature, orginality and importance of their ideas. That the person whose life and death gave rise to the founding of Christianity should be chosen as a subject for this series is understandable. But that Jesus should be described as a 'leading intellectual figure of the past' will strike many people as, to say the least, odd. To the Christian Church he is certainly much more than that, while even unbelievers may argue that he was not an 'intellectual figure' at all. Moreover it could be said that to detach the 'ideas' of Jesus from the rest of what the Bible says about him is a mistaken notion.

This book does not try to detach them. But it does examine his teaching in some detail, and tries to determine the character of that teaching by comparing it with the teaching of Jesus's contemporaries. It also attempts to give an account of modern historians' and theologians' views of Jesus and of the Gospels in which his life is recorded. Most of all, it tries to discuss the evidence about him from a historical point of view, without bringing to bear upon it the theological presuppositions of Christianity. If it does not always provide satisfactory answers, it may at least succeed in raising important questions in the reader's mind.

It begins with a brief study of the Gospels as historical evidence. This is for two reasons: first, so that the reader who does not know the New Testament may have a summary of the Gospel traditions about Jesus readily at hand, and second, so as to show the character of the Gospels as historical documents. I hope that even those readers who know the Gospels well may find some fresh things in this part of the book.

I am not a theologian by training, so I have leant very heavily on those whom I have consulted for advice and criticism, especially Tom Mills, Dennis Nineham, and my father, H. J. Carpenter. Henry Hardy of Oxford University Press has helped me a great deal, and indeed I am grateful to him for asking me to write the book.

Unless otherwise indicated, quotations are taken from the New

English Bible, second edition © 1970, by permission of Oxford and Cambridge University Presses. The following abbreviations refer to books of the Bible:

| | |
|---|---|
| Col. | The Letter of Paul to the Colossians |
| 1 Cor. | The First Letter of Paul to the Corinthians |
| 2 Cor. | The Second Letter of Paul to the Corinthians |
| Deut. | Deuteronomy |
| Ex. | Exodus |
| Gal. | The Letter of Paul to the Galatians |
| Gen. | Genesis |
| Is. | Isaiah |
| Jn. | The Gospel according to John |
| Lev. | Leviticus |
| Lk. | The Gospel according to Luke |
| 1 Macc. | The First Book of the Maccabees |
| Matt. | The Gospel according to Matthew |
| Mk. | The Gospel according to Mark |
| Rom. | The Letter of Paul to the Romans |
| 1 Thess. | The First Letter of Paul to the Thessalonians |
| 2 Thess. | The Second Letter of Paul to the Thessalonians |

# Contents

# 1

## A problem of sources

Jesus did not write any books; or if he did, which seems highly unlikely, they have not survived. This means that an account of his ideas, such as this book is meant to be, faces a special difficulty at the outset. It has to depend for its sources not on his own work, as books on (say) Dante or Pascal or Aquinas can do, but on what he is reported to have said and done. Naturally this introduces an element of unreliability from the start.

And it is not just in the area of his ideas that we are on uncertain ground. Even the simple historical facts about his life are very few. We can, it is true, regard a few things as virtually certain. Jesus was a Jewish religious teacher, and in about A.D. 28–30 he was put to death by crucifixion. When we turn to what happened after that, the facts become more numerous. His followers began to claim that he had risen from the dead and had ascended into heaven, where he had taken his place as the Son of God. Those who held this belief gradually broke away from the main stream of Jewish religion, and came to be known as 'Christians' because of their belief that Jesus was the 'Christ', a Greek word which is the equivalent of the Hebrew 'Messiah' and means 'the anointed one'; the coming of this 'Messiah' had been long expected by Jews. These facts can be deduced from Roman and Jewish writings of the period, which supply enough passing references to the death of Jesus for us to be certain that he really did exist, and was not just (as has occasionally been suggested) a mythical figure invented by Christians. But with regard to what happened before his death, we cannot be at all certain.

In order to find out why this is so, and as a preliminary to our investigation of what may have been the ideas of Jesus — and there must always be some element of 'may have' in it — we need to look at the sources, chiefly the four 'Gospels' found in the Christian Bible, which are Christianity's own account of its founder's life and ideas.* We need to look both at what they say about Jesus and at the ways in which they differ from each other. Then we need to discuss, very briefly, their character as historical documents. After that, we can turn our attention fully to the nature of Jesus's ideas, and their uniqueness and importance.

## Mark's Gospel

The four Gospels (the word 'gospel' means 'good news') were written in Greek, probably in the later decades of the first century A.D.; the earliest surviving manuscripts of any substance date from the fourth century, though there are fragments in existence of earlier origin. Of the four, the one entitled 'According to Mark' is both the shortest and that which most scholars believe to have been written first. I will summarise its contents in more detail than those of the other three Gospels, to give a reader not acquainted with the Bible a fairly full idea of the Christian picture of Jesus, and also to show the theme which runs through it. This theme is Mark's concern to answer the question, 'Who was Jesus?'

Mark's opening words provide an answer to the question at once: 'Here begins the Gospel of Jesus Christ the Son of God.' His account of Jesus's life starts with John the Baptist, a roughly-clad preacher, calling on men to be baptised (ritually immersed in water) in the river Jordan in Palestine, as a sign that they have repented of their sins and are forgiven by God. Among those who come to John for this baptism is a man named Jesus from Nazareth in the Palestinian province of Galilee. John baptises Jesus, and the baptism is accompanied by miraculous signs and a voice from heaven saying to Jesus: 'Thou art my Son.' After his baptism, Jesus undergoes some kind of struggle or temptation in a wilderness with Satan the prince of devils, and then returns to his native district preaching the 'gospel' of God. His message is: 'The kingdom of God

---

* The Bible is the collection of documents regarded by the Jewish and Christian religions as embodying the word of God. It is divided into the Old Testament, the Apocrypha, and the New Testament. The Old Testament consists of those books recognised by the Jews, chiefly the Law (the first five books of the Old Testament) and the writings of the Prophets. The Christian Church, too, recognises the Old Testament as authoritative, and has added to it a New Testament (consisting chiefly of 'Gospels' and 'Letters') which records the life, death and resurrection of Jesus, and the teaching of Paul and other early Christian preachers. The Apocrypha consists of various books regarded as of more dubious authority than the Old and New Testaments. Unless otherwise stated, all 'books' referred to in the following pages will be found in the Bible, of which many translations are available.

is upon you; repent, and believe the Gospel.' He gathers a handful of followers, some of them fishermen on the Lake of Galilee, and goes to the town of Capernaum where on the Sabbath, the Jewish day of abstention from all work (which fell on every seventh day), he teaches in the synagogue, the local place of worship. In the congregation is a man dominated by an evil spirit or devil which makes him suffer convulsions, and this devil calls out to Jesus: 'What do you want with us, Jesus of Nazareth? Have you come to destroy us [i.e. us devils]? I know you who you are — the Holy One of God.' Jesus tells the devil to be silent and come out of the man, and this happens; the convulsions cease and the man is left in peace.

This is only the first of many such actions that Jesus performs. He heals the sick and drives out devils merely by the force of his word and his touch. At one point he heals a man suffering from leprosy, and this causes his reputation to spread widely so that people come from all quarters for cures and exorcisms. He continues to gather disciples, who join his mission as the result of a single command, 'Follow me'. Among them is Levi, a tax gatherer and hence, because of the dishonesty associated with tax collection at the time, someone considered by pious Jews to be a sinner. The Pharisees, one of the principal Jewish religious factions, disapprove of Jesus's association with such men; and they soon find more in his behaviour that they can criticise. As a God-fearing Jew he is expected to keep the religious Law, the code that rules Jewish life, but he and his disciples are observed one Sabbath plucking ears of corn with which to feed themselves as they walk through a field. The Pharisees point out that this is in effect reaping, an activity forbidden on the Sabbath, to which Jesus replies: 'The Sabbath was made for man and not man for the Sabbath.' Such a high-handed attitude to the Law angers the Pharisees, and as a result of this and similar incidents they and their associates begin plotting to dispose of him.

Mark now describes the content of Jesus's teaching. It is characterised by the use of parables (analogy stories) taken largely from rural life. For example, Jesus tells of a sower who scatters seed, of which some comes to grief but some grows into a rich crop. Although he appears to be talking about the kingdom of God, his precise meaning is not clear, and Mark says that Jesus's own disciples are largely puzzled.

Twelve of these disciples have now been appointed to be Jesus's companions. Among them is Simon, to whom Jesus gives the name Peter; also another Simon, who is a member of the Zealots, a political group dedicated to freeing Palestine from Roman control; and Judas Iscariot, who was to be 'the man who betrayed him'. The disciples and Jesus cross the Lake of Galilee by boat. On their journey a storm breaks and they are in peril, but Jesus calmly stands up and tells the wind and water to be still. The storm instantly drops, and the disciples say to one another: 'Who can this be whom even the wind and the sea obey?' Another cause of amazement is the occasion when a large and hungry crowd is plentifully fed by Jesus using only the very small quantity of food there is to be had, five loaves and two fishes. Five thousand people are given enough to eat, and twelve basketfuls of scraps are gathered afterwards. The miracles continue: a blind man is given sight, a deaf man's hearing is restored, and there is widespread curiosity as to who Jesus can be. Eventually he asks his own disciples what they make of his identity, and Peter replies: 'You are the Messiah', that is, the 'anointed one' whom many Jews believed would be sent by God to usher in his 'kingdom' on earth (an idea I will examine later). Jesus tells the disciples to keep this discovery to themselves — in other words, though he does not openly admit that he is the Messiah, he does not deny it. And a few days later three of the disciples realise beyond doubt that this is what he is, for on the top of a mountain they see him miraculously clothed in dazzling white and talking with two great figures from Jewish history, Moses the lawgiver and Elijah the prophet — Elijah was expected to return to earth to announce the arrival of the Messiah.

Yet the Messiah, the inaugurator of God's kingdom on earth, was expected to be a glorious figure, and Jesus is quick to point out that his Messiahship would bring him not glory but suffering. 'He began to teach them that the Son of Man [his own title for himself] had to undergo great sufferings . . . to be put to death, and to rise again three days afterwards. He spoke about it plainly.'

After a time Jesus leaves Galilee and sets out with his disciples for Jerusalem, the capital of the Palestinian province of Judaea and the seat of the great temple which is the centre of Jewish religious life. On the way to Jerusalem he again tells his disciples that he will be arrested and executed, and will rise again, adding: 'For even the

Son of Man did not come to be served but to serve, and to surrender his life as a ransom for many.'

Arriving in Jerusalem, Jesus makes a triumphal entry. The crowd cries, 'Hosanna! Blessings on him who comes in the name of the Lord! Blessings on the coming kingdom of our father David!' In Jerusalem he causes a stir in the courtyard of the temple by driving out the traders who have stalls there; he also attracts attention because of his teaching and his disputes with representatives of the two chief religious parties, the Pharisees and Sadducees. Though they are unable to trap him into voicing dangerous opinions, they nevertheless determine to have him arrested. Meanwhile a great religious festival begins, and Jesus and his disciples meet at night for a meal which traditionally opens it. At this meal Jesus takes bread, blesses it, distributes it to the disciples and says: 'Take this: this is my body.' He also takes a cup of wine, and while they are drinking from it he says: 'This is my blood of the Covenant, shed for many.' (The 'Covenant' was God's promise to the Jews that they were to be his specially favoured people providing they kept his Law.) Jesus then leads his disciples out on to the Mount of Olives, and there, while he is praying, he is arrested by an armed crowd sent by the chief priests and their associates and guided by Jesus's own disciple Judas, who betrays him with a kiss. Jesus is seized and led to the High Priest's house.

There follows an interrogation at which the High Priest tries to find enough evidence against Jesus to warrant a death sentence. Jesus himself keeps silent until the High Priest asks him: 'Are you the Messiah, the Son of the Blessed One?' Jesus says: 'I am; and you will see the Son of Man seated on the right hand of God and coming with the clouds of heaven.' These words recall the seventh chapter of the prophetic book of Daniel, where the Son of Man is a heavenly being, the lieutenant of God; it is prophesied that he will come 'with the clouds of heaven' and be given a glorious rule over all the earth. This heavenly figure is what Jesus now claims to be, and the High Priest responds by accusing him of blasphemy, and calls for his death. But the Jewish authorities (it seems) do not have the power to carry out this death sentence, for they now hand Jesus over to Pilate, the Roman governor, who himself questions Jesus, asking him: 'Are you the king of the Jews?' Jesus replies ambiguously: 'The words are yours', and Pilate is unable to make him answer any further questions. Eventually he confirms the death sentence, and sends Jesus to be crucified, this being the method of execution which Roman law prescribed at the time. Jesus is mocked and beaten by the Roman soldiers, and is taken to the place of execution and fastened to a wooden cross. After hanging from it for six hours he dies, and a Roman centurion who has watched him and heard his last prayers declares: 'Truly this man was a son of God.'

Mark now tells how, thanks to the intervention of a wealthy Jew, Jesus's body is interred in a tomb cut out of rock. Two days later, when the Sabbath is over, three women followers of Jesus come to the tomb to anoint his body. They find that the huge stone which sealed the grave has been rolled away, and they see a young man dressed in white who says: 'He is risen, he is not here; look, there is the place where they laid him.' The women are ordered to tell the disciples that Jesus will go on before them into Galilee, where they will see him. 'Then', Mark continues, 'they went out and ran away from the tomb, beside themselves with terror. They said nothing to anybody, for they were afraid.'

Here, and very abruptly, the earliest manuscripts of Mark's Gospel came to an end. The paragraphs which follow in most printed versions are unanimously regarded as the work of a later writer. These paragraphs tell how the risen Jesus appeared to his disciples, and was then taken up into heaven to be seated 'at the right hand of God'. This extension to the original text seems to have been copied from the other Gospels. But it does show that from an early stage Mark's readers were puzzled by the abrupt ending of his narrative, and felt that they must continue the story to what they regarded as its proper conclusion.

This, then, is in very abbreviated form the outline of Mark's Gospel. As that Gospel forms the basis of two of the others, we need not look at them in so much detail, but need only note their most obvious differences from Mark.

## Matthew's Gospel

Of the remaining three Gospels, that entitled 'According to Matthew' is the one with the most resemblance to Mark. Nine-tenths of Mark's narrative is found in it, and it includes just over half of Mark's actual words. Clearly one of them had copied from the other, and though the question is still open to discussion the usual view is that Matthew used Mark. But he also used a great deal of material which Mark either did not know or decided not to incorporate.

Mark gave no account of Jesus's origins or ancestry, but Matthew begins with a full genealogy. According to this, Jesus had no ordinary list of ancestors: Matthew traces his descent back through twenty-eight generations to David, the most celebrated king in Jewish history, and through another fourteen to Abraham, the patriarch from whom all Jews were believed to be descended. He then explains that while this accounts for the origins of Jesus's nominal father, Joseph, the truth is that Jesus was not the physical son of Joseph at all, but was conceived while his mother was a virgin, as the result of a direct act of God—'Before their marriage she found that she was with child by the Holy Spirit.' This happened, says Matthew, in order to fulfil the ancient prophecy, 'The virgin will conceive and bear a son.' (The source of this prophecy is the seventh chapter of the prophetic book of Isaiah, and modern commentators point out that 'virgin' is actually a mistranslation, found in the Greek text which Matthew used, for the original Hebrew which meant 'young woman'.)

Matthew says Jesus was born at Bethlehem in Judaea 'during the reign of Herod'. He means Herod I, who ruled Palestine as a puppet-king under the Romans and who died in 4 B.C. As to Bethlehem, Matthew explains that Jesus's birth there fulfils the prophecy, 'Bethlehem in the land of Judah . . . out of you shall come a leader to be the shepherd of my people Israel' — an adaptation of verses from the fifth chapter of the book of Micah. Matthew no doubt also had in mind that Bethlehem was the home town of King David.

Matthew tells how after the birth of Jesus a group of 'magi', which means either wise men or magicians (or both), come to visit the child, being led to him by a moving star. Because of their journey, Herod learns of the birth of this child 'who is born to be King of the Jews', and is so perturbed that he orders the massacre of all infants in the Bethlehem district. But Jesus escapes death because Joseph is warned in a dream to flee with the child and its mother into Egypt, and stay there until Herod's death. This, says Matthew, 'was to fulfil what the Lord had declared through the prophet: "I called my son out of Egypt." ' Similarly, Matthew sees the slaughter of the innocent Bethlehem children as fulfilling the words of the prophet Jeremiah, 'Rachel weeping for her children'.

A modern reader will probably be intrigued by these frequent declarations by Matthew that events in Jesus's life are fulfilments of prophecies, are indeed taking place *in order* to fulfil those prophecies. This seemingly odd notion is actually quite in keeping with Jewish thought, for it was a fundamental belief that nothing of importance could happen which had not been promised by God and foretold in those writings now known as the Old Testament. Because they believed this, Jewish writers were constantly searching the Old Testament for sayings which could be interpreted as prefiguring recent events. This sometimes led to the assumption that those events had taken place so that the prophecies might be fulfilled. Indeed in a case such as Herod's supposed slaughter of the children, which is not recorded in any other source, we may suspect that the existence of the prophecy led to the invention of the event.

Although Matthew reports that Jesus was born in Bethlehem he knows of the tradition that he came from Nazareth in Galilee, and he explains this by saying that Joseph was warned not to return to Judaea and took the family to Nazareth instead. Even here Matthew adds: 'This was to fulfil the words spoken through the prophet: "He shall be called a Nazarene." ' As it happens, on this occasion no such prophecy can be traced; perhaps here Matthew, faced with the certainty of the event, has invented the prophecy.

Matthew now takes up the narrative which begins Mark's Gospel, the baptism of Jesus by John the Baptist. Then comes the temptation of Jesus in the wilderness by Satan, mentioned only briefly by Mark. Matthew tells the story in much greater detail. After this he recounts the opening of Jesus's ministry, and makes his first major incident a great sermon preached by Jesus. There is nothing like the 'Sermon on the Mount', as it is usually called from the fact that it is preached on a hilltop, in Mark's Gospel. When Mark records Jesus's teaching he concentrates almost entirely on parables and does not portray Jesus as delivering sets of explicit moral precepts. But the Sermon in Matthew's Gospel is not a parable, though parables and colourful imagery are used within it; it is direct and explicit moral teaching. This raises the question of how it compares with the moral precepts laid down by the Law of Moses, the code of Judaism, and Jesus himself answers that question in the Sermon when he says: 'Do not suppose that I have come to abolish the Law . . . I did not come to abolish, but to complete.' We shall see later precisely what Jesus seems to mean by this.

At the conclusion of the Sermon, Matthew takes up the narrative of Jesus's healing, exorcising and preaching in Galilee, and many of the events that he describes are also found in Mark's Gospel. But they do not always appear at the same point in the story, and there is also a good deal of material in Matthew not found in Mark. This new material is sometimes a longer version of something found briefly in Mark; for instance, where Mark has a few sentences in which Jesus gives a 'mission charge' to his disciples, telling them how to conduct themselves when they travel about preaching and healing, Matthew has a much longer speech in which Jesus, besides giving the disciples practical instructions, warns them about the persecutions they will suffer and exhorts them to carry out their work fearlessly. Matthew also records a number of parables and sayings of Jesus not found in Mark. And there is another more subtle way in which his text differs from Mark's: he shows a concern not found in Mark to relate Jesus's teaching to Jewish religion, showing in what manner it 'completes' the Law.

Despite the differences between the texts of Mark and Matthew the two do present very much the same story, especially in their account of the 'Passion', the trial and execution of Jesus and the events that immediately precede and follow it. But there is one significant difference. When the High Priest asks Jesus if he claims to be the Messiah, the Son of God, Jesus answers not 'I am' as in Mark but 'The words are yours' — that is, you have said it, not me, an ambiguous reply such as Jesus gives Pilate in Mark.

After the death and burial of Jesus the women (in Matthew's version) come to the tomb, see the figure in white, and soon afterwards are met by Jesus himself. He tells them: 'Go and take word to my brothers that they are to leave for Galilee. They will see me there.' The women spread the news of his resurrection, and meanwhile, when the news gets out that his tomb is empty, the Jewish religious authorities spread the rumour that the disciples themselves stole the body. The disciples meet Jesus on a mountain in Galilee, where he tells them: 'go forth therefore and make all nations my disciples; baptise men everywhere in the name of the Father and the Son and the Holy Spirit, and teach them to observe all that I have commanded you. And be assured, I am with you always, to the end of time.' With these words Matthew's Gospel ends.

## Luke's Gospel

The author to Theophilus: Many writers have undertaken to draw up an account of the events that have happened among us, following the traditions handed down to us by the original eyewitnesses and servants of the Gospel. And so I in my turn, your Excellency, as one who had gone over the whole course of these events in detail, have decided to write a connected narrative for you, so as to give you authentic knowledge about the matters of which you have been informed.

Suddenly we are in a different world. Mark and Matthew have little pretension to literary style. Their Gospels are proclamations of Jesus's miraculous nature and his great power and authority, written with little thought of their own roles as authors. But at the head of the Gospel 'According to Luke' we find an urbane, almost suave introduction, a dedication to a noble patron.

This impression is confirmed by the opening of the narrative, for Luke begins his story more subtly than do Mark or Matthew. The first figure to appear in it is Zechariah, an elderly priest whose ageing and barren wife is miraculously made fertile, so that the couple become the parents of John the Baptist. Zechariah's wife Elizabeth is kinswoman to Mary, who is betrothed to Joseph of Nazareth in Galilee, and the miraculous birth of John is paralleled by Mary's even more remarkable virginal conception of Jesus, which is announced to her by the angel Gabriel. In this episode Luke demonstrates that he has a fine taste in poetry, for Mary's lyrical response to the angel's message ('Tell out, my soul, the greatness of the Lord') is in literary terms far beyond anything attempted by Mark or Matthew. And it is equalled by the hymns in which Zechariah greets the birth of his son John, and Simeon, a devout man of Jerusalem, hails the child Jesus as the promised Messiah.

If Luke is a poet he is also a historian. Faced with the problem of explaining how Jesus was said to have been born in Bethlehem but was known to have lived in Nazareth, he adopts an ingenious course. Matthew said that Jesus's parents fled from Bethlehem because of the threat from Herod, but Luke apparently knows nothing of this, or if he does he ignores it. He takes up the point of Joseph's Davidic ancestry, and says that though Joseph lived in

Nazareth he was obliged to journey with his wife to Bethlehem, the home town of the Davidic family, to register there for a census. Luke knows that this census was a historical event: he says it 'was the first registration of its kind; it took place when Quirinius was governor of Syria'. (Actually, though there was indeed a census during Quirinius's governorship, it was not held until A.D. 6–7, which does not tally with Luke's statement that Jesus was born 'in the days of Herod', for Herod died in 4 B.C.)

Luke's artistry is evident too in his narrative of Jesus's birth. Arriving in Bethlehem, Joseph and his wife find no room to lodge in, so Jesus is born in a stable manger. This vivid detail is not found in Matthew; neither is the visit which Luke describes of a band of shepherds who come to see the new-born child. So his nativity story is almost entirely different from Matthew's, though the two are commonly fused to give the traditional Christmas story. Luke also seems to realise, with a historian's and storyteller's instinct, the enormous gap between the birth of Jesus and his baptism; he alone fills this gap with a story of Jesus growing 'big and strong and full of wisdom', and at the age of twelve putting a series of brilliant questions to the religious teachers in the temple at Jerusalem. And when he at last takes up the narrative of Jesus's baptism he sets that too in a historical perspective: he says it took place 'in the fifteenth year of the Emperor Tiberius, when Pontius Pilate was governor of Judaea'.

And then suddenly Luke begins to be a disappointment, at least for the reader who has expected the narrative to go on flowing as easily as this. For when he takes up the narrative that we find in Mark and Matthew he often seems to be losing his grip as a historian-storyteller-poet. It is not that he is any worse at narrating the chief events of Jesus's Galilean ministry than are Mark and Matthew; it is simply that he is no better. The literary promise of the early part of his story is not fulfilled. Instead of sustaining an easy flow he opts for the apparently rather haphazard list of events that is found in Mark and Matthew. On the other hand his narrative does differ considerably from theirs. For example he places the great Sermon given by Jesus much later in the story than does Matthew (and it is given on a plain rather than on a mountain) and his text of the Sermon differs quite substantially from Matthew's. He uses many fewer of the actual words of Mark's Gospel than does Matthew. Moreover there is a long section of his

Gospel which contains incidents and sayings not found in Mark or
Matthew.

His narrative of the 'Passion' of Jesus is much the same as Mark's
and Matthew's, but his account of the resurrection is very different.
The women at the tomb see the risen Jesus himself, and tell the
other disciples what has happened. The scene then changes to the
road leading from Jerusalem to a village named Emmaus, along
which two followers of Jesus are walking and discussing what has
happened. A stranger joins them, and they tell him about the death
of Jesus and the rumour of his resurrection, which they can scarcely
believe. He in reply expounds to them how the raising of Jesus from
the dead was foretold by the prophets. They reach their destination
and invite him to eat with them, and as he says a blessing and
breaks the bread they recognise him as Jesus himself. At this he
vanishes, and they immediately return to Jerusalem and tell the
others what has happened. While they are talking about it, Jesus
is suddenly standing among them. He tells them that he is no ghost
but flesh and blood, and they give him food, which he eats. He then
leads them out of the city to the village of Bethany and blesses
them, and in the act of so doing he departs from them and (it is
implied) ascends into heaven. 'And they returned to Jerusalem with
great joy,' concludes Luke, 'and spent all their time in the temple
praising God.' Actually Luke did not regard this as the end, not if
(as seems to be the case) he was also the author of the 'Acts of the
Apostles'; for that other New Testament book takes up the story
at the point where Luke's Gospel ends, and tells how the Spirit of
God descended on the disciples, and they began their task of
preaching the message of Jesus to the world.

Luke, then, is something of a puzzle, by turns literary and
unsophisticated, close to Mark and Matthew and then departing
radically from them. But he still bears much more resemblance to
them than does the fourth Gospel.

## John's Gospel

'When all things began, the Word already was. The Word dwelt
with God, and what God was, the Word was.' So opens the re-
sounding prologue to the Gospel entitled 'According to John'.

The Gospels of Mark, Matthew and Luke are commonly referred
to by the title 'synoptic', because despite their great differences
from each other the wording of all three is sufficiently identical to

be usefully set out in the parallel columns of a 'synopsis'. But John's Gospel does not fit into this pattern. A few of the incidents from the 'Synoptics' turn up in his narrative and his account of the 'Passion' is substantially the same, but there the resemblance ends. It is not merely that he has different miracle stories and teachings in his account of Jesus's life; his whole portrait of Jesus is based on a different presupposition. He regards Jesus as no less than a manifestation in human flesh of the 'Word' of God, pre-existent since before the beginning of creation. This is expressed in John's prologue, which comes to its climax with the dramatic words 'So the Word became flesh; he came to dwell among us.'

John does not give any account of the birth of Jesus, but begins his narrative with the mission of John the Baptist. He then records a series of miracles and sayings of Jesus, but both show marked differences from those in the Synoptics. The first miracle is not a healing, but the turning by Jesus of water into wine at a wedding-feast. John says that this was the first of Jesus's 'signs'. What he means by this becomes more clear as his Gospel proceeds. To him, the miraculous actions of Jesus are not simply (as they usually are to the Synoptics) wonderful deeds demonstrating the over-whelming authority from God which Jesus possesses, but actions which often have a distinct symbolic meaning. For example, the turning of water into wine means that, just as the wedding party's supply of somewhat inferior wine eventually ran out and was replaced by Jesus's miraculous and splendid vintage, so the Law which governed Jewish life for centuries has outworn its usefulness and is now replaced by the new and better 'wine', the salvation which Jesus brings. And if this interpretation seems forced, it should be noted that in Jewish rabbinical literature wine is regularly used as a symbol for the Law — and incidentally marriage is a common Old Testament metaphor for God's relationship to Israel. Such secondary interpretation of Jesus's actions is not entirely foreign to the Synoptics, but John is more conscious of it, and it governs his selection of incidents.

The sayings of Jesus recorded in John's Gospel are remarkably different from those in the Synoptics. The Jesus of the Synoptics is colourful in his speech and capable of dealing with tricky questions by means, if necessary, of equally tricky answers. He is not so much concerned with his own nature and role as with the immediate demands of the 'kingdom of God', demands which make

the question of his own personality largely irrelevant. When he
does speak of himself it is usually in the third person, as 'the Son
of Man'. But the Jesus of John's Gospel is not like this at all. He
scarcely ever teaches in the lively parables which are so typical of
the Synoptics, nor does he habitually call himself the Son of Man;
he is simply 'the Son', the only Son of God. Moreover he is much
more like God than man, a deity clothed in human flesh but still
undoubtedly a deity. And, after the marked lack on interest in his
own personality shown by the Jesus of the Synoptic Gospels, it is
extraordinary to note how much of John's text is taken up by Jesus's
speeches about himself. 'I am the light of the world . . . I am the
good shepherd . . . I am the bread of life.' With these and other
images he begins the great discourses so typical of him in this
Gospel, discourses which are great sermons about man's relationship to God through Jesus himself, and in which the word 'I' plays
a great part.

Nor is it only the colour of the Synoptics which is missing in
John's portrait of Jesus. Many of the central ideas are not there
either. As the modern theologian John Knox has put it, in his book
*The Death of Christ*:

The Christ of the Fourth Gospel is almost entirely preoccupied with his
own significance to the complete neglect of the great themes of the
righteous will, the abounding goodness, and the imminent kingdom of
God which dominate and give their distinctive character to the utterances
of Jesus in the other Gospels.

This means that on the one hand John provides a peculiarly rich
source of ideas about the nature of Jesus as 'Christ' and 'Son of
God': the Christian religion's own thought about Jesus's nature
undoubtedly owes more to John than it does to the Synoptics. On
the other hand John's portrait has supplied comparatively little to
historians' understanding of Jesus as a man. It is generally considered that his Gospel is a work of spiritual reflection rather than
of reliable history, and in this book it will be to the Synoptics that
we shall usually turn for our information about Jesus, rather than
to John.

## Other sources

These four Gospels are the main sources of information about the
life of Jesus, but there are other documents which ought to be

mentioned very briefly. Most notable among these is a passage in
the first Letter to the Corinthians by the early Christian preacher
Paul of Tarsus. This was probably written quite a lot earlier than
the Gospels, for Paul became a Christian only a few years after the
death of Jesus, whereas the Gospels seem to have originated some
time later. In the fifteenth chapter of this Letter he writes:

> . . . I handed on to you the facts which had been imparted to me: that
> Christ died for our sins, in accordance with the scriptures; that he was
> buried; that he was raised to life on the third day, according to the
> scriptures; and that he appeared to Cephas [Paul's name for Peter], and
> afterwards to the Twelve. Then he appeared to over five hundred of our
> brothers at once, most of whom are still alive, though some have died.
> Then he appeared to James, and afterwards to all the apostles.
> In the end he appeared even to me. (1 Cor. 15. 3–8)

This shows that from a very early stage Christianity was based on
the death and resurrection of an actual person, but of course it tells
us nothing about what Jesus said and did in his lifetime. Indeed in
all of Paul's writings there are only two passages which give us any
explicit information about the historical Jesus. The first is in the
context of Paul's discussion of marriage, where he says: 'A wife
must not separate herself from her husband', and declares that this
ruling 'is not mine but the Lord's', that is Jesus's (1 Cor. 7.10). The
second comes when he is discussing how the congregation to whom
he is writing should celebrate the 'Lord's Supper', the ritual meal
which was a regular activity from the beginning of Christianity.
Paul reminds them that this meal is a tradition which came directly
from Jesus:

> . . . the Lord Jesus, on the night of his arrest, took bread and, after giving
> thanks to God, broke it and said, 'This is my body, which is for you; do
> this as a memorial of me.' In the same way, he took the cup after Supper,
> and said: 'This cup is the new covenant sealed by my blood. Whenever you
> drink it, do this as a memorial of me.' (1 Cor. 11. 23–6)

And that is all Paul has to tell us about the historical Jesus. This
is not as strange as it may seem, because from its beginnings
Christianity regarded Jesus not so much as a person in the past as
a living presence; so that Paul's view of Jesus is set, so to speak,
in the present tense. Moreover Paul, himself a great preacher, was
less concerned to record stories about the life of Jesus (which his
congregations probably already knew) than to emphasise the

meaning of Christianity. Nevertheless it is frustrating that one who was so close to the historical facts tells us so little about them.

Apart from the Gospels of Mark, Matthew, Luke and John and the Letters of Paul, all of which are to be found in that part of the Bible known as the New Testament, there are a number of other early accounts of Jesus's life which have survived. Several of these other Gospels represent traditions about him which were preserved by branches of Christianity whose doctrines differed from the main stream. For example there is the 'Gospel of the Egyptians', which represents Jesus's purpose as being to destroy 'the works of the female', by which is apparently meant the process of reproduction. Another fragment, the so-called 'Secret Gospel of Mark', portrays Jesus as initiating his disciples privately into some kind of sexual rites, while the 'Gospel of the Ebionites' says he made it his aim to terminate all sacrifices in the temple of Jerusalem. It is impossible to take this kind of thing seriously unless one is prepared to discount the whole body of New Testament writings about Jesus. More in harmony with the New Testament tradition are the Gospels known as 'Hebrews', 'Peter', and 'Thomas'. But the first two, of which only fragments exist, seem to be no more than modifications of the Synoptic Gospels, while the third, which is complete, does contain sayings of Jesus not found elsewhere but appears to be merely an imaginative expression of the Synoptics and not to be based on first-hand traditions.

So in our investigation of the life and ideas of Jesus we are left with the four Gospels of the New Testament as our principal sources. How are we to regard them?

## The quest for the historical Jesus

The Gospels themselves imply that they are eyewitness reports. Indeed the Gospel of John actually claims to be the work of an eyewitness, who has usually been identified with John the son of Zebedee, one of Jesus's twelve disciples. As for Luke's Gospel, its author does not say he observed its events himself, but tells us he bases his accounts on traditions handed down by those who did. (Luke himself has been popularly identified with Luke the physician, the travelling companion of Paul, though this tradition is now widely regarded as wrong.) The other two Gospels make no statement about their own authenticity, but at quite an early date traditions grew up about them. A second-century church leader in

Asia Minor named Papias explained Mark's Gospel as originating in the reminiscences of the disciple Peter, who dictated them to a follower named Mark. This soon became the general belief, as did the notion that Matthew's Gospel was the work of the tax-gatherer disciple who is called 'Levi' in Mark but 'Matthew' in Matthew.

Once the early Church had made up its mind to accept these four Gospels as authentic and to reject all others, the question of their reliability was not raised for many centuries. Medieval Christians did not concern themselves with it, and even at the Reformation the issue was scarcely touched on, though the foundations of later investigation were laid by Luther's insistence that the Bible rather than the Church was the real source of the word of God. This led to a more thorough study of what the Bible had originally meant; meanwhile such scholars as Erasmus had begun to investigate the original Greek texts of the Gospels. But it was not until the eighteenth century that it was admitted that the Bible could contradict itself, and might reflect very different points of view. With this came the beginning of real historical investigation.

The fact that Matthew, Mark and Luke tell roughly the same story (though with considerable variations) led the early investigators to look for some kind of 'primal Gospel' which it was supposed must lie behind them all; meanwhile John's very different Gospel was quietly set aside, and the question of its historicity was not discussed. First results for the 'primal Gospel' suggested that Matthew's account was the earliest of the three Synoptics to be written, a view which the early Church had held. But by the mid-nineteenth century the growth of Gospel criticism showed that Mark's account almost certainly preceded the other two, and that Matthew and Luke drew upon it, augmenting their narratives with material presumably based on another tradition about Jesus, to which scholars affixed the name 'Q', perhaps from the German *Quelle*, meaning 'source'.

This led to the assumption that Mark's account of Jesus must be the 'primal Gospel' which everyone was looking for. But further study showed that this assumption presented grave difficulties. If Mark was pure history, it was history of a very odd kind. A great deal was lacking: there was no information about Jesus's birth or early life, and no real explanations of his character and motives. Moreover, while there was no lack of incidents in the narrative, everything was presented as happening in quick succession, so that if it all took place just as Mark said it did the whole series of events would only occupy a few weeks. When this was realised by nine-teenth-century historians there were two results.

The first was that certain people tried to fill the gaps in Mark's narrative by writing conjectural biographies of Jesus, extraordinary books whose contents are summarised in Albert Schweitzer's *The Quest of the Historical Jesus*, and which reflect not so much the personality of Jesus as those of their authors. Among these books were rationalistic attempts to prove that the miracles were not miraculous at all but merely ordinary events misinterpreted by the disciples; allegations that Jesus was a member of a religious secret society which stage-managed (and faked) his death and resurrection; and highly romantic Lives of Jesus whose saccharine sweetness appealed to a vast public. Writings like these were much in vogue for some years — and indeed the same sort of thing is sometimes published today. Needless to say they contribute nothing to the historian's knowledge of Jesus.

The second result of discovering Mark's inadequacy as a biographer of Jesus was that the whole nature of his Gospel was called into question; and a careful study of the original Greek text eventually led to the conclusion that his narrative had been put together from a large number of originally independent stories about Jesus. What Mark himself had done was to assemble these stories into a continuous narrative, providing linking passages where necessary. His Gospel was therefore in no sense a biography, but a loosely-knit collection of independent items. This did not automatically make it less reliable as history. It will be remembered that the early Church believed that Mark had written at the dictation of Jesus's disciple Peter; so could not the disjointed nature of Mark's materials be explained as the fragmentary reminiscences of an old man? Maybe, and some would still hold this view; but there is actually very little in the Gospel which bears the character of an eyewitness's memories. Colourful details are largely lacking, and most events are described very barely, not at all as somebody who had been there might have reported them. Moreover there are many sayings ascribed to Jesus which could only have come from his lips if he had foreseen not just the precise circumstances of his death and resurrection but also the growth of a Church which would worship him, and which would in turn itself suffer persecu-tions for its beliefs. If we do not choose to accept this prophetic element at face value, we may regard this as an indication that Mark's Gospel was not the individual memory of an eyewitness but a general tradition about Jesus preserved corporately in the early Church, a tradition, moreover, that had been embroidered upon by those who preserved it.

These conclusions were reached soon after the 1914–18 war by a group of biblical scholars known as the Form-critics, because of their attention to the detailed literary form of the Gospel materials. The Form-critics' work predictably aroused opposition from more conservative quarters, and this opposition was strengthened by the fact that the Form-critics often exaggerated; for example, they tended to assume that because something *could* have been invented by the early Church then it undoubtedly *had* been. However, the general conclusions of this critical school gradually came to be accepted even in more conservative circles.

What then is the present-day historian's attitude to the Gospels as source material? He will begin by considering Mark, since his is generally agreed to be the earliest Gospel and closest to the original traditions about Jesus. If he has a poor opinion of the accuracy of human memory in general and of a corporate memory (such as the early Church must have used to retain these traditions) in particular, he will be sceptical about Mark's chances of recording the truth. This scepticism will be increased if he is inclined to believe (with most New Testament scholars) that Mark's Gospel was not written down until several decades after the death of Jesus, perhaps between A.D. 65 and 75. And if the historian accepts that Christians would at a very early stage freely elaborate, albeit unconsciously, what had been handed down to them, so as to produce a whole new series of traditions about Jesus, then he will again be sceptical about the accuracy of Mark. If on the other hand he believes that Christians' devotion to the memory of Jesus would make them scrupulous in preserving traditions accurately, and that any invention or elaboration of those traditions would be discouraged, then he will probably allow Mark's Gospel a higher degree of historicity. Perhaps if he is wise he will compromise, for it is after all hard to imagine that this earliest Gospel does not preserve something of the impact that Jesus really made, while at the same time it is unrealistic to suppose that much inaccuracy and departure from historical truth did not occur as a result of the oral transmission of memories from one person to another. Finally, he will take account of the fact that Mark's Gospel, like the other three, was written not simply to inform, but to preach. It is didactic writing, and this influences the selection and presentation of its contents.

But what about the historian's attitude to Matthew and Luke? The view of most biblical scholars is still that the other two Synoptic Gospels used the hypothetical source 'Q', which may have been either a written document or an oral tradition, for much of the material that they did not derive from Mark. But if 'Q' was a document it has disappeared, and when it is conjecturally reconstructed it looks rather an odd piece of work, with no real narrative shape. Moreover if it really did exist it seems that Matthew and Luke knew quite different versions of it, because they used its material very differently. Not surprisingly some discount its existence, and prefer the theory that Luke's resemblances to Matthew are not the product of their using a common source but of Luke's having a copy of Matthew's Gospel in front of him when he wrote.

Where then did Matthew get the material that he did not draw from Mark? And why if Luke copied from Matthew did he make so many changes in the narrative? One explanation has recently been offered which accounts for all this. This is that Matthew wrote a free meditation on what he found in Mark; he took Mark's basic outline and most of his details, but altered where he thought fit, and also invented freely to fill out his account of Jesus to his satisfaction. In the same way Luke based his text on Matthew, but he too invented freely and changed Matthew's narrative when he wanted to.

There is a good deal to support this view. All is explained quite simply without reference to hypothetical sources. But could Matthew and Luke really have dared to invent so much? The New Testament critics who believe they could, cite the long established Jewish practice of *midrash* or free improvisation around sacred themes, a practice which certainly lies behind the composition of many of the Old Testament stories, and suggest that Matthew and Luke as devout Christians in the Jewish tradition would certainly have felt free to compose *midrash* about Jesus. So far this view (which could, of course, be extended even to Mark's Gospel) has not received much support, but it ought to be kept in mind as a possibility. If it is true, then of course Matthew's and Luke's

Gospels are totally unhistorical when they depart from Mark — or at least they can be no more than a reflection of Jesus's general impact, and not a record of what he actually said and did.

As for John's Gospel, the historian will probably regard it as the product not so much of historical tradition as of spiritual reflection. At the same time he will perhaps allow that it may contain a few real historical details. He will certainly accept that it records the Church's beliefs about Jesus, as they developed in later decades after Jesus's death.

Whether the Gospels are history or invention they are virtually our only sources for an examination of the life and teaching of Jesus, so that if we reject them we are left with nothing at all. A proper course is therefore not to dismiss them out of hand but to use them with caution, often very great caution, as we set out on our own quest for the historical Jesus.

# 2

# 'Jesus came from Nazareth in Galilee'

Jesus was certainly called 'Jesus'. The name was so common that the early Church would not have used it of him had it not been his real name. To be strictly accurate, 'Jesus' is the Greek form. The Hebrew original was 'Jeshua', which (like 'Joshua') was a shortened form of 'Jehoshua', meaning 'he whose salvation is God'.

The Gospels give us two sets of information about Jesus's origins. Mark says he came from Nazareth in Galilee, and tells us that in his home town Jesus was referred to as 'the carpenter, the son of Mary, the brother of James and Joseph and Judas and Simon', mentioning that he had sisters too (Mk. 6. 3). Matthew and Luke add to this; they tell us that Jesus was born in Bethlehem, that his nominal father's name was Joseph, and that his mother became pregnant while still a virgin, so that the child was really fathered by God. How we treat this tradition of the virgin birth will depend on our theological views. As to the notion that Jesus was born in Bethlehem, though this may have been simply a conjecture because Bethlehem was David's home town, it could of course be a historical fact. Galilee, on the other hand, remains unchallenged as the place where Jesus was brought up. 'Jesus came from Nazareth in Galilee and was baptised in the Jordan by John', says Mark (1. 9), and there seems to be no reason to doubt the implication that Nazareth was Jesus's home at the time.

## Galilee of the Gentiles

Galilee was the name given to a province in the north of Palestine. Its economy was based on agriculture — the soil was highly fertile — and on fishing in the Lake of Galilee, through which the river Jordan flowed south. About a thousand years before the birth of

Jesus, Galilee had been part of the powerful Jewish kingdom of David. But after the death of David's son and successor Solomon this kingdom was divided once again into the two states of Israel and Judah, its original components. Galilee became part of Israel, the northern state. After a period of peace, in the eighth century B.C. this territory fell to the Assyrians, and its people lost their Israelite identity. The majority of them ceased to worship Yahweh the God of Israel, and turned instead to the Ba'als or heathen deities whose fertility cults had long been popular in the eastern Mediterranean.

The southern state of Judah had Jerusalem, the seat of the great temple built by Solomon for the worship of Yahweh, as its capital. Eventually this kingdom, too, fell to invaders. It was captured by the Babylonians in 587 B.C., and its principal inhabitants were taken in bondage to Babylon. Their captivity there lasted for fifty years, and when they were eventually freed and could return to Judah they were unable to rebuild a nation of any great power. Meanwhile Galilee and the other northern territories that had once been part of the kingdom of David remained in 'Gentile' or non-Jewish hands.

Not until little more than a hundred years before the birth of Jesus did this picture change. In the second century B.C. the powerful Jewish family of the Maccabees managed to free Judah from the Syrians who had by then been controlling it for some time. Eventually they even managed to push the national boundaries outwards until something like the old Davidic kingdom of Israel had been recreated. In the process, Galilee was annexed (104–103 B.C.) and once again became Jewish — and not just in name, for its inhabitants were obliged to be circumcised (the physical sign of Judaism) and to worship Yahweh. The territories around Galilee, however, remained non-Jewish.

The success of the new kingdom was fairly short-lived, for the reigning family was unseated both by internal squabbles and by the Romans, whom it had invited to Jerusalem as a powerful arbitrator to settle those squabbles. Rome installed its own puppet rulers, and itself retained ultimate control of the whole of Palestine. Among these puppet rulers was Herod I, who was styled king. After his death in 4 B.C. his territory was divided among his sons, and one of these, Herod Antipas, took control of Galilee. Though nominally subject to Rome, Antipas actually wielded considerable power.

Galilee, then, had had a chequered history. It had been by turns

Jewish, Gentile, and Jewish again; and the general opinion among the pious Jews of Jerusalem was that it was still more Gentile than Jewish. 'Galilee of the Gentiles' they called it, paraphrasing words from the book of Isaiah (Is. 9. 1; cf. Matt. 4. 15). This is not to say that the Jewish religion had no appeal to the Galileans. Many of them wanted to free their land, and indeed the whole of Palestine, from Roman control; so many in fact that the name 'Galilean' became synonymous for 'rebel'. And like all those who in previous centuries had fought for the freedom and supremacy of the Jewish people, they used the Jewish religion as their rallying point. Nevertheless most other Jews regarded the Galileans in general as rough and rather pagan creatures, 'stupid Galileans', and made a great joke of their incomprehensible northern speech. It was the last area from which a great religious teacher was expected to come.

## The carpenter

Was Jesus really a carpenter by trade? It seems such an odd thing for anyone to invent that most biblical critics have accepted it as fact, though they point out that some doubt is introduced by Matthew calling him not 'the carpenter' as does Mark (6. 3) but 'the carpenter's son' (Matt. 13. 55). There is also the complication that the word in the original Greek (*tektōn*) may mean a worker not just in wood but also in stone and metal, so that 'craftsman' might be a better translation. Speculations as to the precise nature of Jesus's or his father's work vary a great deal, and while some historians imagine him in a simple joinery shop others prefer to think of him as quite a prosperous builder. But it would probably be wrong to regard him as too middle-class socially, because the implication of the words of the people who heard him preach in the Synagogue at Nazareth — 'Is this not the carpenter?' — seems to be 'How can somebody from a background like his be a great preacher?'; though of course they might merely be saying 'How can he pose as a great preacher when he is just a local man we all know?' (see Mk. 6. 3, Matt. 13. 55; cf. Lk. 4, 22).

There is one very important question about Jesus's upbringing. Was he or was he not a trained rabbi?

'Rabbi' is a Hebrew word meaning literally 'my master' (Hebrew continued to be the 'book language' of Judaism even though Aramaic was used in daily speech). After the time of Jesus 'rabbi' came to be the official title for ordained ministers of the Jewish religion who presided in the synagogues. But in his lifetime and before, it had not acquired this meaning, and was used simply as a title of respect for certain recognised scholars who studied and interpreted the Jewish religious Law. In John's Gospel, Jesus is on one occasion addressed as 'rabbi' by his disciples (1. 38). Is this meant to be an indication that he was a scholar with formal training? Probably not, for John glosses the first use of the word 'rabbi' as meaning 'teacher' and the second as meaning 'my master', so in neither case does he seem to imply that Jesus had a formal rabbinical training. None of the other Gospels uses the term 'rabbi' of Jesus, and indeed Luke, with his story of the twelve-year-old Jesus astonishing the trained doctors of the Law with his remarkable knowledge, seems to imply that he was self-taught (or as Luke would have said, directly inspired by God) rather than formally educated. Moreover a formal rabbinical training would in Jesus's lifetime probably have meant spending some years in Jerusalem sitting at the feet of a great teacher, since Galilee at that period is unlikely to have been able to offer anything comparable. There is no record of any such period spent in Jerusalem by Jesus during his early years. On the other hand there is no explicit denial of it, and persons from the artisan and craftsman classes often did become rabbis. Certainly if Jesus did have a formal training in the Law it would explain his fluency in it, and also perhaps his growing discontent with it as an exclusive way of life. Not that he would have had to be formally educated to gain at least a working knowledge of it, for it was all around him.

## The Law and the Prophets

As the son of God-fearing Jews — and despite Galilee's reputation there is no reason to suppose that Jesus's parents were not devout — he would have been taken to the synagogue every Sabbath. For us to regard this as simply 'going to church' in the modern Christian sense would be inadequate, for though there was of course a large spiritual element in the worship of the synagogue it was also a training in Jewish history. This was because the religion of the Jewish people was, and always had been, inextricable from its national history. It was in fact a religion of history.

Yahweh, the God of Israel, was believed to have shown a special concern for the Jewish people since the beginning of time, and the Jews recorded their history in a manner that demonstrated his involvement in it. They told how the first migration of Jews from

Mesopotamia to Palestine had been brought about by Yahweh's summons to Abraham to leave the country of his fathers and to journey to the promised land of Canaan (the earlier name for Palestine). They told how at a later period in Jewish history a great number of their people suffered slavery in Egypt, and were released from that slavery and brought back to Palestine through the power of Yahweh and under the leadership of his servant Moses. Most important of all, they recorded how, during this 'exodus' from Egypt, Yahweh had made a 'Covenant' with the Jews, promising that if they would obey his commandments he would make them supreme above all other nations.

It was believed that the fluctuating fortunes of the Jewish settlers in Palestine after their exodus from Egypt were the direct result of Yahweh's intervention, and of their own fidelity or infidelity to their side of the Covenant. Jewish historians explained the brilliant success of David's kingship as the consequence of Yahweh's power, and they attributed the later decline of Jewish fortunes to Israel's disobedience. Moreover they looked to the future, to the day when at last Yahweh would fulfil his Covenant and make Israel supreme above all other nations.

The books of Jewish history in which these events and their interpretations are recorded are found in that part of the Bible known to Christians as the Old Testament. The Jews in the time of Jesus knew it by a different name, 'the Law and the Prophets'. By 'the Law' they meant the five books supposed to have been written by Moses: Genesis, Exodus, Leviticus, Numbers and Deuteronomy. 'The Prophets' was the collective title for the books of Joshua, Judges, Samuel and Kings — actually historical books but supposed to be by prophetic authors — and those of Isaiah, Jeremiah, and other later prophets. 'The Law and the Prophets' were regarded as beyond doubt holy writings in which divinely inspired authors had recorded the word of God. There were also other historical writings, such as the books of Chronicles, Ezra and Daniel, which were highly esteemed but not treated with quite the same awe.

Readings from the Law and the Prophets were prescribed as part of the worship in the synagogue on the Sabbath. Moreover the Law was supposed to govern every detail of a Jew's daily life. 'You shall have no other gods to set against me. You shall not make a carved image for yourself . . . You should not make wrong use of the name of the Lord your God. Remember to keep the sabbath day holy . . .'.

In such words as these, recorded in chapter 20 of the book of Exodus, Yahweh was believed to have delivered his Law to Moses on Mount Sinai after Moses had led the Israelites out of captivity in Egypt. Nor were these commandments regarded simply as moral precepts for the conducting of a right and holy life. They were one side of a crucial bargain, that Yahweh would reward Israel if it kept the Law.

There was much more to the Law than the Ten Commandments from which the words above are quoted. Through the five books of Moses are found explicit instructions as to how the Israelites should carry out the will of Yahweh — or rather the will of 'The Lord', for Yahweh's name was considered to be so sacred that it was rarely used. 'The Lord' was the term most frequently employed, though the word 'God' alone is often found in the Old Testament.

Here are a few of these explicit instructions, which covered all aspects of daily life:

When one man injures and disfigures his fellow-countryman, it shall be done to him as he has done; fracture for fracture, eye for eye, tooth for tooth; the injury and disfigurement that he has inflicted upon another shall in turn be inflicted upon him. (Lev. 24. 19–20)

Of all animals on land these are the creatures you may eat: you may eat any animal which has a parted foot or a cloven hoof and also chews the cud; those which have only a cloven hoof or only chew the cud you may not eat. (Lev. 11. 2–4)

You shall not eat meat with the blood in it. You shall not practise divination or soothsaying. You shall not round off your hair from side to side, and you shall not shave the edge of your beards. (Lev. 19. 26–7)

Many instructions concerned the offering of sacrifice in the temple at Jerusalem:

When any man among you presents an animal as an offering to the Lord . . . he shall slaughter the bull before the Lord, and the Aaronite priests shall present the blood and fling it against the altar all round at the entrance of the Tent of the Presence. He shall then flay the victim and cut it up . . . and the priest shall burn it all on the altar as a whole-offering, a food-offering of soothing odour to the Lord. (Lev. 1. 2, 5–6, 9)

To us, the Law seems harsh. Not only did it command that murderers and even those who killed accidentally should die, but also 'whoever curses his father or his mother shall be put to death'

(Ex. 21. 17). To take another example, should a man or woman be gored by an ox which was already known to be a dangerous animal but which had not been properly penned up, then 'the ox shall be stoned, and the owner shall be put to death as well' (Ex. 21. 29). Such was the general tone of the Law.

Despite Jewish belief to the contrary, the Law did not in fact originate *en bloc* in the time of Moses. The handiwork of different generations may be seen in its various layers of composition, of which the earliest probably dates from about 850 B.C. and the latest from about two hundred years later. Moreover later Jewish jurists did make some attempt to liberalise the original more severe laws. The result of this was the book of Deuteronomy or 'Second Law', the text of which dates from the seventh century B.C., though it may incorporate earlier traditions. Yet even this later more liberal version of the Law could scarcely be called humane by modern standards:

When a man has a son who is disobedient and out of control, and will not obey his father or his mother, or pay attention when they punish him, then his father and mother shall take hold of him and bring him out to the elders of the town, at the town gate. They shall say to the elders of the town, 'This son of ours is disobedient and out of control; he will not obey us, he is a wastrel and a drunkard.' Then all the men of the town shall stone him to death, and you will thereby rid yourselves of this wickedness. All Israel will hear of it and be afraid. (Deut. 21. 21)

Such drastic measures were probably not still carried out in the time of Jesus. Nevertheless the Law continued to rule severely over Jewish life.

This written Law of Moses dealt with every aspect of Jewish religious and social life, and it might be thought that it left nothing in doubt. But by the time of Jesus there had been in existence for many generations an even more detailed tradition of oral interpretation of the Law. This had begun for the simple reason that no standard text of the Law originally existed, so that it was not always possible to determine precisely what it laid down. Moreover laws sometimes contradicted each other, and at times their application to particular cases was not clear. This meant that skilled interpreters were needed: hence the coming into existence of 'Scribes' or doctors of the Law who had themselves studied the subject thoroughly and could pass their interpretations on to disciples. By the time of Jesus the existence of these Scribes was as much taken for granted as was the Law itself. Moreover the interpretations that they offered had themselves come to be governed severely by precedent and tradition, just as are modern legal judgements. Scribes could no longer interpret freely, but must pass on the teaching of their masters, who in turn had taught what their own master had said. In this way the Scribes' tradition was believed to stretch back to Moses himself. Eventually, some generations after the death of Jesus, this oral interpretative tradition was itself codified and written down in the *Mishnah* ('repetition'), but in his lifetime it still existed only in oral form. This was why young men who were intent on becoming Scribes had to undergo a very severe course of study, listening to their master's words and committing every detail to memory.

We do not know how much of this oral tradition Jesus knew in detail. It is doubtful if, as a Galilean, remote from Jerusalem, he would have been versed in the finer points of legal debate. If there were Scribes resident in his part of Galilee, they would probably have been unsophisticated, provincial men, out of touch with the complex teaching of their Jerusalem counterparts. But certainly the reading aloud of the written Law (in Hebrew, with a translator rendering it into Aramaic) formed the centrepiece of Sabbath worship during Jesus's childhood and early years at Nazareth. Moreover if, as seems likely, he came from a God-fearing family, the whole body of the Law — generally known as the *Torah* or 'teaching' — must have overshadowed his life, much as it did the early years of Paul of Tarsus, who remarked ironically, '. . . except through law I should never have become acquainted with sin. For example, I should never have known what it was to covet, if the law had not said, "Thou shalt not covet" ' (Rom. 7. 8).

After the reading of the Law in the synagogue would come a reading from the Prophets. Nowadays we are perhaps inclined to think of the ancient Jewish prophets simply in terms of their foretelling of the future, and this was of course one aspect of the prophetic calling. But in the history of Israel they had a very practical function: they summoned men back to the worship of Yahweh, and in doing so they strengthened the national resolve and hope for the future. Their role was thus in a sense as much political as it was religious. No better example of this can be found than the anonymous prophet usually known as Second Isaiah, so called because though he composed much of the later part of the book of Isaiah his real name is unknown. He was among the exiles from Jerusalem living in captivity in Babylon during the sixth century B.C., and in the midst of their general despair he promised them a glorious future:

Comfort, comfort my people; — it is the voice of your God; speak tenderly to Jerusalem and tell her this, that she has fulfilled her term of bondage, that her penalty is paid . . . Every valley shall be lifted up, every mountain and hill brought down . . . Here is the Lord God coming in might, coming to rule with his right arm. (Is. 40. 1–2, 4, 10)

Second Isaiah's rallying call to Israel and his vindication of the supreme power of God undoubtedly had a powerful effect on the nation, and helped to rebuild its confidence after exile. Similarly in earlier centuries a long line of other prophets — Jeremiah, Elijah, Samuel, Moses himself — had in their turn guided the fortunes of Israel. But as it happened Second Isaiah was almost the last of the prophets.

After him a few prophetic voices such as Haggai, Zechariah and Malachi still spoke, but they were not of his stature, and with the Israelites' return from captivity towards the end of the sixth century B.C. the prophetic tradition virtually died out. Certainly writings of a prophetic character still emerged, but these were now presented as if they were the work of an earlier age. For example the book of Daniel puports to have been writing during the Babylonian exile, whereas in fact it dates from about four hundred years later, and is really a thinly veiled allegory of the troubles that Jerusalem was going through at the time: Nebuchadnezzar the king of Babylon stands for the Syrian tyrant Antiochus IV who was trying to suppress Jewish religion. Fine as such writings are — and 'Daniel' contributed greatly to the development of later Jewish thought — they do not have the character of the old prophets.

Why had prophecy ceased? The answer is easily found. The Law had really taken its place. In the earlier history of Israel the Law had not really been a law at all but merely a record of current practice. The business of pushing forward the spiritual and ethical frontiers had been left largely to the prophets and their followers — for there were 'schools' of prophecy, and some prophetic books represent the work of a number of people, sometimes spanning many generations. But later the intellectual energy of Judaism had largely been taken over by the Scribes, who studied and interpreted the Law; and they directed this energy towards legal interpretation rather than prophetic utterance. As a result Judaism had become largely a religion of the Law. Meanwhile the disappearance of the prophetic element was greatly regretted. A historian writing in the second century B.C. describes the misery that was then afflicting Israel by saying that it was 'worse than any since the day when prophets ceased to appear' (Macc. 9. 27).

Jesus, then, would have heard the Law and the Prophets read in the synagogue each Sabbath, and it would be a dull young man who would not find excitement in the writings of the Prophets. He too must have regretted, as so many did, the disappearance of prophecy. And he could hardly fail to be gripped by the news, which came one day when he was in his late twenties, that a new prophet had suddenly appeared on the banks of the river Jordan, crying, 'Repent, for the kingdom of God is at hand!'

# 3

## The kingdom of God

### The kingdom of God

The Gospel writers found this new prophet, John the Baptist, such an awkward fact that they can scarcely have invented him. He did not fit into their pattern, and though they tried to imply that he was some kind of reincarnation of Elijah, whose reappearance in Israel was expected by the Jews as a portent of the coming of the Messiah, John the Baptist himself denies this in John's Gospel:

. . . the Jews of Jerusalem sent a deputation of priests and Levites to ask him who he was . . . 'Are you Elijah?' 'No' he replied. (Jn. 1. 19, 21)

As to the notion of Jesus, the sinless Messiah, being baptised by John as a sign that he had repented of his sins and been forgiven, Matthew finds this so uncomfortable that he has Jesus explaining to John the Baptist that it is really only being done 'to conform . . . with all that God requires', which presumably means for show rather than through necessity (Matt. 3. 15). All this leads one to suppose that Jesus's baptism by John is a sound historical fact.

Jesus had already been physically initiated into the Jewish religion by circumcision, which was performed on all male children when they were eight days old. A rite such as baptism would therefore seem to many Jews to be unnecessary. But ritual washings-away of spiritual uncleanness are found in a number of religions, and in Jesus's day something resembling John's baptism was actually practised, along with circumcision, by Gentiles who became Jewish converts. So baptism would certainly not have been a new idea to Jesus. On the other hand the special emphasis John gave to it was obviously thought to be unusual; hence his title 'the Baptist'.

Not long after his baptism and at about the age of thirty, Jesus began to go about in Galilee preaching the message he had heard John announce: 'The kingdom of God is at hand.' What exactly did this message mean?

## A hope for the future

We have already seen that Judaism was a religion of history. It looked back on what God had done for Israel and declared that his deeds in former days proved his power. But it did not content itself with merely looking at the past. How could it, when the great promise of God's Covenant had yet to be fulfilled? On Mount Sinai after Moses had led the Israelites out of Egypt, God promised them that 'out of all peoples you shall become my special possession' (Ex. 19. 5), and this promise had been renewed time and again through the voices of God's prophets. Moreover, at such great moments in its history as the victorious kingship of David and the release from Babylonian captivity, Israel thought it had seen a very real demonstration that God was keeping this Covenant. Admittedly it had not been completely kept; God had not yet utterly fulfilled his promise. However, there was no question but that he would do so. All that was holding him back was the recalcitrance of Israel itself, its refusal to obey his voice and keep his Law. When true repentance was achieved by Israel and the nation at last managed to keep its own side of the Covenant, then would come the time of glory.

But Israel did repent, or at least many of its people did so, very often, and the time of glory did not come. While it was impossible to say that Israel had ever reached a state of complete sinlessness, there were nevertheless many holy men numbered among it. Moreover, however numerous Israel's sins, she had certainly suffered for them, suffered so much that forgiveness and the coming of the glorious time was surely due. And this was exactly what Second Isaiah said was going to happen; in captivity at Babylon he told the Israelites that God declared their nation's sins forgiven: 'she has fulfilled her term of bondage . . . she has received at the Lord's hand double measure for all her sin' (Is. 40.2). And now, he declared, she would at last be raised above all nations:

Now shall all who defy you be disappointed and put to shame; all who set themselves against you shall be as nothing; they shall vanish. You will look for your assailants but not find them; all who take up arms against you shall be as nothing, nothing at all. For I, the Lord your God, take you by the right hand . . . (Is. 41. 11–13)

Yet in the event this was not what happened. Certainly Israel was released from captivity, and the nation to some extent rebuilt itself;

but there was no triumph such as Second Isaiah had promised, and instead a succession of foreign powers interfered with the internal government of the country.

It is conceivable that in the face of this continual frustration of hope, Israel might have abandoned the worship of Yahweh. But it did not. Instead it began to believe that its triumph over other nations would come about not through the natural course of worldly events, but through some kind of supernatural intervention by the deity. The idea grew up, in fact, that Yahweh would fulfil his Covenant not simply by making Israel supreme above nations, but by bringing about the actual end of the world through some kind of cosmic catastrophe. Then would come a great Judgement, in which Yahweh himself would condemn sinners to destruction and would reward the righteous — by which was meant the righteous Israelites. These Israelites would then, at last, be made supreme above all nations. As God's 'saints' they would command the whole earth, or the new earth that had been fashioned. All other peoples would obey them.

This was the sort of thing that many people in Israel came to expect. Not that everyone agreed on the precise details of what would happen. The picture varied greatly from sect to sect. Meanwhile there were always those who refused to allow their hope of Israel's coming triumph to be made so exclusively supernatural, and who continued to expect that in the present world-order a new king David would arrive and lead Israel to victory. There were also a number of people in Israel who had no interest in such things at all, and who regarded them as new-fangled fanciful beliefs which were adulterating the worship of Yahweh and the keeping of his Law.

The ways of referring to the expected intervention by Yahweh varied, but more and more it came to be expressed in terms of Yahweh's 'kingdom'. Israel had always associated its God with kingship, and it was quite natural for it to describe the idea of him intervening directly in the physical world as his appearing in kingly might. Second Isaiah had this in mind when he wrote: 'Here is the Lord God coming in might, coming to rule with his right arm.' (Is. 40. 10)

God's kingly rule and the end of the world which many people believed would usher it in formed the subject of numerous 'apocalyptic' or visionary writings in the centuries before the birth of Jesus. Few of these were thought to have sufficient authority to be added to the canon of Jewish holy writ, but one that did pass the test was the book of Daniel, in the seventh chapter of which is a vision (couched in symbolical terms) of the events which it was believed would lead to the coming of God's 'kingdom'. Daniel sees four huge beasts ravaging the world (the four contemporary world powers), and, as he watches, these beasts are killed or subdued by 'one ancient in years', that is, God himself. Then he sees 'one like a son of man coming with the clouds of heaven', and this 'son of man' (a Jewish tautology for 'man') is given kingly power over the earth, so that all nations serve him. When Daniel asks for an interpretation of this vision he is told that the 'son of man' stands for the righteous Israelites, who will be given sovereignty over the earth.

It will be noted that there is one peculiar feature here, the 'son of man' whose coming 'with the clouds of heaven' ushers in God's kingly rule. We shall need to look at this very carefully later, for it is crucial to the question of Jesus's own role. But for the moment it is enough to note the general features of the Daniel passage: the warring nations which are subdued through the direct intervention of God, and the coming of a 'kingly power' through which God's people in Israel will rule over the whole earth. This was the sort of expectation which existed in Jesus's time. What we do not know is whether most people believed that the kingdom of God (or 'kingdom of heaven', a phrase often used as an alternative) would come soon. Probably this varied from person to person. No doubt many people thought that, while the kingdom of God was something that would certainly arrive one day, only a foolish man would predict that its coming was certainly very near. On the other hand there must have been fanatics, just as there are on street corners today, who made a loud parade of their belief that the long awaited event was about to happen — 'The end of the world is at hand!'

By this criterion, John the Baptist and Jesus were fanatics.

## What did Jesus believe?

Or were they? Not surprisingly, many Christian theologians are uncomfortable about the notion that Jesus went about preaching that God was shortly — very shortly — going to intervene dramatically in the history of the world, in a literally earth-shattering event that would usher in a new age. For of course this did not happen. Both in Jesus's lifetime and afterwards, the world went on very much as it had before. And the idea that Jesus was wrong disconcerts many Christians — though there are some who say that he spoke in the phraseology of his time, and was limited by the contemporary intellectual outlook, which does not (they say) in any way devalue his importance for modern believers.

It is of course perfectly possible to read the Gospels without realising that Jesus was preaching a message about the nearness of the end of the world. Though that phrase 'the kingdom of God' is central to his teaching, and though there are certainly (as we shall see) a number of passages where he specifically refers to the coming crisis, these things do not dominate the Gospels to the exclusion of all else. The reader's attention can easily be drawn away from them to the parables (though these are in fact largely about 'the kingdom'), to the healings and other miracles, and of course to the trial, death and resurrection of Jesus. Moreover the Church from the time of Paul onwards has realised the danger of over-emphasising the 'end of the world' element of Jesus's message, and has drawn attention away from it and focused much more on the importance of Jesus himself. Not until the nineteenth century, when scholars re-examined the Bible in a more candid way than was previously possible, did the realisation dawn that at the centre of Jesus's teaching was this alarming set of notions about a cosmic calamity and the physical coming of the kingdom. Albert Schweitzer's *Quest of the Historical Jesus* (1906) is in fact not just a survey of nineteeth-century writings about Jesus but also an eloquent, though rather exaggerated, plea that we should at last come face to face with the fact that the imminent coming of the kingdom really was what Jesus believed in — in other words that he based his life's work on a mistake.

Naturally the writings of Schweitzer and others who held the same view produced a reaction, one result of which was the work of the English biblical scholar C. H. Dodd. Writing in the 1930s, Dodd put forward the view that while Jesus was certainly talking about the kingdom of God he did not believe that it was about to come, but that *it had begun to arrive already*. Jesus felt (Dodd suggested) that, far from being a merely future event, the kingdom was being made visible on earth in his own work as a healer and preacher. Far from being mistaken, Jesus saw the truth about himself and his role.

Dodd had no great difficulty in making this interpretation seem plausible. He suggested that the words 'the kingdom of God is at hand' (found in the English translations of the Bible up to that time) were a wrong rendering of the original Greek, and that 'the kingdom of God is *upon* you', that is, already arriving, would be better. The New English Bible of which Dodd was a principal translator adopts this rendering (see Mk. 1. 15, Matt. 3. 2, 4. 17). As to the various predictions that Jesus is said to have made of cosmic events which would usher in the kingdom, Dodd regarded these as later interpolations by people who could not help thinking conventionally in terms of a strictly future coming of the kingdom, rather than the 'realised' kingdom which Jesus preached.

Dodd's views require a great deal of selection and re-interpretation of material in the Gospels, and, chiefly for this reason, they have not been widely accepted. So: are we left once again with a Jesus whose expectations were quite plainly of an imminent end of the world, a Jesus who in fact was wrong? And, if so, how crucial was his mistake? Did his message depend entirely on his belief that the end was near, and is it negated by our knowledge that he was mistaken? We shall begin to see the answer when we have examined in some detail the character of his teaching.

# 4

## The Law is not enough

The Gospels are so full of the sayings of Jesus that it ought to be possible to recover the precise nature of his teaching. In fact it is difficult to do so, because of a large number of inconsistencies and even contradictions.

To take one example of this, in Mark 10.9 Jesus forbids divorce unconditionally, with the words: 'What God has joined together, man must not separate.' On the other hand Matthew's version of this saying makes Jesus add a saving clause: 'if a man divorces his wife *for any cause other than unchastity*, and marries another, he commits adultery' (Matt. 19.9). Clearly this alters the whole position.

This kind of confusion often occurs when the attempt is made to recover the details of Jesus's teaching, and nobody can agree on a criterion for resolving it. Are we to accept as authentic only those sayings which reflect Jesus's Jewish background and his debt to the Law, or only those which show his individuality? Associated with this difficulty is the fact that the early Church simply did not take the trouble to record Jesus's teachings as often as one might expect. Paul, for instance, in all his Letters scarcely ever tells his readers what the earthly Jesus specifically taught about something.

In the face of this it is understandable that many historians have despaired of recovering Jesus's teaching. Indeed it is probably foolish to try to reconstruct it in precise detail. On the other hand we cannot really pretend that the problems of the text obscure the character of that teaching, a character which becomes all the more plain when one compares Jesus — as I shall now do — with other Jewish teachers of his time.

### Hillel and Shammai

If one is looking for religious teachers in first-century Judaism with whom to compare Jesus, two figures stand out. They were both

Scribes, that is, their life's work was a study of the Law and its interpretation; and they were both members of the religious group within Judaism known as the 'Pharisees', a name which probably means 'separated ones'. But despite these similarities between the two men, their teaching differed radically.

Hillel came from a poor background and had travelled from the Babylonian 'Dispersion' (Jews living outside Israel) to Jerusalem, where he worked as a labourer in order to keep himself while studying the Law. Eventually he became the leader of a scribal school, which, like the others of its kind, was characterised by its intense discussions on legal issues. Hillel's discussions and those of his disciples were usually carried on with a school of opposing views, led by the severely conservative rabbi Shammai. Hillel was a moral optimist with a faith in humanity and divine justice; he felt that the Law should be an instrument of life-giving rather than of deadly rectitude, and he gave judgement with 'the greater good' in mind, rather than basing his decisions on the niceties of legal interpretation. He was an example of the liberal and reforming element which has always been present within Judaism. In contrast, Shammai typified the Jew who observed the Law scrupulously, with much attention to detailed precepts. He was the kind of Pharisee who believed that God himself studied the Law daily. It was said of him that once at the Feast of Tabernacles, a time when all male Jews were required by the Law to sit within a tabernacle or tent to remind them of their tent-dwelling nomadic days, his daughter-in-law gave birth to a boy. Shammai broke open the roof over the bed where she and the child lay, and built a special booth, so that his grandson might keep the Law and sit (or at least lie) within the tabernacle.

It is revealing to set the teachings of these two men alongside those of Jesus. Like Jesus, they wrote no books, and the record of what they had said was for many years carried solely in the memories of their disciples. Not until the second century were their sayings written in the *Mishnah*.

The comparison is best made topic by topic, choosing crucial areas of Jewish life about which all three men had something to say.

## Marriage, adultery and divorce

The Jews regarded marriage as pre-eminently a means by which a man might produce heirs. Monogamy was not considered an overwhelmingly binding principle, and it was told of Abraham that because his wife was barren he had a child by a slave woman. Wives could be divorced simply on the ground of their infertility; no other reason was necessary for the dissolution of the marriage. Similarly the Scribes considered that the Law's injunction to 'Be fruitful and increase' (Gen. 1. 22) was a command to a married couple that they must have children. The only difference of opinion was over how many children must be born before abstention from further procreation could be allowed. Shammai said a man must have two sons before he and his wife abstained; the more liberal Hillel, who apparently had a higher regard for daughters, said that one son and one daughter was enough.

As to adultery, the written Law was perfectly clear in its command:

When a man is discovered lying with a married woman, they shall both die, the woman as well as the man who lay with her: you shall rid Israel of this wickedness. (Deut. 22. 22)

In fact by the time of Shammai, Hillel and Jesus the death penalty was no longer imposed on persons found guilty of adultery, but the slightest suspicion of unfaithfulness in a wife was enough to expose her to the public shame. Moreover it was taken for granted that in such circumstances the husband would divorce her. The only question was whether the wording of the Law allowed him to divorce her on any other grounds.

What the written Law actually allowed was that when a man had married a wife, if she 'does not win his favour because he finds something shameful in her', then he could write her a note of divorce (Deut. 24. 1). Shammai said that this referred solely to indecency, and that no other cause for divorce could be allowed. Hillel, however, was more liberal in his attitude to the Law — that is, he interpreted it more freely, though the net result was certainly not liberal in the ethical sense. He declared that the wording of the Law meant a husband could divorce his wife merely because small details of her conduct displeased him — even if she just 'spoiled a dish for him'. Moreover a third scribe, Rabbi Akiba, thought that the Law's words 'she does not win his favour' meant that the husband could divorce the wife simply because he had found another woman whom he preferred.

Against the background of these views, the ambiguity in the

Gospel records of Jesus's teaching on divorce becomes comparatively insignificant, and the character of his views stands out clearly. Here is Matthew's version of what he is reported to have said:

Some Pharisees came and tested him by asking, 'Is it lawful for a man to divorce his wife on any and every ground?' He asked in return, 'Have you never read that the Creator made them from the beginning male and female?'; and he added, 'For this reason a man shall leave his father and mother, and be made one with his wife; and the two shall become one flesh. It follows that they are no longer two individuals: they are one flesh. What God has joined together, man must not separate.' 'Why then', they objected, 'did Moses lay it down that a man might divorce his wife by note of dismissal?' He answered, 'It was because your minds were closed that Moses gave you permission to divorce your wives; but it was not like that when all began. I tell you, if a man divorces his wife for any cause other than unchastity, and marries another, he commits adultery.' (Matt. 19. 3–9)

Jesus's method of argument here resembles that of the Scribes. He takes a verse from the written Law as the basis of his judgement: 'male and female he created them' (Gen. 1. 27). To this he adds a second text: 'That is why a man leaves his father and mother and is united to his wife, and the two become one flesh' (Gen. 2. 24). This, he concludes, proves that God wishes marriage to be indissoluble. He even displays something of the subtlety — one could almost say wiliness — of rabbinical exegesis, for the first words of the second text ('That is why man . . .') do not in their original context refer to the first text at all, but to the creation of Eve out of Adam's rib. But then suddenly he departs radically from the Scribes' methods. When his questioners ask him why the conclusion he has reached is in contradiction to the written Law of Moses — they are thinking of the text in Deuteronomy that permits divorce — he does not reply by asserting his case through further scriptural exegesis, as a Scribe would have done, but by saying in effect: 'Moses had to compromise, because he knew you could not keep the ultimate commandment that God had given you.'

If this passage is an authentic record of Jesus's teaching, his approach was radical in the extreme. He is telling the Pharisees that the Law of Moses, which they (and indeed the whole of Judaism) regard as the rule by which everything is governed, is in fact no more than a compromise, the work of a man who knew that God demanded something more. Moreover Jesus reaches this conclusion by confronting the fact that texts from the Law can contradict one another — an extraordinarily daring thing to do, for it was assumed by Jews that the Law could not possibly contradict itself.

Nor is this Jesus's only departure, in this passage, from the Scribal approach. The questioners have set him a problem typical of those which exercised the rabbinical schools, the very question in fact over which Hillel and Shammai debated. They want to know how he interprets the controversial Deuteronomy clause permitting divorce. What precisely does he regard as the grounds on which divorce may be allowed? Jesus responds by not answering the question at all. He tells them that their whole approach is morally completely wrong, that this clause — and by implication others of its kind — is one of the compromises that the Law has regrettably had to make 'because your minds were closed'. Such compromises are not for one moment the *total* will of God. And in the face of all their negative legislation with its prohibitions and conditions and limitations he throws this clear doctrine of marriage: 'What God has joined together, man must not separate.'

After this, it is certainly surprising to find him admitting a saving clause 'for any cause other than unchastity' into his own doctrine. He may of course be simply reflecting current Jewish practice; in other words, divorce on the grounds of adultery may have been regarded as inevitable even by him. Or perhaps the implication is that when a married person commits adultery the marriage has already been destroyed. On the other hand it may be that Matthew, or the earlier oral Christian tradition, has inserted the words 'for any cause other than unchastity' into Jesus's pronouncement so as to make it a particular ruling for the Church, which had perhaps found it impossible to forbid divorce when adultery had taken place. We do not know what the truth is, and for this reason it is most unwise, here and elsewhere, to use Jesus's word as a new Law to govern precise details of behaviour. What matters is the manner in which he approaches the issue, a manner that was startlingly different from that of legalistic Judaism.

## Poverty and wealth

In Mark's Gospel, Jesus is recorded as saying to a rich man: 'sell everything you have, and give to the poor' (Mk. 10. 21). Commentators have pointed out that if this is taken as a literal commandment for everyone it is impractical and unrealistic. Even monastic communities which embrace poverty retain some kind of financial resources with which to make their way of life possible, while for the Christian living in the world and earning his keep this injunction, if taken literally, is clearly absurd. Generosity to the poor may be of paramount importance, but how can people sell *all* that they have? This, at any rate, is how some have responded to these words. But if we want to see why Jesus said them (or is reported to have said them) we need only look at the teachings of his contemporaries to discover what prompted him.

Judaism believed that poverty was pleasing to God, and it included among its number at least one sect, the Essenes, whose members held all property communally and lived somewhat in the manner of poor people. On the other hand riches were regarded as the reward of righteousness. Many Jews led a life of some affluence, especially as farmers, vineyard owners, and cultivators of olive trees, the latter particularly in Galilee where olive oil was a major export. To such as these the Law gave a general injunction:

The poor will always be with you in the land, and for that reason I [Moses] command you to be open-handed with your countrymen, both poor and distressed . . . (Deut. 15. 11)

But what did this mean in specific terms? Over the generations the Scribes established detailed rules for assisting those in need; for example:

A poor man that is journeying from place to place should be given not less than one loaf . . . If he spends the night he should be given what is needful to support him for the night. If he stays over the Sabbath he should be given enough food for three meals. If a man has food enough for two meals he may not take anything from the Paupers' Dish, and if enough for fourteen meals he may not take anything from the Poor-Fund.

Provision was made against starvation, but care was also taken that the poor should not be given more than they needed.

Alongside a system for the relief of poverty in general, Judaism also had strict rules about *peah* or 'gleanings'. This meant that a certain part of crops and of the produce of vineyards and olive groves was set aside for the poor to help themselves. It was definitely implied both in written Law and the oral tradition that when the harvest was abundant or poverty was especially severe, *peah* should be given generously. On the other hand the Scribes also said that 'it should not be less than one sixtieth part' of the harvest, and the nature of the disputes which arose over *peah* suggests that the average farmer was not over-keen to exceed this stipulated minimum, which of course only made a very small demand on him. When plots of grain were sown between olive trees, was it necessary (asked the Scribes) to grant *peah* from each plot individually or just from one to serve for all? Shammai's school said that the sixtieth portion must be taken from each of the plots, a very finicky procedure for the farmer, though arguably the fairest way. Hillel's pupils thought it was enough to calculate what was due on all the plots together, and then to take this amount out of one plot, which would be much easier. This sort of dispute characterised the Jewish poor laws and the people who interpreted them. Against this background, Jesus's attitude to the question of poverty and wealth is a shock:

As he was starting out on a journey, a stranger ran up, and, kneeling before him, asked, 'Good Master, what must I do to win eternal life?' Jesus said to him, 'Why do you call me good? No one is good except God alone. You know the commandments: "Do not murder; do not commit adultery; do not steal; do not give false evidence; do not defraud; honour your father and mother." ' 'But, Master,' he replied, 'I have kept all these since I was a boy.' Jesus looked straight at him; his heart warmed to him, and he said, 'One thing you lack: go, sell everything you have, and give to the poor, and you will have riches in heaven; and come, follow me.' At these words his face fell and he went away with a heavy heart; for he was a man of great wealth. (Mk. 10. 17–22, cf. Matt. 19. 16–22. Lk. 18. 18–23)

To the question 'what must I do to win eternal life?' Jesus first gives the conventional Jewish answer, 'You must keep the Law'; for the commandments he quotes are those six of the Ten Commandments which deal with ethics. But his questioner is not satisfied. He has kept the Law, yet finds that something is still lacking. In answer to this, Jesus says in effect: 'Yes, you are right. God *does* command you to do more than keep the Law which you have known from childhood. You, a rich man, should sell everything that you have and give the money to the poor.'

Compared to the attitude taken by the Scribes, this is remarkable. But we have to ask: is it meant to be a general rule to be kept by all, or is it merely an answer to this particular wealthy man? We really cannot be certain. On the one hand Jesus is not reported to have enjoined compulsory poverty on all his followers. On the other hand the general tone of his ministry seems to have been one of compassion for the poor and outcast rather than for the rich,

and indeed Mark's narrative continues (after this episode) with
Jesus telling his disciples, 'It is easier for a camel to pass through
the eye of a needle than for a rich man to enter the kingdom of God'
(Mk 10. 25) — a saying which the medieval Church found so hard
to accept that it invented a totally fictitious gate at Jerusalem called
the Needle's Eye, so as to soften the impact of Jesus's words.

What we can say for certain is first that Jesus tells the man *to
keep the Law*—we must not miss this—and then he says that
keeping the Law *is not enough*.

## The seventh day

The Law ordered the Jews to keep one day in every seven as a holy
Sabbath, on which no work was to be done. By the time of Jesus
the observance of this Sabbath was governed by minutely detailed
rules, developed by the oral tradition of the Law, which delineated
precisely what constituted work and what did not. For example:

The School of Shammai say: Ink, dyestuffs, or vetches may not be soaked
[on the day before the Sabbath] unless there is time for them to be wholly
soaked the same day. And the School of Hillel permit it. The School of
Shammai say: Bundles of flax may not be put in an oven unless there
is time for them to steam off the same day. And the School of Hillel permit
it.

And here is a rule, one of many, about which there was no dispute,
which delineates precisely what kind of 'work' profaned the
Sabbath:

If a poor man stood outside and the householder inside, and the poor man
stretched his hand inside and put aught into the householder's hand, or
took anything from it and brought it out, the poor man is culpable and the
householder is not culpable. If the householder stretched his hand outside
and put anything into the poor man's hand, or took anything from it and
brought it in, the householder is culpable and the poor man is not culpable.
But if the poor man stretched his hand inside and the householder took
anything from it, or put anything into it and the poor man brought it out,
neither is culpable; and if the householder stretched his hand outside and
the poor man took anything from it, or put anything into it and the
householder brought it in, neither is culpable.

There are more than a hundred such clauses in the *Mishnah*, and
they show that the Sabbath was regarded as a self-justifying
institution, something to be observed for its own sake, without

asking in what way God's will was being served by doing so. The Law ordained that the Sabbath should be observed, and that was enough. There was to be no questioning, no consideration of priorities.

We need to fix this firmly in our minds before we turn to the question of Jesus's attitude to the Sabbath, because the evidence appears at first sight to be contradictory. On some occasions he appears to be taking the prohibition of work on the Sabbath seriously. He does not heal a large crowd of sick people until 'after sunset' on the Sabbath, that is, the hour at which the prohibition was lifted (Mk 1. 32). Moreover he himself is recorded as attending the synagogue and preaching on the Sabbath (Mk. 1. 21; cf Lk. 4. 16 ff). Yet at other times he seems to be attacking the whole Sabbath concept. Mark and the other Synoptics record how he heals a man with a withered hand in the synagogue on the Sabbath (Mk. 3. 1–6, Matt. 12. 9–14, Lk. 6. 6–11). The Scribes and other members of the Pharisaic party regard this as 'work' and thus as forbidden on the Sabbath. In Mark's version, Jesus justifies his actions by asking them rhetorically: 'Is it permitted to do good or to do evil on the Sabbath, to save life or to kill?' At first sight this may seem a slightly obtuse approach to the issue, and it may have puzzled Matthew, for his Gospel records Jesus as saying something rather different:

Suppose you had one sheep, which fell into a ditch on the Sabbath; is there one of you who would not catch hold of it and lift it out? And surely a man is worth far more than a sheep! It is therefore permitted to do good on the Sabbath. (Matt. 12. 11–12)

There is a similar confusion in the story of Jesus and his disciples plucking ears of corn on the Sabbath, which the Pharisees regarded as 'reaping' and therefore forbidden:

One Sabbath he was going through the cornfields; and his disciples, as they went, began to pluck ears of corn. The Pharisees said to him, 'Look, why are they doing what is forbidden on the Sabbath?' He answered, 'Have you never read what David did when he and his men were hungry and had nothing to eat? He went into the House of God, in the time of Abiathar the High Priest, and ate the sacred bread, though no one but a priest is allowed to eat it, and even gave it to his men.'

He also said to them, 'The Sabbath was made for the sake of man and not man for the Sabbath: therefore the Son of Man is sovereign even over the Sabbath.' (Mk. 2. 23–38; cf. Lk. 6. 1–5)

We should note that Jesus justifies his actions first by an allusion
to scripture (the episode of David and his men in the 'House of
God'), which was the Scribal method; then by the general precept
('The Sabbath was made for the sake of man . . .'); and finally by
a statement deduced from this precept, that 'the Son of Man'
(himself) had power even over the Sabbath. His response to the
Scribes is therefore a blend of their own method, of a precept made
on his own authority, and of a statement about the nature of that
authority.

This is Mark's version of the incident, and Matthew apparently
regards it as inadequate, for (unlike Luke, who repeats it virtually
verbatim) his Gospel adds another Scribal-style justification to
Jesus's words:

Or have you not read in the Law that on the Sabbath the priests in the
temple break the Sabbath and it is not held against them? I tell you, there
is something greater than the temple here. If you had known what the text
means, 'I require mercy, not sacrifice', you would not have condemned the
innocent. For the Son of Man is sovereign over the Sabbath. (Matt. 12.
5–8)

The precept about the Sabbath being made for man is entirely
absent here — perhaps because Matthew has found it too shocking
— and the whole issue is becoming cluttered with yet more
allusions to scripture. Paraphrased, Matthew's version reads: 'The
Law says that priests in the temple must work on the Sabbath (to
offer sacrifices and carry out their duties) and nobody condemns
them for doing it. And here, in myself, is something greater than
the temple, so if the temple can override the Sabbath law, so can
I even more.' Jesus then quotes a text from Hosea (6.6) whose
meaning here appears to be: 'It is better to be humane about such
things than to stick to the letter of the Law.' Finally Matthew picks
up Mark's dictum about the Son of Man being lord over the
Sabbath.

This is all very confused and confusing, and not surprisingly
many commentators doubt whether Jesus is really being very
radical. He is after all using all the paraphernalia of rabbinical
Judaism to justify his action. Can he be offering any serious
criticism of the Law?

Quite possibly he is not. He may simply be proving by rabbinical
exegesis that the Law does permit certain exceptions to the Sabbath

rule, though precisely what exceptions is not clear. Or he may be declaring that as Son of Man he is 'sovereign over the Sabbath'. Many commentators have decided that this is so, and one theologian even suggests that the precept should read: 'The Sabbath was made for the Son of Man.' If this latter interpretation is accepted then we are left with a Jesus whose prime concern is to prove that he himself is too great a figure to need to keep the Sabbath rule. Now, this may be exactly what he said. (This is not the place to discuss the vital question of whether he thought he was Messiah or Son of Man; the next chapter will tackle that issue.) If on the other hand we are prepared to give some weight to the precept 'The Sabbath was made for the sake of man . . .' Jesus certainly seems to be being radical towards the Law. And if we then turn back to the earlier incident of his healing the man in the synagogue, we seem to find confirmation that in some circumstances at least Jesus is prepared to set the Sabbath rule on one side.

But in what circumstances? It is no good pretending that these two incidents — the healing of the man and the plucking of the ears of corn — add up to anything like a rule of behaviour. Certainly in both cases some element of human discomfort is involved: the man suffers from his withered hand, the disciples are presumably hungry. But to a modern judgement there seems to be far more moral urgency in the former case than in the latter, and we are left totally puzzled and unable to understand what Jesus is aiming to teach about Sabbath observance.

Of course, modern judgement should not be our criterion. It may be that to the first-century Palestinian mind the two cases could be equated morally. It is also possible that the second incident — the plucking of the ears of corn — had no great significance to Jesus himself, and has been recorded simply because it happened to be the occasion of a dispute with his opponents. We should perhaps be wary of putting too much weight on it.

What, then, can we conclude? Certainly that Jesus was known to have broken the Sabbath law on some occasions, and probably that he did so in order to alleviate suffering. Did he have any consistent attitude to the Sabbath? Very possibly not. We must not let too much hang on the precept that the Sabbath was made for man, partly because it was apparently not original to Jesus — Rabbi Simeon ben Menasya is recorded to have said 'The Sabbath

is delivered unto you, and you are not delivered to the Sabbath' —
and partly because to the modern mind it may suggest the sort of
'humanistic' attitude that was quite foreign to the Jewish mind. We,
with our modern moral outlook, may imagine that Jesus was
saying: 'The Sabbath was made for man to use as he thinks fit, and
man was not made to be the slave of the Sabbath.' No Jew could
have said this. The Sabbath had been ordained by God, and to
keep the Sabbath was to work his will. There was never any
question of *man* being served, either by the keeping of the Sabbath
or by an observance of any other precept. The only question which
a Jew could legitimately ask was: could it be that sometimes God's
will might be obeyed *more fully*, more completely, by setting the
Sabbath rule on one side and fulfilling some other command?
Might there, in other words, be certain occasions when keeping the
established Law was *not enough*?

This, we can now see, is what Jesus is teaching. The healing of
the man with the withered arm exemplifies precisely this. The Law
may forbid all work on the Sabbath, but that is not the sum of
God's will. If Jesus, a healer, is faced with a man who requires his
ministrations, then he will heal him then and there, because God
regards this as more important than the keeping of the Sabbath.
Not to heal the man would be as wrong as to leave a sheep in a
ditch just because it was the Sabbath — something (it seems) that
no farmer, however strict a Jew, would do. When Jesus says 'Is it
permitted to do good or to do evil on the Sabbath?' he means: 'You
can see that God wills me to heal this man. To ignore God's will
would be evil.'

This is not to say that Jesus formulates a rule of Sabbath
behaviour, or that his attitude to the Sabbath rule is necessarily
consistent. Indeed, it *cannot* be consistent. The whole point of his
teaching on this issue (and others) is that fixed rules do not work.
By simply obeying the Law you cannot be certain that you are
carrying out God's commands to the full. Observing the Law may
be good, but it is not enough. The issue must be judged and God's
will must be listened to in each particular case.

## What is uncleanness?

We now come to a passage which has puzzled many commentators.
This is the episode where Jesus comments on the Pharisees'
observance of the laws of ritual purity.

The incident as narrated by Mark (7. 1–23) runs as follows. The Pharisees remark that Jesus's disciples often eat with unwashed hands, and do not observe the rules about purifying dishes and cups in the manner prescribed by the oral tradition of the Law. They ask Jesus why this is so, and he replies that these rules of purification are merely 'the precepts of men' and not the commandments of God. From this he goes on to condemn a way in which the oral tradition has actually superseded the written Law. He says that there are men (presumably Pharisees) who, rather than support their ageing parents, give their money to the service of the temple. This he says is disobedience to the commandment to 'honour your father and your mother'. Then — and this may well be on another occasion — he declares that the elaborate food laws of Judaism which prescribe what may and may not be eaten are based on a misapprehension:

. . . nothing that goes into a man from outside can defile him; no, it is the things that come out of him that defile a man . . . For from inside, out of a man's heart, come evil thoughts, acts of fornication, of theft, murder, adultery, ruthless greed, and malice; fraud, indecency, envy, slander, arrogance, and folly; these evil things all come from inside, and they defile the man.

Mark comments: 'Thus he declared all foods clean.'

Did he? If so, he was, as many commentators have observed, nullifying not just the oral tradition but even the written Law itself, which is very specific about what may be eaten and what may not. There is thus thought to be a contradiction between this and Jesus's remarks earlier in the same passage, where he condemns the Pharisees for *ignoring* the written Law by having too high a regard for the oral tradition. All this has led commentators to suppose that Jesus's criticisms of Judaism were occasional and specific rather than general.

But this is surely missing the point. It is not that Jesus is discussing the relative importance of the written Law and the oral tradition. What he is talking about is — once again — the necessity for realising that the mere keeping of the Law is not enough. People are, he says, failing to observe God's real will. For example they neglect the responsibility of looking after parents in order to be sanctimonious and give their money to the temple. Then again, men scrupulously observe food laws and make sure that nothing 'unclean' goes into their mouths, while all sorts of wicked things come *out of* their mouths. Now it so happens that Jesus's remarks do attack first of all the oral tradition and then the written Law itself, but this is not the point. What he is talking about is men's habit of observing certain rules while ignoring the real demands of God's will. God's Law requires the giving of money to the temple, but God does not wish this to be done at the expense of care for parents. Similarly the food laws ordain what food God wishes his people to eat, but the scrupulous observance of these laws does not exempt men from keeping themselves 'clean' in another sense.

Whether by saying this Jesus really did mean to nullify the food law is not clear. If his disciples really did eat with unwashed hands and did ignore the rules about purifying cups and dishes, and if he himself really did say 'Nothing that goes into a man from outside can defile him', then we might suppose that he did regard this part of the oral tradition as of no value. But we cannot say for certain. What we do know is that here, as in other areas of Jewish life, he believed it to be vitally important that men should be aware that God's will could not be encompassed by the Law alone, either in its written or in its oral form. It was wrong to observe the Law scrupulously while shutting your eyes to God's greater demands.

## 'Love your enemies'

The Law enjoined the Jew to love members of his own race:

You shall not nurse hatred against your brother . . . You shall not seek revenge, or cherish anger towards your kinsfolk; you shall love your neighbour as a man like yourself. (Lev. 19. 17–18)

On the other hand the 'enemies' of the Jews lay everywhere. There were not only those foreign powers who influenced Israel's fortunes for the worse, but also the Palestinian peoples, most notably the Samaritans, who were not in sympathy with Israelite religion. And Judaism did not lightly forget old grudges:

No Ammonite or Moabite, even down to the tenth generation, shall become a member of the assembly of the Lord . . . because they did not meet you with food and water on your way out of Egypt . . . You shall never seek their welfare or their good all your life long. (Deut. 23. 3–4, 6)

In the face of this cautious hostility to outsiders, Jesus, in the Sermon on the Mount in Matthew's Gospel, is reported to have swept away all distinctions:

You have learned that they were told, 'Love your neighbour, hate your enemy.' But what I tell you is this: Love your enemies and pray for your persecutors . . . (Matt. 5. 43–4; cf. Lk. 6. 27–8, 32–6)

The Sermon on the Mount appears to be a collection of sayings of varying authenticity, and we cannot be certain that anything in it was said in precisely that form by Jesus. Commentators have also objected to this particular passage on the grounds that neither the written Law nor the rabbis told the Jews to hate their enemies. But even if this particular saying is a mispresentation of traditional Jewish teaching, there can be no doubt that the *implication* of hating one's enemies was to be found in the Law; and it is entirely in keeping with Jesus's behaviour, as we have observed it so far, that he should tell his hearers that simply to obey the Law's command of loving one's kinsfolk is *not enough*: love must be carried further, until even enemies are embraced by it.

In the same context Jesus tells his hearers that the Law's dictum on revenge is similarly inadequate:

You have learned that they were told, 'Eye for eye, tooth for tooth.' But what I tell you is this: Do not set yourself against the man who wrongs you. If someone slaps you on the right cheek, turn and offer him your left. (Matt. 5. 38–9; cf. Lk. 6. 29–30)

Again the commentators point out that the 'revenge' clause in the Law is not so much *demanding* eye for eye and tooth for tooth as *limiting* revenge to this precise redress of the injury, rather than permitting unbridled vengeance. Moreover by the time of Jesus this direct redress had been superseded by a system of payments for injury. But Jesus's dictum is not based on a misapprehension of the Law. He is not, indeed, necessarily even attacking the principle of compensation. What he is saying is that God's will cannot be circumscribed by the compensation rule. God's commands are far greater than this rule suggests. God wishes that men should give all that is demanded of them and still more, however unjust the demand. By the side of this, the mere observation of the Law is inadequate.

Once again, the temptation to the modern mind is to look for some general rule, some moral principle which Jesus is formulating. Indeed it might appear at first sight that one is being offered here. The command to 'love your enemies' and to turn the other cheek has been used to justify pacifism. We should not assume, however, that Jesus was saying that warfare is sinful. He is not offering a rule for general behaviour; he is not (apparently) even thinking of a particular case. What he is doing, once again, is emphasising that God demands more than just the observance of the Law.

## The thought is enough

The Jewish Law legislated for men's actions but not for their thoughts. Two instances in the Sermon on the Mount suggest that Jesus considered this to be inadequate.

After quoting the commandment 'Do not commit murder', he continues:

Anyone who nurses anger against his brother must be brought to judgement . . . If he sneers at him he will have to answer for it in the fires of hell. (Matt. 5. 22)

The mere conceiving of angry thoughts is in God's eyes the equivalent to an act of murder. There is hyperbole here, for Jesus can scarcely mean that in daily life feelings of anger should be punished as if they were murder; this is perhaps why he invokes 'the fires of hell' as an indication of the divine and supernatural punishment, in contrast to the penalties levied by the courts on actual murder. (Whether Jesus envisaged a literal hell-fire for sinners cannot be determined; the words in the original text — 'the gehenna of fire' — refer to the ravine of Gehenna on the outskirts of Jerusalem where the city's offal was burnt, and which was popularly used in Judaism as a symbol of future punishment.) But the moral lesson is clear. In God's eyes it is not enough merely to obey the Law and abstain from the act of murder. For what is murder but the ultimate expression of anger? And in forbidding murder in the Law, God means to forbid not just this ultimate expression but the whole condition of anger, in the mind as well as in outward actions.

Similarly Jesus declares in the Sermon that it is not only the act of adultery, forbidden by the Law, which merits punishment, but the very thinking of lustful thoughts:

If a man looks on a woman with a lustful eye, he has already committed adultery with her in her heart. (Matt. 5. 28)

It would be wrong to suppose that, during all the centuries of Judaism that preceded the teaching of Jesus, nobody had supposed

that God demanded inner virtue as well as outward good
behaviour. We need look no further than the book of Job in the Old
Testament to see that an inner state of mind, such as Job's patience
in the face of adversity, was considered to be highly valued by
God. It would also be wrong to assume that the antitheses (in the
passages on murder—anger and adultery—lust) between the old Law
and the teaching of Jesus necessarily represent Jesus's own words.
As we have already seen, the Sermon itself is of doubtful authenticity. But there is no doubt that such commands as Jesus is
represented as giving here — commands to men to guard their inner
thoughts as well as their outward behaviour — are part of his
message. The Law, vitally important as it is, does not embrace the
whole of God's demands on men. Those demands are universal,
total; God demands that the inner man shall obey as well as the
outer.

## The golden rule

According to one estimate, the rabbinical oral tradition of exegesis
of the written Law produced 248 commandments and 365
prohibitions. Even the rabbis were aware that some kind of
abbreviation was necessary. It was said that a Gentile once asked
the conservative Shammai how many laws the Jews had, and he
replied: 'Two: the oral and the written Law.' Hillel, who as usual
was more ready to be free with tradition, said there was only one:
'Do not do to another person what is unwelcome to you: this is the
entire Law, and the rest is interpretation.'

It is in the context of this that we should read Jesus's remark near
the end of the Sermon on the Mount:

Always treat others as you would like them to treat you: that is the Law
and the Prophets. (Matt. 7. 12; cf. Lk. 6. 31)

Hillel and he have said almost the same thing. Almost, but not
quite. Hillel's precept is negative, Jesus's is positive: Hillel's is a
restriction on behaviour, Jesus's an injunction to action.

It is easy for a modern reader to be misled by this 'golden rule'
into supposing that Jesus is offering a broad humanistic ethic.
Certainly if the golden rule is detached from its context it had this
appearance. But Jesus and his fellow Jews were not humanists.
They served not man but God, and they did this by obeying the
commandments of the Law and the words of the prophets.

Undoubtedly many of them did so without questioning *why* any particular commandment should be obeyed; their obedience was blind — and was therefore mechanical, for their intellect was not involved in it. It is a characteristic of Jesus's teaching that he praises not this blind obedience, but the kind of *reasoning* obedience which considers *why* God has given some particular commandment to men. And this is the real meaning of the golden rule. It is a reminder that God's demands on men are not mysterious and impenetrable at all: they will be found to be based on the very simplest of rules, the rule that you should behave towards someone as you would wish to treat yourself. The golden rule is not meant to replace all other rules. It is meant to show men how they can obey God's will whether the Law gives them a specific commandment or not. It is a guiding rule for conduct in those areas — and there are many — where the Law is inadequate, and for cases where different parts of the Law conflict.

## Jew, not philosopher

After we have studied those teachings of Jesus which could be called liberal in attitude, it may come as something of a shock to read these words, which Matthew ascribes to him in the Sermon:

I tell you this: so long as heaven and earth endure, not a letter, not a stroke, will disappear from the Law . . . If any man therefore sets aside even the least of the Law's demands, and teaches others to do the same, he will have the lowest place in the kingdom of Heaven. (Matt. 5. 18–19)

Perhaps Jesus did not express it as strongly as this. Matthew may here be reacting against a streak of 'antinomianism' or moral lawlessness in some parts of the early Christian Church. But maybe Jesus did say just this, and it would not contradict the character of his teaching if he did. For, as should by now be evident, he was not trying to offer new precepts which would supersede the Law. He was encouraging his hearers to give a new interpretation to the word 'Law', to realise that God demands *more* of men than the specific requirements set down in the written Law of Moses and elaborated by the rabbis in the oral tradition. And in doing this he did not negate the value of the Law; rather, he showed that beyond the Law there was (so to speak) a higher Law.

What was that higher Law, and how had Jesus come to be aware of it? The answer may seem at first sight banal and misleading; for the truth is that, time after time, the higher Law to which Jesus appeals is *men's consciences*. As the modern theologian H. J. Cadbury puts it, after asking how Jesus arrived at his moral judgements:

Like any other words the words of Jesus find their ultimate sanctions in our own consciences . . . At bottom [there is] a kind of self-validating character in the teachings themselves.

This may seem banal because, after our long search for the source of Jesus's moral judgements, it is a distinct anti-climax to be told that he merely used his conscience, like any modern liberal. And it is misleading because 'conscience' is not a Jewish term. We should not use it to imply that Jesus gave any value to *human* moral judgement. As a Jew, he must have believed that the only moral judge — the only judge of anything — was God. If he thought in terms of anything like a 'conscience', he would presumably have regarded it as the will of God expressing itself clearly in human reason. God was the only judge; but it was wrong to regard the Law as the only mediator of his judgement. His voice spoke clearly in the human mind, for all to hear.

Was this, then, Jesus's distinctive contribution as a teacher? So it will seem to us, though across the gap of centuries we cannot be certain. We might be more definite if we had more contemporary records to show how Jesus compared with other teachers of his time. Certainly the *Mishnah* shows a profound difference of approach between him and the other rabbis, both conservative and liberal; but the *Mishnah*, it must be admitted, is of a later date and only represents one aspect of Judaism, the concern to codify. It is quite possible that there were other religious teachers in the first century whose call to the conscience was much the same as Jesus's. Nor should we be certain that, even if Jesus was distinctive in this respect, it would be this particular feature of his teaching that struck the minds of his hearers as remarkable. As H. J. Cadbury puts it, 'At this distance what seems to us distinctive in Jesus may have been to his hearers commonplace and vice versa.' Cadbury also emphasises that newness, originality — the qualities which the historian is tempted to look for in Jesus — may not have characterised him at all. A great teacher, he suggests, does not so much state things as find remarkable ways of expressing old truths. Cadbury concludes (and we will do well to echo him):

Perhaps more nearly accurate than the words novel, original, unique, for describing any differentia of Jesus, would be such adjectives as radical, intense, extreme.

So far we have concentrated on what is distinctive about Jesus when he is compared with the rest of Judaism. Does his teaching appear to be so remarkable when it is set against, say, the teachings of Plato and Aristotle? What kind of status should we give to Jesus as a philosopher?

The answer must be that such a comparison is meaningless. Greek philosophy thought in terms of man and his ideals. Of what sort were those ideals, and how should man attain them? Were they, as Plato believed, transcendental Forms towards which the educated man could journey, or was 'good', as Aristotle believed, something to be achieved by moderation and conformity with the laws of nature? It is not just that their conclusions were very different from those of Jesus — though indeed both Plato's paternalistic and totalitarian view of the ideal society and Aristotle's self-sufficient and utterly superior ideal man are as different as they could be from anything that Jesus taught. One fundamental difference is that Plato and Aristotle operated with elaborate philosophical models of man and the world, from which they deduced ethical conclusions. Jesus had no such sophisticated system; his method, if it can be described at all, could be called 'inspirational'. Moreover he did not talk of 'ideals' and 'ethics'. He was concerned with man's *obedience* to God, something which the Greek mind could not imagine; for, as Rudolf Bultmann expresses it, the Greek thinker 'recognizes no authority to which there could be any question of obedience; he knows only the law of the perfecting of his own nature by his achievement'. And — as a final point of comparison — we might note that while the Greek thinkers attempted to produce balanced and consistent ethics, in the manner of a modern moralist, this approach seems to have been foreign to Jesus. There is no concern with consistency in his teaching; he was not preoccupied with the construction of a *system*.

But this radical difference between the approach taken by Jesus and the approach of other Western traditions does not mean that nothing can be extracted from Jesus's teaching that can be understood in terms of non-Jewish moral thought, and be seen as original in such an alien context. The idea that it is the spirit in which someone acts that matters rather than the mere conformity of his action to a set of rules, and the belief that it is the inner thought rather than the outward deed that counts in human affairs, are both central in modern European thought; and it is certainly possible that they can be traced back, at least in part, to the influence of Jesus. In so far as these principles are implicit in what Jesus had to say, it is of course true that, as a Jew, he saw their contribution as being towards greater obedience to God; whereas we may see them rather as vital components of any adequate human ethic. This, though, does not rule out their having had any influence outside the world of Judaistic presuppositions.

Yet Jesus himself, as we have seen, was no philosopher; his mind was characteristically Jewish. Even those of his followers who broke away from Judaism and became Christians did not claim that he had formulated an independent system of ethics. Certainly Paul believed that Jesus had made it no longer necessary for his followers to observe every detail of the Law; in a famous phrase he wrote: 'Christ ends the Law and brings righteousness for everyone who has faith' (Rom. 10. 4). But Paul believed that Jesus had done this not by teaching new things, not indeed by his teaching at all, but by dying on the Cross and rising again. Certainly the early Christian Church came, step by step, to abandon the observation of the Law, concurring with Paul when he said that it had been no more than 'a temporary measure' imposed by God until the coming of Christ (Gal. 3. 19). But this was Paul's and the early Church's view, not Jesus's.

Almost in passing, we have stumbled up against a vital fact. Paul believes that Jesus 'ended' the Law *not because of what he taught but because he died on the Cross*. In other words, from the earliest period of the Christian Church Jesus was regarded as something more than just a teacher. This ought to be apparent simply from the difficulty of identifying what was really characteristic about Jesus's teaching. It would appear from the muddled and often contradictory way in which the early Church preserved that teaching that they did not consider it to be the most remarkable thing about him. Possibly they did not regard it as remarkable at all. What seemed to them to be remarkable was that Jesus was Messiah, Son of Man, Son of God. This was what they believed, and what provided the basis of their allegiance.

But what were Jesus's own ideas about himself? Who did *he* think he was?

# 5

# Who did he think he was?

The Christian Church believed, and on the whole still believes, that the answer to this question is perfectly simple. According to the usual Christian view, Jesus believed, or rather knew, that he was the Messiah — though in rather a special sense, better expressed as 'Son of Man'. His followers gradually realised this, and only the stupidity and downright wickedness of other men prevented them from realising it too during his lifetime.

What is likely to be the truth of this view? And indeed what do these terms, 'Messiah' and 'Son of Man', really mean?

## The national Messiah

In chapter 3 we saw how Israel's national ambitions were pushed further and further into the future by continual defeat and failure, so that eventually the simple hope of national triumph was developed into the expectation of an apocalyptic end to the world, after which Israel would at last be made supreme. But not all Jews accepted this. Many clung to the simpler, less supernatural view, and held that a new king David would rise up in their midst, would subdue Israel's enemies and set up his rule in Jerusalem without any end to the present world-order. They constantly looked for the coming of this new David, and frequently thought they had found him. For example, after the return from exile in Babylon in the sixth century B.C. there were many who believed that Zerubbabel the new governor of Jerusalem might be the Messiah; see Zechariah 4. 7: 'How does a mountain, the greatest mountain, compare with Zerubbabel? It is no higher than a plain.' But the hope that Zerubbabel would become a new David came to nothing. Similarly during the second century B.C. the Jewish leader who brought temporary peace with the Syrians, Simon Maccabeus, was regarded by some as having near-Messianic status.

Did Jesus's contemporaries identify him with this national

Messiah? Mark would have us believe so. He records that after
Jesus has performed many miracles which clearly demonstrate his
true nature, he asks the disciples who they think he is, and Peter
answers: 'You are the Messiah' (Mk. 8. 29). Jesus responds by
neither admitting nor denying it, but he gives them orders not to
tell anyone about it. Some time later, when they reach Jerusalem,
Jesus is hailed by the crowd with the words: 'Blessing on him who
comes in the name of the Lord! Blessing on the coming kingdom of
our father David!' (Mk. 11. 9–10; cf. Matt. 21. 9, Lk. 19. 38).
During the trial of Jesus, the High Priest asks him: 'Are you the
Messiah, the Son of the Blessed One?' and Jesus replies, in Mark's
version, 'I am' (Mk. 14. 61–2). And at Jesus's crucifixion the
accusation against him, fixed over his cross, is summed up in the
words: 'The king of the Jews' (Mk. 15. 26; cf. Matt. 27. 37, Lk. 23.
38). Moreover the passers-by taunt him with the words 'Let the
Messiah, the king of Israel, come down now from the cross. If we
see that, we shall believe' (Mk. 15. 32; cf. Matt. 27. 42, Lk. 23. 37).

Could Jesus really have been making political claims? Could he
have regarded himself as the 'king of the Jews' who had come to
set Israel free from Roman rule? The idea is certainly not absurd,
for no one who stirred up the populace in first-century Palestine
could preach a religion which was not felt to be profoundly
associated with national ambitions. The coming of the kingdom of
God, so closely associated with Jesus's message, would certainly be
taken to mean the triumph of Israel. We should not be surprised
that some people regarded him as making a political as well as a
religious challenge to the existing order. Moreover this is all the
more likely to have happened if some of his followers were (as the
Gospels say they were) members of the anti-Roman political group
which came to be known as the Zealots; see Mark 3. 18 (cf. Matt.
10. 4, Lk. 6. 15), which names one of the disciples as 'Simon of the
Zealot party'. But that Jesus himself had any distinctly political
ambitions remains in the realm of improbability. The character of
his teaching as transmitted by the Church shows nothing of such
ambitions, and the Gospels are positive that this was not his own
view of himself. They agree (or at least the Synoptics do, for John
takes a more sophisticated theological view) that he explicitly
renounced political ambitions and instead declared his role to be
one of suffering, describing himself as 'Son of Man'.

## The Son of Man

The words 'Son of Man' are perhaps the most contentious in the Gospels. Theologians cannot agree precisely what meaning Jesus meant to convey by using them — or indeed whether he intended them to have any special significance at all.

The actual words 'son of man' are a typical Hebrew tautology for 'man', and they were certainly sometimes used to mean merely this. A speaker could refer to himself as 'a son of man' without claiming any sort of title, or saying anything other than 'me'. Some biblical commentators believe that this is all that Jesus meant when he used the expression; they say he was in fact calling himself no more than 'a man' or 'this man'.

On the other hand many commentators believe that Jesus meant the term 'Son of Man' to have distinct theological reverberations. They believe, in fact, that when he spoke of himself in this way he was identifying himself with a messianic-style figure who would usher in the end of the world and God's judgement. The chief ground for believing that this is what Jesus meant is the apparent existence of such a figure in the book of Daniel. Despite its claims to have originated during the Babylonian captivity, 'Daniel' was, as we have seen, actually written not much more than 150 years before the birth of Jesus. Here is the passage from it which describes Daniel's version of the coming of the kingdom of God:

I saw one like a son of man* coming with the clouds of heaven; he approached the Ancient in Years [i.e. God] and was presented to him. Sovereignty and glory and kingly power were given to him . . . his sovereignty was to be an everlasting sovereignty which should not pass away, and his kingly power such as should never be impaired. (Daniel 7. 13–14)

This passage in Daniel grew out of that strand of Israel's hope for the future which expected a supernatural end of the world rather than a purely this-worldly national triumph. The exact meaning of the passage is far from clear. It is complicated by the fact that the 'son of man' is here certainly something like an allegorical figure, standing for God's faithful people in Israel. Until recently, it was argued by some theologians that there was a ready-made concept of the Son of Man waiting for the author of Daniel to use, and

* The New English Bible actually reads 'I saw one like a man', but the literal meaning of the Hebrew is 'one like a son of man'.

indeed for Jesus to take over. This Son of Man (it was argued) was
not a human being at all, despite his name; he was a divine and
heavenly creature, created by God before the world was formed;
his face shone like an angel and he was endowed with God's
miraculous power. Until the coming of the kingdom of God he was
being kept hidden in heaven. When the time arrived for the
kingdom to come he would descend to earth accompanied by the
'clouds of heaven'. His coming would be like lightning, and he
would summon all the nations to be judged by himself as God's
representative. This judgement of the living would be accompanied
by the resurrection of the dead, who would themselves be judged.
The righteous, or more particularly the righteous Israelites, would
be delivered into eternal bliss and would be given authority in the
kingdom of God; all other nations would fall at their feet, and at
the feet of the Son of Man, whom they would worship.

But nowadays there is a great deal of doubt about this. Did such
a precise concept of the Son of Man really exist for Jesus to take
over, or were the words 'son of man' in truth a great deal more
ambiguous than this interpretation would suggest? Certainly there
are Jewish texts which do describe the Son of Man on exactly these
terms, but they are of doubtful date, and it would be unwise to
assume that Jesus and his contemporaries knew them and agreed
with them in their use of the term 'son of man'. We do know that
Jesus was well acquainted with the Daniel passage — the book of
Daniel was very highly regarded in his day. But if he was referring
to the Daniel 'son of man' when he called himself by this title, we
cannot say precisely what he meant, so ambiguous is the Daniel
passage; and anyway we have no certainty that on every occasion
when Jesus used the words 'Son of Man' he meant to refer to the
Daniel passage at all.

In order to find some way out of this labyrinth, we need to look
at the various ways in which the Synoptic Gospels use the term Son
of Man (John usually prefers simply 'the Son', implying the Son of
God). In all, the Synoptics employ it nearly seventy times, though
of course many of these are parallel reports of the same incidents.
It is quite an illuminating exercise to divide their uses of the term
into categories.

First, there are the passages where the words 'Son of Man'
certainly refer to the Daniel passage. The most notable of these is
this episode in the trial of Jesus. This is how Mark narrates it:

Again the High Priest questioned him: 'Are you the Messiah, the Son of the Blessed One?' Jesus said, 'I am; and you will see the Son of Man seated at the right hand of God and coming with the clouds of heaven.' (Mk. 14. 61–2)

Matthew presents it like this:

'Are you the Messiah, the Son of God?' Jesus replied, 'The words are yours. But I tell you this: from now on, you will see the Son of Man seated at the right hand of God and coming on the clouds of heaven.' (Matt. 26. 63–4; cf. Lk. 2. 67–70)

Two other passages where a reference to Daniel is implied record Jesus as expecting this coming of the Son of Man to happen very soon. He says to his disciples:

I tell you this: there are some standing here who will not taste death before they have seen the Son of Man coming in his kingdom. (Matt. 16. 28; cf. Mk. 9. 1, Lk. 9. 27)

Indeed Matthew actually records Jesus as promising the coming of the Son of Man with the kingdom of God in a matter of months or weeks rather than years; Matthew's version of the instruction to the disciples before they go off on an independent mission includes these words of Jesus:

I tell you this: before you have gone through all the towns of Israel the Son of Man will have come. (Matt. 10. 23)

How likely is it that these implied references to Daniel are the authentic words of Jesus? We cannot say for certain. But certainly Jesus's alleged answer to the High Priest during his trial does seem rather odd when considered in its context. Up to this point in the narrative Jesus has refused to be goaded by his accusers into making any claims about himself. Now he suddenly declares himself to be Son of Man. We may in fact suspect that the words have been included (in what was after all a highly conjectural report of what may have occurred at the trial) simply to allow Jesus a moment of glory in the face of his accusers, and to give clear grounds for his condemnation. But as to the other passages where Jesus predicts the nearness of his coming as Son of Man, it is certainly hard to explain why they should have been included if they were not based on real sayings of Jesus. By the time the Gospels were written the prediction of a very swift coming of the Son of Man — 'before you have gone through all the towns of

Israel' — had proved untrue, and undoubtedly many of Jesus's
original disciples had died, so that the prediction that some of them
would live to see the coming of the kingdom must have at least
seemed open to question. It is hard, therefore, to see how these
passages could have been pure invention. Very possibly they are
authentic reflections of Jesus's belief that the kingdom would come
soon. On the other hand their very confident character contrasts
oddly with another passage where he says that the date of the
coming of the kingdom simply cannot be foretold.

But about that day or that hour no one knows, not even the angels in
heaven, not even the Son; only the Father. (Mk. 13. 32; cf. Matt. 24. 36)

Altogether we would be unwise to put too much weight on any of
these passages if we are trying to prove that Jesus regarded himself
as Son of Man in a Daniel sense.

Certainly there are also a number of other places where he is
reported as referring to the glorious coming of the Son of Man;
these are found in the 'apocalyptic' or visionary discourse with
which all three Synoptics preface the Passion (Mark chapter 13,
Matthew chapters 24–5, Luke chapter 21). Here, Jesus talks of
events which are to come after his death: false prophets, wars,
rumours of the end of the world, earthquakes, the persecution of
his followers, and (perhaps, though this is not clear) the fall of
Jerusalem in A.D. 70. This speech contains several references to the
'coming' of the Son of Man. But is it authentic? While one or two
commentators think so, the general view is that it is the work of
a later writer or tradition, and certainly it is very much in the style
of other Jewish—Christian apocalyptic books.

These, then, are the sayings in the Gospels where Jesus is
definitely represented as referring to the Daniel-style Son of Man.
And it is a case of 'referring to', not 'identifying with', for the fact
is that all these sayings are in the third person. Jesus never declares
unambiguously 'I am the Son of Man', and very often he could be
talking about a third party:

. . . They will see the Son of Man coming in the clouds with great power
and glory . . . (Mk. 13. 26)

Hold yourself ready, therefore, because the Son of Man will come at the
time you least expect him. (Matt. 24. 44)

. . . everyone who acknowledges me before men, the Son of Man will
acknowledge before the angels of God . . . (Lk. 12. 8)

It is only a presumption that Jesus is here talking about himself. No doubt the writers of the Gospels thought he was, but were they in fact recording sayings in which he had meant to refer not to himself — about whom he was here making no claims — but to the divine being who would eventually usher in the kingdom of God, a being with whom he did not identify himself? This is certainly a possibility.

We come now to the other category of 'Son of Man' sayings in the Gospels: those where Jesus is not so certainly referring to the Daniel concept. In none of these passages is he obviously claiming any special title for himself — rather he might simply be using a commonplace circumlocution for 'mankind' or 'myself'. For example:

The Sabbath was made for the sake of man and not man for the Sabbath: therefore the Son of Man is sovereign even over the Sabbath. (Mk. 2. 27–8)

We can certainly take this to mean '*mankind* is sovereign even over the Sabbath' — an extension of the first part of the precept. In another passage which falls into this category, Jesus is certainly referring to himself when he says 'Son of Man', but he may mean no more than 'me':

'We are now going to Jerusalem,' he said; 'and the Son of Man will be given up to the chief priests and the doctors of the law; they will condemn him to death and hand him over to the foreign power. He will be mocked and spat upon, flogged and killed; and three days afterwards, he will rise again.' (Mk. 10. 33–4; cf. Matt. 20. 18–19, Lk. 18. 31–3)

It ought to be mentioned that most commentators find it impossible to believe that these are the authentic words of Jesus; if he had told his disciples so plainly what was to happen, they would hardly have been cast into despondency by his death, and have been astonished by reports of his resurrection, as the Gospels say they were. But even if the passage were authentic, there is no reason to suppose that the words 'Son of Man' in it — and indeed in the two other very similar predictions of the Passion (Mk. 8. 31, 9. 30–2 and parallels in Matt. and Lk.) — need to be taken to mean more than 'I myself', 'this man'.

On the other hand it is difficult to imagine that the writers of the Gospels, and the many members of the early Church who preserved the traditions on which the Gospels were based, believed that Jesus was making no special claim for himself when he used the term 'Son of Man'. If they had thought the words meant no more than 'I myself', would they have troubled to record them so often? Or can we suppose that every instance of the words 'Son of Man' in the Gospels is an invention by the Church? It is possible, but unlikely. The connotations of the phrase were so vague — far more vague than 'Messiah' — that it seems an improbable thing for anyone to invent totally. It would be more reasonable to suppose that Jesus used the term often enough to impress his hearers. We simply cannot say for certain what he means by it; though we can guess.

## The Suffering Servant

Before we make our guess, we need to look at another view which Jesus may have held about himself. Neither the Jewish national Messiah nor the 'one like a son of man' in the book of Daniel had any suggestions of suffering about them; they were both glorious figures, the victors, not the vanquished. Yet the Gospels portray Jesus as associating his role as Messiah or Son of Man — and note how both terms appear side by side here — with suffering:

. . . he asked his disciples, 'Who do men say I am?' . . . Peter replied: 'You are the Messiah.' Then he gave them strict orders not to tell anyone about him; and he began to teach them that the Son of Man had to undergo great sufferings, and to be rejected by the elders, chief priests, and doctors of the law; to be put to death . . . (Mk. 8. 27–31)

The prophetic element in this passage makes many commentators doubt its authenticity. But even if Jesus did not predict his sufferings in the very literal way depicted by the Gospels, it is not unreasonable to suppose, from the manner in which he seems to have gone to his death, that he believed that by suffering he could in some way make 'atonement', that is, effect a reconciliation between God and man, even 'take away the sins of the world'. Theologians are especially inclined to believe this because of the existence of such a concept in the Jewish scriptures which Jesus knew so well.

The passages in question are all in the book of Isaiah, though modern commentators believe them to be the work neither of Isaiah himself nor even of 'Second Isaiah', but of a third writer or school of writers. These passages are in the form of poems, which have been absorbed into the text of Isaiah. The first three of these poems or 'Servant Songs' (as they are now known) tell of the call of a prophet who is to bring Israel back to the worship of Yahweh; he is also to be 'a light to the nations', a preacher to the whole world (Is. 42. 1–4, 49. 1–6, 50. 4–11). But it is the fourth Song, which concerns us most. Set in the past tense, it tells of the

Servant's miserable life on earth. He was, says the poet, physically unattractive, even hideous, and despised. Moreover he suffered from a foul disease which gave him great agonies. Yet this suffering was a positive element in the work to which he was called. It was in fact a suffering of atonement:

> . . . on himself he bore our sufferings,
>   our torments he endured,
> while we counted him smitten by God,
>   struck down by disease and misery;
> but he was pierced for our transgressions,
>   tortured for our iniquities;
> the chastisement he bore is health for us,
>   and by his scourging we are healed.
> We had all strayed like sheep,
>   each of us had gone his own way;
> but the Lord laid upon him
>   the guilt of us all. (Is. 53. 4–6)

The Servant endured other sufferings too: he died the death of a criminal, and was given an ignominious burial. But the poem ends with the assurance that Yahweh will give the Servant his reward and will show the world his true greatness. He will in fact raise the Servant from the dead, bringing him back to earthly life so that he will 'enjoy long life and see his children's children' (Is. 53. 10). Yahweh declares:

> . . . I will allot him a portion with the great,
>   and he shall share the spoil with the mighty,
> because he exposed himself to face death
>   and was reckoned among transgressors,
> because he bore the sin of many
>   and interceded for their transgressions.

> (Is. 53. 12)

The interpretation of these poems is not easy, but it seems most likely that they were based on a real historical person, a prophet whose personal sufferings were regarded as an atonement for the sins of Israel. A belief in some kind of 'sympathetic' suffering was certainly held by a number of prophets, such as Isaiah himself, who was recorded to have walked naked and barefoot for three years in order to bring down the same disgrace on the Ethiopians and Egyptians, and Jeremiah, who walked about with an iron yoke on his neck in order to illustrate and bring to pass the fate which

awaited Judah, slavery under the 'yoke' of Babylon. Many
prophets indeed regarded the character of their whole lives as a
'sign' of this kind. Jeremiah was forbidden to marry and was made
to cut himself off from society, while Ezekiel was obliged to
undergo physical sufferings as an emblem of the impending ruin of
Jerusalem. In this sense the Servant Songs are part of a wider
tradition.

On the other hand the tradition of prophetic sufferings did not
specifically involve atonement, the notion that such sufferings
might be accepted by God as a kind of ransom for Israel's sins. And
this idea is explicitly present in the Servant Songs. It is true that
atonement was not exactly an unusual idea in Jewish thought: the
sacrifices in the temple at Jerusalem implied it. But the notion of a
man dying on behalf of the whole nation's sins is found most
notably in the Servant Songs, so that if Jesus really believed that
his own suffering and death was an offering for the sins of men he
was probably deriving this idea from these Songs.

This is what more conservative theologians think he was doing.
They believe that he united with the title 'Son of Man' the concept
of the Suffering Servant. He believed, they think, that the kingdom
of God would be ushered in not just by a cosmic crisis but by his
own suffering on the cross, which would atone for the sins of men.
In other words, according to this view Jesus believed of himself
what the Christian Church came to believe about him: that his
death — followed by his resurrection — was itself the great event
through which God declared his mercy to mankind. In a sense it
even took the place of the coming of the kingdom, or was at least
the first stage in the kingdom's arrival on earth.

The great appeal of this view of the historical Jesus is that it
harmonises with the Church's later conceptions of him. On the
other hand it certainly does not fit the evidence very comfortably.
In the Synoptic Gospels there is only one passage where Jesus
explicitly associates his death with atonement or 'ransom':

Jesus called them [the disciples] to him and said, 'You know that in the
world the recognised rulers lord it over their subjects . . . That is not the
way with you; among you, whoever wants to be great must be your
servant . . . For even the Son of Man did not come to be served but to
serve, and to give up his life as a ransom for many.' (Mk. 10. 42–5; cf.
Matt. 20. 25–8)

If Jesus said this, there could be no doubt that he believed that his death on the cross would have an atoning power. But did he say it? One isolated instance seems a slender peg on which to hang so much, particularly as by the time the Gospels were written the Church had certainly developed its own ideas about the crucifixion as an atonement. Most commentators suspect that these words were not spoken by Jesus. (It should be noted that Luke does not include the reference to 'ransom' in his version of the episode.) Yet many who reject the authenticity of this particular passage still assume that Jesus did believe that his death was (or might be) a vicarious sacrifice offered to God on behalf of the sins of men. Is this view justified?

## Moralist or miracle worker?

A historian must surely judge the evidence we have examined to be inconclusive. The Gospels indicate that Jesus did not regard himself as the national Messiah of popular Jewish hopes, but they do not allow us to come to any firm conclusions as to whether he used the words 'Son of Man' as a title for himself, or precisely what he meant by it if he did. Nor do they allow us to say for certain that he regarded his death as having an atoning power, like the death of the Suffering Servant in Isaiah. We are therefore obliged, if we are going to come to any conclusions, to consider other aspects of the issue: we need to ask whether it is psychologically and historically probable that Jesus should have made these claims about himself.

If we judge the psychological issue in purely twentieth-century terms the answer will probably be 'no'. To modern minds it seems that if Jesus did believe himself to be the Son of Man (in the sense of God's vicegerent, sent from heaven), then he must have been quite astonishingly self-assured. Could he really believe that he was a divine being who would one day descend to earth on the clouds of heaven and rule in glory? The modern theologian John Knox asks if it would be 'psychologically possible for a sane person' to think this, and says: 'For myself, I find it exceedingly hard to answer affirmatively.' And to the modern observer's way of thinking, even if Jesus's conception of his role chiefly involved suffering rather than glory — even if, in other words, he thought he was merely the Suffering Servant — was he not still making an immense claim? Knox again finds such a claim incompatible with Jesus's sanity, or at least his modesty; how, he asks, *could* Jesus have believed that his own death could 'take away the sins of the world'? However steeped he may have been in the book of Isaiah, however much he may have been influenced by the Jewish sacrificial outlook, why should he think that he himself was to be the man sacrificed on behalf of all? To Knox, and to our way of thinking in general (if we make no effort to project ourselves back into the century's beliefs), it would have been a vast, an insane claim.

But while Knox's view makes sense in the twentieth century, it is of doubtful relevance to the period of history we are discussing. Given the culture of Jesus's day, people could certainly entertain ideas about themselves which we would regard as insane. The prophets of ancient Israel had made claims about their authority as God's mouthpiece which were, it seems, often accepted; and we may suppose that in Jesus's time for a man to suggest he was the Messiah would not be an utterly outrageous idea. Certainly in the troubled period of Jewish history which followed Jesus's death a number of messianic claimants appeared, most notably Bar Cochba ('Son of the Star'), who led a revolt against the Romans in A.D. 132–5. He claimed to be Messiah, and was widely accepted as such. This is not to say that there would be nothing extraordinary in such claims — witness the outrage of the High Priest when Jesus, during his trial, apparently claimed to be Son of Man in the Daniel sense. But we should not assume that a messianic view of himself would be incompatible with Jesus's sanity.

It ought to be emphasised that Jesus's manner of speaking seems to have been very different from the manner either of the rabbis or of the ancient prophets. The rabbis, as we have seen, took their authority from the exegesis of the written Law, and from the doctrine of their own teachers, which was ultimately derived (they believed) from Moses, and so from God himself. The great prophets of ancient Israel, on the other hand, had claimed to be the direct mouthpiece of God; they often prefaced their sayings with the words 'Thus says the Lord'. Jesus fits into neither of these patterns. At times he does use scriptural exegesis, for instance in his dispute with the Pharisees about the Sabbath (Mk. 2. 25–6). But this is comparatively unusual, and his most characteristic utterances are not primarily based on scriptural interpretation. As to the prophetic style of utterance, he is never recorded as using the words 'Thus says the Lord', or indeed anything like them. This is

the sort of manner in which the Gospels recorded him as introducing his teachings:

I tell you this. . . (Mk. 3. 28 and *passim*)

Take note of what you hear . . . (Mk. 4. 24)

Listen to me, all of you . . . (Mk. 7. 14)

(And there are many examples in Matthew's and Luke's Gospels.)
The phrase 'I tell you this', or, as earlier translations of the Bible
render it, 'Verily I say unto you', appears to have been Jesus's
characteristic way of introducing his precepts. If it was, then
certainly nothing like it is found elsewhere in Judaism, and the
startling effect of the words '*I* tell you' on the ears of pious Jews can
hardly be exaggerated. That a man should simply claim to have
personal authority for making the kind of statements that Jesus
made, and should not derive them from the Law and the Prophets,
or at least maintain that they were the words of God communicated
through prophetic utterance, was tantamount to heresy. So what
prompted Jesus to regard himself as having such authority?

A philosopher might ask if he in fact needed any authority to
make the kind of ethical statement he made. Was it necessary to (as
it were) show any credentials before telling people to behave to
others as you would wish them to behave to you, to love your
enemies, to give your money to the poor? One might suppose such
moral lessons as these to be self-evident. Indeed we have already
admitted that Jesus's moral teachings *are* self-evident, self-
justifying, or at least that they agree precisely with what most of
us find in what we call our consciences. And for this reason the
theologian H. J. Cadbury doubts whether Jesus did in fact
introduce them in the manner recorded by the Gospels. Cadbury
suspects that 'I tell you this' was not his usual habit of speech, but
was introduced in the Gospels so as to contrast his teaching with
the Law (see the Sermon on the Mount in Matthew, where it
certainly has this function). Cadbury writes:

I think he expected his hearers to rely more on themselves than on himself.
At least once he says this explicitly, expostulating with them, 'Why don't
you judge *even of yourselves* what is right?'

If Cadbury is right, this leaves us with a Jesus who states self-
evident moral truth by calling on his hearers to look into their own

consciences. He may have done this. But — as Cadbury himself emphasises — if he did, then there must have been some special reason why people listened to him.

If a man were to get up in the twentieth century and preach a moral message whose kernel was 'You will find the truth in your consciences', he would scarcely command a large audience — unless there was something particularly remarkable about him. How much more, then, must this have been true of first-century Palestine, where there was a tradition of prophetic utterance (albeit a lapsed tradition), and a universal belief in the supernatural. Jesus's moral teaching (as we have it) does not in itself explain the degree of attention he attracted. We simply do not find in it sufficient reason for his being put to death, and for a new religion of enormous power to grow up around his person. The 'liberal Protestant' picture of Jesus as a modest moral teacher may be attractive to us, but such a figure would have cut little ice in the context of first-century Judaism.

How, then, do we explain the impact of Jesus and of the ideas behind his teaching? We are led towards one obvious conclusion — a conclusion which is extremely uncomfortable for most twentieth-century minds, even for many twentieth-century Christians. As H. J. Cadbury puts it, 'Jesus's teaching gained prestige from his miracles. There can be little doubt of that.'

# 6

# *The miraculous kingdom*

The Gospels say very clearly that Jesus performed miracles. They report that he healed the chronically sick, gave sight to the blind and hearing to the deaf, and even brought dead people back to life. They also tell stories of other physical wonders: how he calmed a storm on the Lake of Galilee by the force of his words, how he walked on the water, and how he fed many thousands of people with just a few small loaves of bread and a handful of fishes. How are we to judge such things?

The first point to note is that there are rational explanations of how the stories may have arisen. The account of Jesus miraculously stilling the storm (Mk. 4. 35–41, Matt. 8. 32–7, Lk. 8. 22–5) could have grown out of the Jewish belief that the ability to control the sea and to subdue tempests was a characteristic sign of divine power — see Psalm 89. 9, where God is described as ruling the sea and 'calming the turmoil of its waves', and also the opening verses of Genesis, where the waters represent uncreated chaos. In a rather different way the Old Testament may also have influenced the growth of the story of the Feeding of the Five Thousand (Mk. 6. 30–44, Matt. 14. 13–21, Lk. 9. 10–17, Jn. 6. 1–13). Possibly Jesus concluded an open-air sermon at which a large crowd was present by distributing to each person a fragment of bread as a sign of fellowship with him and God, and in the disciples' memories (or in later tradition) this became an actual meal at which the participants were fully fed by miraculous means — an echo, in fact, of the miraculous feeding of the Israelites in the desert, after they had come out of Egypt, when God sent 'manna' from heaven to sustain them (Ex. 16. 1 ff.).

Certainly where the healing miracles of Jesus are concerned there is much to support the theory that the Gospels told stories about Jesus casting out devils because that is what early Jewish Christians assumed he must have done. The very nature of the kingdom of

God, of which they believed him to be a part, was such that its manifestation on earth would be accompanied by events of this kind. When God came into his kingly power in the world he would (the Jews believed) crush the powers of evil and drive them out. That there were powers of evil to be driven out was actually a recent Jewish belief, dating from about the time of the exile in Babylon, when notions about the powers of good and evil being perpetually at war began to infiltrate Jewish thought from Persian religion. By the time of Jesus these notions were embedded deeply in the Jewish imagination. Earlier, the general attitude to sickness had been that it was a punishment from God, and this belief survived into the first century A.D., but it had been largely displaced by the notion that many diseases were actually caused by a devil taking possession of the sufferer. And so it came to be believed that, when the kingdom of God dawned and all evil spirits were driven from their hiding-places to be destroyed, many sick people would consequently be cured of their maladies. It is this which explains the behaviour (as reported in the Gospels) of the demons whom Jesus casts out. Mark in particular is always reporting that they *recognise* Jesus and are frightened because he is 'the Holy One of God' who has come to destroy them (e.g. Mk. 1. 24). The fact that in this process of driving-out a number of men and women are healed of their afflictions interests Mark rather less.

So we might suggest that Mark — or more accurately the oral tradition that he recorded—actually invented these healing miracles so as to portray Jesus driving out devils and thus showing himself to be the Messiah, the agent of the kingdom of God. There is probably an element of truth in this, perhaps a large element. On the other hand a number of the stories of healing miracles say nothing whatever about devils. For example:

They came to Jericho; and as he was leaving the town, with his disciples and a large crowd, Bartimaeus son of Timaeus, a blind beggar, was seated at the roadside. Hearing that it was Jesus of Nazareth, he began to shout, 'Son of David, Jesus, have pity on me!' Many of the people told him to hold his tongue; but he shouted all the more, 'Son of David, have pity on me.' Jesus stopped and said, 'Call him'; so they called the blind man and said, 'Take heart; stand up; he is calling you.' At that he threw off his cloak, sprang up, and came to Jesus. Jesus said to him, 'What do you want me to do for you?' 'Master', the blind man answered, 'I want my sight back.' Jesus said to him, 'Go; your faith has cured you.' And at once he recovered his sight and followed him on the road. (Mk. 10. 46–52; cf. Matt. 20. 29–34, Lk. 18. 35–43)

It is very likely that stories such as this were influenced by the belief, undoubtedly held by early Christians, that Jesus must have fulfilled such Old Testament prophecies as the passage in Isaiah (42. 18) which promised the giving of sight to the blind. Moreover the Bartimaeus story has symbolic meanings: though Bartimaeus is blind he recognises Jesus as 'Son of David' (Messiah), and when he recovers his sight he 'follows' Jesus, that is, has the spiritual insight to recognise him as Lord. The story also shows how true faith can triumph over all adversity. No doubt these layers of symbolic meaning made the story very useful for preachers in the early Church. Quite possibly indeed the early Church invented it, and many other stories of the same kind, for preaching purposes. Such invention would have taken place gradually. For example, in the earliest days of preaching there might merely be generalised statements about Jesus being able to do wonderful things. A little later, more specific claims might be made, such as 'He could do anything: he could even give sight to the blind and hearing to the deaf.' Later still, a real memory of Jesus giving some sort of help to a beggar at Jericho might become the story of Jesus curing him of blindness.

Undoubtedly this kind of process did occur. Anyone who has collected material for a biography will know how often those close to its subject — his friends and even his family — will unconsciously depart from the strict historical truth in their recollections, even a few years after the events, let alone some decades later. The tendency is to adapt real memories until they are formulated into neat anecdotes with a beginning and end and a distinct point or moral to them. These anecdotes are usually based on some sort of truth, but often only very shakily. That this should happen to recollections of Jesus in the disciples' minds is surely inevitable, especially as they were recounting those memories in order to make claims about what he had done. Moreover many of those who preached about Jesus had never known him when he was alive on earth. Indeed the person who still doubts whether such invention really did take place need only listen to modern sermons. Sooner or later he will hear a preacher making statements about the life and ministry of Jesus which cannot be borne out word by word

by the Gospels. Invention did, and does, take place, albeit unconsciously. On the other hand the historian cannot determine
precisely where it has operated, and to what extent. He can only
have his suspicions, or make allegations. He can prove nothing.

Where the healing miracles are concerned, he would also do well
to avoid the kind of rationalisation in which some nineteenth-
century writers indulged, such as the suggestion that Jesus had a
private supply of mysterious drugs and ointments which produced
miraculous cures. There is rather less absurdity in the notion that
Jesus realised that many of those who begged for help were
psychosomatic sufferers who could be healed merely through their
own faith in the cure and in the power of the healer. Yet could this
really be applied to all those whom Jesus is said to have cured—
epileptics, paralytics, lepers, the blind and the deaf?

We may note, when trying to explain the miracle stories, that
such things had featured in Jewish legend for many centuries. It was
recorded that Moses caused the waters of the Red Sea to move aside
and let the Israelites pass in safety, and that Elijah raised a widow's
son from death and summoned fire down from heaven on an altar.
The Old Testament is full of such stories. Moreover the holy man
who was said to work miraculous cures and control the elements
was not an entirely uncommon figure in the time of Jesus. For
example, Honi the Circle-Drawer was said to have brought rain
to end a drought, and Hanina ben Dosa supposedly worked
miraculous cures, some of them, like the cures of Jesus, being per-
fomed at a distance from the sufferer. This indicates that Jesus's
reputation as a miracle-worker, healer and exorcist was by no
means unique even in the first century A.D. It was part of the
vocabulary of the time for expressing how remarkable someone
was.

But this does not mean that we can dismiss the miracles as a
totally fictitious part of the Gospels; or at least, if we do this we
are rejecting an enormous and highly distinctive part of the
tradition about Jesus. If we label the miraculous element as fiction
and discuss Jesus purely in terms of his teachings we may be
satisfying the demands of those modern minds which do not accept
the supernatural, but we are doing violence to the historical record.
We are also leaving ourselves with a 'non-miraculous' Jesus whose
extraordinary impact on his contemporaries becomes inexplicable.
His teachings on their own are not enough to explain the

impression he caused. A more honest historian will say that undoubtedly the miracle stories in their present form include a large element of elaboration and invention; but he will also say that something happened which gave rise to those stories. He will also suggest that it was this 'something', this 'wonder-worker' element in Jesus, which gave authority to his teaching. People listened to him because they were astonished by what he did.

But what did he do? What would we have seen if we had been there? We simply cannot say, because we can only study what happened during Jesus's ministry by reading accounts of it written by people with a very different outlook from that of the twentieth-century historian. Jesus's observers believed in a God who had intervened directly in history with miraculous actions, and would do so again. They believed in devils who inhabited the bodies of men, and who could be cast out by an agent of God. They believed that persons acting as God's representatives, such as the prophet Elijah, had already raised dead people to life, and that this could happen again. Their presuppositions were, in other words, entirely and utterly different from the presuppositions of a modern rationalist. Whatever happened during Jesus's ministry, they saw it against this background, and their account of it was based on these beliefs. If we had been there, we might have come to very different conclusions. We (with *our* presuppositions) might have talked not about miracles but about psychosomatic cures and the remarkable impact of a charismatic personality. We might have seen not supernatural events but the reactions of supernaturally minded people, who were deeply impressed by a man who behaved as if he were the agent of God.

For Jesus believed all these things too: we must not forget that. He was no modern rationalist. He shared the beliefs of his contemporaries, and if they believed that he could perform miracles it seems highly likely that he believed it too. This is not to say that he necessarily presented himself in public primarily as a miracle-worker; the indications are rather the opposite. He is never reported as discussing the miracles; rather, his usual habit is to try to persuade people to keep quiet about them — 'He gave them strict orders to let no one hear about it' (Mk. 5. 43) is his typical reaction after performing a miraculous cure. This may be explained by Mark's belief that Jesus simply wished to keep his messianic status a secret, something that Mark is always emphasising in his Gospel.

But it might also reflect that Jesus was himself startled or overawed by whatever cures he did perform. He certainly does not seem to have wished to advertise his powers. Yet we should not suppose from this that he did not believe in the cures, and perhaps in other miraculous events too. The indications are that, in this respect at least, the modern rationalist would have found him a very uncongenial figure: a supernaturalist, a believer, in fact, in his own miraculous powers, a thoroughly Jewish and first-century figure, not a twentieth-century liberal Protestant at all; certainly 'a man for others' (as he has sometimes been called), but also somebody who believed himself to be the special agent of God.

For we may guess, from the dominant role played by the miracles in the Gospels, and from the constant emphasis on Jesus's messianic status and his alleged use, time after time, of the words 'Son of Man', that he did not reject all suggestions that he was some kind of Messiah, but admitted, if only tacitly, that he had been in some way specially appointed by God for the furtherance of the coming of the kingdom. He seems to have rejected any identification of himself with the national, political Messiah; but we may well suppose that he did adopt the term 'Son of Man' to describe himself, perhaps because of the very ambiguity which puzzled us when we discussed its use as a title. He must surely have realised that it evoked echoes of 'one like a son of man' in Daniel, but that on the other hand it could also be taken as nothing more than a tautology for 'myself'. It may have seemed to him that this imprecise term was an ideal title for him to use in a ministry which was quite unlike anything previously known in Judaism, and which perhaps surprised even him in the dramatic turns it took. But that he felt he had some special relationship to God, some messianic role or 'sonship' which manifested itself in miracles and gave powerful authority to his teaching, we cannot doubt. Moreover his teaching itself was largely concerned with the miraculous, with the wholly marvellous and inexplicable power of God and his kingdom: this emerges clearly from the area of Jesus's teaching which we have so far neglected, the parables.

## Why Jesus taught in parables

The Gospels record that Jesus taught largely in parables, vivid stories designed to express an idea or to illustrate a point; and there is no reason to doubt this. It was a common method of teaching

among the rabbis, as can be seen from the *Talmud* ('teaching'), the
chief work of the Jewish post-Biblical literature. This does not
mean, of course, that Jesus told precisely those parables that the
Gospels record him as telling. Many of the parables found in
Matthew and Luke do not appear in Mark's text, and while they
may have been derived from reliable sources there is always the
possibility that they are inventions, perhaps even compositions of
Matthew and Luke themselves. For example a number of the best-
known parables — the Good Samaritan, the Lost Sheep, the Lost
Coin, the Prodigal Son, the Unjust Steward, Dives and
Lazarus — appear in Luke's Gospel alone, a fact which must raise
doubts about their authenticity, though they certainly reflect
the spirit of Jesus's teaching (Lk. 10. 30–7, 15. 3–16, 13, 16. 19–31).
So we must, as usual, exercise caution. On the other hand we
may decide to accept at least the outline of some of the parables
as reflecting the real teachings of Jesus, especially those parables
which appear in all three Synoptic Gospels and which deal with
the central issue of his mission, the kingdom of God. Indeed these
'parables of the kingdom', as they are usually called, would
seem to be crucial to Jesus's teaching, since they are the
only substantial sayings of Jesus which Mark includes in his
Gospel.

Why should Jesus apparently have set much of his teaching in the
form of parables? Mark answers this very oddly to modern ears,
by saying that Jesus chose the parabolic method because he wanted
his teaching to be understood only by his close followers; he used
parables (says Mark) to cloak his meaning and confuse the rest of
his audience (Mk. 4. 10–12; cf. Matt. 13. 10–12, Lk. 8. 9–10). We
are unlikely to accept this as a true account of Jesus's motives. It
would be strange that Jesus, preaching in public, should want to
confuse his audience deliberately. The passage in Mark also shows
the influence of the 'gnostic' type of religion, whose initiates believe
they have a *gnosis* or secret knowledge which is denied to others,
and though 'gnosticism' seems to have appealed to Mark there is no
reason to suppose he is recording a trait in the historical Jesus.
Mark's explanation of Jesus teaching in parables is also motivated
by his doctrine of the 'messianic secret', his notion that Jesus was
not universally recognised as Messiah because he kept his messianic
status concealed.

If we reject Mark's account of why Jesus used parables, what is
the real explanation? Perhaps it is the very opposite of what Mark

suggests. Jesus was preaching for much of the time not to educated intellectuals but to the common people, especially the poor and outcast. His audience's attention could be best held by telling them stories. Statements about the kingdom of God would attract notice more easily if they were set in picture language. So he chose the imagery of daily life in Galilee — the farmer sowing, the vineyard owner hiring his labourers, the crops springing up in the field — to picture the workings of the kingdom.

Indeed there is every reason to suppose that this was Jesus's own mode of thinking. Very probably he himself was not highly educated, and we should not expect his mind to work exclusively in abstractions. Obviously he was capable of clear thought and reasoning; his disputes with the Pharisees (if they represent historical conversations) show a very nimble mind at work, a mind quite capable of dealing with learned people. But we may suspect that for much of the time he himself thought in parables.

Nevertheless there remains the fact that, though the parables are simply stories, their precise meaning is often far from clear. This is not just because of the passage of time between Jesus and ourselves; Mark says that the disciples themselves had to ask Jesus to explain the parables because they did not understand them (Mk. 4. 10).

This difficulty is greatest with many of the short figurative sayings ascribed to Jesus, a large proportion of which have become detached from their original contexts. For example, all three Synoptic Gospels report Jesus as saying something on the lines of 'Salt is a good thing; but if the salt lose its saltiness, what will you season it with?' (Mk. 9. 50). But none of the three agrees with the others either on the saying's place in Jesus's ministry or on its precise meaning. They record it so as to give it both a different context and a different emphasis (Matt. 5. 13, Lk. 14. 34–5). The meaning obviously depended on the precise circumstances in which the saying was uttered.

Indeed it is not just these shorter sayings that present problems of interpretation. In many parables, while the general meaning may be clear the significance of the various details of the story is not at all clear. An example is the parable of the Sower (Mk. 4. 3–9), where the footpath, the birds and the sun do not have any obvious significance. For a time it was fashionable in theological circles to say that if only we could recover the precise circumstances in which the parables were told by Jesus — the 'life situation' or *Sitz im Leben* as Form-critics in Germany have called it — we would understand exactly what he meant.

But would we? Very often we are probably looking for too close a correspondence between the details of the parables and the precise details of Jesus's message. Many parables probably contain no more than a broad general meaning; they are not detailed allegories at all. And besides, in our careful search for the correct interpretation of each parable, are we not perhaps missing the point? Might it not be true that at least some of the parables have no precise abstract meaning at all? Might Jesus not have taught in parables because he himself could not express in any other way what he was trying to say?

## The miraculous kingdom

Jesus's task was to preach about the kingdom of God. But he did not do this in purely abstract terms, for he had a conception of it which did not communicate itself so much to the intellect as to the imagination. He did not say 'The kingdom of God *is* so-and-so', but 'The kingdom of God is *like* such-and-such'. Indeed in many of the parables we find him urgently trying to communicate in this way his most central belief about the kingdom.

What was this belief? We see it very clearly if we remind ourselves what Judaism had traditionally thought about the kingdom of God. The Jews felt that a hard-and-fast line separated them from it. At present the kingdom existed strictly in another world, where God was in his glory. One day, perhaps soon, that glorious kingdom would come to earth. When it did arrive, only the righteous people in Israel would be admitted to it. This meant that Israelites must in the meantime try to achieve that righteousness by keeping the Law.

Jesus did not think in these terms at all. Certainly he did not doubt that the kingdom would one day come to earth. Almost certainly he expected it to happen soon. But this future coming of the kingdom — which was after all a long-standing feature of Jewish hopes — was his *presupposition* rather than his *message*. His message was a call to decision, a call to men to repent of their sins, a call to them not merely to keep the Law but to meet the universal and total demands that God was making of them. This was the message, and it gained its tremendous urgency — an urgency that can be seen in all his teachings—because he believed that the kingdom of God might come to earth at any moment, and that there was no possible way in which men could understand its workings. Jewish tradition had regarded the kingdom as something whose nature could be understood or at least guessed at by men, something almost *predictable*. Jesus totally rejected this. He told his hearers that they must regard the kingdom as something utterly and totally mysterious.

This can be understood more easily if we look at some examples. Jewish writers in late Old Testament and early Christian times were fond of picturing the coming of the kingdom of God in terms like this, taken from the book of Ezra, not in the Bible:

Suddenly the sun will shine by night and the moon by day. From the trees will drip blood, stones will cry out. The nations will fall into tumult, the heavenly regions into chaos; and there shall come to power one whom dwellers on earth expect not. The birds fly away, the sea of Sodom brings forth fish, and roars at night with a voice, which many do not understand, though all hear. At many places the abyss opens, fire bursts forth and blazes long, then the wild beasts forsake their haunts. Women bear monsters, in fresh water salt is found.

It is true that this sort of prophecy of the end is found on Jesus's lips in the apocalyptic discourses before the Passion (Mark chapter 13, Matthew chapter 24, Luke chapter 21). But the argument for regarding these discourses as not authentic is very strong. Much more characteristic of Jesus elsewhere in the Gospels is this warning to his hearers not to indulge in this sort of speculation:

The Pharisees asked him, 'When will the kingdom of God come?' He said, 'You cannot tell by observation when the kingdom of God comes. There will be no saying, "Look, here it is!" or "there it is"; for in fact the kingdom of God is among you.' (Lk. 17. 20–1)

These last words might be taken by an incautious commentator to mean that 'the kingdom of God' was not a supernatural power but an inward spiritual state in men. It would be less misleading to render the original Greek as: 'for in fact the kingdom of God is [suddenly] in your midst'—in other words, the kingdom will suddenly come upon you when you least expect it. For this is Jesus's view of the kingdom. He sees it as something not at all to be described in normal terms, but as thoroughly unpredictable, unknowable, other-worldly and miraculous:

The kingdom of God is like this. A man scatters seed on the land; he goes to bed at night and gets up in the morning, and the seed sprouts and grows — how, he does not know. (Mk. 4. 26–7)

'How, he does not know': to the first-century mind there can have been few things more mysterious than the germination and sprouting of a seed. As the celebrated theologian Rudolf Bultmann reminds us:

Such a parable must not be read in the light of the modern conceptions of 'nature' and 'evolution'. The parable presupposes that the growth and ripening of the seed is not something 'natural', within Man's control, but that it is something miraculous. As the grain springs up miraculously and ripens without human agency or understanding, so marvellous is the coming of the Kingdom of God.

The same message is found in other parables of the kingdom:

How shall we picture the kingdom of God, or by what parable shall we describe it? It is like the mustard-seed, which is smaller than any seed in the ground at its sowing. But once sown, it springs up and grows taller than any other plant, and forms branches so large that the birds can settle in its shade. (Mk. 4. 30–2; cf. Matt. 13. 31–2, Lk. 13. 18–19)

The kingdom of Heaven is like yeast, which a woman took and mixed with half a hundredweight of flour till it was all leavened. (Matt. 13. 33)

There are few things stranger to the unscientific mind than the workings of yeast, which mysteriously and relentlessly alters the nature of an entire lump of dough. Just so will the kingdom come to earth — in a way which cannot be understood or foretold by men.

And because the coming of the kingdom could not be foretold, because its nature was wholly incomprehensible and miraculous, men must not remain idle a moment longer. It might not come, of course, for a long time: we should not suppose that Jesus would necessarily have been disconcerted had he learnt that nearly two thousand years after his lifetime the 'coming' had still not happened. As he himself is reported to have said, no one, not even he, could predict it. It was not in fact the actual *event* of the coming of the kingdom that concerned him. The dramatic happenings which would accompany its arrival did not interest him, nor did he speculate as to what the kingdom would in itself be like. The kingdom concerned him because its coming presented man with a call to decision, a call to repent and be saved. 'The kingdom of God is at hand; *repent*, and believe the good news.'

The news that the kingdom is imminent is of course good, but it is also a demand that men face up to the huge, unlimited, total moral demands which God is making of them. They must mend their lives *now*. Hence the urgency of Jesus's call to the disciples: 'Follow me.' There is simply no time to be lost. So it is that the kingdom, while it may be an entirely future event, acts on men at the present moment, determining the nature of their lives now. A sense of urgency, a need to prepare, to be ready, must be communicated to everyone. As Jesus himself expresses it according to Mark:

Keep awake, then, for you do not know when the master of the house is coming. Evening or midnight, cock-crow or early dawn — if he comes suddenly, he must not find you asleep. And what I say to you, I say to everyone: Keep awake. (Mk. 13. 35–7)

# 7

## 'I have come to set fire to the earth'

If Jesus had not died by crucifixion in Jerusalem, his teaching might well have been forgotten. The Christian Church grew up because Jesus was executed — and because his followers believed that after his death he came back to life again. So, though this book is mainly concerned with the ideas of Jesus, we need to conclude by looking at the events leading up to his death and supposed resurrection, and to ask, what kind of influence did Jesus finally come to exert, both over Christian believers and over non-believers?

Jesus's ministry was apparently first conducted in his home district around Nazareth. Later he seems to have gone further afield in Galilee, but even then he preached only in country places and avoided cities such as Tiberias, apparently setting up a temporary home in the small town of Capernaum on the shore of the Lake of Galilee (see Matt. 4. 13). He seems to have taken care that his words should reach the ears of those whom society thought of as outcasts: blind beggars, people subject to epileptic fits (who were regarded with fear and horror because they were thought to be possessed by demons), and even lepers, who were banished by Law from all normal human contact. It was apparently to such as these, rather than to the affluent who were the mainstay of Judaism, that he directed his mission. As he is reported to have declared: 'It is not the healthy that need a doctor, but the sick' (Mk. 2. 17).

The essence of his message, as we have seen, was an urgent call to repentance, a call to meet the universal and total demands that God was making. It was an urgent message because Jesus believed that the wholly miraculous and incomprehensible kingdom of God might dawn at any moment. It was not in any sense a gentle message, because the demands being made on his hearers were immense. But it was also, at least by implication, a message of love, for to those who accepted the call to repentance and tried to meet God's demands, salvation would be complete. In this sense the message was truly a 'Gospel', 'good news'. And this love which God gave to men who repented was shown in the works of healing which Jesus performed. The healings were in this sense symbolic in that they were acts of forgiveness; the removal of sickness and infirmity signified the casting out of sin. Before healing a paralysed man Jesus says to him: 'My son, your sins are forgiven' (Mk. 2. 5).

The consequence of all this was that man, in the message of Jesus, was brought into a new relationship with God. This relationship was to be one of direct contact. Traditionally, as we have seen, Judaism feared the very name of Yahweh and used it only rarely; 'the Lord' was the usual way of referring to the deity. But to Jesus, Yahweh seemed less like a lord than a father, and this was how he began to talk about him and pray to him:

Whoever does the will of my heavenly Father . . . (Matt. 12. 50)

Father, thy name be hallowed . . . (Lk. 11. 2)

The Gospels record that the actual word he used to address God was *Abba* (Mk. 14. 36), an Aramaic term for 'Father'. And he was explicit in telling his followers that this was how they too must address God:

When you pray, go into a room by yourself, shut the door, and pray to your Father who is there in the secret place . . . This is how you should pray: 'Our Father in heaven, thy name be hallowed; thy kingdom come, thy will be done, on earth as in heaven . . .' (Matt. 6. 6, 9–10)

As to the geographical limits of his mission, Jesus apparently restricted his work to Jewish soil, for his whole message was based on Judaism. There is no reason to suppose that he did not share the belief of his contemporaries that the kingdom of God, when it came to earth, would be peopled first and foremost by the chosen Israelites; 'Gentiles' or non-Jews would play only a secondary part in it. Later, when there existed a Christian Church that was no longer exclusively Jewish, the Gospels tried to suggest that Jesus had made at least brief journeys into the Gentile territories surrounding Galilee, and that he had even preached in Samaria, whose inhabitants, though their religion was related to Judaism, were held in deep suspicion by the Jews (see e.g. Mk. 7. 24 ff., Jn.

4. 4 ff.). But Matthew was probably nearer the truth when he recorded Jesus as saying to his disciples: 'Do not take the road to Gentile lands, and do not enter any Samaritan town; but go rather to the lost sheep of the house of Israel' (Matt. 10. 5–6).

Though Jesus preached first of all in Galilee, it was imperative, if he was to make more than a purely local impact on Judaism, that he take his message to Jerusalem, the capital of Judaea and also the seat of the temple, the only place where the full sacrificial cult of Yahweh could be practised — for sacrifice was never offered in the provincial synagogues, which were simply meeting-houses for prayer and readings. Moreover it was in Jerusalem that the great scribal schools such as those of Shammai and Hillel were established; and it was to Jerusalem that thousands of pilgrims came several times a year for the great Jewish religious festivals. Moreover, during the Galilean stage of his ministry Jesus had almost certainly met opposition from representatives of the established sects of Judaism, especially the Pharisees, and he may have wanted to face the opposition in full force in Jerusalem.

Mark and the other Synoptics would have us believe that at every stage of his preaching and healing work in Galilee his steps were dogged by 'Scribes and Pharisees' who voiced their disapproval of his message and behaviour. We are unlikely to accept this as historically very accurate; little is known about the extent to which the Pharisaic movement and its scribal experts penetrated and influenced Galilean Judaism in the first century, but it seems improbable that its representatives should have been at hand with quite such regularity to comment chorus-fashion on the words and deeds of Jesus. They come in pat on cue in a way which resembles a stage play rather than real life. But we should not assume from this that no kind of Pharisaic opposition to Jesus had materialised in Galilee. If his success was anything like as great as the Gospels report, he would have quickly been seen as a challenge to established Judaism in general and probably to the Pharisees' scrupulous observance of the oral tradition of the Law in particular. Jesus may in fact have seemed to be yet one more example of the anti-Pharisaic element which was already present in Judaism. While many Pharisees were undoubtedly good and worthy men, their insistence on scrupulous observance of the oral Law was regarded, at least in some circles, as hypocrisy; a contemporary text speaks of them as men whose 'hands and hearts were busy with uncleanness and whose mouth did speak proud things, and who said, Draw not near me lest you defile me!' Whether Jesus himself made similarly critical remarks about the Pharisees we cannot say for certain, but the Gospels certainly record him as doing so:

Alas for you Pharisees! You pay tithes of mint and rue and every garden-herb, but have no care for justice and the love of God. It is these you should have practised, without neglecting the others . . . you lawyers [i.e. Scribes], it is no better with you! For you load men with intolerable burdens, and will not put a single finger to the load. (Lk. 11. 42, 46)

Whether or not Jesus spoke in these actual terms, they certainly represent the character of his message, and the Pharisaic party and its Scribes must have regarded him as a radical challenge.

Undoubtedly therefore he went to Jerusalem knowing both that he would be able to preach to a wider audience, and that he would meet opposition. It is indeed not impossible that he actually foresaw arrest and execution. There was a certain tradition in Judaism of the voice of prophecy being suddenly and violently silenced; prophets had been executed and otherwise persecuted, and one had even been stoned to death in the court of the temple itself. So, even if we do not accept the very explicit Gospel predictions by Jesus of his trial and death, we may imagine that 'he set his face resolutely towards Jerusalem' (Lk. 9. 51) with a distinct awareness that he might have some sort of ordeal to undergo. Perhaps most of all he was anxious to communicate his vital message to the whole of Judaism before, as he feared and expected, he was forcibly made silent. As Jesus himself expressed it in Luke's Gospel (12. 49–50), 'I have come to set fire to the earth, and how I wish it were already kindled! I have a baptism to undergo, and what constraint I am under until the ordeal is over!'

## Jerusalem: trial and death

It is possible (as John's Gospel in fact alleges) that Jesus made not one but a series of visits to Jerusalem; at all events, his work certainly ended there. The Gospel accounts of his activities in the city are extremely bare, but it is clear that he preached in the temple, and had a series of encounters with the Pharisees and the Sadducees.

The Pharisees were not the conservatives of Jerusalem. Indeed, with their emphasis on the oral rather than the written Law, and with their belief in such things as the resurrection of the dead, they were comparatively almost radical. The real conservatives were the Sadducees (the meaning of whose name is obscure), who accepted only the written Law and rejected the oral tradition, and did not believe in immortality. At the time of Jesus they were the ruling party, having a majority on the Sanhedrin (the parliamentary judicial council) and wielding considerable power under the Romans. They were opposed to any political ferment among the populace, which they saw as a threat not merely to the Romans, but to their own authority.

The Gospels record a few disputes between Jesus and the Pharisees and Sadducees in Jerusalem. The Sadducees question him about his views on immortality and resurrection (Mk. 12. 18–24), and the Pharisees ask him an awkward question about whether Jews should pay taxes to Rome (Mk. 12. 14–15). In both cases his answers are ingenious but evasive; it appears that he did not wish to be drawn into a debate. He also avoids giving any direct answer to the question, put to him by the religious authorities, 'By what authority are you acting like this?' (Mk. 11. 28). He replies:

I have a question to ask you too; and if you give me an answer, I will tell you by what authority I act. The baptism of John: was it from God, or from men? Answer me. (Mk. 11. 29–30)

The questioners are unable to give a judicious answer, and are silenced.

We may suggest that such disputes were in fact more numerous and protracted than the Gospels suggest, and that in Jerusalem Jesus faced a serious challenge to his authority and message from the established religious factions, who united temporarily for the purpose. As to his teaching in the city, no substantial account is preserved, and we have only brief glimpses of him 'teaching the people in the temple and telling them the good news' (Lk. 20. 1). What interests the Gospel writers much more is his attitude to the temple itself.

All four Gospels record that he went into the outer courtyard of the temple and drove out the traders and money changers who had stalls there. They also report that this accident was violent in character; Mark says he 'upset the tables' (11. 15) and John that he 'made a whip of cords and drove them out' (2. 15). The implication is that he objected to the secularisation of the temple; but it is not very clear why he should do so, for the traders were there solely to sell commodities needed for sacrifice, while the money changers exchanged Greek and Roman coins for the Jewish currency required for payment of the temple dues. We can draw no definite conclusions. It is of course possible that Jesus publicly attacked, in some form or other, the whole nature and function of the temple. That he should do so would not be very surprising. Sacrifices were controlled by minutely detailed regulations, and he might have expressed impatience with the notion that this sort of practice was *enough* as a way of worshipping God. There is also the accusation reportedly made in his trial that he said: 'I will pull down the temple, made with human hands, and in three days I will build another, not made with hands.' (Mk. 14. 58). This is overlaid with a prediction of Jesus's own resurrection after three days, and in that form we may regard it as improbable. But it seems possible that behind it there lies some real attack made by Jesus on the temple.

Was Jesus, during his time in Jerusalem, publicly identified as the Messiah? All four Gospels record that his entry into the city was accompanied by the acclamations of a crowd who hailed him as Messiah; even John, who usually ignores the political implications of Jesus's role, records that they cried 'God bless the king of Israel!' (Jn. 12. 13). We may suspect that, whatever Jesus's own wish to dissociate himself from political claims, he was being increasingly identified with the hoped-for national Messiah who would free Israel from Roman rule. This would certainly help to explain the authorities' concern to suppress him.

The Synoptic Gospels say that Jesus, knowing very well that he was about to be arrested, presided over a meal attended by his twelve disciples, at which he instituted the breaking and eating of bread and the sharing of a cup of wine (as a 'New Covenant'), which afterwards became the central rite of the Christian Church. The precise historicity of this 'Last Supper' cannot be determined, and not all commentators accept that Jesus meant there to be any special ritual meaning in his actions. But this meal was certainly a part of the tradition about Jesus from the earliest days; it is one of the very few details of Jesus's life which Paul mentions to his readers (1 Cor. 11. 23–6), and some event almost certainly took place. Indeed, if we assume that Jesus suspected that his arrest was near, it would be natural that he should wish to conclude his ministry in some formal fashion. He may simply have wished to institute a symbolic meal which was to remind men of the close 'communion' with God which he had always emphasised in his ministry. Or if, as seems likely, he saw his twelve disciples as the patriarchs of a 'new Israel' — twelve was the number of the legendary tribes of ancient Israel — he may indeed have wished to make a new form of Covenant between God and his chosen people. Whether he really saw the bread and wine as in some sense his own body and blood (as the Gospels say he did) cannot be determined.

It is not at all clear from the Gospels on what ground Jesus was arrested. The implication seems to be that the authorities had no particular charge in mind but were determined to silence him at all costs, and intended to trump up accusations when he was in custody. This seems somewhat unlikely in view of the detailed rules which governed Jewish judicial procedure, and (bearing in mind that the Law expressly forbade 'false witness') it is hard to accept the Gospel picture of a string of witnesses extravagantly and inefficiently perjuring themselves in order to get Jesus convicted. In fact the Gospels say that grounds of conviction were not found until he himself claimed, during the trial, to be the Son of Man who would come on the clouds of heaven — an unambiguous reference to the book of Daniel. We have already seen that there are reasons to doubt that Jesus made such a claim on this occasion; nor, if he did, was it technically blasphemy (a cursing of the divine name), so that one may wonder if it would have been enough to condemn him to death. In these and many other particulars the Gospel accounts of the judicial proceedings against Jesus are unsatisfactory and puzzling.

In fact the part that the Romans played in the proceedings is likely to have been greater than the Gospels indicate. That Jesus was executed by crucifixion indicates that it was beyond doubt the Romans who actually put him to death — it was the Roman method of capital punishment at the time: the Jews, when they were allowed to execute criminals, practised stoning. It is indeed possible that the Jews may have played no part at all in Jesus's arrest, trial and death. If he was being publicly acclaimed in Jerusalem at festival time as 'king of the Jews', the Romans may have regarded this as a sign of political insurgence, and may have decided that a summary execution was the best way of dealing with it. This is borne out by the words fixed by the Romans over Jesus's cross during his execution, words which indicated the charge against him: 'The king of the Jews' (Mk. 15. 26 and parallels). As to why the Gospels shifted the blame from the Romans to the Jews, this can be explained by the fact that Christianity in its first centuries was very much under the shadow of the Roman Empire, and did its best to minimise the grounds for conflict with Rome; moreover after the Jewish wars of the mid-first century the Jews were disgraced in the eyes of the Empire. There is also the fact that quite early in its history the Christian Church split with Judaism, and came to regard it with hostility. From this it was perhaps only a short step to blaming the Jews for Jesus's death. On the other hand it should be noted that the Gospel emphasis on the part played in Jesus's death by the Jewish religious leaders is so strong that it is hard to dismiss it entirely. Moreover the small detail of Peter waiting in the High Priest's courtyard during the trial (Mk. 14. 53 ff.) indicates, at least to those who believe that Peter's reminiscences played some part in shaping the Gospel traditions, that there were Jewish judicial proceedings against Jesus.

So we do not know precisely who was responsible for Jesus's arrest, trial and execution; nor do we know what was in his mind as he went to his death. Those who hold that he identified himself with the Suffering Servant believe that he regarded his suffering as an atonement for the sins of men; those who do not will make no such claim for him. But we can be reasonably certain that he regarded his death as having some positive bearing on his message. He had, after all, preached that the demands of God were utterly uncompromising. Clearly he believed that those demands should be met even if the result were persecution and death. Perhaps there was also in his mind the realisation that by dying — especially by dying the death of a criminal — he was talking to its ultimate limit the willingness to place himself among social outcasts that had always marked his mission. Whether he expected to return to life again after he had died, or envisaged a glorious 'coming' back to earth as Son of Man in the Daniel sense, we do not know. Such ideas are certainly not incongruous with his belief in the miraculous nature of the kingdom of God.

As to the execution itself, the Gospel account of it is largely written to show how in its details it fulfilled Old Testament prophecies. Passages from Psalms 22 and 69 (poetic cries of dereliction) and from Isaiah chapter 53 (the Suffering Servant) have been woven into the narrative so as to demonstrate that everything took place 'according to the Scriptures'. There is little to suggest that Jesus's disciples were able to give any real first-hand report of what happened, and indeed the probability is that by this time they were in hiding, frightened, desolate, and themselves in fear of execution. Bearing this in mind, it is all the more remarkable that they soon came to believe that Jesus was no longer dead but had been raised to life again by God.

## The resurrection

Quite apart from the physical possibility of a resurrection, which must remain a matter for belief or disbelief, many commentators find the Gospel accounts of Jesus's appearances to his disciples after his death extremely hard to accept on grounds of internal consistency and logic, let alone the very puzzling fact that Mark's Gospel (apparently the earliest) comes to an end so abruptly and inconclusively with the description of the frightened women leaving the empty tomb. Moreover there is no reason to assume without question that the detail of the empty tomb, on which the story largely depends, was an early part of the resurrection tradition. Paul makes no mention of it in his account of the resurrection (1 Cor. 15. 3ff.), an account which he introduces as 'the facts which had been imparted to me', and which therefore probably predates the Gospels by at least twenty years. The Gospels say that Joseph of Arimathaea, a rich Jew, obtained the body with Pilate's permission and buried it in his own tomb, but this might be legend. Jesus could have been buried not in any marked grave but in some common burial ground for criminals, so that there was no tomb to be found empty.

On the other hand we must realise that to reject the Gospel accounts of the resurrection and to explain what happened as an experience in the minds of Jesus's disciples presents its own difficulties. It was certianly a very remarkable thing if a group (probably a small group) of frightened men could change its mind and believe that what had appeared to be final defeat was in fact victory. Certainly there are many other instances in history of celebrated persons being supposed to be alive after their death. Such a thing, for example, was often believed of Hitler and other exceptionally evil men, the force of whose personality was so great that the news of their death was simply not accepted by many people. But this is not the same as belief in a resurrection.

Nor can the belief in the resurrection be explained, as can many things in the Gospels, as a 'fulfilment of prophecy'; for no such thing had been prophesied. Certainly the Servant Songs declared that God would raise his Servant from the dead and would restore him to bodily life, so that he would 'enjoy long life and see his children's children' (Is. 53. 10), but this was not at all what was being claimed for Jesus. Indeed when the early Church began to preach that Jesus had risen from the dead on the Sunday morning after his death it had some difficulty in making it seem that the Old Testament really had foretold that such a thing would happen. The nearest text that could be found to a prophecy of such a resurrection was Hosea 6. 2: '. . . after two days he will revive us, on the third day he will restore us, that in his presence we may live'. The truth is that, as the theologian C. F. Evans puts it, 'Resurrection is certainly not something which could have been arrived at by reflection on the Old Testament.'

Those who regard mythology as having a profound influence on human thought will look for a different source for the resurrection belief. From them comes the suggestion that it grew from the ancient notion of the Dying and Rising God, a figure found in early mythologies, including those of Egypt, Mesopotamia, and pre-Jewish Palestine itself. Traces of this figure can (it has been argued) even be found in the Old Testament. But it is hard to imagine how this mythological notion might have had a practical effect on the minds of Jesus's disciples at this moment of crisis.

The historian who does not believe in the resurrection will conclude that the belief in it grew up because of a spontaneous change of mind by the disciples, a decision by them that Jesus was not dead after all. But, even if this is the explanation, one thing must not be missed. Such a belief about Jesus is the most enormous tribute to the force of his personality in his lifetime.

## The Lord Jesus Christ

The result of this belief in the resurrection was that a new religion grew up, centred on the person of Jesus. 'Christianity', as it soon came to be called, was not simply a religion which incorporated his teachings; it was religion *about* him, and about his death and resurrection in particular. It declared that these events were a special self-revelation of God in the field of history, that they had atoned for the sins of mankind, and that all who believed in God and in his Son 'the Lord Jesus Christ' could attain eternal life in God's kingdom. It was a religion of salvation, and Jesus's actual teachings in Galilee and Judaea were only one aspect of his importance as the central figure in it. 'Jesus saves' was the message of Christianity, and his death and resurrection were the chief events by which this was believed to have happened. As Paul expressed it, ' . . . if Christ was not raised, then our Gospel is null and void' (1 Cor. 15. 14).

It would seem very much as if this Gospel of Paul and other early Christians was markedly different from the 'good news' that Jesus preached during his ministry. Indeed many theologians believe that Paul and other early Christian preachers were the true founders of Christianity, in that it was they rather than Jesus himself who constructed a religion around his person. How true this is depends, of course, on our view of Jesus. But if we do not regard him exclusively as a teacher, and accept that he admitted (if only tacitly) the claims of his disciples that he was God's special agent, then we must allow some measure of continuity between Jesus and the early Church.

It is very difficult to assess the exact degree to which the historical Jesus influenced Paul and other early preachers. Certainly it appears from his letters that Paul was not greatly concerned to base his own teachings on what Jesus had taught. He felt he was being guided by Jesus as the living Lord, not by the specific sayings of the Jesus who had walked in Palestine. In fact he often departs dramatically from Jesus's teachings; for example, instead of demanding that his congregations should sell all that they possessed and give to the poor he wrote: 'There is no question of relieving others at the cost of hardship to yourselves' (2 Cor. 8. 14). On the other hand Paul's letters are addressed to those already instructed in the Christian faith, and we cannot say for certain how much new converts would have been told about the actual life and teachings of Jesus. Moreover it would be hard to imagine that the Gospels were written in a climate of declining interest in Jesus himself; they seem to indicate rather the opposite.

Nevertheless there was undoubtedly a tendency in the early Church to centre Christian faith not so much on what Jesus *had* done during this earthly ministry but on the salvation he could offer to Christians *now*. Early preachers spoke of the glorious Jesus of the present — and of the future, since the Church confidently expected his return 'on the clouds of heaven' to judge the living and the dead and to inaugurate God's kingdom on earth. Paul wrote of the day when our Lord Jesus Christ is revealed from heaven with his mighty angels in blazing fire. Then he will do justice upon those who refuse to acknowledge God and upon those who will not obey the gospel of our Lord Jesus. They will suffer the punishment of eternal ruin, cut off from the presence of the Lord and the splendour of his might, when on that great Day he comes to be glorified among his own and adored among all believers . . . (2 Thess. 1. 7–10)

Paul, at least at first, expected that the 'great Day' would happen in his own lifetime; early in his work as a preacher he talked of 'we who are left alive until the Lord comes' (1 Thess. 4. 15). But the years passed and the glorious event did not occur; and, though the Church never abandoned the hope of Jesus's Second Coming — it believes in it still — it began to shift the emphasis of its teaching away from this hope for the future, and more towards the belief that Jesus could offer salvation to believers *now*. One result of this change of emphasis was John's Gospel, which, much more than the Synoptics, emphasises Jesus's role as Saviour of the world. It is possible to see in the Synoptic picture of Jesus, despite the many problems of the narrative, a historical person. John shows us not a Jesus of history but the Word of God made flesh, the saving Christ whose call is to all who believe in him. 'I am the light of the world. No follower of mine shall wander in the dark; he shall have the light of life' (Jn. 8. 12).

From this point onwards until modern times it becomes virtually impossible to distinguish the influence of Jesus himself from the influence of Christianity. Up to the nineteenth century Jesus's message was only perceived through the medium of the Church. Even the Reformation, which challenged established ideas about the Church's authority, returned not to the specific teachings of the historical Jesus but to the Pauline theology of personal salvation through Jesus as Lord. Until the beginnings of modern historical research the distinction was not really made between the ideas *of* Jesus himself — his actual teaching — and ideas *about* him, by which is meant Christianity's belief in him as Saviour.

Indeed at certain periods in the Church's history it can be said that the followers of Jesus drastically misinterpreted his teachings or overlaid them with views of their own. The Christian belief that salvation was a gift from God and could not be achieved by the works of men led to a tendency, particularly in the early years of Christianity, to ignore the ethical demands of religion and concentrate on its mystical aspects. As J. L. Houlden puts it:

As salvation was not to be found in the life and activity of this world but only by escape into a wholly mystical present or an otherworldly future, ethics lost their force and significance. God held the initiative, only God could act in this cause; why then should man concern himself with duties dictated solely by his bodily existence?

This streak of 'antinomianism' or moral lawlessness arose partly because some early Christians misinterpreted the assertion made by such preachers as Paul that Jesus had 'ended' the Law. Antinomianism was, of course, a complete perversion of what Jesus himself had taught: his message was not that God made no ethical demands, but that the demands were total and unlimited, and could not be circumscribed by the Law. In fact antinomianism did not become a dominant feature of Christianity; Paul and his contemporaries took much trouble to oppose it, particularly when it led (as it often did) to sexual licence; see 1 Cor. 6. 12–20, where Paul attacks those who say, in the name of Jesus Christ, 'I am free to do anything.' But the fact that the antinomians could — however erroneously — claim the authority of Jesus for their licentious behaviour shows how much his teaching was subject to misinterpretation.

Nor were such distortions of Jesus's message confined to the early Church. At many times in the history of Christianity there have been sects of believers who have regarded scrupulous moral purity as being of paramount importance for salvation — the exact opposite, in fact, of antinomianism; and again this has been done in the name of Jesus. The Puritans of seventeenth-century England are a particularly obvious example of this, and something of the kind can also be found in those present-day 'evangelical' Christians, especially in the United States, who regard abstinence from tobacco and alcohol as a *sine qua non* of faith in Jesus. Needless to say, there is no evidence that the historical Jesus endorsed such attitudes, which resemble those of the Pharisees rather than that of Jesus himself and his followers.

It may be objected that these are extremes, and that within the central stream of Christianity the message of Jesus remains largely unimpaired. This may be so, and certainly the Gospels are read at every celebration of the 'Lord's Supper', so that in this central act of worship Christians are constantly reminded of the sayings and actions of Jesus himself, at least as the Gospels recorded them. On the other hand it cannot be said that the Church concerns itself very much to emphasise the radical character of Jesus's ethical teachings. What matters to it is Jesus's power to save *now*: he is the living Lord, rather than just a historical figure on whose teachings the Church is based. This means that his influence on his followers is quite different from that of Muhammad or Gautama, the teachers — and they claimed to be no more than teachers — who founded Islam and Buddhism.

If we ask what has been the influence of Jesus outside the Christian Church, the question is very difficult to answer. Certainly there have been occasions when Christian ethics — and thus perhaps ultimately the teachings of Jesus — have shaped world events. Slavery was eventually abolished in Western society in the nineteenth century largely as a result of pressure from Christians. On the other hand the early and medieval Church supported slavery as an institution — 'Slaves, give entire obedience to your earthly masters,' wrote Paul (Col. 3. 22) — and it may be said in general that Christianity has often been content to accept the moral *status quo* of its time, only changing its moral outlook as society itself does so.

In the humanities and the arts the figure of Jesus has certainly been of great importance. From early and medieval times until very recently the great majority of European moral thinkers and artists often drew in one way or another on Christian beliefs. Works as diverse as Dante's *Divine Comedy* and Bach's *St Matthew Passion*, as well as whole schools of European religious painting, testify to the imaginative appeal of Jesus and of the Church who worshipped him. Yet it can scarcely be said that this reflects the intellectual achievement of the historical Jesus. Here too it is Jesus as Saviour, as the central figure in a religion of salvation, that has caught hold of men's minds.

Now the picture has changed, and the decline of religious belief in many areas of Western society, together with the increase of historical research into the events behind the Gospels, means that the influence of Jesus is today rather different. Outside the Church, Jesus sometimes appears as a figurehead for movements which profess no religious belief about him, but are attracted by what they regard as his anti-establishment message of love and compassion. To them he appeals because (they say) he rejected fixed rules and attacked moral hypocrisy. Such an interpretation of Jesus is dubious to say the least; though he was certainly a radical, he opposed not established society in general but specific religious abuses of his day, and while he preached love and compassion he balanced this with enormous moral demands; nor did he reject moral rules so much as declare them to be inadequate. It has to be said that modern movements of this kind which claim to follow the message of Jesus are not really doing so at all. Meanwhile within Christianity there is a steadily increasing tendency, at least in radical quarters, to reject the whole supernatural framework of religion as mythical, not literally true, and this has been accompanied by an attempt to posit some other kind of philosophical system in which the teachings of Jesus, 'de-mythologised', might make sense. In particular, existentialism has been offered by many theologians as an alternative to the old Judaeo–Christian picture of God, Heaven and Hell; and this existential interpretation of Jesus and Christianity is at present finding wide acceptance in theological circles. It must be said, however, that it has largely failed to communicate itself to those not acquainted with the intricacies of modern philosophy, and it certainly lacks the direct, immediate, and ultimately *simple* character of the message of Jesus himself.

It is because of this simplicity of his teaching that Jesus has, despite all the confusions and perversions of his message over the centuries, continued to have a powerful influence on the human mind. He was not a philosopher; he did not construct any complete system of ethics; nor did he speak in moral abstractions which can be straightforwardly detached from the context of his religious beliefs. But in the manner of his teaching, his refusal to compromise when faced with any moral dilemma, his emphasis on the universality and totality, the unlimitedness of moral demands on men, there is a force which crosses all religious barriers and appeals to us whether or not we subscribe to his religious beliefs. This, we feel instinctively, is how moral problems should be attacked. We may find that in practice it is often impossible to do so; and certainly he taught in hyperbole. Yet despite the inconsistencies in his teaching, despite the fact that it was never designed as a detailed rule for daily life, it has a sharpness and immediacy which makes the teaching of almost every other moralist (however sane and wise and well balanced) seem pale by comparison. Jesus was not just a moral teacher: this book has tried to emphasise that fact. His appeal was just as much charismatic as intellectual. But in the field of moral teaching his forcefulness has had no equal.

# Sources and further reading

Among the many modern translations of the Bible, *The New English Bible* (Oxford University Press and Cambridge University Press, 1970) is particularly recommended. Those who wish to study the original Greek of the New Testament will find a number of editions available, among them one which prints a literal English translation between the lines of the Greek; this is *The R. S. V. Interlinear Greek-English New Testament* (Samuel Bagster & Sons Ltd., 1958).

There are many modern commentaries on the Gospels. These vary greatly both in the viewpoint of the commentator and the detail into which they go. The Pelican New Testament Commentaries provide a good cross-section of modern opinion, and that on Mark's Gospel by D. E. Nineham (Penguin, 1963) has been invaluable in the writing of this book. A more conservative view of Mark and of the reliability of the Gospels in general is taken by V. Taylor in *The Gospel According to St Mark* (Macmillan, 1953); his commentary is worth studying both for this and for the great detail in which he examines the original Greek. Matthew's Gospel is perhaps best studied with the aid of the commentary by H. Benedict Green (New Clarendon Bible, Oxford University Press, 1975), and John's Gospel with the aid of the commentary by Barnabas Lindars (New Century Bible, Oliphants, 1972). There are many commentaries on Luke, of which one of the best is still that by J. M. Creed (Macmillan, 1930).

Studies of Jesus and the New Testament are so numerous that only a very few of those available can be mentioned here. The following books are included simply because they were a help to the present writer. *A Short History of Religions* by E. E. Kellett (Penguin, 1962) provides an admirable survey of religions in the ancient world, while John Bright's *A History of Israel* (S.C.M. Press, 1972) and Bo Reicke's *The New Testament Era* (A. &. C. Black, 1969) give a good summary of the historical background to Christianity. The teachings of the rabbis Hillel and Shammai, whose work has been contrasted in this book with the teaching of Jesus, are found in the *Mishnah*, translated by Herbert Danby (Oxford University Press, 1933). As regards Jesus himself, two of the best books on the character of his teaching and of his ministry in general are Rudolf Bultmann's *Jesus and the Word* (Fontana, 1958) and H. J. Cadbury's *Jesus: What Manner of Man?* (Macmillan, 1947), while J. L. Houlden's *Ethics and the New Testament* (Mowbrays, 1975) is a useful summary of the difficulties of disentangling what Jesus really taught, and of the moral differences between the authors of the different New Testament books. On the subject of Jesus's messianic claims and the background to those claims, S. Mowinckel's *He That Cometh* (Blackwell, 1959) is the best summary of the traditional view, while the more radical view that Jesus meant nothing extraordinary by his use of the term 'son of man' is argued by Geza Vermes in *Jesus the Few* (Fontana, 1976), a book which is full of fascinating detail about the Jewish background to Jesus's ministry. The trial and death of Jesus are discussed fully in John Knox's *The Death of Christ* (Collins, 1959); on this subject see also *Roman Society and Roman Law in the New Testament* by A. N. Sherwin-White (Clarendon Press, 1963). The resurrection and the problems surrounding the Gospel accounts of it are discussed very usefully in C. F. Evans's *Resurrection and the New Testament* (S.C.M. Press, 1970).

The history of Gospel studies is a subject in itself. The best introduction to it is *The New Testament: the History of the Investigation of its Problems* by W. G. Kümmel (S.C.M. Press, 1973), while Robert Grant's *A Historical Introduction to the New Testament* (Fontana, 1971) is a handy paperback summary of the subject. Recent New Testament studies which have influenced the writing of this book include John Drury's *Tradition and Design in Luke's Gospel* (Darton, Longman & Todd, 1976) and Michael Goulder's *Midrash and Lection in Matthew* (S.P.C.K., 1974). And finally mention must be made again of that fascinating volume by Albert Schweitzer, *The Quest of the Historical Jesus* (3rd edition, A. & C. Black, 1954), with its timely reminder that 'There is no historical task which so reveals a man's true self as the writing of a Life of Jesus.'

# MUHAMMAD

MICHAEL COOK

# *Preface*

It is unlikely that Muhammad would have warmed to the series in which this book appears, or cared to be included in it. Its very title smacks of polytheism; the term 'master' is properly applicable only to God. He might also have resented the insinuation of intellectual originality. As a messenger of God, his task was to deliver a message, not to pursue his own fancies.

My own reservations about writing this book arise from different grounds. Muhammad made too great an impact on posterity for it to be an easy matter to place him in his original context. This is both a question of historical perspective and, as will appear, a question of sources. The result is that the only aspect of the book about which I feel no qualms is the brevity imposed by the format of the series. The attempt to write about Muhammad within such a compass has brought me to confront issues I might not otherwise have faced, and in ways which might not otherwise have occurred to me.

I give frequent references to the Koran (K), and occasional references to the *Sira* of Ibn Ishaq (S); for details, see below, p. 367. For simplicity I have transcribed Arabic names and terms without diacritics; note that the 's' and 'h' in the name 'Ibn Ishaq' are to be pronounced separately (more as in 'mishap' than in 'ship').

My thanks are due to Patricia Crone, Etan Kohlberg, Frank Stewart, Keith Thomas and Henry Hardy for their comments on a draft of this book; and to Fritz Zimmermann for a critical reading of what might otherwise have been the final version, and for a substantive influence on my understanding of Muslim theology.

# Contents

# Introduction

The Muslim world extends continuously from Senegal to Pakistan, and discontinuously eastwards to the Philippines. In 1977 there were some 720 million Muslims, just over a sixth of the world's population. The proportion might have been a great deal higher if the Muslims of Spain had applied themselves more energetically to the conquest of Europe in the eighth century, if the sudden death of Timur in 1405 had not averted a Muslim invasion of China, or if Muslims had played a more prominent role in the modern settlement of the New World and the Antipodes. But they have remained the major religious group in the heart of the Old World. In terms of sheer numbers they are outdone by the Christians, and arguably also by the Marxists. On the other hand, they are considerably less affected by sectarian divisions than either of these rivals: the overwhelming majority of Muslims belong to the Sunni mainstream of Islam.

There are many Muslims at the present day whose ancestors were infidels a thousand years ago; this is true by and large of the Turks, the Indonesians, and sizeable Muslim populations in India and Africa. The processes by which these peoples entered Islam were varied, and reflect a phase of Islamic history when different parts of the Muslim world had gone their separate ways. Yet the core of the Islamic community owes its existence to an earlier and more unitary historical context. Between the seventh and ninth centuries the Middle East and much of North Africa were ruled by the Caliphate, a Muslim state more or less coextensive with the Muslim world of its day. This empire in turn was the product of the conquests undertaken by the inhabitants of the Arabian peninsula in the middle decades of the seventh century.

The men who effected these conquests were the followers of a certain Muhammad, an Arab merchant turned prophet and politician who in the 620s established a theocratic state among the tribes of western Arabia.

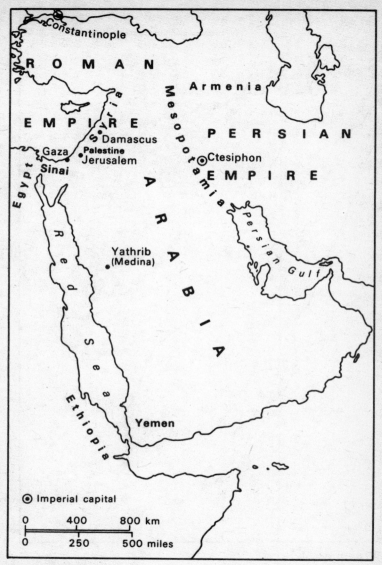

The Middle East

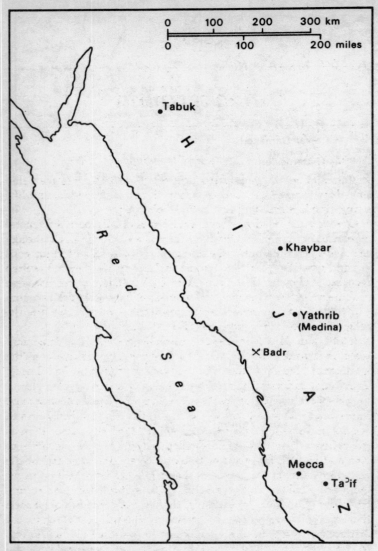

Western Arabia

# 1

# *Background*

## Monotheism

Muhammad was a monotheist prophet. Monotheism is the belief that there is one God, and only one. It is a simple idea; and like many simple ideas, it is not entirely obvious.

Over the last few thousand years it has probably been the general consensus of human societies that there are numerous gods (though men have certainly held very different views as to who these gods are and what they do). The oldest societies to have left us written records, and hence direct evidence of their religious beliefs, were polytheistic some five thousand years ago; by the first millennium B.C. there is enough evidence to indicate that polytheism was the religious norm right across the Old World.

It did not, however, remain unchallenged. In the same millennium ideas of a rather different stamp were appearing among the intellectual élites of the more advanced cultures. In Greece, Babylonia, India and China there emerged a variety of styles of thought which were noticeably more akin to our own abstract and impersonal manner of looking at the world. The tendency was to see the universe in terms of grand unified theories, rather than as the reflection of the ill-coordinated activities of a plurality of personal gods. Such ways of thinking rarely led to denial of the actual existence of the gods, but they tended to tidy them up in the interests of coherence and system, or to reduce them to a certain triviality. (Consider, for example, the view of some Buddhist sects that the gods are unable to attain enlightenment owing to the distracting behaviour of the goddesses.) What they did not do was to pick out from the polytheistic heritage a single personal god, and discard the rest.

This development was to be the contribution of a conceptually less sophisticated people of the ancient Near East, the Israelites.

Like other peoples of their world, the Israelites possessed a national god who was closely identified with their political and military fortunes. Like others, they experienced the desolation of defeat and exile at the hands of more powerful enemies. Their distinctive reaction to this history was to develop an *exclusive* cult of their national god, eventually proclaimed as the only god in existence — in a word, as God.

Had monotheism remained a peculiarity of the Israelites (or as we can now call them, the Jews), it would not have ranked as more than a curiosity in the history of the world at large. As it happened, this situation was drastically changed by a minor Jewish heresy which became a world religion: Christianity. Its primary spread was within the Roman Empire. By the fourth century after Christ it had been adopted as the state religion; by the sixth century the Roman Empire was more or less solidly Christian. At the same time Christianity had spread unevenly in several directions beyond the imperial frontiers. There were, for example, Christian kingdoms in Armenia and Ethiopia; and although the Persian Empire held fast to its ancestral Zoroastrian faith, it contained within its borders a significant Christian minority, particularly in Mesopotamia. West of India, no major society was unshaken by the rise of monotheism, and only the Persians stood out against it.

## Arabia

South of the Roman and Persian Empires lay the world's largest desert. This area is divided into two unequal portions by the Red Sea: to the west lies the Sahara, and to the east Arabia. The Arabian peninsula is a vast rectangle, some 1,300 miles long and 750 wide, stretching south-east from the Fertile Crescent (i.e. Syria and Mesopotamia). Its predominant feature is its aridity. This is slightly offset in the north, where desert gives way to semi-desert and even to steppe, and still more in the south, where a mountainous terrain receives a measure of summer rain. But between these marginal zones lies the bulk of Arabia, and for the most part it is desert relieved only by scattered oases.

In comparison with the Fertile Crescent, Arabia was accordingly a land of deprivation. Agriculture, the basic economic activity of mankind between the neolithic and industrial revolutions, was largely confined to the oases; and even the rainfall agriculture of the Yemen was derisory by comparison with what could be achieved across the Red Sea in Ethiopia. Much of Arabia was fit only for pastoralism, and a nomadic pastoralism at that.

These conditions did much to shape the character of Arabian society. Civilisation, with its cities, temples, bureaucracies, aristocracies, priesthoods, regular armies, and elaborate cultural heritages, requires a substantial agricultural base. With the partial exception of the Yemen, such an edifice could not be built in Arabia. Arabian society was tribal, in the oases as much as in the desert. There were pariah groups excluded from tribal society, and 'kings' who were almost but not quite above it; but by the standards of the Fertile Crescent, Arabian society was egalitarian and anarchic. By the same standards the culture of Arabia was simple, if not threadbare; its principal legacy is its poetry.

The isolating peninsular geography of Arabia, and the mobility of pastoralists within it, contributed to another significant feature of Arabian society, its homogeneity. To a surprising extent, the Arabian desert was the land of a single people, the Arabs, speaking a single language, Arabic. This cannot always have been so. The Arabs do not appear by name before the ninth century B.C., and were not the first nomadic pastoralists of the area; but by the time of Muhammad, any earlier diversity had been obliterated north of the Yemen.

Although Arabian society was very different from the settled societies of the Fertile Crescent and beyond, it was by no means deprived of contact with the outside world. Yet these contacts, though ancient, had wrought no transformation on either side; their effects were most pronounced in the border areas where the two patterns interacted.

We may begin by looking at the military and political aspect of this relationship. A nomadic tribal society is warlike and highly mobile; but it is also allergic to large-scale organisation. As raiders, the tribesmen of Arabia were accordingly a persistent nuisance to the settled world; but they were rarely a serious military threat. The Nabatean Arabs built up a kingdom on the edge of the desert which in 85 B.C. occupied Damascus, and an Arab queen of the later fourth century invaded Palestine; but such events were exceptional. They might lead to the creation of Arab statelets, and encourage penetration by Arab settlers, but they initiated no massive and enduring conquests. A state governing a settled society, by contrast, is capable of organised military effort on a large scale, and may adopt a more or less forward policy of frontier defence against nomadic raiders. It has, however, neither the means nor the motive for conquering a desert. An eccentric Babylonian king had once spent several years in the western Arabian oases, and a Roman expedition had blundered through the Arabian desert on its way to the Yemen; but again such episodes were exceptional. Under normal conditions, the political influence of outside powers was confined to frontier areas, where it might lead to the formation of Arab client principalities and the use of their troops as auxiliaries. It is true that a certain departure from this pattern seems to have arisen from the imperial rivalries of the centuries preceding the career of Muhammad. In this period the Persians established a hegemony over the Arabs on an unprecedented scale. They were entrenched in the east and south, and even had some presence in the oases of central Arabia. But it is hard to imagine this yoke as a heavy one in inner Arabia, least of all in the west, and it scarcely appears in the story of Muhammad's life.

Another significant form of contact with the outside world was trade. The Islamic sources remember a trade in silver to Persia from south and central Arabia, in close connection with the Persian political hegemony. In the west they describe an Arab trade with southern Syria of which the staple commodity would seem to have been leather. By the standards of the international trade of the day, both the silver and, still more, the leather trades were doubtless rather trivial. Frankincense, the great Arabian export of antiquity, had long ago lost its market in the Roman Empire; and coffee, the only other Arabian export of consequence before the arrival of oil, had not yet appeared. At the same time the bulk of the peninsula played no part in international transit trade; it was naturally cheaper to ship goods round the peninsula than to transport them across it. But such trade as there was sufficed to ensure that a knowledge of the civilised world and its proceedings existed far into Arabia.

## Arabia and monotheism

The Arabs were polytheists. The pattern of their religion was simple — the Arabs did not, for example, provide their gods with expensive housing such as was standard in the Fertile Crescent, and so far as we know they developed little in the way of a religious mythology. But simple as it was, such indications as we have suggest that it had been remarkably stable over a long period; thus Allat, a goddess prominent in the time of Muhammad, is already attested by Herodotus in the fifth century B.C. In the centuries preceding the life of Muhammad, however, external influences were beginning to disturb this ancient polytheism. Predominantly, this influence was monotheist; despite the Persian hegemony, the impact of Zoroastrianism seems to have been slight outside the north-east.

As might be expected, the Arabs were affected by the rise of Christianity, and more particularly by the sects which came to predominate among their settled neighbours. In Syria, the prevailing doctrine from the fifth century was that of the Monophysites; this sect achieved a considerable following among the Arab tribes of the northern desert. In the Persian Empire the Christian population was mainly Nestorian, and to a lesser extent this sect held an analogous position among the neighbouring Arabs. It was also active along the Arab side of what in political terms was very much the Persian Gulf. In the Yemen we hear most of Monophysites, matching as it happened the form of Christianity which prevailed in Ethiopia.

There was also a considerable, and probably much older, Jewish presence in western Arabia. The Islamic tradition describes substantial Jewish populations in several of the western oases, in the region known as the Hijaz, and this has some confirmation from archaeology. In the Yemen a Jewish presence is likewise attested. There is evidence that it was in contact with the Jews of Palestine, and it seems to have achieved some local influence; in the early sixth century a Yemeni king martyred Christians in the name of Judaism.

Despite this Christian and Jewish penetration, Arabian society was still predominantly pagan; but an awareness of monotheism in one or other of its forms must have been widespread.

If we imagine ourselves for a moment in sixth-century Arabia, what long-term expectations could we reasonably have entertained? First, that if the Arabs had never in the past been a serious military threat to the outside world, they were unlikely to become one now. Second, that the escalating rivalry between the leading foreign powers, the Romans and the Persians, would lead if anything to a tightening of their grip on whatever was worth

controlling in Arabia. And third, that despite the persistence of
paganism and the presence of Judaism, it was only a matter of time
before Arabia became more or less Christian. In the event, the
triumph of monotheism in Arabia took a form which rendered each
of these plausible expectations false.

# 2

# Life

The life of Muhammad is the subject of a wealth of Muslim narrative sources. Of these the most successful in the Muslim world, and the best-known outside it, is a life of the Prophet composed about the middle of the eighth century by a certain Ibn Ishaq. We possess it in the edition of a minor scholar two generations his junior. Much, though not all, of what is said in this chapter derives from this work. My aim here is simply to present the traditional account in outline — not, at this point, to interpret it or assess its reliability.

## Mecca

Muhammad was born into the Arab tribe of Quraysh in the southern Hijaz. Quraysh are defined as the descendants in the male line of a certain Fihr ibn Malik, who lived eleven generations before Muhammad. They were a noble lineage, but not at first a particularly successful one. For several generations they lived scattered among a wider tribal grouping, and did not function as a political unit. Nor did they possess a territorial centre; Mecca, a local sanctuary of great antiquity, was in other hands. Five generations before Muhammad, this situation was remedied by an enterprising member of the tribe called Qusayy. He put together an alliance, and by war and diplomacy obtained possession of the Meccan sanctuary. He was then able to ingather his scattered fellow-tribesmen and to settle them in Mecca. They held him in such respect that he was virtually their king — a position which was not enjoyed by any of his descendants. Thus was established the society into which Muhammad was born.

But how, one might ask, did the newly settled Quraysh make ends meet? Mecca is situated in a notoriously barren valley, which as such is quite unsuited to supporting a settled population. The answer appears in the third generation before Muhammad, when

Hashim, grandson of Qusayy and great-grandfather of the Prophet, took steps to establish Quraysh as merchants of international standing. He initiated the two caravan journeys of the year, one in the summer and one in the winter. He made a friend of the Roman Emperor and obtained protection for merchants of Quraysh in Roman territory; he himself died in the Palestinian town of Gaza. His brothers obtained similar concessions from the rulers of Persia, the Yemen and Ethiopia, and at the same time arrangements were made to secure the safety of Meccan trade in the territories of the intervening Arab tribes. In this way was created the mercantile economy in which Muhammad himself was in due course to play a part.

Despite these developments, Quraysh remained very much a part of the local scene. Socially and culturally, they were well integrated into the world of the neighbouring pastoralists, with whom their relations were close and on balance friendly. Mecca itself was a city only in name. In the generation before Muhammad, most of its dwellings were still mere huts constructed of palm-branches; dramatic redevelopment overtook the town only in the very different conditions of the early Islamic period.

Mecca also remained a sanctuary, and so a centre of pilgrimage. In the eyes of the tradition, as we shall see, it had originally been a monotheist foundation, but by the period which concerns us it was effectively a pagan sanctuary. Qusayy, at the time of his take-over, had left the rites of pilgrimage unchanged, but had made practical arrangements for the feeding of the pilgrims. This responsibility was in due course inherited by the Prophet's grandfather, who also rediscovered and restored the spring originally associated with the sanctuary. In Muhammad's youth the central shrine of the sanctuary, the building known as the Ka'ba, was reconstructed; Muhammad himself participated at a crucial juncture. There were also stirrings of monotheism in the generation before Muhammad, with three of the four men affected ending up as Christians; but Mecca remained an overwhelmingly pagan society.

## Early life

Muhammad was born at an uncertain date around A.D. 570. (At his death in 632, he was aged sixty-three or sixty-five according to one's choice of authorities.) He did not receive his mission as a prophet till the age of forty (or forty-three or forty-five), i.e. around the year 610.

Prior to this there was, as might be expected, no lack of pointers to his future greatness. At his birth there issued with him a light by which his mother could see the castles of Bostra in Syria. Prophecies regarding his future role came from Arab soothsayers, from Jews, and from Christians of various kinds. On one occasion he accompanied his uncle Abu Talib on a caravan journey to Syria; a Christian monk recognised the boy for what he was, and advised his uncle to take great care to protect him from the Jews.

Yet at a more mundane level his prospects during much of this period were anything but assured. His father died before, or not long after, he was born. Soon after birth he was handed over to foster-parents in an impoverished neighbouring tribe for two or three years; he then returned to his mother, who herself died when he was six. After being cared for by his grandfather for a couple of years, he went to live with the family of Abu Talib, and this uncle became in effect a father to him. Then as a young man he was retained by Khadija, a wealthy widow, to act as her commercial agent in the trade with Syria; he did well, and in due course she saw fit to marry him. He was thus, at this stage, a somewhat marginal figure, who owed such success as he had achieved as much to his older and richer wife as to his own position in society.

## Mission

Eventually Muhammad was given his prophetic mission. He had been in the habit of spending one month of each year on the nearby Mount Hira'. This, it would seem, was a religious custom of pagan times; while there, he might be joined by his family, and would feed such of the poor as came to him. One night while he was residing on the mountain in this fashion the angel Gabriel visited him in his sleep, and ordered him to recite; in response to Muhammad's puzzlement he then taught him a passage of the 96th chapter of the Koran, which appropriately begins with the command 'recite!'. The experience was in two ways characteristic of what followed: Gabriel was to be the normal channel of communication between God and Muhammad, and it was in such fragments that what was to become the Muslim scripture, the Koran, was gradually revealed to him. At the time, however, Muhammad found the experience disturbing, and concluded that he must be either a poet or possessed — in either case the victim of a malign spirit. But a local Christian perceived that Muhammad's experience was comparable to that of Moses, and inferred him to be 'the prophet of this people'; while a careful experiment devised by Muhammad's wife Khadija established that his supernatural visitor was indeed an angel and not a devil.

After receiving his mission, Muhammad spent fifteen (or thirteen, or ten) years in Mecca. During this period the episodic revelation of scripture continued, and a simple ritual and morality were developed. The ritual consisted of a number (fixed at five) of daily prayers, to be performed in a state of ritual purity attained by washing; the practical details were demonstrated to Muhammad by Gabriel. The morality comprised such principles as abstaining from theft and fornication. This was also the time when Muhammad was vouchsafed a remarkable supernatural journey. One night while he was sleeping in the sanctuary in Mecca, he was taken by Gabriel to Jerusalem; there he met Abraham, Moses and Jesus, and led them in prayer, after which he was taken on a visit to heaven. His subsequent description of the layout of Jerusalem was confirmed, presumably from personal experience, by one of his followers. At the same time, the authenticity of his mission continued to be confirmed by a variety of Christians, not least of whom was the ruler of Ethiopia.

In the course of this period Muhammad made a considerable number of Meccan converts. At first (if we follow Ibn Ishaq) these converts were confined to his immediate family: Khadija, his wife; 'Ali, a young son of Abu Talib whom Muhammad had taken into his household at the time of a famine; and Zayd, a slave whom he had manumitted. For three years the incipient religion continued to be a private matter. Then God ordered Muhammad to make it public, and it rapidly acquired a local following, and became the talk of Arabia.

The reaction of the pagan Meccans to this development was initially a tolerant one. There was no reason, as one of them put it, why a man should not choose a religion for himself as he pleased. There was some mockery and cynicism — suggestions that Muhammad had actually received his supposedly divine message from human sources — but there was no real trouble until Muhammad began to disparage the local pagan gods. This was considered offensive. Even then, the pagans showed great willingness to compromise; they offered to make Muhammad a king, or to obtain suitable medical treatment for his psychic condition. Certainly on the one occasion when Muhammad temporarily yielded to the temptation to allow the pagan gods a place in his religion, the move was in human terms a dramatic success. But it was not monotheism. Muhammad reverted to the purity of his message, and relations between his followers and their pagan fellow-tribesmen became bitterly hostile.

What follows is crucial for Muhammad's career, and must be seen against the background of tribal politics in a stateless society. Since the days of its founder Qusayy, the Meccan polity had lacked a central authority; it was made up of a number of descent groups whose mutual relations could easily degenerate into civil war. To some extent, the spread of the new religion reflected these divisions: it was strongest among the Banu Hashim, the descendants of Hashim, to whom Muhammad himself belonged; and it was weakest among their leading rivals, the Banu 'Abd Shams. This situation lay behind the boycott which the pagans for some two or three years imposed on the Banu Hashim and their nearest relatives, refusing intermarriage or commercial dealings with them until such time as they came to their senses in the matter of Muhammad. But alignments were not in fact as clearcut as this suggests. Leading members of the Banu Hashim remained pagans, while at the same time a good many members of other descent groups converted to Muhammad's religion.

The question for the Muslims was who, in this stateless society, would protect them. The most exposed were clearly those outside the Prophet's own descent group. They were wide open to attack by members of their own descent groups, and there was nothing in the circumstances which Muhammad could do to protect them. It was in response to this situation that Muhammad sent a party of his followers to take refuge in Ethiopia, where they succeeded in obtaining the protection of the ruler. For a long time Muhammad's own position was relatively secure; thanks to the strong personal commitment of his pagan uncle Abu Talib, he enjoyed the protection of his own descent group. But in due course Abu Talib died, and Muhammad's problem now became acute.

His only recourse was to look outside Mecca for the protection he needed — an expedient already foreshadowed in the Ethiopian episode. But the Ethiopian ruler was obviously too distant to

provide protection in Arabia itself, and Muhammad began his
search nearer home. A visit to the neighbouring town of Ta'if
proved a fiasco; its only happy moment was the recognition of
Muhammad's prophethood by a Christian slave from Nineveh.
Thereafter Muhammad presented himself at fairs as a prophet in
search of protectors, and made overtures to a number of tribes; but
he was always turned down. Finally deliverance came from the
north.

## The hijra

Medina, or Yathrib to use its pre-Islamic name, was a very different
sort of place from Mecca. It was one of a number of agriculturally
rich oases in the Hijaz. Like others of these oases, it had an ancient
Jewish population. These Jews were tribesmen well assimilated to
the Arabian environment. At a later date Arabs had settled
alongside the Jews; they constituted the tribes of Aws and Khazraj,
and had come to dominate the oasis. Like Mecca, Yathrib lacked
a central authority. Unlike Mecca, it was disturbed by recurrent
civil strife. It was these features of the oasis that were to give
Muhammad his opening.

On one occasion when he was advertising his cause at a fair,
Muhammad had the good fortune to identify a small group of
Khazraj. He invited these six men to sit down with him, and
proceeded to expound his religion. The group responded positively
for two reasons. Their close relations with the Jews of their city had
familiarised them with the notion that a new prophet was about to
appear; and they saw Muhammad's cause as one in which the
people of Yathrib might be united, a solution to their domestic
political problems. 'If God unites them in it', they added to
Muhammad, 'no man will be more powerful than you' (S 198).

It was some time before anything came of this project; but
eventually Muhammad reached a firm agreement with a larger and
more representative group of tribesmen from Yathrib. The
tribesmen pledged themselves to protect him as they would their
own families, and showed themselves willing to accept the risks
which that entailed — in particular the likelihood of military
confrontation with Quraysh. Muhammad then ordered his Meccan
followers to leave the city and emigrate to Yathrib. He himself
stayed behind until such time as he received God's permission to

defend it was roundly defeated by some three hundred Muslims (reinforced by angels) at Badr. Subsequently, however, it looked as if Muhammad had taken on more than he could handle. The next two rounds were fought in the immediate neighbourhood of Medina: in the third year Muhammad suffered his major defeat at Uhud; and in the fifth he was defending Medina itself. In the following year, however, we find him attempting a peaceful pilgrimage to Mecca; the Meccans prevented him, but a truce was negotiated between the two parties. Thereafter the tide turned, leading in the eighth year to the surrender of Mecca and Muhammad's triumphant entry into the city which had rejected him.

As his fortunes improved, Muhammad achieved military successes in other directions as well. In the seventh year he had taken possession of two major Jewish oases of the Hijaz, Khaybar and Fadak. The conquest of Mecca led on to a consolidation of his power in the southern Hijaz: an alliance of hostile tribes was defeated nearby at Hunayn, and the oasis of Ta'if submitted. In the aftermath of these successes, the Arab tribes at large more or less voluntarily submitted to Muhammad's authority.

One theatre of Muhammad's military activities had a particular significance for the future. In the far north-west, tribal Arabia bordered on the Roman Empire. Early in the eighth year of the *hijra*, before the conquest of Mecca, Muhammad had sent an expedition to this region without success. In the following year he himself went as far as Tabuk, but without confronting the Romans. In the eleventh year he planned to send an expedition into Roman territory in Palestine, but his death intervened. Within a generation of his death these small beginnings had issued in the Muslim conquest of the Middle East.

## The faith

Muhammad's years in Medina were also important in more narrowly religious terms. They saw a spread of his religion closely associated with his military success. Among the pagan Arabs, resistance to his message — as opposed to his political authority — was rarely deep-rooted, though the attachment of the people of Ta'if to their pagan idols was something of an exception. The Jews and Christians of Arabia (particularly the former) proved more stiff-necked — whence Muhammad's prescription on his death-bed to the effect that they be expelled from Arabia. Outside Arabia, Muhammad addressed himself to the rulers of the day with varying results. The king of Ethiopia wholeheartedly accepted Muhammad's message; the Roman Emperor privately conceded its truth; the ruler of Persia tore up the letter he was sent. Meanwhile lesser imitators of Muhammad had appeared in eastern and southern Arabia, a backhanded compliment to the success of his mission.

At the same time Muhammad's religion was itself elaborated and perfected. He continued to receive revelations, and by the time of his death the entire content of the Koran had been revealed. The basic rituals and duties of Islam were established or further refined: washing, prayer, alms-giving, fasting, pilgrimage. Numerous prescriptions on matters of religious law were revealed to Muhammad as part of the Koran, or otherwise stipulated by him. On the occasion of the conquest of Khaybar, for example, he declared the eating of the flesh of the domesticated ass forbidden.

A particularly dramatic moment in the development of the religion was the changing of the direction in which the believers prayed. This took place in the second year of the *hijra*. Previously they had faced Jerusalem in prayer, like the Jews; from now on they faced towards their own sanctuary of Mecca. This reorientation was eventually complemented by Muslim possession of the sanctuary itself. At the time of the conquest of Mecca in the eighth year, Muhammad purged the sanctuary of its pagan idols; and in the tenth year he demonstrated in detail the Muslim rites of pilgrimage.

In the eleventh year of the *hijra* (A.D. 632) Muhammad was taken ill in Medina and died. He left behind him nine widows and an Egyptian concubine. By the latter he had had a son, Abraham, who died in infancy; of his other children, four daughters survived him.

# 3

## *The monotheist universe*

In the following four chapters I shall set out the fundamental ideas
associated with Muhammad's mission. I shall draw primarily on
the Koran, which we have already met as the corpus of the
revelations received by Muhammad through Gabriel at sundry
times. I shall also make use of the abundant traditions which relate
what Muhammad said and did, and are preserved in Ibn Ishaq's
biography and other such sources; occasionally I shall fill out the
picture with views ascribed to early Muslims but not directly
attributed to Muhammad. Any substantial use of these non-
Koranic materials will be indicated. How far the resulting picture
can be considered to represent the actual teaching of Muhammad
is a question to be taken up in a later chapter.

### The universe in a nutshell

There are two components of Muhammad's universe: God and the
world. Of these, God is the more remarkable. He is eternal — He
has always existed, and always will. He is omniscient: not a leaf
falls without His knowledge. He is omnipotent: when He decides
something, He has only to say 'Be!' and it is. Above all, He is
unique: He is one, and there is no other god but Him; He has no
partners in His divinity. Furthermore, He is merciful and beneficent
— but for reasons we shall come to, He is frequently angry.

The rest of the universe — the seven heavens, the earths, and
their contents — was created by Him and belongs to Him. This feat
of creation was achieved in six days (though the days in question
would seem to have been divine days, each equivalent to a
thousand human years). The basic structure of the world is fairly
simple, although the scanty Koranic data have to be completed
from tradition. The lower part, which was created first, consisted
originally of a single earth which God then split into seven. The
seven earths are arranged one above another like a stack of plates;

we inhabit the top one, and the devil the bottom one, which is hell. Above the earths God placed an analogous stack of heavens; the lowest heaven is our own sky, the topmost is Paradise. The scale is generous by terrestrial standards: the standard distance, that between any two neighbouring plates, takes five hundred years to traverse, and larger dimensions are encountered at the top and bottom. The whole structure is said to have posed serious under-pinning problems, to which colourful solutions were found; but these and other details need not detain us. God, in so far as He may be said to be in any particular place, is at the top of the world. Having created it, He did not leave it to run itself, or delegate the responsibility to others. Rather He continues to attend to it in every detail. He holds back the sky to prevent it falling on the earth; and He it is who makes rain to fall and trees to grow.

The world contains more than one form of intelligent life; but it is mankind which receives the lion's share of divine attention. The human race is monogenetic: we all descend from Adam, who was made from dust, and his consort, who was fashioned from him. We too belong to God. Tradition, slightly adapting a Koranic passage, relates that after creating Adam God rubbed his back, and there issued from him the souls of all future humanity. God then called them to bear witness, asking: 'Am I not your Lord?', to which they replied 'Yes, we bear witness' (K 7.171).

Despite this admission, the record of human conduct has to a large extent been one of disobedience to God. In the varied reper-toire of human disobedience, one sin is particularly prominent: the failure to accord to Him the exclusive worship which is His due. This sin of polytheism is one into which men keep falling, and which then acquires for them the spurious authority of ancestral tradition. Hence the repeated dispatch of divine messengers to prise men loose from the ways of their fathers and revive their primordial allegiance to God alone. The story of these reminders, and the mixed reception they met with, makes up the core of human history; we shall take it up in the following chapter.

Sooner rather than later, this history will end in a cataclysmic destruction of the world as we know it. The sky will be split, the stars scattered, the earth pounded to dust. The entire human race will be brought back to life — an easy matter for God to bring about, as the Koran insists. He will then proceed to judge men according to their deeds with the aid of balances; the saved will spend the rest of eternity amid the colourful delights of Paradise, while those found wanting are consigned to the pains of hell.

## The universe in comparative perspective

In these basic outlines, Muhammad's universe does not differ radically from those of other monotheist faiths. What comment it requires will accordingly depend on whether the reader is himself from a monotheist background. If he is, it will be enough to identify the more significant points of comparison. If he is not, he may legitimately find the entire conception puzzling; and this is perhaps where we should begin.

Historically, monotheism is descended from the polytheism of the ancient Near East. Near Eastern gods were often human beings writ large: they had bodies of human shape, quarrelled, behaved irresponsibly when drunk, and so forth. The God of the Old Testament was not given to such undignified behaviour, but He retained considerable traces from this past. The Bible speaks of Him as creating man in His own image, and as taking a day's rest after the labour of creation; and it treats in detail of the manner in which the Deity is to be housed and supplied with food. The tendency in monotheism has, however, been away from such a human conception of God, and towards a more transcendent one. Muhammad's God in some respects illustrates this trend. Admittedly the Koran still speaks freely of God's 'hand', and refers to Him settling into His throne; but it strongly denies that He found the work of creation tiring, and Islam does not accept the notion that God created man in His own image.

This dehumanisation of God had one rather serious implication, and we can best identify it by going back to the Mesopotamian myth which explains the creation of man. Even after the basic work of creation had been done, it must be understood, the running of the universe made heavy demands on the gods; and as might be expected, it was the junior gods who were saddled with the drudgery. Under these conditions, serious labour unrest developed among the junior gods, and a critical situation was defused only when discussions among their seniors issued in the creation of a substitute race, namely mankind. Since then men have done the hard work, and by and large the gods have lived a life of leisure. The whole story turns on the assumption that the gods have needs close enough to our own to be immediately intelligible to us, and that their powers to satisfy these needs, though considerable, are not unlimited.

The monotheist God, by contrast, needs nothing and nobody: 'God has no need of the worlds' (K 3.92), and 'no need of you' (K 39.9); and if He were to need anything, He has only to say 'Be!' and it is. What then can be the point of His having human servants, or indeed a created world at all? Yet the Koran often refers to such servants of God, and explicitly assures us that God did not create heaven and earth for fun; had He wished to amuse Himself, He could have done so without resorting to the creation of an external world. But by the same token, the world cannot be considered to meet any other divine need. The strong and often immediate sense of God's purposes that characterises monotheism thus fits badly with the sublimer notions it has developed about His nature.

The reader who is himself from a monotheist background will of course be inured to this tension. He should also find the basic conception of Muhammad's universe a familiar one; it is not so distant from that found in the first chapter of the Book of Genesis, and ultimately derives from it. Other features have parallels in monotheist cosmology as it existed closer to the time of Muhammad. Thus the seven heavens, the five-hundred-year module, and the underpinning arrangements can all be matched from Jewish tradition. Similarly homespun ideas were also current among the Christians of the Middle East; here, however, they were under strong pressure from the very different style of cosmological thought represented by Greek philosophy. A sixth-century Nestorian Christian found it necessary to write at length to defend his traditional monotheist image of God's world against this pernicious influence. The same influence was later at work in the Islamic world, but not in the period which concerns us.

The feature of Muhammad's universe which is most likely to strike a non-Muslim monotheist as alien is a certain bleakness in the relationship between God's power and human action. This point is intimately related to the general tension within monotheism that we have already explored: on the one hand God frequently engages in behaviour that can be understood in much the same way as our own (e.g. He keeps sending messengers to disobedient communities with warnings they mostly disregard); and on the other hand, He is an omnipotent God who can realise His wishes immediately (e.g. He could if He wished have all men believe in Him). The first conception suggests that men act of their own free will and sooner or later get their deserts for it. The second suggests that human acts, like other events, take place because God in His omnipotence has decreed that they will. The two conceptions do not go well together, if indeed they are compatible at all.

In the circumstances, there are two obvious ways to respond to the dilemma. One is to cut back the operation of God's omnipotence to allow at least a minimal domain for the freedom of human choice; for if men are not given enough moral rope to hang themselves, we are confronted with the unwelcome implication that their sin and damnation are the fault of God. This, essentially, was the option chosen by the other monotheist faiths of the day. The second course is to stand unflinchingly by God's omnipotence, and to allow human free will to be swamped by it; this, essentially, is the direction in which Islam inclines. God 'leads astray whom He will and guides whom He will' (K 16.95). He has created many men for hell, and pledged His word to fill it. The unbelievers will not believe, whether Muhammad warns them or not, for 'God has set a seal on their hearts' (K 2.6). This idiom was not new in monotheism; the God of Exodus repeatedly hardened the heart of Pharaoh the better to display His signs (see for example Exod. 7.3, and compare Rom. 9.17–18). Nor is it one consistently used in the Koran. Thus Muhammad is told to say: 'The truth is from your Lord; so let whosoever will, believe, and let whosoever will, disbelieve' (K 18.28). Such verses were duly cited by the proponents of the doctrine of human free will in Islam. But for better or worse, they fought a losing battle.

# 4

# *Monotheist history*

Early Muslim scholars assigned to this world a duration of some six or seven thousand years. By the standards of ancient Indian or modern Western cosmology such a figure is breathtakingly small, but it agreed well enough with the views of other monotheists. Of this span, it was clear that the greater part had already elapsed — perhaps 5,500 out of 6,000 years. Muhammad's mission thus fell decidedly late in the day. He himself is said to have told his followers, with reference to the prospective duration of their community: 'Your appointed time compared with that of those who were before you is as from the afternoon prayer to the setting of the sun.' The formulation is problematic, but there is learned authority for the view that it represents about one-fourteenth of the total.

An early scholar who reckoned the age of the world at 5,600 years avowed that he knew about every period of its history, and what kings and prophets had lived in it. We can disregard the kings; it is the prophets who constitute the backbone of monotheist history. The list given below shows the most important of them. (The dates, which may be taken to represent years elapsed since the expulsion of Adam from Paradise, have the authority of Ibn Ishaq; but conflicting opinions abound on such details.)

| | |
|---|---|
| Adam | — |
| Noah | 1200 |
| Abraham | 2342 |
| Moses | 2907 |
| Jesus | 4832 |
| Muhammad | 5432 |

A chronology of this kind is not to be found in the Koran; but all the prophets listed here appear there, and their order in time is clearly envisaged as shown.

## *Adam to Jesus*

Every name in the list bar the last is familiar from the Bible. The first four names are major figures of the Pentateuch, and as such the common property of Judaism and Christianity. The parts they play in the Koranic view of monotheist history are more or less in accordance with their Biblical roles — though a good deal of material is altered, added or lost. Adam remains the common ancestor of humanity, and is expelled from Paradise with his consort for eating forbidden fruit. Noah is the builder of the ark whose occupants alone survive the flood in which God destroys the human race. Abraham is still the father who nearly sacrifices his son to God. Moses confronts Pharaoh, leads the Israelite exodus from Egypt, and meets God on Mount Sinai; to him is revealed a scripture, the Pentateuch. Other Old Testament figures also appear, notably Joseph, David and Solomon.

All this is familiar. Yet there are differences, and of these the most significant is a subtle shift of emphasis. The original Biblical figures play roles of considerable diversity; the Koran, by contrast, has a tendency to impose on them a stereotyped conception of the monotheist messenger. Thus in the Koran, Noah's mission is to warn his polytheist contemporaries to worship God alone; whereas in the Bible their sin is moral corruption rather than polytheism, and Noah has in any case no message to deliver to them.

With the next name on the list we come to a specifically Christian figure. As might be expected, the Jesus of the Koran is still recognisable as the Jesus of the New Testament: he is styled the Messiah, is born of a virgin, works miracles, has disciples, is rejected by the Jews, and eventually ascends to heaven. There are, however, divergences. For no obvious reason the Koran insists that Jesus was not really crucified; and there is no sense of his mission being addressed to an audience wider than the Children of Israel. But the crucial point of divergence is the insistence that Jesus, though a messenger of God, was not His son, still less God Himself. He is accordingly quoted in the Koran as denying his own (and his mother's) divinity. Closely related to this emphasis on the humanity of Jesus is the rejection of the Christian doctrine of the Trinity: it is unbelief to say that God is 'the third of three' (K 5.77), for there is but one God. The Koranic doctrine of Jesus thus establishes a position quite distinct from that of either the Jews, who reject him, or the Christians, who deify him. Here, then, we have a parting of the ways.

It will be evident from this that the Koranic respect for Moses and Jesus does not extend to the bulk of their followers. The Koran does have some friendly things to say of the Christians, despite its strong sense of their fundamental error with regard to the status of their founder. But it also advances a good deal of miscellaneous polemic against them — they consider Mary, the mother of Jesus, to be divine; they hold themselves to be sons of God; they are riven by sectarianism; and so forth.

The Jews receive considerably more attention than the Christians. There is a long appeal to the Children of Israel to fulfil their covenant with God, and to accept Muhammad's message confirming the revelation that had already come to them; some of them would seem to have responded positively. There is a large amount of polemic. Misdeeds of the Biblical Israelites are raked over, such as their worship of the golden calf; the Jews are accused of speaking slanderously of Mary, the mother of Jesus, and are said to be among the most hostile of men towards the true believers. Many of the charges are petty or obscure (e.g. the curious allegation that the Jews consider Ezra to be the son of God), and in general there is more bad feeling towards the Jews than there is towards the Christians. But by contrast, the polemic is not focused on any central issue of doctrine — other than the Jewish refusal to accept Muhammad's own credentials.

Before leaving this stretch of monotheist history, a negative point implicit in all this should be brought out. The Koran is much concerned with the missions of the various monotheist messengers; but it displays little interest in whatever structure of religious authority may have existed in the intervals between these prophetic episodes. Aaron appears in the Koran as the brother of Moses and a participant in the events of his career, but never for his role in the establishment of the Israelite priesthood. The case of the twelve disciples of Jesus is similar: they never figure as the nucleus of the Christian Church. Admittedly the Koran has a few things to say about the rabbis and monks of contemporary Judaism and Christianity, and it once mentions Christian priests. It is clear that these figures are thought to have legitimate roles to play in their respective communities; but they tend to be a bad lot, and to be worshipped by their followers in the place of God. One verse refers to monasticism as an institution; it describes it as an innovation of the Christians, not a divinely imposed duty, but does not reject it out of hand. Yet the attention given to these matters is slight.

## The role of Arabia

From this survey, it might appear that Arabia played no role in monotheist history until the coming of Muhammad himself. In fact there are two Koranic conceptions which serve to endow Arabia with a monotheist past in its own right; one is rather modest, the other extremely bold.

The first conception is that of the ethnic warner. The idea is that God sends to every people a messenger, usually of their own number, who warns them in their own language to worship God alone; they regularly disregard the warning, and God destroys them in some spectacular fashion. We have already seen the shift of emphasis whereby the Koran presents Noah's career in this light. There is in fact a whole cycle of such stories which appear and reappear in the Koran; what concerns us here is that this stereotype is also extended to Arabia. To take a single example, a certain Salih (a good Arabic name) was sent to Thamud (an attested people of ancient Arabia) with such a message; they ignored it, and were destroyed by a thunderbolt, or some equivalent expression of divine irritation. These Arabian warners are unknown to Jewish or Christian tradition, and their presence in the Koran does something to place Arabia on the monotheist map. But by their very nature, they make no mark on the grand scheme of monotheist history. The episodes are parochial side-shows, and establish no continuing monotheist communities; all that is left is some archaeological remains and a cautionary tale.

The other conception, the 'religion of Abraham', is of a quite different calibre. Its starting-point is the Biblical account of Abraham and his sons. According to the Book of Genesis, Abraham was married to Sarah; but she only bore him a son, Isaac, in their extreme old age. At that time Abraham already had a son, Ishmael, by an Egyptian concubine named Hagar. This had led to considerable ill-feeling between the two women, and already while Hagar was pregnant she had run away into the wilderness. On this occasion an angel had found her by a spring, and sent her home with somewhat qualified promises for the future of her unborn son. When eventually Isaac was born to Sarah, Hagar was

sent packing together with her son. This time her water supply ran
out, and the child was about to die of thirst when again an angel
intervened. Hagar was promised that a great nation would arise
from her son, and was miraculously shown a well. Thereafter, we
are told, God was with the lad; he grew up in the wilderness and
had twelve sons, from whom were descended the twelve Ishmaelite
tribes. But for all that, Abraham's heir was Isaac, the ancestor of
the Israelites; it was with Isaac, not Ishmael, that God made His
everlasting covenant.

The message of this colourful narrative of patriarchal family life
is a simple one. Abraham was the common ancestor of the Israelites
and the Ishmaelites — or as posterity would put it, of the Jews and
the Arabs. Thereafter sacred history was concerned only with the
Israelites; the Ishmaelites might be a great nation, but in religious
terms they were a dead end.

Much of this picture was accepted by Islam. Muslim scholars
thought in the same genealogical idiom, and considered the Arabs
(or more precisely, the northern Arabs) to descend from the sons
of Ishmael. Equally, as we have seen, Islam accepts the Israelite line
of sacred history running from Isaac to Moses and on (in the
Christian view) to Jesus. Where Islam departed radically from the
Biblical conception was in opening up the Ishmaelite dead end,
thereby creating a second line of sacred history that was specifically
Arabian.

One Muslim tradition describes the aftermath of the quarrel
between Sarah and Hagar. Abraham took Hagar and Ishmael to an
uninhabited spot in the wilderness, and left them there. Hagar's
water-skin was soon empty, and her child was about to die when
Gabriel appeared; he struck the ground with his foot, and a spring
gushed forth. The uninhabited spot was Mecca, and the spring was
Zamzam, the water-supply of the Meccan sanctuary which we met
in connection with Muhammad's grandfather. Other traditions
depart more strongly from the Biblical narrative. God ordered
Abraham to build Him a sanctuary where He would be
worshipped. Abraham was at first in some perplexity as to how to
proceed, but was supernaturally guided to Mecca, accompanied by
Hagar and Ishmael. There Abraham and Ishmael built the
sanctuary and established the rites of pilgrimage to it. Abraham
seems in due course to have departed to resume his Biblical career;
but Hagar and Ishmael remained, and at their deaths were buried

in the sanctuary. Some say that Ishmael was the first to speak in pure Arabic. He was also a prophet in his own right — and the ancestor of a prophet, Muhammad.

The Arabs thus inherited from their ancestor a monotheist faith and sanctuary. In the course of time, however, this heritage was greatly corrupted. As Mecca became overcrowded with Ishmael's rapidly multiplying descendants, groups of them would move away and subsequently fall into local idolatry. Idols even appeared in the sanctuary itself (Hubal, the most noteworthy, being acquired by a leading Meccan while travelling on business in Moab). In the meantime, the descendants of Ishmael had lost possession of their sanctuary to others, not to regain it till Quraysh settled in Mecca five generations before Muhammad. Yet for all that the Arabs had lapsed into pagan superstition, monotheism remained their birthright.

The elaborate narrative traditions drawn on here are not to be found in the Koran, but the basic conception is present in force. The Koran emphasises that Abraham was a monotheist long before there was such a thing as Judaism or Christianity. 'Abraham was neither a Jew nor a Christian; but he was one of the true religion *(hanif)* who submitted to God *(muslim)*' (K 3.60). That Abraham is here described as, in effect, a Muslim is no surprise; the Koran uses similar language of other monotheists (e.g. Noah, Joseph, the Queen of Sheba, the disciples of Jesus). Its tendency to link the term *muslim* with Abraham in particular is nevertheless a pronounced one. The term *hanif* is also significant. Although its exact sense is obscure, the Koran uses it in contexts suggestive of a pristine monotheism, which it tends to contrast with (latter-day) Judaism and Christianity. It associates the idea strongly with Abraham, but never with Moses or Jesus.

Abraham in turn bequeaths his faith to his sons, warning them to be sure that when they die, they do so in a state of submission to God *(muslim)*. He prays that they may not succumb to the worship of idols, and asks God to raise up from his and Ishmael's posterity a people *(umma)* who submit to God *(muslim)*. Abraham's religion accordingly remains valid for his descendants. The Koran frequently recommends it, and tells the believers that their religion is that of 'your father Abraham'. (The phrase is to be taken literally; this is not the Christian image of 'our father Abraham' as the *spiritual* ancestor of all believers, whatever their actual descent.) At the same time the story of the building of the sanctuary by Abraham and Ishmael has a prominent place in the Koran; and Abraham speaks of the settlement of some of his posterity in a barren valley beside it (i.e. Mecca).

The effect of these ideas is simple but crucial: they endow Arabia and the Arabs with an honoured place in monotheist history, and one genealogically independent of the Jews and Christians.

## The role of Muhammad

The view of sacred history just analysed is in some ways a very consistent one — relentlessly monotheist, and by Biblical standards rather stereotyped. It nevertheless puts side by side two notions between which there is a certain tension. On the one hand there is the conception of a linear succession of monotheist messengers, among whom the founders of Judaism and Christianity find their places. Yet on the other hand we have the idea of an alternative, Arabian monotheism in a line branching off from Abraham. These two conceptions are closely linked to the role, or roles, which the Koran ascribes to Muhammad.

The least adventurous role is that of an ethnic warner. Muhammad's mission is to 'warn the mother of cities (i.e. Mecca) and those round about her' (K 42.5); those to whom he is sent have received no previous warning. The parallel with the earlier ethnic warners is explicit: 'This is a warner, of the warners of old' (K 53.57). This simple conception is a prominent one in the Koran, and each retelling of the cautionary tales about earlier warners helps to underline it. Yet it does not quite fit. For one thing, we find in these passages references to Muhammad as the recipient of a revealed book. Aptly, this scripture is an 'Arabic Koran' — a common Koranic phrase, and a characteristic example of the Koranic emphasis on Arabic as the language of Muhammad's mission. Yet the revelation of a scripture is not a motif that appears in the cautionary tales of earlier warners. And for another thing, Muhammad's people did in the end listen to him, an outcome for which the model of the ethnic warner hardly provided.

A more ambitious conception of Muhammad's role arises out of the religion of Abraham. This pristine monotheism having fallen on evil days, Muhammad could be seen as a messenger sent to restore it. Such a need had been anticipated by Abraham himself. In the course of the major Koranic account of the foundation of the sanctuary, we read that Abraham prayed in these terms on behalf of his descendants: 'Lord, send among them a messenger of their own number who may recite your signs to them, teach them the Book and wisdom, and purify them' (K 2.123). A little later, it is stated that such a messenger has now been sent — a clear reference to Muhammad.

This gives Muhammad a definite position in the structure of monotheist history, and one that goes well with the Arabian setting. But it does not really define his position with regard to the main line of succession, and in particular to Moses and Jesus. It is here that a third conception of Muhammad's role appears. This conception is nicely illustrated in a Koranic sketch of the history of scriptural law: first the Pentateuch was revealed, i.e. to Moses; then Jesus was sent, and to him was revealed the Gospel, confirming the Pentateuch; then the Book (i.e. the Koran) was revealed to Muhammad, confirming what had already been revealed. Conversely, the Koran describes the earlier scriptures as foretelling the coming of Muhammad: he is inscribed in the Pentateuch and the Gospel, and his future mission was part of the good news announced by Jesus. Muhammad is thus authenticated as a new prophet with a new scripture in the direct line of succession to Moses and Jesus.

He is accordingly much more than just a local Arabian prophet. The Koran, after speaking of the endorsement of Muhammad in the Pentateuch and Gospel, goes on to refer to him as 'the messenger of God to you all' (K 7.157); and from this it is but a short step to conceiving him as God's messenger to mankind at large (K 34.27). In practice, as the Koran makes clear, it is not the will of God that mankind should again become the 'one community' they originally were; He guides whom He wills, and by the same token He leads astray whom He wills. But for all the persistence of error, there is now but one true religion for all mankind.

This assertion gains poignancy from the fact that Muhammad is not just the most recent of the prophets, but also the last — the 'seal of the prophets', in a Koranic phrase which has come to be understood in this sense. Tradition has it that Muhammad, comparing his role to those of the earlier prophets, likened himself to the final brick to be laid in the corner of an edifice otherwise completed. His career is accordingly the last major event in monotheist history before the end of the world.

## The future

We may end this account with a brief relation of the future course of history as it appeared to early Muslims. This is not a topic treated in the Koran; but it is abundantly (and by no means consistently) treated in early tradition, from which what follows is selected.

The future is nasty, brutish and short. The Muslim community will break up into a mass of conflicting sects, just as the Children of Israel had done before them. Sedition will follow sedition like strips of the darkest night, and the living will envy the dead. Eventually God will send a redeemer, a descendant of Muhammad. This redeemer, the Mahdi, will receive allegiance at the sanctuary in Mecca, whence his emigration *(hijra)* will be to Jerusalem; there he will reign in justice. Yet this interlude will last less than a decade. Thereafter Antichrist (the Dajjal) will appear from Iraq, reducing the Muslims to a remnant making their last stand on the peak of a mountain in Syria. In the hour of their need, Jesus will descend to earth in armour and lead them against Antichrist, slaying him at the gate of Lydda in Palestine; then Jesus will reign in justice and plenty, exterminating the pig and breaking the crosses of the Christians. Yet this too will pass, giving way to the final horrors of human history. At the last a wind takes up the souls of the believers, the sun rises in the west, and history gives way to the cataclysmic eschatology of the Koran.

# 5

---

## *Monotheist law*

---

The Koranic view of history is in some ways rather repetitive. Successive messengers arrive with the same doctrinal message. There is, however, a certain ringing of changes with regard to the outward form and precise content of the messages. Sometimes they are in writing; sometimes, apparently, they are not. What is more, the various revealed books, while of course confirming each other in general terms, may differ significantly in points of detail. God tells Muhammad that 'to every term there is a book' (K 13.38), that is, each age has its scripture; in it God erases or confirms what He pleases, the 'mother of the Book' (presumably a kind of archetype) being with Him. In other words, the content of revelation is liable to change from one prophetic epoch to another.

The field in which this instability is most marked is divine law — law which God Himself makes and unmakes. To each community God assigned its particular way; thus each has its own way of slaughtering (or sacrificing) animals, and yet 'their God is one god' (K 22.35). Whereas the truth of monotheist doctrine is timeless, the validity of monotheist law is a more relative matter. Even within the Koran itself, the Muslim scholars found scriptural support for the view that earlier verses could be abrogated by later ones.

### Law before the Koran

The pivotal event in the Koranic view of the history of law is the revelation of the Pentateuch to Moses. There is little indication that law played much part in God's dealings with mankind before this event. We learn incidentally that God had revealed the duties of prayer and almsgiving to Abraham, Isaac and Jacob, and that Ishmael imposed them on his family; but for the most part Abrahamic law remains as shadowy as the scripture with which the Koran occasionally endows him. With Moses, we are on firmer ground. The Pentateuch contains the 'judgement of God', and by

it the Prophets judged the Jews. Some of its concrete legal
stipulations are cited — a couple of dietary laws, for example, and
the principle of 'a life for a life'. The Pentateuch (or the set of tablets
which God gave to Moses) deals fully with all questions; in it are
guidance and light.

There is nevertheless a strong sense in the Koran that the yoke
of the Pentateuchal code was an unduly heavy one, and that this,
though God's responsibility, is the fault of the Jews. This idea finds
clear expression with regard to dietary law. The Koran insists that
dietary prohibitions of divine origin were first introduced in the
Pentateuch: 'Every food was lawful to the Children of Israel, except
what Israel (i.e. Jacob) forbade to himself, before the revelation of
the Pentateuch' (K 3.87). That God then forbade to the Israelites
foods previously permitted to them was a punishment for their own
misdeeds.

The tendency since the revelation of the Pentateuch has accordingly been for God to ease the yoke of the law. The mission
of Jesus is conceived in a manner rather similar to that of Moses,
in the sense that the scripture revealed to him, the Gospel, is a law-
book according to which his followers are to be judged. Yet at the
same time it is part of his mission 'to declare lawful to you some
of what was forbidden to you' (K 3.44). Muhammad's role is
similarly conceived, and is perhaps thought of as going further in
the direction of liberalisation. Much, of course, is carried over from
earlier dispensations; thus the obligation to fast is laid upon the
believers 'as it was laid upon those who were before you' (K 2.179).
Dietary law, however, is drastically pruned: the prohibitions are
reduced to a few key points, and these provisions are expressly
contrasted with the more elaborate restrictions which God had
imposed on the Jews. The case of the Sabbath is similar. Without
question it had been imposed on the Jews, and one verse which was
to cause a considerable theological flurry tells how God metamorphosed Sabbath-breakers into apes. Yet this did not mean that
the Sabbath was binding on Muhammad's own community. It had
been imposed only on 'those who differed concerning it'
(presumably the Jews), and — so the context seems to imply —
forms no part of the religion of Abraham.

Historically, this Koranic perspective on the history of law is in
some ways an apt one. Law was a late starter in religious history.
The gods of the ancient Near East did not usually concern

themselves with legislation, and law was not a central feature of the culture of their priests. The salience of law in ancient Israelite religion was thus unusual — and still more so the later elaboration of the Biblical heritage into the law-centred culture of the Jewish rabbis. It is also legitimate to think of a trend towards liberalisation, and to place both Jesus and Muhammad within it. Yet there is a fundamental difference here which the Koran, in bringing Jesus firmly into line between Moses and Muhammad, has glossed over. The Gospel is not a law-book. Its message is rather that the Law is not enough; and the followers of Jesus soon went on to infer that most of it was not necessary at all. The dietary code of the Pentateuch still stands in the Christian Bible as 'appointed to be read in churches', but it would be bizarre, indeed sinful, for Christians to observe it. Christianity, in short, is not a law-centred religion. Islam, for all its liberalisation, unmistakably remains one, and in this it is supported by the legal content of the Koran.

## Koranic law

In the early Islamic period there was a school of thought which saw the Koran as the sole and sufficient basis of Islamic law. God Himself, it was argued, describes the Koran as a book which makes everything clear. The consensus of Muslim scholars, however, was against this view. Too much is left unsaid in the Koran; for example, it tells the believer to pray, but omits essential information as to how he should do it. The bulk of Islamic law as it actually evolved is thus non-Koranic in substance. Some of what is missing is supplied from the innumerable traditions regarding the sayings and doings of Muhammad. A typical example of such a tradition was given in Chapter 2: at the conquest of Khaybar, Muhammad is said to have declared the eating of the flesh of the domesticated ass forbidden. At the same time, the lawyers had to rely, in one way or another, on their own legal reasoning. All this would bulk large in any survey of Islamic law as such; here, however, I shall focus on such law as there is in the Koran.

Although it does not add up to a comprehensive law-code, the Koranic treatment of law covers a wide range of subject-matter. In the first place, it deals with specifically religious rituals and duties: washing, prayer, almsgiving, fasting, and pilgrimage to the sanctuary. The treatment is uneven; thus the instructions on the fast are fairly full, whereas no indication is given as to how much alms a believer should give. It is nonetheless clear from the way in which the topics are treated that God's interest as a lawgiver is not confined to generalities. For example, the believer in preparing himself for prayer is specifically instructed to wash his arms up to the *elbows*, and to wipe his feet to the *ankles*. In the second place, the Koran discusses a range of less narrowly religious aspects of law: marriage, divorce, inheritance, homicide, theft, usury, the drinking of wine, and the like. Again, the treatment is uneven: thieves are to be punished by having their hands cut off, but the fate of the unrepentant usurer is not prescribed (though he receives a dire warning that he will find himself at war with God and His messenger). The scope and character of this material suffices to define Islam as a legally oriented religion.

A more concrete sense of the nature of Koranic law can best be gained from examples. I shall accordingly outline what the Koran has to say on three specific legal topics: the rites of pilgrimage, dietary restrictions, and the status of women.

1. The Koran gives considerable attention to the rites of pilgrimage, yet what it has to say is not intelligible as it stands; I shall accordingly supply in brackets a minimum of non-Koranic material from early sources. We can best begin with the layout of the sanctuary in its widest sense. We have already encountered the Ka'ba. (This is the cubic building towards which Muslims pray; in one corner is set a black stone of peculiar sanctity.) To it we must now add (working outwards from Mecca): Safa and Marwa (two hillocks within a few hundred yards of the Ka'ba); an unnamed place of sacrifice (at Mina, a few miles from Mecca); the 'holy waymark' (Muzdalifa, a couple of miles further out); and 'Arafat (a hill located twelve miles out of Mecca). We shall encounter these places in reverse order.

The main form of pilgrimage is that known as the *hajj*. Its performance (once in a lifetime) is a duty for those able to undertake it. It takes place (annually) in the holy month (of Dhu 'l-Hijja). Three main components of the rites are referred to in an unambiguous fashion in the Koran. (There are of course others, including the central rite of the entire pilgrimage: the pilgrims go out to 'Arafat and wait there till sunset.) The Koranic rites are: (i) The pilgrims (then) 'rush' from 'Arafat (to Muzdalifa, the 'holy waymark'); they then again 'rush' from the 'holy waymark' (i.e. from Muzdalifa to Mina). (ii) They sacrifice (at Mina, whereupon they shave their heads before proceeding to Mecca itself). (iii) They then circumambulate 'the ancient house' (i.e. the Ka'ba). (They do this seven times, if possible kissing or touching the black stone. In fact pilgrims are likely to have performed this ceremony once before, on first arriving in Mecca before going out to 'Arafat.) If they want, they can also circumambulate Safa and Marwa. (Thereafter, there are further but less arduous rites back at Mina.)

During the *hajj* the pilgrims are in a special ritual state (which they leave by stages towards the end of the rites). They may not hunt, though they may fish. They must abstain from quarrelsome behaviour and lascivious talk (such as telling a woman one's intentions towards her when the pilgrimage is over). (In fact sexual relations are excluded altogether; at the same time the pilgrims wear special clothing, and may not cut their hair or nails, or use perfume.)

Two points are worth noting about the entire ritual complex. The first is that the rites, though physically demanding, are simple; there is little that cannot be done by the ordinary believer who knows his religious duties. (Even the sacrifice at Mina, where one might have expected some kind of priesthood to be at work, is performed by the pilgrims themselves.) The second point is that the meaning of the rituals is more than a little opaque, and that the Koran shows little disposition to interpret them. Why 'rush'? and why spend so much of a visit to God's house in a set of locations several miles from it?

2. As we have seen, the Koran takes an interest in the place of dietary prohibitions in the history of monotheist law. This is no accident; dietary law as it appears in the Koran is a thoroughly contentious issue. There is frequent polemic against those who falsely ascribe dietary regulations to God. Devils are at work inspiring their friends to dispute with the believers, and troublemakers are engaged in leading people astray. The malice of the troublemakers consists in alleging that God has prohibited foods which are in fact perfectly lawful. (This, incidentally, is surprising in an Arabian context; historically one might have expected it to be the other way round.) Accordingly, the believers are repeatedly urged to eat the good things which God has given them, and are not to declare them forbidden. No sin accrues to an honest believer on account of what he eats; or more exactly, God has spelt out those few things that are in fact forbidden, leaving no ground for misplaced zeal in dietary matters.

As this suggests, the Koran tends to list forbidden rather than permitted foods. Its concern, as will appear, is always with meat; vegetarians have no problems other than the prohibition of wine, which does not concern us here. We can consider the Koranic rulings under two heads.

First, what animals are forbidden as such? The only one named is the pig; cattle — in a wide sense — are expressly permitted. (Does God then intend to allow the eating of hares, shellfish, lizards and mermaids? Such questions received much attention, and a variety of answers, from the Muslim scholars.)

Second, in what ways can the meat of a permitted animal become forbidden? The implicit but fundamental point is that animals have to be slaughtered in a proper ritual fashion (though fish and locusts were generally considered an exception to this). Thus carrion is forbidden, as is the victim of a beast of prey, or an animal killed by strangling; again implicit here is the principle that the mode of slaughter must shed the animal's blood, the eating of blood as such being expressly forbidden. More specifically religious is the prohibition of meat consecrated to (gods) other than God, or sacrificed on pagan altars; this in fact extends to whatever has not had the name of God invoked over it (i.e. as part of the ritual of slaughter). On the other hand, there is no objection to 'the food of those to whom the Book was brought' (K 5.7). (This clearly refers to Jews and Christians. Presumably 'food' includes meat; so at least the scholars of Sunni Islam have held, though others have denied it.)

The Koran regularly adds to its lists of forbidden foods an assurance that these provisions can be overridden in cases of dire need. It is better to eat carrion than to starve.

3. The status of women is extensively treated in the Koran. God's views on this matter are on the whole unfashionable at the present day. Women are not equal, and are to be beaten if they get out of hand. As in ancient Israel, polygamy and concubinage are allowed, and women are easily divorced; with regard to the extent of polygamy, the Koran speaks of believers taking two, three or four wives. (But with the single exception of Muhammad himself, they may not take more.) Within this framework, there is a good deal of provision intended to secure the decent treatment of women. For example, there is compulsory financial provision for widows for a year after the death of the husband; and men are

advised, politely but firmly, that when they die their widows will have every right to remarry after a specified interval. Women are also accorded a significant place in the inheritance system; they receive shares — generally at half the corresponding male rate — in the estates of their parents and near relatives.

Other provisions are concerned with the problems of ritual purity and public decency to which the existence of women gives rise. Thus men are enjoined to separate themselves from menstruating women. (By sleeping in separate beds? or in the same bed but with separate sheets? or simply by abstaining from full intercourse? Here, as often, God's words left the scholars with much to discuss; on this question they tended to a liberal view.) When in public, women should cover their bosoms (the Koran does not mention their faces). The punishment for adultery is a public flogging for both parties; it takes four witnesses to prove such a charge. (There is no mention of stoning in the Koran as we have it, though Muhammad is said to have inflicted this penalty on adulterers when the issue was forced on him.)

The general question to which these examples give rise is the sense in which Koranic law is monotheist. In a basic way, much of it is not, in the sense that there is little about its actual content which is *intrinsically* monotheist. What the Koran has to say of the status of women does not follow from the postulate that God is one, and could just as well be conjoined with polytheism or atheism. This is also true for much of the concrete detail of dietary law, with the exception of the provisions regarding the religious aegis under which an animal can validly be slaughtered. The case of pilgrimage is different, since it is a form of worship; and those aspects of the ritual which are performed around the Ka'ba have a strong monotheist association, inasmuch as this sanctuary was appointed by God and established by His prophet Abraham. With other aspects of the ritual, however, the association is a good deal looser. In general, what is monotheist about Koranic law is not its content but its form — not what God says but the fact that it is He who says it.

# 6

## Monotheist politics

The traditional biography of Muhammad presents his career as a remarkable combination of religion and politics, and this combination can fairly be seen as the key to his success. As we saw, he made little headway as a prophet until he became a successful politician; but at the same time, his political opportunity turned on his credentials as a prophet. His religion and his politics were not two separate activities that came to be entangled; they were fused together, and this fusion was expressed doctrinally in the distinctive vocabulary of monotheist politics that pervades the Koran. The theme of this vocabulary is quite literally revolution, the triumph of the believers against the pervasive oppression of unbelief.

### The oppressed

From the numerous Koranic references to the oppression to which believers are exposed, we may pick out one particularly evocative term: *mustad'af*. Literally it means 'deemed weak'; an apt translation might be 'underdog', but here I shall settle for the less colourful rendering 'oppressed'. Like the rest of the terms to be discussed in this chapter, it is a loaded one; and like most of them, it is not confined to the context of Muhammad's own career. Striking examples of its use are to be found in the Koranic version of the story of Moses and Pharaoh. Here Pharaoh's iniquities include oppressing a section of the population (i.e. the Israelites). God, however, wishes an end to this injustice: 'We desire to be gracious to those who have been oppressed in the land, . . . to make them the inheritors, and to establish them in the land' (K 28.4–5); and in due course His promise comes true. Here, then, the term identifies a group whose very wretchedness in the present marks them out for future deliverance. It is similarly applied in the context of Muhammad's own career. God reminds his followers — now home and dry—that they had once been 'few, oppressed in the land' (K 8.26), but that He had then given them refuge and come to their aid.

The situation of the oppressed is thus one which can engage some divine sympathy, but in itself it is not enough. It will not excuse spineless resignation. This point is dramatised in Koranic accounts of the day of judgement when all unbelievers get their deserts. The weak among the unbelievers will then try to blame the strong: they were oppressed, they say, and only followed their oppressors in unbelief. Yet this whining will avail them nothing. A clue to what they might have done to escape their predicament is suggested by a prayer which the Koran places in the mouths of the oppressed in relation to Muhammad's mission: 'lead us out from this city of oppressors' (K 4.77). The moral is to get up and go. It is expressed with some brutality by angels who in one passage engage in dialogue with the souls of certain people who are contemptuously described us having 'wronged themselves'. The angels ask for their account, and receive the plaintive reply: 'We were oppressed in the land.' To this the angels retort: 'Was God's earth not wide enough for you to emigrate somewhere else in it?' (K 4.99).

## Hijra

The word for 'emigrate' used by the angels derives from a root we have already met in the terms *hijra* and *muhajirun*. The Koran does not, as it happens, make use of the noun *hijra* to refer to the act of emigration, or apply the notion to Muhammad himself; but the participle *muhajirun*, and related verbal forms, are frequently applied to his followers. Thus the Koran speaks of those who emigrated after being oppressed or persecuted, and of those who emigrate 'in the way of God', leaving their homes behind them. There are numerous promises that God will reward such emigrants. Sometimes their departure is presented as a matter of expulsion rather than choice, but it is always construed as a positive act. It is also tantamount to joining Muhammad's community. Those who merely believe, but have yet to emigrate, have little or no claim on its loyalty.

As it happens, the Koran does not use the term in the context of the Mosaic exodus from Egypt. It does, however, apply it in an Abrahamic context, where it seems to be Abraham himself who declares: 'I am an emigrant *(muhajir)* unto my Lord' (K 29.25). The reference is presumably to his separation from his idolatrous people and his journey to the Holy Land, and the term thus acquires a place in the 'religion of Abraham'.

## Jihad

We saw in Chapter 2 how tradition presents the *hijra* as the turning-point of Muhammad's career. In Mecca his role had been confined to calling people to God, and he had been obliged to endure patiently the maltreatment to which this exposed him. But shortly before the *hijra*, a verse was revealed to him permitting him to make war and shed blood: 'Permission is granted to those who fight because they have been wronged. God is well able to come to their aid — those who have been driven out of their homes unjustly' (K 22.40). Soon afterwards, Muhammad emigrated, and from Medina he was able to avail himself of the new permission to good effect. In itself, of course, emigration did not have to lead to war; those of Muhammad's followers who had previously emigrated to Ethiopia in what came to be known as the 'first *hijra*' had been peaceful refugees. In Muhammad's case the link was nevertheless a strong one, and the Koran often refers in one breath to emigration and war.

War against the unbelievers (*jihad*, literally 'effort') is accordingly a prominent theme in the Koran. God not only permits it, He orders it to be waged till His cause prevails. Not all injunctions on the subject are as aggressive as this; there are indications that the unbelievers should be left to start the war, and that hostilities may be terminated or interrupted by peace agreements. In the case of Jews and Christians, honour is satisfied if they pay tribute. Yet the general atmosphere is one of enthusiasm. Although not everybody is obliged to participate in the war, the lukewarm are strongly encouraged to do so. Those who go out and fight will earn from God a far greater reward than those who sit at home. Twenty steadfast believers will defeat two hundred unbelievers, and a hundred will overcome a thousand. (The next verse, however, revises these ratios in a less optimistic direction.) Those killed in the war should not be spoken of as dead: even now they are alive. They have struck a bargain with God: 'God has bought from the believers their selves and their substance in return for Paradise; they fight in the way of God, killing and being killed . . . Who is more true to his covenant than God?' (K 9.112). At the same time,

God's intimate involvement is emphasised by His practical aid on the battlefield. At Badr, where God gave Muhammad and his followers victory, He reinforced them with an army of angels, and on other occasions he sent to their aid 'armies you did not see'. That this is holy war is likewise evident in the way in which its needs can override other religious values. Thus fighting in the sacred month is pronounced an evil, but of less weight than the evil the war is directed against.

As might be expected, the Koran refers to religious war in earlier contexts of monotheist history. It appears as a religious duty in ancient Israel in an account of the establishment of the monarchy — though the performance of the Israelites as described here is unimpressive, as it had also been when Moses had called upon his people to enter the promised land. Other prophets seem to have been better served; there were numerous prophets for whom myriads fought unflinchingly against the unbelievers, to be rewarded for it in both this world and the next. An aspect of religious war which is not mentioned in earlier contexts is the division of the spoils; this is a matter to which the Koran devotes some attention, and tradition has Muhammad declare himself the first prophet to whom booty was made lawful.

Alongside the war against the unbelievers without, the Koran also reflects a struggle against the hypocrites (*munafiqun*) within the community. Though they had accepted Muhammad's message, they harboured unbelief in their hearts. They were lazy in performing the duty of prayer, sceptical about Muhammad's revelations, politically unreliable, and destined (some slight hopes of repentance apart) for eternal punishment in the lowest level of hell. One passage envisages a definitive break with them, after which they will be liable to be taken and killed wherever they are found; and in others, Muhammad is told to fight them — and the unbelievers at large — without remorse. The phenomenon of hypocrisy does not explicitly appear in the Koran as one which earlier prophets had to contend with.

## The umma

Unlike the 'first *hijra*' to Ethiopia, Muhammad's emigration led to the creation of a politically autonomous community. This emerges most clearly in a document transmitted by tradition which we have already encountered, the 'Constitution of Medina'. It is there declared that 'the believers and Muslims of Quraysh and Yathrib, and those who follow them, join them and fight alongside them' are 'one community (*umma*) to the exclusion of all other people' (S 231–2). They are to stand united against whatever troublemakers appear in their midst; they are to be mutual friends (the term has a more political connotation than this English rendering carries); and any serious dispute is to be referred to God and Muhammad. In short, the document constitutes a community and designates an authority within it.

Much of this picture can also be elicited from the Koran. The believers are told not to take unbelievers rather than other believers as friends. Muhammad's followers and helpers are affirmed to be friends one of another. There are frequent demands for obedience to 'God and His messenger', and the believers are instructed that 'if you quarrel about anything, refer it to God and the messenger' (K 4.62).

It would be a mistake to see this community as an egalitarian one. Human inequality is a common theme in the Koran, both inside and outside the community. Yet if we leave aside the inferior status of women and slaves, the Koran endorses no inequalities among the believers other than those of religious merit. Thus it emphasises that those who do not participate in holy war cannot be considered the equals of those who do, and asserts generally that 'the noblest among you in the sight of God is the most godfearing' (K 49.13). But there is nothing here to underwrite a privileged position for an aristocracy or priesthood, and the political atmosphere is strikingly lacking in pomp and ceremony. Muhammad is told that he should take counsel with the believers when problems arise; the believers are instructed not to raise their voices above that of the Prophet, and not to shout at him in the way they shout at each other. It is of a piece with this immediate relationship between Muhammad and his community that neither Koran nor tradition speaks of any formal and continuing structure of authority interposing between them. (Contrast the elaborate hierarchy of administrators of tens, hundreds etc. which the Bible tells us was established by Moses to take routine matters off his hands.) There are intermediate powers only where Muhammad himself is not present, as when he appoints commanders of expeditions, governors of distant tribes, or a temporary deputy during an absence from Medina.

Taken together, these ideas suggest a simple and powerful model of political action against the oppression of an unbelieving society. The remedy for the victims is in the first instance to emigrate. This in turn leads to the creation of a new and autonomous polity, the act of emigration placing both physical and moral distance between the old and the new. The new community then embarks on a remorseless struggle against its enemies, the unbelievers without and the hypocrites within. The monotheist context of these notions gives them force and definition. There is only one God, and men are either His friends or His enemies. 'Now is the way of truth manifestly distinguished from error . . . God is the friend of the believers, bringing them out of darkness into light; but the friends of the unbelievers are idols, who bring them out of light into darkness' (K 2.257–9). Manifest distinction is but a step from armed confrontation: 'The believers fight in the way of God, the unbelievers in the way of idols; so fight the friends of Satan!' (K. 4.78). Then assuredly the oppressors will know 'by what overturning they will be overturned' (K 26.228).

These ideas are not notably eirenic, and to anyone brought up on the New Testament they will seem very alien. In the face of persecution, Jesus neither resisted nor emigrated. He created no new polity, at least not in this world, he waged no holy wars, and he gave a most evasive answer when after his resurrection his followers suggested that the time might have come to 'restore again the kingdom to Israel' (Acts, 1.6). If Christians want to be political activists, they cannot in good faith take their values from the life of their founder.

Muhammad has a good deal more in common with Moses, an altogether less dovish Biblical figure. The story of Moses tells of a people who lived in bondage in Egypt, were led out by their God and His prophet amid scenes of fearsome devastation, and went on to live a nomadic life in the wilderness in preparation for the conquest of the land God had promised them — a conquest eventually achieved with no small amount of slaughter. Here, then, is politics in a style more akin to Muhammad's.

There is nevertheless a significant difference of idiom. The Biblical account of the exodus, the wanderings and the conquest identifies the peoples involved in ordinary ethnic terms. The people whom Moses leads out of Egypt are the 'Children of Israel', and remain so irrespective of whether they worship God or the golden calf.Their enemies are referred to in the same way: Egyptians, Amorites, Perizzites and so forth. The Koran, by contrast, is not given to speaking in this manner; its categories are ideological rather than descriptive. God's people are 'those who submit' to Him, 'those who believe', 'the friends of God'; against them are ranged 'the hypocrites', 'the unbelievers', 'the polytheists', 'the enemies of God', 'the friends of Satan'. Terms like *muhajirun* and *jihad* are similarly ideological; they have no parallel in the Biblical narratives, which use the same commonplace vocabulary to describe the comings, goings and battles of all and sundry. In short, the Bible does no more than tell a story of monotheist politics, whereas the Koran might be said to provide something approximating to a theory.

What this theory meant for posterity is a question that can only be touched on here. It takes no great insight to see that Muhammad's tribal polity was in some ways an anomalous paradigm for the world that resulted from the very success of Islam — a vast territory populated mainly by peasants, and dominated by cities and states such as Arabia had never seen. Under such conditions the Muslims could no longer function politically as the single community they had once been, and the nature of the Muslim state had undergone drastic change. As part of a doctrinal adaptation to these altered circumstances, key notions of Muhammad's politics were widely held no longer to apply; in the mainstream of Sunni Islam the view was thus usually taken that the duty of *hijra* had ceased when Muhammad conquered Mecca. Yet there remained Muslims who engaged in vigorous re-enactments of his ideas, often in tribal environments akin to his own, and several of Muhammad's notions are very much alive at the present day.

This chapter, and the preceding one, have emphasised how much in the life of Muhammad's followers is subject to divine norms. This does not, however, mean that all human action without exception is subject to direct prescription by God, and that no scope is left for purely human choices. The point is nicely dramatised in an exchange which tradition describes between Muhammad and a certain Hubab shortly before the battle of Badr. When Muhammad had halted his troops, he was accosted by Hubab, who asked: 'Prophet, this position we've taken up, is it one revealed to you by God from which we can neither move forward nor back, or is it just a matter of judgement and tactics?' When Muhammad replied that it was a purely tactical matter, Hubab went on to give him some advice: 'Prophet, this isn't the right place to be. Get everyone moving so we reach the water-supply closest to the enemy.' Muhammad promptly did so, depriving the enemy of water, and won the battle (S 296–7). Even believers do not attain victory simply by being on the side of the angels.

# 7

## *The sources*

Two rather different types of source-material have been drawn on in the preceding chapters: Koran and tradition. The Koran is a scripture with a fixed content and — within narrow limits — an invariant text. Tradition is more amorphous. It is whatever the Muslim scholars have handed down, formally by a process of oral transmission, in practice as a vast literature. It embraces all aspects of the sayings and doings of early Muslims, and comprises many different genres; within it a particular tradition may recur in a variety of contexts and in numerous variants. The early narrative accounts of the life of Muhammad form a small if significant part of this body of material, and it is with them that we can best begin a closer look at our sources.

### *The narrative sources*

We possess a fair number of works of scholarship written in the ninth century or so which include, often within some larger framework, accounts of Muhammad's life. These works are not free literary compositions. Their authors were compilers who drew on a mass of earlier literature which is otherwise mostly lost. Good Muslim compilers are responsible scholars who tell us to whom they owe their materials, and thereby enable us to reconstruct something of the sources they were using. There are, however, limits to this reconstruction. The rules of the game allow the compiler a freedom of wording in reproducing his source which may be considerable, and do not oblige him either to quote in full or to indicate his omissions. Since he normally quotes in units of a few lines to a couple of pages, and then frequently switches to a different source, we may be left pretty much in the dark as to the overall structure of his sources. Moreover, the conventions of transmission require that the compiler quote men, not books; whether the authority in question had in fact written on the subject, or is merely a source of oral information, is not usually apparent from the way in which the compiler refers to him.

A partial exception to these remarks is Ibn Hisham (d. 833). What he did was to confine himself to the work of one and only one of his predecessors, Ibn Ishaq (d. 767). More precisely, he edited that portion of Ibn Ishaq's work which dealt with the life of Muhammad, using the version transmitted to him by one of his teachers. Yet he too proceeded by quoting his material in the customary blocks; and he was scrupulous enough to warn his readers in general terms that he had omitted a good many things from a variety of motives. We also possess a considerable volume of citations from Ibn Ishaq in sources independent of Ibn Hisham. An unusually deviant body of such material bearing on the early period of Muhammad's life has recently been published, and brings home both the extent of Ibn Hisham's omissions, and the difficulty at any given point of reconstructing the exact words of Ibn Ishaq. Yet if our image of Ibn Ishaq's work is blurred, and likely to remain so, we still know a great deal about it, and it is on this basis that at several points in this book I have referred without hesitation to Ibn Ishaq as having said this or that.

Ibn Ishaq's biography of Muhammad, though in the long run easily the most successful, was far from being the only one produced in his day. For example, we possess a shorter and simpler biography which may stem from the scholar Ma'mar ibn Rashid (d. 770), and which is preserved for us in the same kind of way as Ibn Ishaq's work. Further biographies were written in the second half of the eighth century. We may perhaps include here the work of Waqidi (d. 823); a large part of it survives, and what is lost is represented by extensive quotations.

At some point in this discussion we have to descend to detail, and comparing Waqidi with his predecessors is an instructive way to do it. Let us take a point which in itself is quite trivial: when and how did 'Abdallah, the father of Muhammad, die? Ibn Ishaq tells us that 'Abdallah died while his wife was pregnant with Muhammad — though in one line of transmission a statement has been added to the effect that he may rather have died when Muhammad was twenty-eight months old, and that God knows best which is right. Ma'mar likewise (if we take the account he transmits to be essentially his own) has 'Abdallah die while Muhammad is still in the womb, and is able to give a short account

of the circumstances: 'Abdallah had been sent by his own father,
'Abd al-Muttalib, to lay in stores of dates in Yathrib, and died
there. Two further scholars of this generation are quoted by a
ninth-century compiler for the view that 'Abdallah died when
Muhammad was twenty-eight months old, or perhaps it was seven.
The conclusion to be drawn from this range of opinions is obvious:
the scholars of the first half of the eighth century were agreed that
'Abdallah had died early enough to leave Muhammad an orphan;
but as to the details, God knew best.

By the later eighth century times had changed, and it was Waqidi
who knew best. Waqidi knew that 'Abdallah had gone to Gaza on
business, had fallen ill on the way back, and died in Yathrib after
leaving the caravan he was with to be nursed by relations there.
Waqidi was further able to specify 'Abdallah's age at death and the
exact place of his burial. Naturally he also knew when the event
took place, namely while Muhammad was still in the womb. He
was aware that this was not the only account of the matter, but
pronounced it the best. This evolution in the course of half a
century from uncertainty to profusion of precise detail is an
instructive one. It suggests that a fair amount of what Waqidi knew
was not knowledge. Similar effects have been demonstrated in
Waqidi's treatment of the course and chronology of much later
events in the biography of Muhammad.

What kind of sources lie behind the works of Ibn Ishaq and his
generation? Since most of the research in this field remains to be
done, I shall proceed here by setting out two contrasting positions;
my own sympathies lie with the second.

Our starting-point is the fact that the writers of Ibn Ishaq's day
are in the habit of naming their sources, just as the ninth-century
compilers do. Often they give a whole chain of such sources
reaching back to an eyewitness of the event in question, and for one
event we may be able to collect several accounts going back
through distinct chains to different eyewitnesses. Such chains of
authorities (*isnad*s, as they are called) are in fact a salient
characteristic of Muslim tradition in general. A legal ruling of
Muhammad, or an interpretation of a Koranic verse by one of his
leading followers, will be quoted with such a chain, and a spurious
tradition will be equipped with a spurious chain.

Two questions now arise in connection with our narrative
sources. First, how far are the chains of authorities to be taken as

genuine? Second, are we to take it that the authorities named in these chains were (like Ibn Ishaq and his likes) the authors of books?

One view, which does not lack for adherents, is that the chains are genuine and the authorities are authors. Thus we can simply extend back the kind of reconstruction that works for the biographies of Ibn Ishaq's day. For example, he and his contemporaries make frequent reference to Zuhri (d. 742), a major figure of the previous generation. An energetic researcher could then collect all the quotations relating to the life of Muhammad that are given on Zuhri's authority, and hope to emerge with something like a reconstruction of his work. It would of course have to be conceded that the further back we go, the more blurred our reconstructions are likely to become. But this is a small price to pay for the overall assurance of the reliability of our sources. If these sources preserve for us a literature that reaches back to the contemporaries of Muhammad, and if they preserve the testimony of numerous mutually independent witnesses, then there is little room for the sceptic in the study of Muhammad's life.

The other view is that false ascription was rife among the eighth-century scholars, and that in any case Ibn Ishaq and his contemporaries were drawing on oral tradition. Neither of these propositions is as arbitrary as it sounds. We have reason to believe that numerous traditions on questions of dogma and law were provided with spurious chains of authorities by those who put them into circulation; and at the same time we have much evidence of controversy in the eighth century as to whether it was permissible to reduce oral tradition to writing. The implications of this view for the reliability of our sources are clearly rather negative. If we cannot trust the chains of authorities, we can no longer claim to know that we have before us the separately transmitted accounts of independent witnesses; and if knowledge of the life of Muhammad was transmitted orally for a century before it was reduced to writing, then the chances are that the material will have undergone considerable alteration in the process.

Which of these positions, or what middle course, lies closest to the truth is something which — to borrow the idiom of the Muslim scholars — God knows best. Thus to return for a minute to Zuhri, the sources are bewilderingly inconsistent about his literary activity: we are told that he was a prolific writer who wrote down all the traditions he heard, and we are told that he never wrote anything at all, and left no book behind him. Setting side by side quotations from Zuhri given in different sources produces, in my own experience, similarly inconsistent results; and sometimes one finds striking verbal similarities between two versions of an event ascribed to Zuhri, only to encounter the same echoes in versions ascribed to quite different authorities.

The most interesting hypothesis which has been advanced, and one which accounts rather well for this and other effects, is that the eighth-century authors drew much of their material directly from the specialist story-tellers of early Islam, the *qussas*. We should then think in terms of a common repertoire of material in circulation among these story-tellers, rather than of hard and fast lines of individual transmission. If, as is plausible, we assume that this story-telling remained a living source for the authors of scholarly biographies as late as the time of Waqidi, we can readily explain Waqidi's superior knowledge as a reflection of the continuing evolution of this oral tradition.

Story-telling is an art, not a science, and signs of this art are commonplace in the biography of Muhammad. For example, one element in the repertoire was clearly a story of a frightening encounter between the woman who suckled the infant Muhammad and some person or persons whose spiritual expertise enabled them to divine his future greatness. Whether the encounter is with Jews, Ethiopian Christians, or an Arab soothsayer, is nevertheless a point which varies from one version of the story to another. Similar floating anecdotes occur later in Muhammad's life. The details again are trivial, but the overall implications are not. We have seen what half a century of story-telling could achieve between Ibn Ishaq and Waqidi, at a time when we know that much material had already been committed to writing. What the same processes may have brought about in the century before Ibn Ishaq is something we can only guess at.

In this situation, how is the historian to proceed? The usual practice is to accept whatever in the sources we lack specific reason to reject. This may be the right approach; doubtless there is a historical core to the tradition on Muhammad's life, and perhaps a little judicious selectivity is enough to uncover it. Yet it may equally be the case that we are nearer the mark in rejecting whatever we do not have specific reason to accept, and that what is usually taken for bedrock is no more than shifting sand. We can best pursue the question when we have first discussed the Koran.

## The Koran

Tradition describes Muhammad as receiving his revelations bit by bit, and this seems to find support in some (though not all) of the relevant Koranic statements. As we now have them, however, Muhammad's revelations are in the form of a book. There is a rich body of traditions as to how the Koran was collected and edited to yield the text we have today, and two points are more or less common ground: that the task was not accomplished by Muhammad himself, and that it was completed at the latest in the reign of the Caliph 'Uthman (ruled 644–56). This apart, the traditions are not a model of consistency. We learn that some of Muhammad's followers already knew the whole Koran by heart in his lifetime — yet subsequently it had to be pieced together out of fragments collected from here and there. We are told that Muhammad regularly dictated his revelations to a scribe — yet the scripture was later in danger of being lost through the death in battle of those who had it by heart. It was collected and made into a book by the first Caliph; or by the second; or by the third, 'Uthman. Alternatively, it had already been collected before the time of 'Uthman, and he merely had the text standardised and other versions destroyed. The last of these traditions has tended to prevail, but the choice is a somewhat arbitrary one; the truth may lie anywhere within the limits of the discordant traditions, or altogether outside them.

Turning to the book itself, its structure needs some elucidation. Outwardly it is clear enough: like the Bible, the Koran comes in chapters (*sura*s) and verses (*aya*s) — though not 'books'. The verses often rhyme, but they are not the verses of poetry. The *sura*s are composed of anything from three to nearly three hundred verses apiece, and are arranged in roughly descending order of length. A *sura* is usually named by some catchword appearing in the text; thus the second is 'the Cow', because of a reference to a sacrifice of a cow which Moses demanded of the Israelites. None of this has much to do with content, and at this level the Koran is strikingly lacking in structure. A *sura* of any length will usually take up and dismiss a variety of topics in no obvious order, and a given topic may be treated in this way in several *sura*s. The largest effective units of structure thus tend to be blocks of verses which the formal organisation of the text does nothing to demarcate. Within such blocks, trivial dislocations are surprisingly frequent. God may appear in the first and third persons in one and the same sentence; there may be omissions which, if not made good by interpretation, render the sense unintelligible; there are even what look like grammatical errors. Whatever is behind these puzzling features, their preservation in our texts points to extraordinarily conservative editing, as if things had been kept just as they fell.

Yet alongside this conservative editing we also find evidence of a much freer handling of the raw materials of the Koran. This presumably reflects an earlier stage in their history. There are, for example, clear cases of interpolation. Thus in the fifty-third *sura*, the basic text consists of uniformly short verses in an inspired style, but in two places this is interrupted by a prosaic and prolix amplification which is stylistically quite out of place. Another significant feature is the frequency with which we find alternative versions of the same passage in different parts of the Koran; when placed side by side, these versions often show the same sort of variation as one finds between parallel versions of oral traditions. Whatever these phenomena mean, they presuppose very different processes from those at work in the final editing. It is also obvious that the Koran contains material in more than one style, and much effort has been expended on the elaboration of a relative chronology of the revelation on the assumption that short and inspired passages are likely to be older than long and prosaic ones.

Taken on its own, the Koran tells us very little about the events of Muhammad's career. It does not narrate these events, but merely refers to them; and in doing so, it has a tendency not to name names. Some do occur in contemporary contexts: four religious communities are named (Jews, Christians, Magians, and the mysterious Sabians), as are three Arabian deities (all female), three humans (of whom Muhammad is one), two ethnic groups (Quraysh and the Romans), and nine places. Of the places, four are mentioned in military connections (Badr, Mecca, Hunayn, Yathrib), and four are connected with the sanctuary (three of them we have already met in connection with the rites of pilgrimage, while the fourth is 'Bakka', said to be an alternative name for Mecca). The final place is Mount Sinai, which seems to be associated with the growing of olives. Leaving aside the ubiquitous

Christians and Jews, none of these names occurs very often: Muhammad is named four or five times (once as 'Ahmad'), the Sabians thrice, Mount Sinai twice, and the rest once each. Identifying what the Koran is talking about in a contemporary context is therefore usually impossible without interpretation, which in previous chapters I have on occasion tacitly supplied. For such interpretation we are naturally dependent mainly on tradition. Without it we could probably infer that the protagonist of the Koran was Muhammad, that the scene of his life was in western Arabia, and that he bitterly resented the frequent dismissal of his claims to prophecy by his contemporaries. But we could not tell that the sanctuary was in Mecca, or that Muhammad himself came from there, and we could only guess that he established himself in Yathrib. We might indeed prefer a more northerly location altogether, on the grounds that the site of God's destruction of Lot's people (i.e. Sodom) is said to be one which those addressed pass by morning and night (K 37.137–8).

The Muslim scholars sought to relate the Koran to traditional information on Muhammad's life on two levels. First, they made a broad distinction between what was revealed in Mecca and what was revealed in Medina. Thus one early scholar is quoted for the rule of thumb according to which everything mentioning the 'communities' and 'generations' (i.e. of the past) is Meccan, and everything establishing legal obligations and norms is Medinese. This distinction has been broadly accepted by most modern scholars. Secondly, the Muslim scholars dealt in detail with the occasions on which particular passages were revealed. Thus Ibn Ishaq, treating the time when Muhammad had newly arrived in Medina, remarks that much of the revelation used to come down with reference to the Jewish rabbis, who kept asking him tricky questions. Ibn Ishaq then goes on to specify contexts for the revelation of numerous passages in these altercations between God and the Jews. In the face of many traditions of this kind, it is hard to dissent from the view of 'Abida al-Salmani, a scholar of the late seventh century, who is said to have refused to interpret a verse on the ground that those who had known the occasions of the revelation of the Koran had passed away. Most modern scholars discard the bulk of this material as without foundation, but retain some of the historically more significant links which it purports to establish between Koranic references and historical events.

The problem in such cases is how to distinguish between genuine historical information and material that came into existence to explain the very Koranic passages that concern us. An example will help to make this clear. In the third generation before Muhammad, as we saw in Chapter 2, Hashim and his brothers are said to have laid the foundations of Mecca's international trade. In the first place, tradition relates that Hashim initiated the two caravan journeys, that of the winter to the Yemen and that of the summer to Syria; these are known as the 'two *rihlas*', the word *rihla* simply meaning 'journey'. In the second place, he is reported to have led the way in a process whereby each brother went to negotiate with the ruler of one of the neighbouring states for the security of Meccan trade in their domains; at the same time, each brother on his way back made arrangements for the protection of commerce with the tribes along his route. These latter arrangements with the tribes went by the name of *ilaf*. There are naturally other versions of these traditions, sometimes differing considerably, but we can leave the variants aside.

Both these institutions are mentioned in the Koran. The first two verses of the 106th *sura* read: 'For the *ilaf* of Quraysh, their *ilaf* of the journey (*rihla*) of the winter and the summer.' Koran and tradition thus appear to support each other's testimony in a most reassuring fashion, and confirm the historicity of these two foundations of Meccan trade. Yet by itself, the Koranic reference would not tell us much; *ilaf* is scarcely a term known outside this context, and a *rihla* could be any kind of journey. If we now turn to the commentators, we begin to have doubts. For one thing, it emerges that there was uncertainty as to how to read the word *ilaf* (the Arabic script being sparing in its marking of vowels) — which is surprising if the term was well-known. More important, there was a wide range of opinion among the commentators as to what the term meant, and it was not even agreed that the meaning had to do with commerce. It is as if future historians confronted by the term 'Common Market' in a twentieth-century document should speculate whether it meant a market catering to the needs of both sexes, or perhaps rather one frequented by the lower classes. Such a break in the continuity of the understanding of the Koran is not isolated. Many *suras*, for example, begin with mysterious combinations of letters of the Arabic alphabet which must once have meant something to someone, but were already as opaque to the early Muslim scholars as they are to us.

It would seem, then, that as far as the commentators were concerned, God knew best what He meant by the term *ilaf*. Yet it is hard to believe that if *ilaf* was in fact a fundamental institution of Meccan trade, and was referred to as such in the Koran, the early commentators (many of them Meccans themselves) could have been so much at sea. The alternative hypothesis is that what we mistake for economic history is no more than the blossoming of one particular line of speculation to which an obscure Koranic verse has given rise. (Even the presumption that the 'journey of the winter and the summer' was commercial is uncertain; a distinguished authority who lived locally is quoted for the view that the reference is to a practice among Quraysh of spending the winter in Mecca and the summer in the nearby town of Ta'if.) Here too we have a phenomenon which may have far-reaching implications for Muhammad's biography.

## External evidence

In this situation it would obviously be helpful to have some early sources that have not been transmitted within the Muslim tradition, or at least reflect only the earliest phase of it. A cave with some contemporary documents and diaries would meet the need admirably — but this is something we do not have, and probably never will. What we do have is nevertheless worthy of attention. It consists of two kinds of sources: Muslim material preserved archaeologically, and hence unaffected by the later development of tradition, and non-Muslim sources preserved in the literatures of non-Muslim communities. None of the material is earlier than the beginning of the conquest of the Fertile Crescent in 633–4, and much that is of interest is some decades later, but it can still take us behind the Muslim tradition in its eighth-century form. On the Muslim side, we can learn something from such sources as administrative papyri, coins and inscriptions, especially for the last years of the seventh century; the earliest datable papyrus fragments of religious content come only in the first half of the eighth century. On the non-Muslim side, we have a small body of material in Greek and Syriac dating from the time of the conquests, and further Syriac material from later in the century. An Armenian

chronicler writing in the 660s gives us the earliest narrative account
of Muhammad's career to survive in any language. In Hebrew, an
eighth-century apocalypse has embedded in it an earlier apocalypse
that seems to be contemporary with the conquests.

What does this material tell us? We may begin with the major
points on which it agrees with the Islamic tradition. It precludes
any doubts as to whether Muhammad was a real person: he is
named in a Syriac source that is likely to date from the time of the
conquests, and there is an account of him in a Greek source of the
same period. From the 640s we have confirmation that the term
*muhajir* was a central one in the new religion, since its followers
are known as 'Magaritai' or 'Mahgraye' in Greek and Syriac
respectively. At the same time, a papyrus of 643 is dated 'year
twenty two', creating a strong presumption that something did
happen in A.D. 622. The Armenian chronicler of the 660s attests
that Muhammad was a merchant, and confirms the centrality of
Abraham in his preaching. The Abrahamic sanctuary appears in an
early Syriac source dated (insecurely) to the 670s.

Secondly, there are the major points on which this material is
silent. It gives no indication that Muhammad's career unfolded in
inner Arabia, and in particular makes no mention of Mecca; the
Koran makes no appearance until the last years of the seventh
century; and it is only then that we have any suggestion that the
adherents of the new religion were called 'Muslims'. Since there is
not much of this material anyway, such silences do not mean very
much. We should nevertheless note that the earliest evidence from
outside the tradition regarding the direction in which Muslims
prayed, and by implication the location of their sanctuary, points
much further north than Mecca. Equally, when the first Koranic
quotations appear on coins and inscriptions towards the end of the
seventh century, they show divergences from the canonical text.
These are trivial from the point of view of content, but the fact that
they appear in such formal contexts as these goes badly with the
notion that the text had already been frozen.

Thirdly, there are the major disagreements. Two are chrono-
logical. The first is that the Armenian chronicler's account of the
foundation of Muhammad's community places it by implication
several years after 622; here, however, the Islamic tradition has the
support of the papyrus of 643. The second is that the earliest Greek
source, which is dated to the year 634 and unlikely to be much

later, speaks of Muhammad as still alive — two years after his
death according to the Muslim tradition. There are indications that
this impression was widely shared by the non-Muslim communities
of the Fertile Crescent. The other two major disagreements are of
considerable doctrinal interest, and relate to Muhammad's
attitudes towards Palestine and the Jews.

To begin with the Jews, we have already seen how tradition
preserves a document, the 'Constitution of Medina', in which
Muhammad establishes a community to which believers and Jews
alike belong, while retaining their different faiths. The document is
anomalous and difficult, and could well be authentic in substance.
Be that as it may, tradition goes on to recount a series of breaks
between Muhammad and the Jews of Yathrib whereby the Jewish
element was eliminated from the community several years before
the conquests began. The early non-Muslim sources, by contrast,
depict a relationship with the Jews at the time of the first conquests
such as tradition concedes only for the first years of Muhammad's
residence in Medina. The Armenian chronicler of the 660s describes
Muhammad as establishing a community which comprised both
Ishmaelites (i.e. Arabs) and Jews, with Abrahamic descent as their
common platform; these allies then set off to conquer Palestine.
The oldest Greek source makes the sensational statement that the
prophet who had appeared among the Saracens (i.e. Arabs) was
proclaiming the coming of the (Jewish) messiah, and speaks of 'the
Jews who mix with the Saracens', and of the danger to life and limb
of falling into the hands of these Jews and Saracens. We cannot
easily dismiss this evidence as the product of Christian prejudice,
since it finds confirmation in the Hebrew apocalypse referred to
above. The break with the Jews is then placed by the Armenian
chronicler immediately after the Arab conquest of Jerusalem.

The other major disagreement between the Muslim tradition and
the non-Muslim sources is the place of Palestine in Muhammad's
scheme of things. Palestine is far from unimportant in tradition (we
saw how it tends to recover its centrality towards the end of time).
Yet in the traditional account of Muhammad's career, it is already
demoted in favour of Mecca in the second year of the *hijra*, when
Muhammad changes the direction of prayer of his followers from
Jerusalem to Mecca. Thereafter Mecca is the religious focus of his
movement, as it is also the main object of his political and military
aspirations. In the non-Muslim sources, by contrast, this role is

played by Palestine, and provides the religious motive for its conquest. The Armenian chronicler further gives a rationale for this attachment: Muhammad told the Arabs that, as descendants of Abraham through Ishmael, they too had a claim to the land which God had promised to Abraham and his seed. The religion of Abraham is in fact as central in the Armenian account of Muhammad's preaching as it is in the Muslim sources; but it is given a quite different geographical twist.

If the external sources are in any significant degree right on such points, it would follow that tradition is seriously misleading on important aspects of the life of Muhammad, and that even the integrity of the Koran as his message is in some doubt. In view of what was said above about the nature of the Muslim sources, such a conclusion would seem to me legitimate; but it is only fair to add that it is not usually drawn.

# 8

## *Origins*

To understand what Muhammad was doing in creating a new religion, it would be necessary to know what religious resources were available to him, and in what form. In a sense, of course, we know perfectly well; we possess rich literary remains from the Jewish and Christian traditions, and we know something about the paganism of Arabia. But beyond this point the going gets difficult. We might like to think of Muhammad as a well-travelled merchant acquainted with the same forms of the monotheist tradition as are familiar to us. Or we might think of him as a man of more local horizons who was in contact with some Arabian byways of monotheism which have otherwise left no trace. The first view makes him a man of considerable doctrinal originality, whereas on the second view he might have found much that to us is distinctively Islamic already present in his Arabian environment. The trouble is that we are not well placed to decide between two such hypotheses. For example, we would dearly like to know what sort of Judaism was current in pre-Islamic western Arabia; but evidence of this is scarce within the Islamic tradition, and non-existent outside it. For the most part, we are reduced to the crude procedure of comparing Islam with the mainstream traditions of Judaism and Christianity, and trying to determine which elements came from which. The answers are often convincing, but they fail to tell us in which form these elements came to Muhammad, or he to them.

### The Koran

One way of approaching the question is through the Koran, which has been ransacked for parallels with the religious traditions of the day — not to mention others which may already have been extinct. The results of this research can perhaps be summarised as follows. First, nothing resembling the Koran as such is to be found in any

other tradition; the book remains *sui generis*, and if it had
predecessors, we know nothing of them. Secondly, there is no lack
of elements in the Koran for which parallels can be found
elsewhere, and these parallels are sometimes impressive. Thirdly,
this evidence points in a bewildering variety of directions, and
conforms to no simple pattern. The examples which follow should
serve to bring this home.

As might be expected, Jewish influence is prominent. It can, for
example, be seen in the way in which Biblical narratives are told
in the Koran. Thus the story of the efforts of Potiphar's wife to
seduce Joseph in Egypt appears in the Koran with the addition of
a curious anecdote: the woman is irritated by the tittle-tattle of her
peers, so she invites them to a banquet, gives each of them a knife,
and orders Joseph to come before them; when he does so, they cut
their hands (K 12.31). This story comes from post-Biblical Jewish
tradition, and indeed it is only in the light of the Jewish original
that the Koranic narrative becomes intelligible: the woman had set
the gossips to cut up fruit with their knives, and they cut themselves inadvertently while staring at the good-looking Joseph.

We can take another example of Jewish influence from the
vocabulary of religious law. The Koran enjoins the giving of alms,
often conjoined with prayer as a basic duty of believers. The term
for alms, *zakat*, is a loan-word in Arabic. In form it could be of
either Jewish or Christian origin. But if we turn to the meaning, the
field narrows. It is in Jewish texts from Palestine that we find the
corresponding form used in the sense of the merit which accrues
from good works; and in particular, we find a verbal form from the
same root used in the sense of 'to give alms'. Christian usage, by
contrast, offers no such parallel.

Other Koranic elements are definitely Christian in origin.
Obvious examples are the material relating to the life of Jesus, and
the legend of the Seven Sleepers of Ephesus (who appear in the
Koran as 'the people of the cave'). Some of the religious loan-words
found in the Koran are definitely or probably Christian; thus the
term used for 'hypocrite' (*munafiq*) seems to be an Ethiopic Christian
loan-word. These examples of Christian influence could easily be
extended.

There is also the possibility of influences from other known
monotheist groups. Thus the profession of faith that 'there is no
god but God', and the emphasis on His having no companion, find

their best (though not their only) parallel in Samaritanism, an archaic Jewish heresy which survived mainly in Palestine. But the real joker in the pack is the spectre of Judaeo-Christian influence. In the early Christian centuries there existed groups of Jewish Christians. Such groups combined an acceptance of the mission of Jesus with a retention of their Jewish observances; Jesus was for them no more than a man. We do not know what happened to these groups, but we do have an account which places a community of Jewish Christians in Jerusalem in the later seventh century. If such a group had influenced early Islam, this might account for much of the Koranic view of Jesus that we outlined above. On the other hand, it would not go well with the Koranic denial of the death of Jesus on the cross. This denial was a well-known Christian heresy (Docetism), and its primary appeal was to those who regarded Jesus as God, and were accordingly disturbed by the idea that God should have died. (Since the Koranic Jesus is so emphatically human, the appearance of this doctrine in the Koran is on any showing a puzzle.)

None of this excludes influences from outside the monotheist tradition. In particular, some Koranic prescriptions are more than likely to be endorsements of religious customs of pagan Arabia. A clear case is the practice of circumambulation which the Koran enjoins in connection with the rites of pilgrimage to the sanctuary. Muslim tradition presents this as a ritual that was current in pagan times, and a Christian source attests it (though not at a sanctuary) among the pre-Islamic Arabs of Sinai. Another case in point is the Arabian institution of a holy month or months, likewise associated with pilgrimage to a sanctuary, during which fighting is forbidden. As we saw, this custom is endorsed in the Koran, subject to the overriding demands of holy war. Here too, Muslim tradition describes the institution as one of pagan times, and the point is confirmed by a Greek account from the sixth century.

## Key doctrines

It may be more interesting to approach the question of origins by picking out a couple of key elements of Muhammad's preaching and asking where they may have come from.

One quite fundamental idea is that of the 'religion of Abraham'. That this was not an invention of Muhammad's is indicated by the Islamic tradition: rightly or wrongly, it depicts adherents of the idea in both Mecca and Yathrib before the coming of Muhammad. Outside Arabia, we know that the idea had occurred, if only as armchair theology, to Jews and Christians. Long before Muhammad, the apocryphal Book of Jubilees (a Jewish work preserved by Christians) had outlined a religion of Abraham which the patriarch had imposed on all his sons and grandsons — including by implication the Arabs. The Jewish rabbis considered (and unsurprisingly rejected) the notion of an Ishmaelite claim to Palestine by virtue of descent from Abraham. Sozomenus, a Christian writer of the fifth century, reconstructs a primitive Ishmaelite monotheism identical with that possessed by the Hebrews up to the time of Moses; and he goes on to argue from present conditions that Ishmael's laws must have been corrupted by the passage of time and the influence of pagan neighbours.

But did the Arabs themselves get to hear of these intriguing ideas? Here Sozomenus has something further to tell us. He remarks that (at a date later than his reconstructed history of the decay of the religion of Abraham) some Ishmaelite tribes happened to come in contact with Jews, and learnt from them about their 'true' origin, i.e. their descent from Ishmael; they then 'returned' to the observance of Hebrew laws and customs. Even at the present day, he adds, there are some Ishmaelites who live in the Jewish way. What Sozomenus is here describing is Arabs who adopted Jewish observances, not by becoming Jews, but by rediscovering their own Ishmaelite descent. All that is missing from this conception of the religion of Abraham is the Abrahamic sanctuary. This evidence is not lightly to be set aside: Sozomenus was a Palestinian from Gaza, and a casual remark indicates that he even knew something of Arabic poetry. We have no evidence that would show any direct link between this early religion of Abraham and Muhammad's message nearly two centuries later, but it is at least a confirmation that Muhammad was not the first in the field, and an indication of the use to which the Jewish brand of the monotheist tradition could be put by the Arabs.

Another fundamental feature of Muhammad's preaching is the set of political ideas which cluster around the notion of *hijra*. Although the Koran does not use *muhajir* in a Mosaic context, there are, as we saw, other points at which these ideas are linked to the story of Moses, and the overall analogy is striking. Likewise the Armenian chronicler makes a point of Muhammad's familiarity with the story of Moses. Yet in the seventh century this story was ancient history. The one context in which it was politically alive was Jewish messianism, a religious expectation which continued to fire occasional rebellions against a world dominated by gentiles. Here the career of the messiah was seen as a re-enactment of that of Moses; a key event in the drama was an exodus, or flight, from oppression into the desert, whence the messiah was to lead a holy war to reconquer Palestine. Given the early evidence connecting Muhammad with Jews and Jewish messianism at the time when the conquest of Palestine was initiated, it is natural to see in Jewish apocalyptic thought a point of departure for his political ideas.

In contrast to the diversity of origins that marks the Koranic material at large, both these points go well with the view that Muhammad owed more to Judaism than to Christianity. This would not be surprising. Both the Islamic tradition and — still more — the external sources portray him as having more to do with Jews than with Christians.

# Conclusion

The Muslim profession of faith affirms that 'there is no god but God, and Muhammad is the messenger of God'. Only the first half of this affirmation conveys a substantive message; the second half merely identifies the bearer. In this sense, the burden of Muhammad's preaching was simply monotheism. Such an insistence was not superfluous in the seventh century. In Arabia, where an old-fashioned polytheism still flourished, it dramatically accelerated the penetration of the peninsula by monotheist influence. Outside Arabia, it had some purchase in the lands which the Arabs went on to conquer. Although authentic pagans were now in short supply, Zoroastrians and Christians were not immune to the challenge of a strict monotheism. The Zoroastrians worshipped not only the good god of their dualist cosmology, but sundry other deities as well; and while it may be true that the three persons of the Christian Trinity add up to one God without companions, the arithmetic is elusive, and not only to the theologically untrained. Only in the Jewish case does the monotheist polemic of Islam seem somewhat contrived. Muhammad, then, had a point. But this point was no more than the perennial message of monotheism, and as such it neither was, nor was intended to be, distinctive. It was what Muhammad made of this ancient verity that mattered; and in his day this meant what he made of it for the Arabs.

## Muhammad and the Arabs

The reader may recollect that four Meccans are said to have experienced a revulsion from paganism in the generation before Muhammad, and that three of them ended up as Christians. The fourth, Zayd ibn 'Amr, is a more interesting figure. He set out from Mecca in quest of the religion of Abraham, and travelled to the Fertile Crescent. The choice was natural: where else could he hope to find such a treasury of religious expertise? Once there, he went about questioning monks and rabbis, but all to no purpose. Eventually he found a monk in the uplands to the east of Palestine who had something to tell him: there was no one at present who could guide him to the religion of Abraham, but a prophet was about to be sent to proclaim this religion — and would arise in the very land from which Zayd had set out. Zayd did not care for what he had seen of Judaism and Christianity, and he now set off on the long road back to Mecca. The Arab had wandered in vain; the truth was about to be revealed on his own doorstep.

With this we may compare the reactions of the Arabs and Jews of Yathrib to Muhammad's mission. As we saw, the first response came from the six men of Khazraj. They took Muhammad seriously because they had heard from their Jewish neighbours that a new prophet was about to appear. More precisely, tradition tells us that the Jews expected this prophet to lead them against the Arabs; so the Khazrajis were understandably anxious to appropriate Muhammad before the Jews could do so. Later we hear much of the hatred which the Jews felt for Muhammad. What they could not abide was that God had favoured the Arabs by choosing His messenger from among them. One Jew declared with a certain logic that he recognised Muhammad to be a true prophet, and would nevertheless oppose him as long as he lived.

These stories present two sides of the same coin. What was gall to the Jews was balm to the Arabs. The Jews, the original holders of the monotheist patent, now found themselves expropriated; the Arabs discovered that the truth they had humbly sought from the superior religious insight of monks and rabbis was in fact their own. Today such expropriations and discoveries take place under the banner of nationalism, but the motivation behind them is one which can come into play whenever men confront the problem of remaining themselves while adopting the beliefs of others.

What Muhammad also did for the Arabs of his day was to effect a powerful fusion between his monotheism and their tribal politics. His achievement can be seen as a revival of the radically monotheist polity enshrined in the story of Moses. By the time of Muhammad, the Jews had for long lived the life of a dispossessed minority; their messianic attempts to restore their political fortunes were sporadic and short-lived. Christianity had fared differently. It had put itself out to assure the Roman authorities that it was not a subversive religion, and in due course these authorities had come to see it as one which might do the state some service. Thereafter the Roman Empire was Christianised, much to the disgust of its pagan aristocracy; but it was in no sense a monotheist creation.

Against such a background, it was a very considerable innovation to bring about the rule of God and His prophet over an independent community of believers.

It was no accident that Muhammad achieved this in Arabia, with its predominantly pastoral and stateless tribal society. He had the good luck to be born into an environment which offered scope for political creativity such as is not usually open to the religious reformer. But it was clearly more than good luck that he found in this society the key to a hitherto virtually untapped reserve of power. The pastoral tribes of Arabia were of necessity mobile and warlike, but their military potential was normally dissipated in small-scale raiding and feuding. Muhammad's doctrine, and the use he put it to, brought to this society a remarkable, if transient, coherence of purpose. Without it, it is hard to see how the Arabian tribesmen could have gone on to conquer so substantial a portion of the known world.

The Arab conquests rapidly destroyed one empire, and permanently detached large territories of another. This was, for the states in question, an appalling catastrophe, but it need not have marked the end of the road. Political unity did not come easily to the Arab tribesmen, and within decades of Muhammad's death they had fought two major civil wars. It was not unreasonable to suppose that the Arab domination would simply disintegrate, leaving as little residue as did that of the Goths in Europe. In any case, tribal conquerors are usually less civilised than the settled populations they subject, and accordingly end up by adopting the culture of their subjects. Of this too there were signs in the early period of Arab rule. Had the Arabs either disintegrated politically or capitulated culturally in this formative period, the minor religious movement initiated by Muhammad in western Arabia would not have become one of the world's major civilisations. That the Arabs were able to withstand the countervailing pressures so successfully in the generations following the death of their prophet is remarkable. It is hard to imagine that they could have done so had their hegemony not derived meaning and purpose from the monotheist polity which Muhammad had created among them, and the monotheist faith which he had made their own.

Something of this meaning and purpose can perhaps be conveyed by a numismatic comparison. Jesus, who like Muhammad was often asked awkward questions, was once challenged by the

Pharisees to say whether it was lawful 'to give tribute unto Caesar'. Jesus had them show him a coin, and asked in return: 'Whose is this image and superscription?' When they answered that it was Caesar's, Jesus gave his famous reply: 'Render therefore unto Caesar the things which are Caesar's; and unto God the things that are God's' (Matt. 22.15–22). It was an apt and prudent distinction, a dignified solution to the problem of confuting the Pharisees without giving offence to the local representatives of imperial Rome. Over six hundred years later, and some sixty years after the death of Muhammad, the Caliph 'Abd al-Malik — who did as much as anyone for the political unity and cultural autonomy of the Arabs — likewise gave his attention to the matter of coins, their images and superscriptions. A silver coin struck in the year 79 (A.D. 698–9) is a good example of the results of his deliberations. There is no image, but there is an abundance of more or less Koranic superscription. On the obverse is the legend: 'There is no god but God, alone, without companion'; and on the reverse: 'Muhammad is the messenger of God, whom He sent with guidance and the religion of truth, to make it supreme above all others, whether the polytheists like it or not.'

## Muhammad and the wider world

As we saw, there are already indications in the Koran that Muhammad's message was in principle directed to all mankind. One of his immediate followers was in fact a Persian, a certain Salman, who had abandoned the religion of his father, left his native land, and come to Arabia in search of the religion of Abraham. Within a century or two of Muhammad's death, the religion of Abraham was spread far beyond Arabia, and large numbers of converts to Islam had appeared among the conquered peoples. At first conversion tended to go hand in hand with Arabisation — in other words, the converts were assimilated into the society of their conquerors. But in both social and geographical terms, Islam soon spread well beyond the reach of such Arabisation. Today, the Arabian prophet is recognised as the messenger of God among a great variety of peoples, and the Arabs themselves account for less than a sixth of the world's Muslims. It is of course true that Muhammad's religion, with its Arabian sanctuary and Arabic Koran, retains a strong Arab colouring; unlike Christianity, it did not break with the milieu in which it was born. Yet the Arab identity of Islam has inevitably faded with the centuries, and Islam is now many things to many men.

There is no place in this book for an analysis of the way in which Muhammad's legacy was developed, extended, attenuated and transformed among generations born at times and places increasingly removed from his own. Even the Caliph 'Abd al-Malik had never met Muhammad; since his day over forty generations of Muslims have lived and died, and the history they have made can hardly be laid at the door of a man who claimed neither to possess the treasures of God nor to know the future, and followed only what was revealed to him.

Nor is there any place here for a consideration of the absolute value of Muhammad's message. He saw himself, according to the tradition, as the last brick in the edifice of monotheist prophecy. Today we live in a landscape littered with the fallen masonry of such edifices; what are we, for whom bricks are but clay, to see in Muhammad's contribution to this scene? Any answer to such a question is bound to be intensely arbitrary, and I shall therefore seek only to identify that quality of Islam which has most worked on me in the writing of this book. Both Judaism and Christianity are religions of profound pathos — Judaism with its dream of ethnic redemption from present wretchedness, Christianity with its individual salvation through the sufferings of a God of love. In each case the pathos is indeed moving; but it is a pathos which too easily appeals to the emotion of self-pity. Islam, in contrast, is strikingly free of this temptation. The bleakness which we saw in its conception of the relationship between God and man is the authentic, unadulterated bleakness of the universe itself.

# Further reading

Two of the primary sources on which this book is based are readily available in English.

There are many translations of the Koran. I have made most use of that by A. J. Arberry (*The Koran interpreted*, first published in two volumes, London and New York, 1955, but more easily accessible in the Oxford University Press series 'The World's Classics', London, 1964). Contrary to what the title might suggest, it gives a bare (but palatable) translation, which delicately conveys the obscurities of the original without resolving them. An old translation which has worn very well is that of George Sale (*The Koran*, London, 1734, many times reprinted). The great virtue of Sale's translation is that it presents the text in a context of traditional Sunni interpretation, while making it clear by the use of italics and footnotes what is, and is not, contained in the text itself. The standard European translation today is a German one by R. Paret. My references to the Koran are by *sura* and verse: 'K 2.10' means the tenth verse of the second *sura*. There is more than one way of numbering Koranic verses; I follow that of G. Flügel's edition of the Koran, since it is used by Arberry.

The *Sira* of Ibn Ishaq as transmitted by Ibn Hisham has been translated into English by A. Guillaume (*The life of Muhammad*, London, 1955), and my references (as: 'S 154') are to the pages of his translation. It is, however, too bulky a book for all but the most intrepid beginner; an annotated translation of Ma'mar ibn Rashid's account as transmitted by 'Abd al-Razzaq ibn Hammam would be a welcome addition to the literature.

Turning to modern writing, there is no lack of introductory works. Thus for the life of Muhammad, there are readable accounts by W. M. Watt (*Muhammed: prophet and statesman*, London, 1961, itself an epitome of two larger volumes by the same author) and by M. Rodinson (*Mohammed*, London, 1971). A shorter account that carries the story through to the conquests is F. Gabrieli, *Muhammad and the conquests of Islam*, London, 1968. For the Koran, a useful introduction is *Bell's Introduction to the Qur'ān*, revised by W. M. Watt (Edinburgh, 1970). For a survey of Islam which relates Muhammad to the subsequent evolution of the religion, see I. Goldziher, *Introduction to Islamic theology and law*, Princeton, N.J., 1981 (a translation of an old but excellent German work which also covers Sufism and sectarian divisions, both of them topics excluded from the scope of this book).

There is a large volume of modern research on the topics covered in this book, but a surprising lack of up-to-date standard works.

There is no such thing as a critical edition of the Koran. There used to be a standard work on the Koran in German (T. Nöldeke and others, *Geschichte des Qorāns*, second edition, Leipzig, 1909–38), and it remains indispensable for serious study; but with the steady appearance of new material (which may well continue into the coming century), the work in question is becoming obsolete in many particulars. Much the same is true for Muhammad's life, where again the standard work was in German (F. Buhl, *Das Leben Muhammeds*, Leipzig, 1930, originally published in Danish). The reader who wishes to go beyond the few English works mentioned in this note will, however, find much information and current bibliography in relevant articles of the second edition of *The Encyclopaedia of Islam*, Leiden and London, 1960– (e.g. the recently published article 'Ḳurʾān'; 'Muḥammad' is yet to come).

A few references may be added for the more recondite information used here and there in this book. For the external sources discussed in the last section of Chapter 7, references will be found in Chapter 1 of Patricia Crone and Michael Cook, *Hagarism: the making of the Islamic world*, Cambridge, 1977. For Sozomenus' account of the religion of Abraham (above, p. 360), see his *Ecclesiastical History*, VI, 38; I owe my knowledge of this passage to Patricia Crone. For the Jewish usage of the verb *zakki* in the sense of 'to give alms' (above, p. 358), see for example *Leviticus Rabbah*, 34.5–14 (in the new edition of M. Margulies, Jerusalem, 1953–60); this testimony seems to have been overlooked by Islamicists.

# Index

(Entries relate to central characters as follows: pp. 1–85 the Buddha; 91–179 Confucius; 187–280 Jesus; 299–366 Muhammad.)